THE SOCIAL CONDITION
AND EDUCATION OF THE PEOPLE

The Development of Industrial Society Series

Joseph Kay

THE
SOCIAL CONDITION
AND EDUCATION
OF THE PEOPLE

in England and Europe

Volume 1

IRISH UNIVERSITY PRESS
Shannon   Ireland

First edition London 1850

This I U P reprint is a photolithographic facsimile of the first edition and is unabridged, retaining the original printer's imprint.

© *1971 Irish University Press Shannon Ireland*

All forms of micropublishing
© *Irish University Microforms Shannon Ireland*

ISBN 0 7165 1565 2 Two volumes
ISBN 0 7165 1566 0 Volume 1
ISBN 0 7165 1567 9 Volume 2

T M MacGlinchey Publisher
Irish University Press Shannon Ireland

PRINTED IN THE REPUBLIC OF IRELAND BY
ROBERT HOGG PRINTER TO IRISH UNIVERSITY PRESS

The Development of Industrial Society Series

This series comprises reprints of contemporary documents and commentaries on the social, political and economic upheavals in nineteenth-century England.

England, as the first industrial nation, was also the first country to experience the tremendous social and cultural impact consequent on the alienation of people in industrialized countries from their rural ancestry. The Industrial Revolution which had begun to intensify in the mid-eighteenth century, spread swiftly from England to Europe and America. Its effects have been far-reaching: the growth of cities with their urgent social and physical problems; greater social mobility; mass education; increasingly complex administration requirements in both local and central government; the growth of democracy and the development of new theories in economics; agricultural reform and the transformation of a way of life.

While it would be pretentious to claim for a series such as this an in-depth coverage of all these aspects of the new society, the works selected range in content from *The Hungry Forties* (1904), a collection of letters by ordinary working people describing their living conditions and the effects of mechanization on their day-to-day lives, to such analytical studies as Leone Levi's *History of British Commerce* (1880) and *Wages and Earnings of the Working Classes* (1885); M. T. Sadler's *The Law of Population* (1830); John Wade's radical documentation of government corruption, *The Extraordinary Black Book* (1831); C. Edward Lester's trenchant social investigation, *The Glory and Shame of England* (1866); and many other influential books and pamphlets.

The editor's intention has been to make available important contemporary accounts, studies and records, written or compiled by men and women of integrity and scholarship whose reactions to the growth of a new kind of society are valid touchstones for today's reader. Each title (and the particular edition used) has been chosen on a twofold basis (1) its intrinsic worth as a record or commentary, and (2) its contribution to the development of an industrial society. It is hoped that this collection will help to increase our understanding of a people and an epoch.

The Editor
Irish University Press

THE

SOCIAL CONDITION

AND

EDUCATION OF THE PEOPLE.

VOL. I.

LONDON:
SPOTTISWOODES and SHAW,
New-street-Square.

THE

SOCIAL CONDITION

AND

EDUCATION OF THE PEOPLE

IN

ENGLAND AND EUROPE;

SHEWING

THE RESULTS OF THE PRIMARY SCHOOLS,
AND OF THE DIVISION OF LANDED PROPERTY, IN
FOREIGN COUNTRIES.

BY

JOSEPH KAY, ESQ. M.A.

OF TRINITY COLLEGE, CAMBRIDGE;
BARRISTER-AT-LAW;
AND LATE TRAVELLING BACHELOR OF THE UNIVERSITY
OF CAMBRIDGE.

" The best way to help the Poor is to enable them to help themselves."
" The object of all Government should be the happiness of the *majority*
of the people."

IN TWO VOLUMES.

VOL. I.

THE PEASANT PROPRIETORS.

LONDON:
LONGMAN, BROWN, GREEN, AND LONGMANS,
PATERNOSTER-ROW.
1850.

TO

THE RIGHT HONOURABLE

THE LORD JOHN RUSSELL, M.P.,

FIRST LORD OF THE TREASURY,

&c. &c.

My Lord,

When you addressed the Electors of the City of London, upon assuming, at the command of Her Majesty, the office of First Minister of the Executive Government, you announced, that the Administration, over which you were called to preside, would apply itself to the amelioration of the social condition of the people.

Your Lordship's Government has sought to fulfil this great promise, on the one hand, by the reduction of the public burthens, by the removal of commercial restrictions, and by the consequent diminution of the price of the necessaries of life; and, on the other hand, by the diminution of the hours of labour, by the improvement of the sanitary regulations of the towns, by the institution of local courts and cheaper forms of legal procedure, and by the decisive indications, which have been given, that the power of the Government will be zealously applied to the creation of a comprehensive and efficient system of National Education.

These measures have spread, among large classes of the operative population, a confidence in the disposition of the Executive Government to promote their well-being, which I trust a further development of the same policy may tend to increase.

In the belief, that your Lordship's Government will persevere in the introduction of progressive measures for the improvement of the social condition of the nation, and as a slight indication of the respect and gratitude with which, in common with so many of my countrymen, I have witnessed your Lordship's unwearied, enlightened, and disinterested efforts to promote the happiness and prosperity of the poorer classes of this country, I venture to dedicate this work to your Lordship.

I remain, my Lord,

Your Lordship's very obedient Servant,

JOSEPH KAY.

3. Churchyard Court, Inner Temple, London,
March 1. 1850.

PREFACE.

I CANNOT commit this work to the press without expressing the sincere gratitude I feel to the under-mentioned gentlemen, all of whom have aided me in my inquiries abroad. Many of them spent several days, and some of them several weeks, in accompanying me in my examination of their schools and colleges, and in explaining to me the organisation of the different European systems of National Education, the modes of educating and supporting the teachers, the methods of instruction pursued in the schools, and the effects of the daily education given to the children of the poorer classes, upon the social condition of the people.

Poor and unworthy as this return is, for the kindness which these gentlemen have shown me, I hope I may be allowed to preface this work by at least acknowledging, how much I am indebted for the assistance given me by —

His Excellency the Chevalier BUNSEN, the Ambassador of
  Prussia;

Dr. EICHHORN, late Minister of Public Instruction in
  Prussia;

M. SALVANDY, late Minister of Public Instruction in France;

The Minister of the Interior in the kingdom of Saxony;

The late Minister of the Interior in the kingdom of Bavaria;

The Minister of the Interior in the kingdom of Wirtemberg;

The late President of the Diet of Switzerland;

The Minister of Public Instruction in the canton of Berne;

The Director of the Normal College at Versailles;

The Principal of the central College of the Frères Chrétiens
  of France;

Dr. DIESTERWEG, late Director of the Normal College at
  Berlin;

Professor FREDERIC VON RAÜMER, of Berlin;

The Director of the Normal College at Potsdam;

Dr. HENNICKE, the Director of the Normal College at
  Weissenfels;

The Professors of the Normal College at Weissenfels;

Professor OTTO, Director of the Normal College at Dresden;

The Director of the Normal College at Vienna;

The Director of the Normal College at Carlsruhe;

M. GAUTHEY, late Director of the Normal Colleges at
  Lausanne;

M. VEHRLI, Director of the Normal College at Kreuitz-
  lingen;

The Professors of the Normal College of Zurich;

The Director of the Normal College of Solleure;

The Director of the Normal College near Hofwyl;

The Professors of the College at Argau;

The Directors of the Normal Colleges of St. Gall;

M. DE FELLENBERG, Principal of the Great Schools at
  Hofwyl;

The Directors of the Schools in Lucerne ;

The Director of the Schools at Vevay ;

The Director of the Schools of the canton of Zug ;

LE PÈRE GIRARD, of Fribourg ;

LE CHANOINE GOTTRO, of Fribourg ;

Counsellor STIEHL, the Inspector General of Prussia ;

DR. DIETERICI, Chief of the Statistical Bureau in Berlin ;

DR. BRUGGEMAN, Member of the Council of Education in Berlin ;

Professor HINTZ, of Berlin ;

DR. PERTZ, King's Librarian at Berlin ;

DR. JULIUS, of Hamburg ;

The Teachers of the great Primary Schools in Berlin ;

The Teachers of the Primary Schools in Dusseldorf, Elberfeld, Aix-la-Chapelle, Cologne, Bonn, and Weissenfels ;

The Teachers of the Primary Schools of Dresden and Munich ;

HERR PETERS, of Bonn ;

HERR LOHRER, of Carlsruhe ;

The Teachers in the Rauhe Haus, near Hamburg ;

The Professor of Music in the Normal College of Brühl, in Prussia ;

The Teachers of the Primary Schools at the Hague ;

The Director of the Pauper Colony in the North of Holland ;

The Teachers in the Schools connected with this Colony ;

The Director of the Institution for the Education of Protestant Nurses, and of the Primary Schools, near Dusseldorf.

CONTENTS

OF

THE FIRST VOLUME.

CHAPTER I.

THE SOCIAL CONDITION OF THE POOR IN FOREIGN COUN-
TRIES, AND THE RESULTS OF THE SUBDIVISION OF THE
LAND.

The higher and middle classes in England and Europe. — The poorer
classes in England and Europe.—The happy condition of the German
poor the result of two causes: 1. The schools — 2. The subdivision
of the land. — The condition of a people entirely the result of its
institutions. — The conduct of the German people during the revolutionary times a proof of their intelligence and conservative character.
— The preparation for life through which a German peasant passes:
1. In the schools — 2. In the barracks — 3. In the villages. — The
causes which have led to the subdivision of landed property in France,
Germany, Switzerland, Holland, Belgium, Denmark, &c.—The causes
which have led to the accumulation of land in a few hands in Great
Britain and Ireland. — The description of the condition of the poorer
classes in foreign countries.

1. *The Intelligence of the Poor Abroad.*

2. *The Education of the Peasants, combined with the Subdivision of Land,
tends to strengthen their Prudence, Foresight, and Economy.* — The laws
prohibiting marriage in certain cases in Switzerland. — Opinions of
Reichensperger and Thaer. — Statistics of the age of marriage in
Geneva, Vaud, Prussia, and England. — The postponement of mar-
riage does not necessarily increase the immorality of the peasants. —
Opinions of Mill, Laing, Sismondi, Rau, Quetelet, and Legoyt. —
Statistics showing the rate of the increase of population in different

CHAP. II.

THE CONDITION OF THE POOR IN ENGLAND.

THE

SOCIAL CONDITION

AND

EDUCATION OF THE PEOPLE.

CHAPTER I.

THE SOCIAL CONDITION OF THE POOR IN FOREIGN COUN-
TRIES, AND THE RESULTS OF THE SUBDIVISION OF THE
LAND.

The higher and middle classes in England and Europe. — The poorer
classes in England and Europe.—The happy condition of the German
poor the result of two causes : 1. The schools — 2. The subdivision
of the land. — The condition of a people entirely the result of its
institutions. — The conduct of the German people during the revolutionary times a proof of their intelligence and conservative character.
— The preparation for life through which a German peasant passes :
1. In the schools — 2. In the barracks — 3. In the villages. — The
causes which have led to the subdivision of landed property in France,
Germany, Switzerland, Holland, Belgium, Denmark, &c. — The causes
which have led to the accumulation of land in a few hands in Great
Britain and Ireland. — The description of the condition of the poorer
classes in foreign countries.
1. *The Intelligence of the Poor Abroad.*
2. *The Education of the Peasants, combined with the Subdivision of Land,
tends to strengthen their Prudence, Foresight, and Economy.* — The laws
prohibiting marriage in certain cases in Switzerland. — Opinions of
Reichensperger and Thaer. — Statistics of the age of marriage in
Geneva, Vaud, Prussia, and England. — The postponement of marriage does not necessarily increase the immorality of the peasants. —
Opinions of Mill, Laing, Sismondi, Rau, Quetelet, and Legoyt. —
Statistics showing the rate of the increase of population in different
countries. — The parish of Montreux. — Opinion of Nicholls. — The
small amount of pauperism in some of the Protestant cantons of
Switzerland.

VOL. I.

in the canton of Schaffhouse. — Von Knonau's description of the peasants' houses in the canton of Schweitz. — Symon's description of the peasants' houses in the cantons of St. Gall and Appenzell. — Chambers's opinion of the condition of the Swiss peasantry.—Mügge's description of the improvement of the condition of the peasantry in the canton of Vaud since the abolition of the feudal laws. — Sismondi's description of the social condition of the peasant proprietors of Switzerland. — Laing's description of the social condition of the peasant proprietors of Switzerland. — Nicholls's description of the houses and social condition of the small proprietors of Belgium. — Reichensperger's opinion of the effect of the subdivision of land upon the peasants of Prussia. — The difference between the state of the houses of the peasants in those parts of Germany where the land is divided, and in those parts where it is not divided. — The causes of the miserable condition of the houses of the peasantry in countries where the land is in the hands of a few persons.

7. *The Education of the Poor and their improved Social Condition tend to give them Habits of Neatness and Cleanliness.* — The dress of the German and Swiss poor is much neater and much more respectable than that of the English poor.

8. *The Education of the Poor and the Division of the Land in Germany, Switzerland, &c., have tended to improve the Character of the Amusements of the poorer Classes.* — One generally true index of the condition of the poorer classes of any country is the character of their amusements. — Tavern frequenting now the only amusement of the English poor. — The character of our beer-houses and gin-palaces. — The character of the village inn in Germany. — Mr. Banfield's description. — The amusements of the peasants of many parts of Germany are of a higher character than those of the lower part of our middle classes. — The universality of education in music in Germany. — The village bands. — The singing and chanting in the churches of Germany. — The garden concerts of Germany. — The mingling of different classes of society at these concerts. — The pleasure gardens. — The public promenades near the towns. — The village fêtes of Germany. — The dancing. — The respect for property, and the absence of enclosures, enable the townspeople in Germany to enjoy walks through the fields. — The little respect shown for landed property in our manufacturing districts.

9. *The Education of the Poor and the Subdivision of Land tend very materially to improve the Health and Social Comforts of the Poorer Classes.* — The promenades and public gardens, and their effects. — The gardens of the small shopkeepers and labourers of the provincial towns, and their effects. — Reichensperger's opinion. — The well-ventilated school-rooms and the dry play-grounds, and their effect. — The food of the German poor. — Reichensperger's opinion. — The increase in the consumption of bread by the Prussians, as shown by Banfield's

statistics. — The increase in the consumption of meat by the Prussians since the division of the lands. — The increase in the general consumption of the Prussians since the subdivision of the land, as shown by the Report of the Prussian Minister of Statistics. — Opinions of the Minister. — Reichensperger's opinion of the improvement of the social condition of the people of the Rhine province. —Von Knonau's account of the food of the poor in the canton of Zurick. — Pupikofer's account of the food of the poor in the canton of Thurgovie. — Im Thurm's account of the food of the poor in the canton of Schaffhouse. — Professor Vulliemin's account of the food of the poor of the canton of Vaud.

10. *The Education of the Peasants and the Division of the Land tend to render the Peasants very Conservative in feeling.* — The peasant proprietors of France — of Germany — of Switzerland. — Their conduct during the late political revolutions. — What would be the effects of free trade in land in Ireland.—The necessity of introducing a conservative element into the operative classes of the manufacturing districts.

11. *The Education of the Peasants and the Division of Land foster a Spirit of healthy and active Independence in the People.* — The effects of our system of landed tenures in undermining the prudence and independence of the peasants.

12. *The Freedom of the Land from the Old Feudal Restrictions, and the Existence of an effective System of Registration, enable the small Shopkeepers to acquire Land.* — The great advantage of making it possible for our shopkeepers to acquire land.

13. *The Division of Landed Property reduces that intense Competition for Wealth which distinguishes English Life.* — The intense competition of the different classes in England reacts very unfavourably upon the poor. — *The results of the great property system in Ireland.— The present condition of Ireland. — The causes of that condition. — The remedy for Irish misery.*

14. *The Opinions of great Writers on the Results of the Division of Landed Property in France.* — Mill. — Napoleon and his Ministers. — Reichensperger. — Sismondi. — Troplong. — Chaptal. — Giraud de Barante. — De Carné. — Buret. — Chevalier. — De Dombasle. — C. Dupin. — Gasparin. — Villeneuve Bargemont. — Passy. — De la Farelle. — Report of the Central Agricultural Congress. — Bertin. — Points upon which all travellers in France are agreed.

IN 1844 the Senate of the University of Cambridge honoured me by appointing me Travelling Bachelor of the University, and by commissioning me to travel through Western Europe in order to examine the social condition of the poorer classes of the different countries.

During the last eight years I have travelled through Prussia, Saxony, the Austrian Empire, Bavaria, Wirtemburg, the Duchy of Baden, Hanover, Oldenburg, Lombardy, Switzerland, France, Belgium, and Holland, as well as through England, Wales, and parts of Scotland and Ireland. I undertook the greater part of these journeys in order to examine the comparative conditions of the peasants and operatives in these several countries, the different modes of legislating for them, and the effects of these different modes of legislation upon their character, habits, and social condition.

I have ventured to believe that it will not be wholly uninteresting or unprofitable to some of my own countrymen, if I publish some of the information I collected during my different tours through Europe.

It is important that we should make ourselves acquainted, as far as possible, with the state of the poorer classes in the countries of Western Europe; for there is much to learn from the results of the systems of legislation pursued by their governments and people.

We are much too apt to look down upon foreign nations, and to imagine that all our institutions are superior to theirs, and that each class of our people is more prosperous and happy than the corresponding class of any foreign country.

English noblemen and English merchants visit foreign lands, and find, that there is no other country on the face of the globe, where the aristocracy and the merchants are so wealthy, where their houses are so luxurious, where the elegances, comforts, and conveniences of life are so numerous, or where the position of the *rich man* is so enviable as in England. They see no ports and harbours so crowded with shipping, and no cities so thronged with equipages and commerce, as those of England; no palaces and country-houses so luxurious, no magazines so vast, and no shops so well stocked as those of England; no metropolis so wonderful or so wealthy, and no provincial towns so flourishing and prosperous as the metropolis and provincial cities of England; and, in a word, no exhibition of vast territorial or commercial wealth comparable to that which they have been accustomed to look upon in England.

If the object of Government is to create an enormously wealthy class, and to raise to the highest point the civilization of about one-fifth of the nation, while it leaves nearly three-fifths of the nation sunk in the lowest depths of ignorance, hopelessness, and degradation, then the system hitherto pursued in Great Britain is perfect; for the classes of our aristocracy, our landed gentry, our merchants, manufacturers, and richer tradespeople, are wealthier, more refined in their tastes, more active and enterprising, more intelligent, and, consequently, more prosperous than the corresponding classes of any other country in the world.

But, if we have enormous wealth, we ought to remember that we have enormous pauperism also; if we have middle classes richer and more intelligent than those of any other country in the world, we have poor classes, *forming the majority of the people of this country*, more ignorant, more pauperised, and more morally degraded than the poorer classes of most of the countries of Western Europe. And here it is where Englishmen might well afford sometimes to forget their pride in their own country, and to learn a lesson from other lands.

It is this side of the foreign picture which I propose in this work to describe : not that I forget wherein our country is first among the nations, but because I remember wherein other countries have outstripped us ; and because I believe more good is done by exposing our negligence, and by examining the grounds of our prejudices, than by idly flattering ourselves that we have done all that we can, and that the results are fully satisfactory.

I do not hesitate, then, to affirm, — and the proof of this affirmation I shall immediately show, — that the moral, intellectual, and social condition of the peasants and operatives of those parts of Germany, Holland, Switzerland, and France, where the poor have been educated, where the land has been released from the feudal laws, and where the peasants have been enabled to acquire, is very much higher, happier, and more satisfactory than that of the peasants and operatives of England ; and that, while these latter are struggling in the deepest ignorance, pauperism, and moral degradation, the former are steadily and progressively attaining a condition, both socially and politically considered, of a higher, happier, and more hopeful character.

I think it will appear from the following pages, that the remarkable improvement which has been witnessed in the condition of a great part of the German and Swiss poor since 1800, has been the result of two causes ; viz. —

1st. The admirable and long-continued education given to *all* the children ; and,

2d. The division of the land among the peasants.

The examination of foreign countries, and of history, clearly shows, that the moral, intellectual, and physical condition of *any* people, no matter what their race, is almost entirely the result of the laws and institutions under which they live; and that this condition is capable of indefinite improvement, by an improvement of those laws and institutions.

There is no better, or more remarkable illustration of the truth of this remark, nor any which is more frequently quoted in foreign countries, than the difference between the character and habits of Irishmen in their own land, and their character and habits in the United States, in the British Colonies, and in the British army.

In his own country, exposed to the wretched under-lessee system, and under-agent system of Ireland; to the discontented spirit of a priesthood, which we have treated as if we desired to render it inimical to our government; to the galling sense of foreign rule, suggested by the presence of English soldiers ; and to the irritating thought that his rent goes to aggrandise the splendour of a distant capital, and that the hall of his landlord is deserted, the Irishman becomes discontented, idle, rebellious, and criminal. Send him to Australia, to the States, or to any English colony, where he can make himself, by industry, a proprietor of land, and where he is not shackled by middle-age legislation, and he becomes immediately the most energetic and conservative of colonists. He there acquires faster than any one

else; he effects more in a day than any one else; he is
more untiring in his perseverance than any one else;
and he forces his rulers to write home to England, — as
the Governor of South Australia did but a few years
ago, — that the Irish are the most enterprising, successful, and orderly of all the colonists of those distant
lands. Put the Irishman in the English army, or
in the manufacturing districts of England, and similar
results invariably follow. In the army he makes a first-
rate soldier, while in Lancashire, where he is sure to
earn as much as his day's labour is worth, where the
galling misgovernment of his own country does not
affect him, where he enjoys his property securely, and
where he is put on a level with the English labourer,
he at once becomes a formidable rival of the Englishman under every respect, and one of the most successful
of the operatives. On the railway works of England,
the same result is visible, all showing that, as far as the
Irish are concerned, they might be made, and would
certainly become, the best of citizens, if they only had
the best of institutions under which to live.

But the truth of the position, that the character of
a people depends almost entirely upon the character of
the political and social institutions under which they
live, is still more remarkably demonstrated in Germany
and Switzerland. The people of the Romanist cantons
of Switzerland have not been nearly so well educated as
the people of the Protestant cantons; the schools are
not so numerous or so good in the former as they are
in the latter. The teachers of the former cantons
have not been nearly so carefully and liberally trained

as the teachers of the latter. The Roman church dispenses a much greater quantity of alms to beggars in the former, than the Protestant church does in the latter cantons; and the consequence is, that the peasants of the Romanist cantons are much more superstitious, much less intelligent, and have much less independence of mind, than the peasants of the Protestant cantons.

The result of these different systems of treating the poor has been just what might have been expected. No one, who travels through Switzerland, with his eyes open, can fail to notice the very different appearance of the people in the Romanist and in the Protestant cantons. In most of the former, beggars are very numerous, the peasants are poorly dressed, many of the children are dirty and ragged, many of the farms are negligently cultivated, and the general appearance of the people shows them to be dull, feeble, and dependant. In the Protestant cantons, on the other hand, where, as I shall afterwards show, all the people are most carefully and liberally educated, where begging is forbidden by the laws, and where the church does not dispense nearly so much indiscriminate alms and ill-judged relief, few or no beggars are to be seen; the people are well dressed and very respectable in appearance; the children are always clean, neat, and intelligent in their expressions and manners; the little properties are beautifully tilled; the houses are very clean, roomy, well-furnished, comfortable, and in good order; and the whole look of the peasants is that of an active, thriving, and contented people. I have often heard travellers remark upon the surprising difference between the appearance of the peasants of the Protestant cantons of Berne, Vaud, Geneva, Thurgovie, Zurick, and Neuchatel, and that of the peasants of the Romanist cantons of Friburg, Schweitz, Uri, and Unterwalden ; yet the inhabitants of many of these cantons, the social conditions of whose people differ the most, are people of the same race, — they speak the same language, they live in the same climate, and amid the same scenes, and they intermix much with each other. Whence then arises this singular difference in their condition? It arises solely from the difference in their political and social institutions and habits.

In Germany the same truth stares us in the face. Saxony and Bohemia lie side by side. The majority of the people of these two countries speak the same language, profess the same religion, and belong to the same race ; but the condition of the peasants of the two countries is as different as can well be imagined.

In Saxony, which I have visited and carefully inspected twice, there is very little pauperism; the people are well and comfortably clad—ragged or badly patched clothes are seldom, I might truly say, never seen; beggars are hardly ever met with; the houses of the peasantry are remarkably large, high, roomy, convenient, substantially built, constantly whitewashed, and orderly in appearance; the children are always clean, well dressed, and very polite in their manners; there is little or no difference between the appearance of the children of the poor and of the rich; the land is perhaps better cultivated than in any other part of Europe; and the general condition of the peasantry

more prosperous than that of any other I have seen,
except it be that of the peasantry of the cantons of
Berne, Vaud, and Neuchatel in Switzerland, or of the
Rhine Provinces of Prussia.

In Bohemia, on the other hand, a totally different
spectacle presents itself, and one which cannot fail to
strike any intelligent traveller with astonishment. The
moment he has crossed the Saxon frontiers, the traveller finds himself surrounded by crowds of beggars of
the most miserable appearance, who strongly remind
him of the sight which meets his eyes in Ireland ; while
even those peasants, who do not beg, are very poorly
dressed, wear no shoes or stockings, and often appear
in rags. The cottages are very small and wretched;
the villages are generally only collections of the most
miserable wooden cabins of one story in height, and
crowded together as closely as possible ; and the land
itself is only half cultivated, and presents about the
same contrast to Saxony, as Ireland does to England.

But what is the cause of this difference ? It is easily
explained. In Saxony the people are admirably educated
by teachers of great erudition and practical good sense,
who have been for many years past engaged in awaken-
ing and directing the intelligence of the children, and
in teaching them to think. In Bohemia, although there
are plenty of schools, the instruction given in them is
much inferior to that given in the Saxon schools, and
is planned so as to make the people good subjects;
while that of Saxony is planned so as to make the
Saxon peasants intelligent citizens. In Saxony the
land is divided among the peasants, the entail laws

having been repealed, so that the peasants feel strongly
interested in the cultivation of their little properties,
and study how to make them as productive as possible.
In Bohemia the land is divided among great nobles,
who leave their estates in the hands of agents, and
carry off all their rents to spend them in the distant
metropolis of Vienna. The peasants of Bohemia, therefore, like the peasants of Ireland, feel no interest in the
soil or in its proper cultivation, as they derive no benefit from it, and as they are deprived of any chance of
acquiring land, and of raising themselves in the social
scale ; while those, who can think at all, are exasperated
by seeing the fruits of their labour and of their country
spent among strangers at Vienna.

I travelled through one part of Bohemia with a
Saxon. He pointed out the beggars to me, and the
poor dress of the peasants, and said, with pride, " You
will not see such sights in my country, Sir. Our peasants are owners of their own little estates, and have
been steadily improving in their social condition ever
since we repealed our entail laws and allowed the land
to be subdivided among them, and ever since we began
to educate the children as we now educate them. Our
people are all well educated, have got libraries in their
villages, and are contented, because they are intelligent and know that their success in life depends upon
their own exertions, and that there is nothing to prevent their succeeding if they are only prudent. But
these poor Bohemians have no strong stimulus to be
prudent and industrious, for they have no interest in the
soil : they are the serfs of the great lords at Vienna."

It seemed to me that there was some similarity between the cases of the Bohemian and the Irish peasantry.

I travelled through another part of Bohemia, in company with a very intelligent Prussian landlord, with whom I had a great deal of conversation. He said to me, " What a strange spectacle it is to see this fine country so badly cultivated, and the peasants so poorly housed. Look, too, what great tracts are left entirely uncultivated. You do not see any thing like this in those parts of Prussia, where the peasants are educated proprietors. There they are prosperous, and the land is beautifully cultivated. Here a great part of the land is waste, while the peasants are the miserable serfs of great lords who spend their rents at a distance from their estates. If Bohemia were only cultivated like Prussia, it would be one of the richest countries in Europe. But it never can be properly cultivated under the present system." This was a remarkable opinion to be uttered by a German landlord. But so it is. The different effects of these different systems of legislation are so conspicuous, that no one who is commonly intelligent can fail to remark it ; while no one who does perceive it, can meet it in this case by the old argument, " it is the difference of race which occasions this difference in the condition and character of the people." The truth is, race has little or nothing to do with the degradation of either the Bohemian, the Austrian, or the Irish peasantry. In each of these cases it is entirely the result of bad social and political institutions.

Even in Prussia*, the difference between the condition of the peasants in those parts of the country, where the land is subdivided, and in those parts, where the peasants are merely day-labourers on the great estates of rich landowners, is very remarkable. In the former, as I shall show hereafter, the peasants are prosperous, hopeful, and industrious, are dressed comfortably, have roomy and well built houses, and have all the manners and appearance of independent men; while in the latter, they are pauperised, wretchedly lodged, miserably clothed, and exhibiting no symptoms of improvement. All Prussian authorities agree in this statement. There are not, however, many large estates in Prussia; and the latter description of peasants is becoming rarer every day.

Germany and Switzerland are peculiarly instructive and interesting countries to a traveller, who visits them in order to study the effects of different political and social institutions on the characters of nations. In each country, people of the same race have been exposed to the influence of institutions of the most varying character, and in each, as I shall show hereafter, the different results, invariably and without exception, prove that the more liberal the institutions, the better will be the people; that the social condition of the people is generally the direct and immediate result of its institutions, and that it is capable of an amelioration, of which

* In some able articles, published in the National-Zeitung in 1849, it is shown that " a comparison of the statistics of the different provinces proves that the larger and the fewer the estates, by so much the less prosperous invariably is the condition of the peasantry."

in England we can have no conception; that the institutions, which alone can effect this end, are those which teach the people how to raise themselves, and which make it possible for the people to raise themselves by perseverance and temporary self-denial, and not such, as favour one class more than another, or such as keep one class for ever in the leading-strings of another. Independence, perfect independence, unshackled independence of action, is absolutely necessary to the success and improvement of one class as much as to that of the other.

This independence cannot exist, where a class is uneducated, and unable to understand its interests or how to make the most of its resources. Ignorance is a greater thraldom than oppression; for oppression does stimulate to opposition; whereas, ignorance cramps and palsies efforts, by concealing the view of the advantages to be gained by industry.

Some persons, perhaps, will think that the turbulent conduct of the people of the great towns of Germany, since the commencement of the year 1848, does not speak much for the contentment or character of the poorer classes of Germany. It may seem strange to those who do not know Germany; but to myself the conduct of the people of that country, since the outbreak of the different revolutions, is one of the strongest proofs of the great intelligence and strong conservative feeling of the poorer classes of Germany that could possibly be adduced. My reasons for thinking so are simply these. A political change has been effected in Germany, greater and more sudden than almost any that history records. In the beginning of 1848 there was not even the semblance of political liberty. There was neither liberty of speech, nor liberty of action, nor freedom of the press. The people were treated like children. The governments did every thing for them, and suffered them to take no part worth speaking of in the direction of national affairs. The will of each sovereign was law in its fullest and widest sense. The newspapers were not allowed to print any articles of criticism upon any matter of internal politics. Every sentence which was destined for the press, whether for a book, or for a newspaper, or pamphlet, had to be subjected, before it was printed, to a censor appointed by government, who cut out every thing which he thought ought not to be printed. In the Austrian empire, not only were the newspapers prevented publishing any original articles on internal or external politics, but they were also prohibited publishing any news about foreign political matters; so that the Austrian people were kept in the strangest and most complete state of ignorance about the progress of events in foreign countries, as well as of every political event which took place in the different provinces of their own empire. The Austrian papers contained articles of literary criticism, notices of court proceedings, accounts of the fêtes of foreign courts, incidents of travel, articles on music; and this was nearly all. Such was the depressing influence of this strict censorship, that even the literary articles were so miserably poor as not to be worth reading. Austrian literature had sunk to the lowest ebb, for nothing like free thought could express itself in print.

In Austria, too, no person could move from his
native town to another without a written order of the
police. If he attempted to do so without an order, he
was always detected at the entrance of the town, and
stopped and punished. The native of one town, before
he could pass the gates of another, had to produce his
permission, to show it to the police, and to get it
entered into a book kept on purpose.

No foreigner was ever allowed to enter into any
Austrian town or city, until he had shown and delivered
his passport to the police, told them where he was
going to lodge, and received a ticket from them. He
could not leave the town again, until he had got his
ticket again exchanged for his passport.

Except in one or two provinces, there were no public
courts of justice in Germany, and no juries. Every
political and every civil offender was examined in closed
courts, before judges appointed by the central power,
and convicted and sentenced by the judges. In Austria,
every man was liable to be dragged suddenly from his
home and family, and confined at the will of the police
in some distant dungeon, while his poor family was
often left uncertain whether he was dead or alive, or
where he was concealed.

In Austria, every Roman Catholic (and nearly the
whole population are Roman Catholics) was *obliged* to
confess himself to his parish priest at certain fixed
periods every year. The priests were *obliged* to inform
the police who neglected to confess at the appointed
times, and these persons were heavily punished. One
of the priests in Vienna told me, that this system was

introduced in order to keep the people in check, and to find out every commencement of political plots. No one was safe, as he might be betrayed by some superstitious or incautious neighbour at the next confessional.

Immense numbers of police and spies were kept in the pay of the governments. In some parts of Germany, and more especially in Austria, no one dared to speak on political matters before a stranger, and scarcely before a friend. As the people often said to me, "*we are never sure whom we may be addressing.*" A few incidents of my own travels will best show to what extent this wretched system was put in force.

In 1846 I spent some weeks at Bonn, in Prussia. I there made acquaintance with a student of great ability, and the son of a member of the Prussian government. He informed me, as of a matter of course, that the students were not allowed to discuss politics freely at their parties. He said, that only a few days before there had been an evening party of some students; that one of them had got a little excited with beer, and had spoken rather freely about political matters ; that the police had *somehow or other* heard of it, and that the student had been summoned to the police bureau the next morning, and had been told, that if he ever repeated his offence, he would be heavily punished and expelled the university.

At Berlin, in the same year, I was walking one afternoon with two young professors. We had been discussing for some time the state of political feeling in Germany, and the political wants of the people, when my companions suddenly put a stop to the conversation. Not understanding their reason for doing so, I endeavoured to renew it; when they answered me, " We had better change the conversation, Sir; just before us there are two of the police; and in Prussia, we never talk politics when we are in sight of any of the police."

In 1847, I dined with about 200 of the National Guard of Dresden: many of them were gentlemen, and others shopkeepers of the city. After dinner we had, as in England, a good many toasts and speeches: several of these latter were political. It was very curious to hear them. All the opinions of the speakers were clothed in enigmatical language; and though nothing was intended beyond what is spoken in our House of Peers every day, still no one ventured to mention reforms in the laws, except in an indirect kind of way. The hints were all understcod, and were cheered all the more, from the general feeling of the danger which the speakers ran in giving utterance, even in this enigmatical manner, to their opinions. A man, who sat beside me, told me, in answer to my questions, that it would not be safe to discuss political matters in a freer vein, and in more undisguised language. It is to be remembered that in this country, Saxony, there was no free press. The papers were not allowed to publish any thing that the government disapproved. No book was printed, out of which the government had not previously cut out every sentence it disliked.

In the same year I was travelling by rail from Leipsig to Dresden. In the same carriage were three Germans. I entered into conversation with one who was sitting near me. In the course of the conversation, I said, in an inquiring way, " I hear that Prince John has been very unpopular in Leipsic, ever since the Leipsic riots." The German did not answer for a short time, and then, coming up close to me, he said, in a low tone of voice, " It is always better, Sir, to avoid politics in a railway-carriage, in Germany, when there are third parties present. We generally make a point of not talking politics at such times. I hope you will excuse my observation." I bowed, and turned the conversation. This was in Saxony, of the freedom of which country we have heard so much.

In 1846, I was travelling in the north of Bavaria, on the Nuremberg line of railroad: there were four Germans in the same carriage in which I was seated : two of them I knew ; the others were strangers to us all. I had been talking in German to my friends, for some time, when the conversation turned upon Munich, and the great expenditure of the King upon art. I asked how the King had obtained all the money necessary for his great works, and whether it was true that many parts of the internal administration were suffering from want of means. My friends instantly addressed me in French, and said, " If you wish to talk about political matters, it will be advisable to speak in. French. We do not know the persons who are present, and it is never safe to talk politics before a stranger." We continued our conversation, therefore, in French.

In Austria, the people would never talk with me upon political matters. If a stranger addressed them on such subjects, it instantly produced a lull in the conversation, and an expression of countenance which said, " Who are you? do you know in what land you are travelling? do you want to betray us?"

In Austria, and the greater part of Germany, neither the upper, middle, nor lower ranks of the people were allowed to interfere in any manner in political affairs. They were not told what the government intended to do; nor, when done, were they allowed to criticise, or even pass an opinion upon, the line of policy adopted. The people of Austria, and of many parts of Germany, enjoyed no kind of training whatever in political matters; neither the training to be derived from reading dissertations upon political matters, nor even that to be derived from reading the political histories of foreign lands. In Austria, and many parts of Germany, all thought, and still more all discussion, upon political matters was prevented, and effectually stifled, by spies and police. Owing to this, the people of Austria and of other parts of Germany were literally babes in political knowledge and political experience.

Is it, then, to be wondered at, that when this wretched system crumbled away under the moral earthquake of the French Revolution of 1848, the German people, wholly inexperienced as they were, should have committed extravagances, and that they should have shown that they did not know how to use the power with which they suddenly found themselves invested?

Do Englishmen forget how much bloodshed and civil strife it cost us to escape from the trammels of tyranny, and to establish a constitutional government?

In two short months the old tyrannies and governments of Germany fell to pieces. For several months afterwards, there was literally no government in the greater part of Germany and Austria. The people found themselves suddenly without masters, and discovered that the reins of government, which they had never handled, and which they had never been taught to handle, were thrown to them.

The wonder is, — not that riots and bloodshed ensued in the great cities, but that the whole of Germany and Austria was not convulsed by a horrible civil war. I am firmly persuaded, that if it had not been for the great intelligence of all ranks of the people, and also for the great subdivision of the landed property among the peasants themselves, we should have witnessed a revolution in Germany, much more terrible than any thing of the kind that has ever occurred in Europe; for never before did any people emerge so suddenly from such an extreme of political thraldom, into such an extreme of political freedom. Of all proofs of the beneficial effects of education, and of a system of peasant proprietors, I know none more undeniably satisfactory than the conduct of the German peasants during these late revolutionary times. When my readers consider from what a state of political bondage they suddenly broke loose, and what an absolute freedom from restraint they suddenly attained, they will surely grant that they exhibited but little of that wild revelling in liberty, which usually follows the sudden bursting loose from long-endured and galling tyranny, and which might, if history be any guide, have naturally been expected.

There is no people on the face of the earth, morally and intellectually considered, so well fitted for and so deserving of the enjoyment of real liberty as the Germans. All classes of the inhabitants of Prussia and Saxony are as far advanced in the scale of civilization as our shop-keeping classes. All they require is experience in the exercise of political privileges. This they never enjoyed before the year 1848, so that it is not to be wondered at that many excesses and follies have been committed in their first experiments in political liberties. These excesses may, in their case — as in the case of all nations in all times, — lead to the temporary suspension of their unfolding freedom; but that suspension will be only temporary. The masses of the German people are so intelligent that it will be impossible for any of the German governments to run counter to public opinion for any length of time. Ever since the governments began, in 1815, to educate the peasants, public opinion has been growing stronger and stronger with the growth of intelligence, and the governments have been obliged to secede, year by year, more and more from their old ideas and from their old pretensions. If it had not been for the education of the people, the absolute forms of government would have lasted in Germany for centuries to come; for the people, before the schools were built, were asleep and stupid, and were not goaded into any longing for liberty by actual miseries like those, which produced the Revolution of 1789 in France. Education has taught

the German peasants to desire political freedom, and
has fitted them for its enjoyment. When the change is
once effected, and the first commotions necessarily attendant on that change are over, and when the Germans
have had a little experience in political affairs, they will
prove themselves more deserving of unrestricted liberty
than any nation upon earth.

As I have already said, the moral, intellectual, and
physical condition of the peasants and operatives of
Prussia, Saxony, and other parts of Germany, of Holland, and of the Protestant cantons of Switzerland, and
the social condition of the peasants in the greater part
of France, is very much higher and happier, and very
much more satisfactory, than that of the peasants and
operatives of England; the condition of the poor in the
North German, Swiss, and Dutch towns, is as remarkable a contrast to that of the poor of the English towns,
as can well be imagined; and that the condition of the
poorer classes of Germany, Switzerland, Holland, and
France is rapidly improving.

The great superiority of the preparation for life, which
a poor man receives in the countries I have mentioned,
to that which a peasant or operative receives in England,
and the difference of the social position of a poor man in
these countries to that of a peasant or operative in England, seem sufficient to explain the difference which exists
between the moral and social condition of the poor of
our own country and of the other countries I have
named.

In Germany, Holland, and Switzerland, a child begins
its life in the society of parents, who have been educated

VOL. I.

and brought up for years in the company of learned and gentlemanly professors, and in the society and under the direction of a father, who has been exercised in military arts, and who has acquired the bearing, the clean and orderly habits, and the taste for respectable attire, which characterise the soldier. The children of these countries spend the first six years of their lives in homes which are well regulated. They are during this time accustomed to orderly habits, to neat and clean clothes, and to ideas of the value of instruction, of the respect due to the teachers, and of the excellence of the schools, by parents, who have, by their training in early life, acquired such tastes and ideas themselves.

Each child, at the age of six, begins to attend a school, which is perfectly clean, well ventilated, directed by an able and well educated gentleman, and super-intended by the religious ministers and by the inspectors of the government. Until the completion of its four-teenth year, each child continues regular daily attend-ance at one of these schools, daily strengthening its habits of cleanliness and order, learning the rudiments of useful knowledge, receiving the principles of religion and morality, and gaining confirmed health and physical energy by the exercise and drill of the school play-ground. No children are left idle in the streets of the towns; no children are allowed to grovel in the gutters; no children are allowed to make their appearance at the schools dirty, or in ragged clothes; and the local authorities are obliged to clothe all whose parents cannot afford to clothe them.

The children of the poor of Germany, Holland, and

Switzerland acquire stronger habits of cleanliness, neatness, and industry at the primary schools, than the children of the small shop-keeping classes of England do at the private schools of England, and they leave the primary schools of these countries much better instructed than those who leave our middle-class private schools. After having learnt reading, writing, arithmetic, singing, geography, history, and the Scriptures, the children leave the schools, carrying with them into life habits of cleanliness, neatness, order, and industry, and an awakened intellect, capable of collecting truths, and of reasoning upon them.

At the age of twenty all the young men, having been educated as above mentioned, enter the army, and, for two or three years, go through all the exercises of a severe military discipline, and through all the precise and orderly drill of soldiers. All are subjected to this course. In the barracks is continued the discipline which was commenced in the playgrounds of the schools. They learn to walk uprightly, to go through all military manœuvres, and to act in concert; they strengthen their previously acquired habits of good dressing, cleanliness, neatness, and order; they harden their muscles by exercise and severe drill; they learn how to use arms; by being moved from barracks to barracks, and from province to province, they become better acquainted with their own country, and see more of life and of the world, than if they had been confined, as peasants generally are, to the narrow circle of a parish or provincial town; they strengthen their patriotic sentiments by learning to regard themselves as members of their country's army, and as capable of aiding to defend their fatherland; they acquire manly and masculine ideas and habits, by being for three years accustomed to the severest daily drill and exercises, by being taught to look the hazards of a soldier's life in the face, and by being habituated to the use of the instruments of death; they acquire manners of courtesy by their relations with their officers, and gain that manly and self-confident feeling, which is the consequence of practice in the use of arms. Habits thus acquired become a second nature which can seldom be shaken off afterwards. The dissemination of such habits among the people must be productive of great good. The dispersion of Cromwell's army diffused among the English people a leaven of manly vigour, active industry, intelligent subordination, and courageous independence. In Germany and Switzerland, the constant diffusion among the people of soldier-citizens with such habits as those I have mentioned, tends inconceivably to raise the character of the lower orders of society.

It must not be supposed that the character of the soldiers of foreign armies is like that of our own. In our country, the soldiers are generally men of habits not sufficiently steady and industrious to enable them to succeed in the ordinary avocations of life, or men who do not like to depend upon their own independent exertions. They are too often the worst specimens of our peasants, or of the idle populations of our towns. Their barrack life is not distinguished by any strict morality; on the contrary, the neighbourhood of a regiment with us is proverbially bad, and is carefully avoided by families. This is not to be wondered at. The sober domestic man, who loves a home, will not, in England, choose a soldier's life, where he must, in the majority of cases, either give up all idea of marrying, or separate from his wife, and leave her unprotected and alone. It is, therefore, the men who do not care for wives or domestic comforts who generally, with us, seek the army. Whilst, therefore, it may be fairly questioned whether it is not better for the community to draw away from the villages and towns the class of men, who most naturally and generally seek the army in England, and to subject them to a severe daily drill, and to constant surveillance; and, although it may be, that this class of men make the bravest and the most daring soldiers; yet it is not to be wondered at, that their barrack life is dissolute, notwithstanding strict watchfulness on the part of the officers, nor is it great matter of wonder, if such men often contaminate and injure one another. Our barrack life would not, therefore, be likely to improve the people.

But it is different in Germany and Switzerland. The men who are each year enlisted there, are all the youths of the nation who have attained their twentieth year. All must enlist. Soon after their education in the schools is completed, they begin their education and exercises in the barracks. The drill is severer than ours; the surveillance in the barracks is stricter; the character of the young men who enter them is incomparably better. The shopkeeper's son, the artizan's, the peasant's, the doctor's, the lawyer's and the farmer's, *all* enter the ranks of the army together, serve side by side, wear the same dress, live in the same barracks, and are subjected to the same discipline. The barrack life in these countries is but a continuance of the school life, with this difference, that the discipline is stricter, that physical training takes the place of mental training, and that the soldiers are older than the scholars.

No parent, therefore, fears sending his sons to the barracks in these countries, more than he does sending them to the schools. The young men find, on entering the barracks, their relations, their old associates, and the sons of their father's friends; and they find themselves subjected to a stricter discipline than that of any school or college of their own or of any other country.

After the most careful attention to this subject, the results of the military systems of Germany and Switzerland appeared to me to be admirable. The drill of the army is so severe, that a peasant is only too happy to exchange it for his simple duties in the country. It does not breed any discontent, nor does it at all unfit a young man for the duties of his after life; but it returns him to his parish and his home a manly, orderly, gentlemanly, and hard-working citizen.

True it is, that three years spent in the army are so much cut out of a man's professional life, but they are well spent in gaining what the exercises of those years confer.

The system tends also to prevent improvidently early marriages, as the young men do not marry until their term of barrack discipline is past; and it thus acts as a very powerful and very healthy check upon the too rapid increase of population.

It tends also very much to improve the race of the lower classes of the citizens. A soldier accustomed to good dress, to great cleanliness, and to gentlemanly associates, seeks a better-looking and more ladylike style of wife, than a poor boorish peasant, who has been brought up all his life without any or with very little instruction, in dirt, and among the lowest classes of the farm girls of a country village. Where the tastes of the men improve, the girls will always strive to raise themselves up to the standard which the men require; and so it happens, that the school and army training of the peasants of Germany and Switzerland tends most remarkably to civilise the women of the lowest classes of society. An Englishman, taken to the markets, fairs, and village festivals of these countries, would scarcely credit his eyes were he to see the peasant girls who meet there to join in the festivities; they are so much more lady-like in their appearance, in their manners, and in their dress, than those of our country parishes.

I hope it will not be supposed, from what I have said about the discipline in the barracks in Germany and Switzerland, that I intend to infer, that such an institution would suit our people or our habits. I have only narrated a simple fact, viz., that such an institution exists abroad, and is productive there of good results. If I had passed it over in silence, it would have been said, that I joined with other writers in condemning it and its effects. I have not wished to expose myself to such an imputation, and therefore, at the risk of offending some to whom such an institution is peculiarly odious, I have ventured to show how it seemed to me to work abroad.

When the young men leave the army after their three years' service as soldiers, and when they return to their native parishes, they find themselves in the following position. They are well educated, healthy, strong, and active. Nearly all the land is divided into small estates, and is held and cultivated by peasants. The process of conveying an estate from one owner to another is very simple and cheap. Great numbers of small estates in all parts of the country are constantly in the market to be sold. Each young man finds that many of his friends and relations, who had left the army some years before himself, have bought houses and plots of land, and are engaged in farming for themselves. The young peasant, stimulated by his desire to get married and to become a householder and a proprietor, hires himself to a farmer who requires a labourer, learns farming, lays by his savings; and if he has no old relation to whose property he would naturally succeed in the course of time, after some years saving, he invests his little capital as a first payment towards the purchase of a house and farm, raises the remainder of the price by way of mortgage, and enters into possession, paying off the mortgage by regular instalments. Sometimes the purchase is hastened and facilitated by his marriage with a young woman, who brings with her some small amount of saved earnings towards the purchase. The desire to acquire the possession of a house and farm tends very greatly to restrain early marriages, and stimulates very greatly the

energies, hopes, and exertions of the peasants. Doubtless, there are many peasants who cannot make up their
minds to present self-denial, to postponement of marriage, and to doubled exertion, in order to attain what
seems at first a distant good; but the knowledge that
it is possible to buy a farm, if such present self-denial
is exercised, and the desire to purchase one, operate
with such force, that in most parts of Germany, Holland, Belgium, Norway, Denmark, Switzerland, the
Tyrol, North Italy, and France, the greatest part of the
land belongs to the farmers and peasants, who cultivate
it for themselves.

Even the labourers in the small towns of these
countries often possess outside the towns small gardens
or plots of land, to which they resort in the evenings in
order to cultivate them, or to carry away their produce
for the use of their families.

Every peasant, who possesses one of these estates,
becomes interested in the maintenance of public order,
in the tranquillity of the country, in the suppression of
crimes, in the fostering of industry among his own
children, and in the promotion of their intelligence. A
class of peasant proprietors forms the strongest of all
Conservative classes.

Such is a sketch of the social situation, and of the
preparation for life, of a peasant of Germany, Holland,
and Switzerland. Before I describe the condition of
the peasants and labourers of these countries, let me
just glance at the preparation for life, which the majority of our poor receive. Of the children of the poor,
who are yearly born in England, vast numbers never

receive any education at all, while many others never enter any thing better than a dame or a Sunday-school. In the towns they are left in crowds until about eight or nine years of age, to amuse themselves in the dirt of the streets, while their parents pursue their daily toil. In these public thoroughfares, during the part of their lives, which is most susceptible of impressions and most retentive of them, they acquire dirty, immoral, and disorderly habits; they become accustomed to wear filthy and ragged clothes; they learn to pilfer and to steal; they associate with boys, who have been in prison, and who have there been hardened in crime by evil associates; they learn how to curse one another, how to fight, how to gamble, and how to fill up idle hours by vicious pastimes; they acquire no knowledge except the knowledge of vice; they never come in contact with their betters; and they are not taught either the truths of religion or the way by which to improve their condition in life. Their amusements are as low as their habits. The excitements of low debauchery too horrible to be named, of spirituous liquors, which they begin to drink as early as they can collect pence wherewith to buy them, of the commission and concealments of thefts, and of rude and disgusting sports, are the pleasures of their life. The idea of going to musical meetings, such as those of the German poor, would be scoffed at, even if there were any such meetings for them to attend. Innocent dancing is unknown to them. Country sports they cannot have. Read they cannot. So they hurry for amusement and excitement to the gratification of sensual desires and appetites. In this manner,

filthy, lewd, sensual, boisterous, and skilful in the commission of crime, a great part of the populations of
our towns grow up to manhood. Of the truth or falsehood of this description any one can convince himself,
who will examine our criminal records or who will
visit the back streets of any English town, when the
schools are full, and count the children upon the door-
steps and pavements, and note their condition, manners,
and appearance, and their degraded and disgusting
practices.*

The state of things is better in the country villages;
but it is generally better, more from the absence of the
corrupting influences always to be found in town streets,
than from the presence of corrective influences.

Many town parishes are without any schools at all;
the instruction given in most of the schools, which are
established, is miserable in its character; infant schools
are terribly needed in almost every town in England.
Efficient teachers are needed everywhere. Every child
in Germany and Switzerland remains in school, or continues to receive education, from the age of six to that
of fourteen, and often to that of sixteen or seventeen;
while in England, even of those children who do go to
school, few remain there beyond the age of nine or ten.
If all this be true, is it to be wondered at, that the dress
of our peasants, their manners, their appearance, their
amusements, their manner of speaking, their cleanliness,
the character of their houses, the condition of their

---

* Lord Ashley informs us, (see Chap. II. of this work,) that there are
80,000 poor children such as these in London alone.

children, and their intelligence, should be all miserably
inferior to those of the peasants of Germany, Holland,
and of some parts of Switzerland and France?

I confess that to me it seems to be a sufficiently reasonable conclusion, that such should be the case; but
whether reasonable or not, such it undoubtedly is.

I shall now attempt to give my readers a sketch of
the condition of the poor in Germany, Holland, and
Switzerland, and to show how far the training which a
poor man goes through in these countries, combined
with the division of the land, has tended to improve the
intelligence, the habits, the appearance, the manners and
customs, the amusements, the political character, and
the happiness of the poorer classes.

In order that my readers should the better understand, what has occasioned the division of the land
among the people in Germany, Holland, Denmark,
Norway, Switzerland, the Tyrol, North Italy, and
France, I shall be obliged, very briefly, to state the
difference of the laws relating to property in land in
Great Britain and Ireland and in the countries I have
mentioned above.

In Great Britain and Ireland the laws relating to property in land are either the direct creations of the feudal
system, or modifications of that system, varying in character as little as the change of times and circumstances
will allow.   They form one of the most difficult and intricate parts of our jurisprudence, being compounded of
ancient feudal regulations, couched in quaint and technical language, of modifications engrafted upon the old
system by the monastic orders, and of statutes modi-

fying the stringency of the old restrictive laws, or restraining the liberality of the monastic interpretations.

They are so technical, and are based upon so much antiquated learning, and upon so many almost forgotten customs, that it is quite impossible for any one, who has not made himself master of a great deal of the old learning connected with them, to understand them. If a system had been expressly devised, in order to keep every one but the studious part of the legal profession ignorant of its objects and meaning, none could have been better fitted to effect this end than our present landed property laws. It is most astonishing that, in this age of reforms, no one has attempted to codify and simplify these laws. When we see the beautiful simplicity and clearness of the foreign codes, enabling any unprofessional person to understand their general meaning and effect; and when we look at our own system, which keeps every one, but a part of the legal profession, in absolute darkness as to the rights and privileges of an owner of land, which often renders it very difficult and expensive for a proprietor to find out, what his real power over his own property is, and which tends so greatly to fetter and impede the sale of land, by rendering its conveyance from man to man so difficult and expensive; and when we remember, how many centuries this system has existed, we see another singular instance of the difficulty and slowness, with which the most useful and necessary national reforms are effected.

These laws were framed, and have been retained, for the express purposes of keeping the land in the hands of a few proprietors, — of depriving the peasants and small shopkeepers of any part of it, and of the influence which its possession confers, — and of supporting a great landed proprietor class, in order to uphold the system of aristocratic government, and to give greater strength and stability to the Crown.

It would be very difficult, in a work like the present, to give persons who have not studied these laws any correct idea of their extraordinary intricacy, or of the way in which they tend to prevent the subdivision of the large estates among the shopkeeper and peasant classes; but it is necessary for me to attempt some faint sketch of them, in order that my readers should have something like a true idea of the cause of the subdivision of land in foreign countries.   This I shall do as shortly and as distinctly as possible.

In Great Britain and Ireland, in Russia, and in some parts of Austria alone, as many of my readers are aware, the land is still divided,, and, so to speak, tied up, in few hands and in immense estates; and in these countries alone the old laws relating to landed property, which emanated from the feudal system, and which tend to prevent the subdivision of estates, still continue in force. These laws effect this end by means of the extraordinary powers which they confer upon owners of land.   They enable an owner of land to prevent the sale of the land by himself during his own life, by his creditors, and by any successor or other person for many years after his own death.

They enable an owner of an estate in *fee simple* (*i. e.* of an estate which the owner can sell so as to give the purchaser full powers of selling it to whomsoever he pleases), not only to dispose of his land during his own lifetime, and to leave the whole estate in it to any one he pleases after his death, but to do very much more. They enable him, if he has not been prevented by the settlement or will of a former proprietor, to grant by his settlement, or to leave by his will, different interests in his land to a number of persons, and so to arrange the succession to the ownership of the property by his settlement or will, that no person or persons shall be able to *sell* any portion of the land, until some person, who was an infant at the time of making the settlement, or at the death of the person having made the will, has grown up, married, and had a son, and until that son has attained the age of twenty-one years, and not even then, so as to confer a right to the immediate possession of it, unless all those, who have any interest in the land prior to that of the last-mentioned son, are dead, or join in the sale.

Let me give an example to explain this more clearly. Supposing A to be the owner of an estate in fee simple, and B, C, and D, his nephews ; and suppose D to be the youngest of his nephews, and to be only *one year* old, when A makes a settlement of his estate. A is empowered by our laws to grant his estate to his nephew B for his life; and, after B's death, to C for his life ; and, after C's death, to D for his life ; and, after D's death, to D's eldest son in fee or in tail ; or, if D should leave no son, to the unborn child of some one else in fee or in tail. If D grows up to manhood, marries, and has a son, the estate cannot be sold, until

that son has attained his twenty-first year, and not even
then, unless all the persons, entitled to the estate before
him, are dead, or join with him in the sale.

It may be stated, generally, that these laws enable
an owner of land, by his settlement or will, so to affect
his estate, that it cannot possibly be sold, in many cases
for about *fifty*, and, in some cases, for even *sixty, seventy,*
or *a hundred* years after the making of the settlement
or will.

However advisable it may be, that the estate should
be sold for the sake of all those who are interested in it,
such is the state of the law, that in many cases this is
impossible, owing to the terms of the settlement or will
of some former proprietor, who died, it may be *fifty,
sixty, seventy,* or *eighty* years ago.

Our law is not content with giving the living man
full power over the land, but it gives his corpse, so to
speak, a controlling power long after breath has de-
parted, and after the circumstances of the family or
nation have changed.

Owners of land are also enabled in certain cases to
make long leases of their land, and to introduce into
these leases, clauses, which prevent the land being under-
let or sold, or treated in any of the excepted manners
mentioned in the lease. Such leases often affect the
land for many years; sometimes for several generations
after the death of those who made them; and often prevent improvements, which the progress of science, long
after the decease of the person who so affected the land,
has rendered not only possible but expedient.

Owners of land are also in certain cases allowed to

create all sorts of curious interests or estates in their lands.   If A be an owner of an estate with full powers of disposition, he may sell it for his own lifetime only, or he may sell it to B for A's, or for B's, or for another person, C's, life, or for a certain number of years; and he may sell the succession to the estate after B's death to another person, C, for his own life, or for the life of some other person, or for a number of years, and so on for any number of persons who are living at the time of the settlement; and afterwards he may settle the succession to the land, after the deaths of all the former persons, upon the child or children of some infant not yet out of its nurse's arms; or he may make the same sort of arrangements by his will.

When such settlements or wills as these have been made, the property cannot be sold, or treated contrary to the terms of the settlement or will, until the unborn child has been born and has attained the age of twenty-one years; and not even then, unless all the persons entitled to the property before him, have died, or unless they agree with him in making such disposition.   Besides this, an owner of an estate *in fee* may mortgage his land, so as to charge it, not only for his own lifetime, but so as also to burden it with his debts for years, and sometimes for several generations, after his own death; or he may mortgage it to a number of people in succession, giving to each of the several mortgagees and to their families certain rights and claims over the estate, which may, and often do, endure for several generations after the person, who so mortgaged the property, has been gathered to his fathers.

There is another part of our system of laws relating to land which ought to be noticed, — this is the system of *primogeniture*.   If a man possesses an estate *in fee* [*] in England, and dies without having settled his land, and without having made a will devising it, the law of England prescribes, that all the land shall, after the death of such person, except in certain rare exceptional cases, descend in *one undivided mass*, either to the eldest of his sons, if he has any, or, except in certain cases, if he has no sons living at the time of his death, to the nearest of his relations, according to a table of affinities prescribed by law.

The effect of this part of our system of laws is, that in nine cases out of ten the whole estate in fee of a deceased person, who has not made a settlement or will, descends *undivided* and *undiminished* in size to some one of his children or relatives; so that if a father, who possessed an estate in fee, die leaving six sons, and without having made a will, the eldest son by the law of England would take the *whole* estate, while the younger children would receive no share of it whatever. This is only a consequent part of the old feudal system, which was framed with the express design of preventing the subdivision of estates, and by this means of depriving the middle and lower classes of any share in the land of the country, and of keeping up the wealth and power of a rich ruling class of territorial aristocracy.

The consequences of the great powers given by our

---

[*] That is, an estate which he can sell if he pleases, so as to give the purchaser full powers of disposing of it.

law to proprietors over their estates, and of the system of primogeniture, are singular and numerous. I will briefly enumerate some of them.

1. It causes the land to accumulate in the hands of a few proprietors; it prevents it selling, in the generality of instances, in small estates; it has for the last two hundred years tended gradually, but continually, to merge all small freehold properties in the great estates, until the old race of yeomen freeholders and small copyholders, who, eighty years since, were to be found all over our island, has almost entirely disappeared; it thus deprives the farmers, the shopkeepers, and the peasants of almost every chance of purchasing small plots of land, except for building purposes, in the neighbourhood of the towns; it promotes a system of large farms, and by so doing lessens the number of small farms, and renders it every year more and more difficult for a peasant to rent a farm and to raise himself to the next step in the social scale; and *it thus deprives the peasant of all strong motives to exercise exertion, self-denial, economy, or prudence, renders his prospect hopeless, and condemns him to pauperism.*

2. It tends in many instances to cheat creditors of landlords of their just claims. If a man purchase land and get deeply into debt, and afterwards marry, and if upon his marriage, and while he is still in debt, he makes a settlement of his property in consideration of his marriage, and afterwards die, not having paid his debts, and leaving no money or other property besides the land, or not sufficient money wherewith to pay his debts, his creditors cannot sell a

bit of the land so settled, and have no means of recovering their debts, although they were induced to
trust him before his marriage by seeing him in possession of the property.

If, too, a man has a great house and estate, which
belong to him for his *lifetime* only, under his own or
some prior settlement, and if shopkeepers and tradesmen, seeing him in possession of this great house and
estate, allow him to run up long accounts with them, believing him to be able to pay any amount of claim upon
him, and if this wealthy owner die very much in debt
and leaving no money, the poor creditors, who had no
means of learning, whether the land belonged to him
for more than his own life or not, cannot, after his
death, recover a farthing of their debts, even if their
debtor was possessed during his lifetime of a million
acres of land.

3. It tends also in very many instances to keep
large estates out of the market for fifty, eighty, or
one hundred years, when, if it had not been for these
laws, the proprietor would either have been compelled
to sell them by his own extravagance, or by his bad
and unskilful farming or management; or when he
would have voluntarily sold either part of them, in
order to obtain capital wherewith to cultivate the other
part better, or the whole of them, in order to engage
in other pursuits more congenial to his tastes.

4. It induces unprincipled proprietors to be tenfold
more careless, than they otherwise would be, about
the education of the child, who is to succeed them;
for they reason, with great truth, that whatever their

own extravagance, the child will take the property, which is settled upon him, unaffected by his father's debts, and, whatever the child's extravagance and folly, he will not be able to dissipate the property or to lower the social station of the family. It thus often puts into the influential places of the land men, whose early education and habits have rendered them totally unfit to be intrusted with any influence whatever, and who never would have enjoyed that influence if it had not been for this state of the law ; and it thus often sets up as examples for society, persons of depraved tastes and corrupted morals.

If a proprietor is extravagant, this state of the law, in the vast majority of cases, saves his estate from being sold either by himself or his creditors ; and if he is prudent, it often enables him to add to the property, to entail, in many cases, again, and so to hand it, undivided and increased in extent, through several successive hands again.

5. It supports a large body of old men and young men, who are not obliged to work for their living, — who are kept by the laws in their positions, however unworthy of those positions they may be, — who have never been obliged to study or improve their minds, — who have therefore often grown up in ignorance and frivolity, — who are so rich as to enable them to exercise an immense influence in the state, and to make their own conduct and manners the standard for all thoughtless and weak-minded men, and who, therefore, more than any other class, foster habits of extravagance, effeminacy, luxury, and immorality.

An idle man is a public nuisance, and ought to be chased out of the hive of men. He fosters almost invariably immorality and vice. What shall we say, then, of a system which supports a crowd of idle men, and puts these idle men into the most influential places in the land?

6. It emancipates the heir almost entirely from the influence and authority of the father. Wherever the settlements are in force, and where the father has only the life estate, the son knows that his father cannot disinherit him, but that he is sure to succeed to the property, whatever his father's wishes may be. He knows that his chance of succeeding to the lands does not depend upon his being dutiful or undutiful, moral or profligate, industrious or idle.

The father cannot in such a case interfere with the son's interest in the estate. He cannot stimulate the eldest son to exertion or honourable conduct by the fear of the property being left to one of the other children. However unworthy the eldest son may be, in such a case he cannot be prevented succeeding to the estate.

A strict settlement, therefore, diminishes, and in fact destroys, the inducements, which would otherwise have actuated the eldest child in some degree, and it tends to render him idle, careless, disrespectful towards his father, and often profligate in his habits; and having done this, it puts him into one of the most influential places in the country, as an example to the nation.

7. It tends very greatly to retard the progress of agriculture, and it does so in several ways.

A young man, brought up in expectation of being at

some future time the possessor of a great estate, does not feel obliged to work hard, and does not therefore generally acquire studious or industrious habits ; but, on the contrary, generally becomes fond of pleasure, amusements, luxury, and of many habits necessarily entailing considerable expenditure. As the heir to an estate has not, however, generally a large income until he enters into possession of the estate, so, during the life of the prior possessor, he is often obliged to borrow largely, in order to find means wherewith to gratify his luxurious habits. It is not generally difficult for him to do so, if he will engage to pay a handsome per-centage for the advance.

In this way many owners of land have burdened themselves with heavy debts, long before they have entered into enjoyment of their estates, and are then obliged to lay by a great part of each year's income in order to pay off their prior incurred debts. Such a man, therefore, is often unable to advance any capital towards the improvement of the cultivation of his estate, especially as he has been taught in his youth to consider it necessary, that he should afterwards keep up a certain " style" of living and expenditure. Thus many of our landowners, even when they are sufficiently intelligent, are not able to find sufficient spare capital to enable them to embark in many improvements.

Besides, their early luxurious education is not well qualified to enable them to devote themselves afterwards to practical farming, or to give them any taste for such an employment. A merchant, who had brought up his son in the gaieties of London fashion until he was

thirty or thirty-five years of age, would not expect,
afterwards, to find him able to apply to the dry and
laborious duties of business, or to prosecute these duties
with any success. So, it cannot be expected, that a
young nobleman, or the son of an owner of landed
property, who has been brought up in gaiety and idleness, until he is between thirty and forty years of age,
should afterwards, in the generality of cases, practise
farming or agriculture with any great success, even
when he has sufficient ready capital, in addition to his
personal expenditure, to enable him to do so. But no
matter how unable or how unwilling the landlord may
be to farm his lands in a profitable or skilful manner,
this system of laws prevents him, in many instances,
selling his lands to those, who would farm better than
himself, and who would feel more interest in the cultivation of the lands; and it thus often prevents a landlord engaging in some other occupation, for which he
was better fitted than for farming.

Nor is inability on the part of the landlord compensated by the ability of the steward. There is not one
steward in a hundred, who *can* feel as much interest in
the improvement of his master's property, as he would
feel if he himself were the owner; and the less the
interest he feels in the property, the less labour will he
devote to its improvement. This is universally true.

An estate, which is managed by a steward, no matter
how intelligent the steward may be, is scarcely ever so
well cultivated as an estate, which is cultivated by an
intelligent owner himself. But under the system of
which I am speaking, the owners are generally so

brought up, as to know as little as possible about farming, to dislike all business-like employments, and to look down upon them as something with which it would dishonour them to meddle.

If, then, this system tends both to diminish the proprietors' stocks of ready capital, and to destroy their fitness and willingness for the occupation of agriculture, it surely cannot be a matter of surprise, if agriculture suffers; for it is clear, both from the actual state of things and from evident causes, that a farmer, who holds a farm without a lease of it, will never feel so safe in laying out his capital and labour upon the improvement of the land, and will never be so willing to do so to any extent, as if the land were his own, or even as he would do if he held it under a lease.

Let any one ask himself, If I were a farmer and had no lease of my farm, or only a lease of it for seven or ten years, should I be willing to expend three or four hundred pounds upon its improvement? The answer will be always in the negative; but if he were owner, he would not only have no objection to expend upon improvements, but he would feel interested in doing so.

8. The extraordinary powers given to owners of land in England, render it necessary, in framing the settlements or wills, to make long and expensive deeds or writings, and to provide in those deeds or writings for many circumstances which may possibly occur in future years; for after the making, in the generality of instances, no alteration or provision to meet such circumstances can be made. An owner of land in Great Britain and Ireland knows, when he makes a settlement or will, that he is

VOL. I.

about to regulate the succession to the land, and the rights of numerous parties to it, for many years, and often for several generations after his own death. He knows, that, in many cases, after he has once made his settlement, or after his death, if he has made a will, no possessor of the land will be able to do anything with it, except what he is permitted to do by the deed or will. It becomes necessary, therefore, in framing these deeds and wills, to make provision for all sorts of contingencies which may happen many years after the maker's death; and hence it becomes absolutely necessary to introduce numerous, lengthy, and carefully worded clauses, providing for all kinds of contingencies, conferring all kinds of powers, and guarding against all chance of misconstruction.

9. This system of mortgages, long leases, and intricate settlements and wills, which bind the land for many years after they are made, renders it often very difficult, and very expensive for a purchaser, even when he can find a small plot of land for sale, to discover what the real state of the title to the property is. It is often affected by so many ancient deeds, mortgages, and leases, which are scattered in so many hands; and it is often so difficult to find out whether all the persons entitled under the old deeds and wills are dead, or whether their title to the property is extinguished, that the mere inquiry into the title of a small plot of land, and the legal expenses attendant thereon, are often quite sufficient to deter a man, who is not rich, from venturing to invest money in the purchase of a plot he would otherwise have been glad to buy. And such is the effect of

the strange force given by these old feudal laws to the settlements and wills of dead proprietors, that the search into the title of a small farm of five or six acres may sometimes be quite as expensive as a search into the title of an estate of several thousands.

Sometimes too a piece of land is affected by different deeds in the hands of different persons, as, for instance, by different mortgages. It very often happens that no reference is made in one of these deeds to some one or more of the others; so that a purchaser of land can never be perfectly sure that, after his purchase is completed, some other deed may not be found in the hands of another person, giving him also a claim upon the land.

As an instance of this, I may mention the following fact. One of my friends purchased, a short time since, a small estate in the south of England. Prior to the purchase, he caused a most careful search to be made into the state of the title of the land. His attornies informed him that they could discover no incumbrance of which he was not already aware. He accordingly paid down the purchase-money, and the former proprietor had a deed made, transferring the land to him. The former proprietor then became a bankrupt and left the country. A short time afterwards, my friend was informed, that the estate he had purchased was mortgaged in 1200*l.* to another person, who produced the mortgage deed, and claimed the money due to him from the estate, and my friend was obliged to pay the money.

This is only a single instance of what all lawyers know constantly occurs in this country.

This state of the law has had the effect, throughout Great Britain and Ireland, of gradually accumulating the land in the hands of fewer and still fewer proprietors ; of retaining the same estate for many years, and often for many generations, in the hands of the same family ; of depriving the shopkeepers, farmers, and peasants, of any chance, in general, of purchasing lands ; of progressively increasing the size and lessening the number of the farms, and thus of depriving the peasants more and more every year of any chance of even renting a farm.

As long as the proprietors of land are allowed to tie up the land, for so many years after their own deaths, by their settlements and wills, so long will it be quite impossible materially to lessen the expense of conveying a piece of land from one person to another ; so long will the greater part of the land remain, as at present, accumulated in great estates, and in the hands of a few proprietors ; and so long will it continue quite impossible, in the great majority of instances, for the small shopkeepers, and, still more, for the peasants, to buy land, or to invest their savings therein.

A system of registration would somewhat lessen the expense of the *search* for titles ; but its effects would be very slow, so long as the settlements and wills were allowed to have such effect on the land as at present. Conveyances and wills would continue just as lengthy as at present. Many years would elapse, before even the expense caused by the examination of titles would be lessened, and the utmost, which could ever be effected by such a system, would do but little towards lessening the expense of conveyances, though it would make titles *safer* than at present.

Now, in Germany, Holland, Switzerland, Lombardy, the Tyrol, Denmark, Norway, Belgium, France, and in a great part of Italy and America, the law does not allow the proprietor of land a power of preventing his property being sold after his own death.   In all these countries the old feudal system of primogeniture, entails, long settlements, and intricate devises of land, invented in order to keep great estates together, to preserve the great power of the feudal aristocracy, and to prevent the lands getting into the hands of the shopkeeping and peasant classes, have been, since the first French Revolution, entirely swept away.

In *all* these countries every proprietor of land is allowed to sell or dispose of it as he likes during his own *lifetime*.

In *all* these countries, if the proprietor dies without having sold his land, and without having made a will, the law divides the land, after his death, among his wife and *all* his children, instead of giving the whole estate to the eldest son.

In *some* of these countries the proprietor is allowed to devise his land to whomsoever he will ; but even in these cases he cannot prevent his successor disposing of it as he pleases.

In France, Switzerland, and the Rhine provinces, however, the proprietor (although he may dispose of his land as he chooses *during his lifetime*) cannot devise it, as the law gives each of his children a right to a certain share of all the land their father dies possessed of.   If the division of the property would be inconvenient, or would cut it up into too small portions, the whole estate is sold, either to one of the children or to a stranger, and the proceeds divided among the children.

This system of forced subdivision would seem, *prima facie*, to be as great an evil as a system of forced accumulation, if it were not that nearly all accounts agree * in proving that the average size of the estates in France does not go on decreasing, but that it is, on the contrary, *increasing* throughout the greater part of the country, as it is found, that the estate is always sold, when it is inexpedient to divide, and as there are many of the merchants and richer farmers who are always striving to accumulate large estates.

The best and soundest plan, however, is to give the proprietor power to leave his land to whomsoever he will, but to deprive him at the same time of all power of preventing his successor from selling any portion of the land, and of leaving his successors any other than the whole estate in the land devised to them.

But, whichever of these systems is pursued, it tends rapidly to divide the lands among the middle and lower classes, to render titles very simple, and, joined with systems of registration, such as those in force in foreign countries, to enable a man to purchase land without having to expend much upon the mere conveyance.

Whenever an owner of land in these countries is a spendthrift, an idler, or a man who does not know how to live within his income, he gets into debt, and, in the end, his land is sold by himself or by his creditors. Whenever, too, a man does not like agriculture, or

---

* See the authorities on the French system collected at the end of the chapter.

the care of an estate, and whenever a man dies leaving several children, who want each of them to obtain their share of their father's property in money, and not in land, the land is sold.

The conveyance of the land, in these countries, from man to man, is very simple and very cheap. Two causes contribute to produce this result.

1. The deeds of transfer are very short and simple.

No man can subject his estate to the long settlements and singular arrangements, to which an English proprietor can subject his land: he can only affect his land during *his own lifetime.* The consequence is, that it is not necessary to make provision in the deeds for so many contingencies, or for so many changes in the property, or for such long future arrangements as in England. The foreign deed does not generally do more, than convey away simply and briefly the whole of the seller's interest, and does not, as is the case generally in England, convey some limited interest in the land, and then make arrangements, how the rest of the interest in the land is to pass from hand to hand for the next fifty or eighty years, and for all the contingencies which may arise during that time.

2. There is no need to expend any money in examining the title of land in the foreign countries I have mentioned.

In most of these countries there are, in each of the provinces, registration courts, where all the changes in the right to, or ownership of, every parcel of land in the province is entered in a book under the name or description of the land. No mortgage, lease, conveyance, or writing affecting land is allowed, by the laws of these countries, to have any validity, unless it is entered in the books of the registration office of the province in which the land is situated; so that a purchaser knows that he can always easily, without any expense, and in a few minutes, discover what the state of the title of the land he thinks of buying is; and he knows that no mortgage or other incumbrance, which is not copied in the registry book under the description of the piece of land which he thinks of purchasing, can turn up afterwards and affect his land, as the law, as I have said before, does not allow any validity whatsoever to any writing affecting the land, which is not registered in its proper place in the registry books of the province in which the land is situated.

Owing to these several causes, the land in these countries is very much divided, and is in the hands of a great number of proprietors. In Belgium, Holland, Germany, Switzerland, the Tyrol, France, North Italy, Denmark, and Norway, the majority of the estates vary from 300 acres to 1 acre in size. M. Lullin de Châteauvieux estimates the average size of the holdings of the 3,900,000 poorest proprietors of France at eight acres and a half.*

The small number of large estates in Prussia at the present time may be seen from the statement of the Prussian Minister of Statistics, made in the Prussian chambers in the month of October, 1849. He is represented to have said, that he had endeavoured to

---

* Mill's Political Economy, vol. i. p. 577.

obtain returns of the number of persons in the Prussian kingdom possessing clear annual incomes of more than 1200*l.* ; that, after a careful scrutiny, he had ascertained that the number was only 474, and that these proprietors were distributed throughout Prussia in the following proportions : —

In the Province of

Prussia, the Number of such Proprietors was					-	35
Posen,	-	-	-	-	-	60
Pomerania, -	-	-	-	-	-	60
Silesia,	-	-	-	-	-	120
Brandenburg	-	-	-	-	-	70
Saxony,	-	-	-	-	-	50
Westphalia,	-	-	-	-	-	41
Rhine Province,	-	-	-	-	-	38
Total	-	-	-	-	-	474

To illustrate still more clearly the great subdivision of landed property in Prussia, Dr. Shubert, in his excellent work on the Statistics of the Kingdom of Prussia, informs us, that there are in Prussia —

257,347 estates, each of which is between 240 acres and 50 acres in size;
314,533 estates, each of which is less than 50 acres in size; and
668,400 persons (without reckoning the owners of the above-mentioned estates), some of whom have each of them, a small house of their own, whilst the remainder are labourers for others, and do not possess a house or any land of their own, but are allowed by their masters a field for the support of one or two cows.

Owing also to the impossibility of tying up the land by settlements, mortgages, long leases, or wills, and to the great simplicity and cheapness of the mode of conveying an estate from a seller to a purchaser, a great many estates of all sizes, and situated in all parts of these countries, are constantly changing hands, or being offered for sale in the markets.

From these causes, people of all classes are able to become proprietors. Shopkeepers and labourers of the towns purchase gardens outside the towns, where they and their families work in the fine evenings, in raising vegetables and fruit for the use of their households; shopkeepers, who have laid by a little competence, purchase farms, to which they and their families retire from the toil and disquiet of a town life; farmers purchase the farms they used formerly to rent of great land-owners; while most of the peasants of these countries have purchased and live upon farms of their own, or are now economising, and laying by all that they can possibly spare from their earnings, in order therewith as soon as possible to purchase a farm or a garden.

It is this, fact which more than any other, distinguishes the social state of these countries from that of Great Britain and Ireland. The position of the peasant in the first-mentioned countries admits of hope, of enthusiasm, and of progress, for he knows that if he is economical and prudent, he may make himself a proprietor, and may climb the social ladder. The position of the peasant in the last-mentioned countries is one of hopelessness, discontent, and stagnation; for what motive has he to induce self-denial, energy, and prudence; and what chance has he of improving his position in the world?

It is possible for the poorest young man in Germany, Switzerland, the Tyrol, Belgium, Holland, France, Denmark, Sweden, and Norway, to purchase a garden or a farm, if he is intelligent, prudent, and self-denying. It is a safer and more agreeable investment than that of a little shop, which is the only one open to a poor peasant in England. It seems to be inherent in man's nature to wish to possess land; and it is certain that there is no other inducement, which has half its force, in leading the poor man to give up present gratification for its sake. Few men will defer their marriage, or deny themselves the excitement of the tavern, or of the gambling-table, for the sake of becoming a shopman; but millions of peasants are at this moment on the continent of Europe putting off their marriages, abstaining from the use of spirits, and from immoral gratifications, working double hours, striving with double diligence to please their employers, refraining from the strife of politics, and availing themselves of every opportunity of saving money, in the hope of purchasing a garden or a farm.

Let it be remembered, that the subdivision of the old feudal estates, and the creation of the peasant proprietor class, and of systems of public registration of titles of landed property, have been effected since the outbreak of the first French Revolution. The old feudal laws, which enabled the landed proprietors of France to prevent their estates being sold for several generations after their deaths, were entirely repealed in 1789; those of Prussia, in 1811; and those of Holland, Belgium, Denmark, Saxony, Nassau, Bavaria, Wurtenburg, Baden, and Switzerland, at different times since the commencement of the present century. Before this great change was effected in the countries I have mentioned above, the condition of the peasants in several of them was, at least, as bad as that of the Irish peasantry in the present day.   Thus, Arthur Young says, speaking of the condition of the French peasantry just prior to the subdivision of the great estates, which existed in France before the first French Revolution, " It reminded me of the miseries of Ireland."

If any one will read Mr. Alison's description of the French peasantry prior to the Revolution, he will see that it is but a faithful picture of the Irish peasantry of the present day.   The condition of the peasantry in many parts of Germany was no better.   Indeed, it was so bad in Prussia, that the government was obliged to take from the proprietors their feudal powers of preventing their successors selling their lands, in order to save the nation from being ruined, as the Roman empire was, by the utter degradation of the poorer classes.

In Germany it was as in France, of which country, Mr. Alison (vol. i. p. 134.), quoting the authority of Arthur Young, says, " With a very few exceptions, the peasantry were in the most indigent condition; their houses dark, comfortless, and almost destitute of furniture ; their dress ragged and miserable ; their food the coarsest and most humble fare."

I am going to show, both from my own observation, and from many excellent authorities, what the state of the peasantry of those countries is at the present day, now that their governments have educated all the children, and have enabled the peasants to acquire land.

It ought to be borne in mind, however, that if the improvement in the state of the peasants of these coun-

tries has been so great since 1800, as I shall show it to
have been, it is only reasonable to infer, that when the
older and more uneducated generations, who were
brought up under the old degrading system, have died
away, and have given place to the younger and better
educated ones, who have been brought up altogether
under the present improving system, and when the
present system itself, which has already produced such
vast effects, has been allowed to work upon the people,
unimpeded by the last remains of the old demoralising
system, the effects will be still greater and still more
surprising than at present.

Those peasants abroad, who have attained the age of
fifty, began their lives under the old system, never received in their youth any education, were never taught
by free institutions to feel, that their fate was in their
own hands, but were demoralised in their youth by contact with demoralised peasants, such as those whom
Arthur Young describes.

As might have been anticipated, the difference between
the appearance, manners, and condition of the peasants of
Germany and Switzerland, who are more than fifty
years of age, and those of the peasants, who have not
yet attained the age of thirty-five years, is still singularly apparent.   A traveller, who did not know the
causes of this difference, would return home with the
most mistaken ideas of the progress of civilisation among
the poorer classes of foreign countries.   There is, in
general, a clear and broadly defined difference between
the peasants of more than fifty years of age, and those
of less than thirty-five years of age, — a difference

which cannot escape the observation of any, but a careless or mere pleasure-seeking traveller. The peasants,
who have not attained the age of thirty-five years, are
better dressed, cleaner, more polite in demeanour, and
more intelligent and respectable in appearance than
those who are more than fifty years of age. They belong to different and very distinct systems of civilisation, and they each bear the stamp of the system under
which they have grown up.

The fact that this difference has not been kept in
view by travellers on the Continent, has been the cause
of many of the contradictory reports, which we have
heard. I wish it to be clearly understood, that when I
speak of the civilisation and happy social condition of
the peasants of Germany, Holland, and Switzerland, I
limit all my remarks to the class of peasants, who have not
attained the age of thirty-five years, — to that class, in
short, which has enjoyed the advantages of an excellent
education, and which has grown up under the combined influences of the schools, and of the subdivision
of landed property.

If other writers would observe this distinction, there
would be no difference between our reports. My conviction is, that even those peasants of Germany, Switzerland, and Holland, who have attained the age of
fifty, are much more civilised and in a much better social
position and condition than our own peasants, but that
they are not so much superior to our own peasants as
those, who are below the age of thirty-five years.

I shall now describe the condition of the poorer
classes of foreign countries under different heads.

1. *The Intelligence of the Poorer Classes in Foreign Countries.*

As I have before stated, every child in Germany, Holland, and Switzerland, for the last twenty or thirty years, has been receiving a good education. Of the men and women under thirty-five years of age, nine tenths are well educated. They can *all* read, write, cipher, sing, and chant. They *all* know the Scripture history, and nearly all the outlines of the history of their own country. Throughout all parts of these countries, there are many of the poorest people who have learned more than this, and who know something of the general principles of science, or of the principles of some particular science.

In subsequent parts of this work, the reader will find many statistics to prove the truth of this statement, and to show how this great result has been obtained. I may, however, in this place, mention that, four years ago, the Prussian Government made a general inquiry throughout the kingdom to discover how far the school education of the people had been extended, and it was then ascertained that, out of all the young men in the kingdom who had attained the age of twenty-one years, *only two in every hundred were unable to read.* This fact was communicated to me by the Inspector General of the Kingdom.

The poor of these countries read a great deal more than even those of our own country who are able to read. It is a general custom in Germany and Switzerland, for four or five families of labourers to club together, and to subscribe among themselves for one or two of the newspapers, which come out once or twice a week. These papers are passed from family to family, or are interchanged. Sometimes one set of families in a village takes in one paper, and another set another paper. These are exchanged, when each has been the round of its own set. When the press of North Germany was less free than it is at present, these papers did not contain many original articles on political matters; but they contained the political news of foreign countries, descriptions of wonderful works in process of erection, accounts of new inventions, lives of celebrated men, and articles on subjects of interest to the peasant farmers. The existence of the great class of poor readers had produced a class of cheap papers suited to meet the demand. The German press teems with cheap provincial papers published for the peasants, and filled with the news and information most interesting and useful to the peasant readers. Almost every little town publishes one or two such journals, which strive to outvie each other in cheapness, and in the amount of interesting information compressed within their pages.

In the country villages it is often difficult for the peasants to obtain books. But means of supplying the demand are being discovered. Professor Frederick von Raumer informed me, that they were endeavouring to establish village libraries in connection with the schools, so as to provide the peasants with books for their evening reading. Wherever there is a demand there will always be a supply; and it will soon be a trade common to the German, Swiss, and Dutch villages, to keep village lending libraries for the peasants.

In the towns, where the poorer classes are even still more intelligent than in the country, it is not difficult for the poor to obtain books as well as papers. In the towns, therefore, of Germany and Switzerland, the poor read a great deal. Indeed, it will be hardly credible to English ears, when I inform them how the poor of these towns amuse and instruct themselves in their leisure hours, and during the long winter evenings. I was assured by Dr. Bruggeman, the Roman Catholic Counsellor in the Educational Office in Berlin, and by several teachers and other persons, that not only were the interesting works of German literature perused by the poorest people of the towns, but that translations of the works of Sir Walter Scott, and of many other foreign novelists and writers, were generally read by the poor.

I remember one day, when walking near Berlin in the company of Herr Hintz, a professor in Dr. Diesterweg's Normal College, and of another teacher, we saw a poor woman cutting up in the road logs of wood for winter use. My companions pointed her out to me, and said, " Perhaps you will scarcely believe it, but in the neighbourhood of Berlin, poor women, like that one, read translations of Sir Walter Scott's novels, and of many of the interesting works of your language, besides those of the principal writers of Germany." This account was afterwards confirmed by the testimony of several other persons.

Often and often have I seen the poor cabdrivers of Berlin, while waiting for a fare, amusing themselves by reading German books, which they had brought with them in the morning expressly for the purpose of sup-

plying amusement and occupation for their leisure
hours.

In many parts of these countries, the peasants and
the workmen of the towns, attend regular weekly
lectures or weekly classes, where they practise singing
or chanting, or learn mechanical drawing, history, or
science.

As will be seen afterwards, women as well as men,
girls as well as boys, enjoy in these countries the same
advantages, and go through the same school education.
The women of the poorer classes of these countries,
in point of intelligence and knowledge, are almost equal
to the men.

The intelligence of the poorer classes of these countries is shown by their manners. The whole appearance of a German peasant who has been brought up
under this system, i. e. of any of the poor who have
not attained the age of thirty-five years, is very different to that of our own peasantry. The German,
Swiss, or Dutch peasant, who has grown up to manhood under the new system, and since the old feudal
system was overthrown, is not nearly so often as with
us distinguished by an uncouth dialect. On the contrary, they speak as their teachers speak, clearly, without hesitation, and grammatically. They answer questions politely, readily, and with the ease which shows
that they have been accustomed to mingle with men of
greater wealth and of better education than themselves.
They do not appear embarrassed, still less do they appear gawkish or stupid, when addressed. If, in asking
a peasant a question, a stranger, according to the polite
custom of the country, raises his hat, the first words of

reply, are the quietly uttered ones, " I pray you, sir, be covered." A Prussian peasant is always polite and respectful to a stranger, but quite as much at his ease as when speaking to one of his own fellows.

2. *The prudential Habits of the Peasant Proprietors. — The General Diffusion of Education, combined with the Subdivision of the Land, tends very remarkably to increase the Prudence, Forethought, and Economy of the Poor.*

A poor man in Germany, France, Holland, and Switzerland is, from his education, intelligent enough to be able to calculate his chances. He knows, when he begins his life, that if he defers his marriage for some years, he will be able to save, and to acquire land. He knows that if he marries early in life, he cannot hope to save enough to enable him to buy a farm or a garden of his own, and that if he does not buy one, he will occupy a lower and less comfortable social position than his neighbours. The fact of so many of his friends possessing small estates of their own, and the pleasure of owning one himself, stimulates him with double ardour to seek to obtain a small plot of land also, and to consent to present self-denial for the sake of attaining this strongly desired end. The consequence is, that the poor of these countries do not marry nearly so early in life as the English poor, and do not consequently rear such large families. In some parts of Switzerland, as in the canton of Argovie for instance, a peasant never marries before he attains the age of twenty-five years, and generally much later in life; and in that canton the

women very seldom marry before they have attained
the age of thirty.   Indeed, so strongly do the people of
Switzerland understand from experience the expediency
of their sons and daughters postponing the time of their
marriages, that the councils of state of four or five of
the most democratic of the cantons, elected, be it remembered, by universal suffrage, have passed laws, by
which all young persons, who marry before they have
proved to the magistrate of their district that they are
able to support a family, are rendered liable to a heavy
fine.   In Lucerne, Argovie, Unterwalden, and, I believe, St. Gall, Schweitz, and Uri, laws of this character have been in force for many years; but I mention them rather as symptoms, than as causes of the
prudence and self-denial of the peasantry.   Nor do
the division of land and the cheapness of the mode of
conveying it from one man to another encourage the
providence of the labourers of the rural districts only.
They act in the same manner, though, perhaps, in a
less degree, upon the labourers of the smaller towns.
In the smaller provincial towns, it is customary for a
labourer to own a small plot of ground outside the
town.   This plot he cultivates in the evenings as his
kitchen-garden.   He raises in it vegetables and fruits
for the use of his family during the winter.   After his
day's work is over, he and his family repair to the
garden for a short time, which they spend in planting,
sowing, weeding, or preparing for sowing or harvest,
according to the season.   The desire to become possessed of one of these gardens operates very strongly in
strengthening prudential habits, and in restraining im-

provident marriages. Some of the manufacturers in the canton of Argovie told me that a townsman was seldom contented until he had bought a garden, or a garden and house, and that the town-labourers generally deferred their marriages for some years, in order to save enough to purchase either one or both of these luxuries.

I have no doubt in my own mind that the effect of the subdivision of land, after it has proceeded to such a length that the smallest of the estates is sufficient to support a peasant's family in comfort, but not large enough to support two average-sized families (and beyond this the subdivision will not proceed, as I shall show hereafter), is to retard the too rapid increase of population more than any scheme that could be invented, and to retard it in a thoroughly healthy manner.

Among our middle classes a young man will not generally marry as soon as he becomes his own master, if he perceives, that, by waiting, he will be able to secure for his wife and for himself a higher and more comfortable position in society. The hope of getting a larger or a more certain income operates among the middle classes in the majority of instances, by making a young man remain unmarried a few years, and sometimes many years, longer than he otherwise would do.

But among our lower classes no such thought interferes with marriage. As soon as a young peasant can earn his miserable pittance of from seven to nine shillings a week he marries, and thereby increases his own sufferings, and involves his poor young wife and his family in the same pauperism with himself. What good, in the present state of our laws, would a peasant gain if he deferred his marriage? None which is perceptible to his understanding. He knows that, if he could save, he would not be able to make use of his little capital. He knows that all avenues of rising in the world in his own native village are closed to him. He knows that he must die in the same position in which it pleased God he should be born. Having therefore no incentive to self-denial, he practises none. He marries as soon as he can, and generally by so doing doubles his own difficulties and miseries, and soon increases the poor-rates of his parish.

But, abroad, the peasants know, that if they wait a few years and save, they and their future wives and families will be happier, more respected among their neighbours, and in a more comfortable position in the world, and that they will realise their day-dream, and call a small farm their own. It is not surprising, then, that the peasants do not marry so young in foreign countries as they do here and in Ireland.

Counseller Reichensperger, writing in the midst of the small proprietors of Prussia, says * : — "The desire to found a family is so strong an actuating principle in man's nature, that none but the most powerful considerations, such as the possibility of supporting a wife and children, can restrain the rapid increase of population. These considerations have a very different significance, according to the circumstances of the persons affected by them. Whilst the day-labourer or

* Die Agrarfrage.

operative considers a future family provided for, and therefore marries, when he can only reckon upon annual wages to the amount of from 80 to 100 thalers; the man in a better social position will see a hundred comforts and necessaries beyond what would have satisfied the poorer man, and without which he considers it impossible to secure a suitable income for himself and for his family. If he cannot see a certainty of securing such an income, and if he cannot calculate with certainty upon providing his children with a social position in life equal to his own, he will, as daily experience shows, forbear, at least for a time, to marry, or, at least, such considerations will not remain without influence upon the future greatness of his family.

" The egotistical wish of persons desirous of marrying not to sink into a lower social position, and the desire of parents to support their children respectably, form the most influential and the most legitimate obstacle to the ever-threatening danger of over population. These natural and honourable feelings almost always influence those, who have themselves experienced the value of possessions and of a social position, so as to protect them against too early marriages and against too numerous families.

" The day-labourer and operative, who have no possessions of their own except their own capability of working, are not affected by the healthy check which I have mentioned above. Every such person leaves his children, however many he may have, in a position similar to his own, and he therefore feels no moral impediment to the founding or increasing of his family, although in reality, owing to the increasing competition of the labourers, the future wages will be lessened.

" It is these labourers, entirely without possessions, whether they live in the towns or in the country districts, — whether they are found in the factories or behind the plough, — who are the really dangerous members of society; since the increase in their numbers is restrained, not by the sufficiency or insufficiency of the means of subsistence, but only by the extent of their physical powers. The real ground of their dangerous character lies in their freedom from any moral restraint, caused by the hopelessness and poverty of their social position. The evils, with which the position of these classes threaten society, can only be avoided, by removing the helplessness and destitution of their social position.

" The simplest, most efficacious, and most legitimate means, by which to attain this great end, is to free landed property from all restrictions preventing its sale, and gradually, and by means of the natural sale of the lands, to enable the labourers to acquire property."

A. Thaer, in his "Englishen Landwirthshaft," p. 104., says, " The population will grow more rapidly on great estates than on small ones, because day-labourers are more thoughtless about their future than independent peasant proprietors, and, therefore, bring up larger families in the hope of being able to get them supported upon the estate."

Speaking of Geneva, Mr. Chadwick says * : — " It is

* Report on the Sanitary Condition of the Labouring Population of Great Britain, p. 175.

proved in a report of M. Edward Mallet, one of the most able that have been made from the registries of the city of Geneva, that the increase of the population of that city has been followed by an increase in the probable duration of life.

"The probabilities of the continuance of life in Geneva were, to every person born, —

				Yrs.	Mths.	Days
Towards the end of the 16th century	-		-	8	7	26
In the 17th century -	-	-	-	13	3	16
1701—1750	-	-	-	27	9	13
1751—1800	-	-	-	31	3	5
1801—1813	-	-	-	40	8	0
1814—1833	-	-	-	45	0	29

"The progression of the population, and the increased duration of life, had been attended by a progression in happiness. As prosperity advanced, *marriages became fewer and later ;* the proportion of births were reduced ; but greater numbers of the infants born were preserved, and the proportion of the population in manhood became greater.

"It is the practice in Geneva for female servants to delay marriage, until they have saved enough to furnish a house, &c. In illustration of this state of things, it is stated that, in 290 out of 956 marriages, *the female was at the time of marriage older than the male.* In the early and barbarous periods, the excessive mortality was accompanied by a prodigious fecundity. In the few last years of the seventeenth century a marriage still produced 5 children and more, the probable duration of life attained was not 20 years, and Geneva had

scarcely 17,000 inhabitants. Towards the end of the
eighteenth century, there were scarcely 3 children to
a marriage, and the probabilities of life exceeded 32
years. At the present time, a marriage only produces
2¾ children, the probability of life is 45 years, and
Geneva, which exceeds 27,000 in population, has arrived
at a high degree of civilisation and of ‘prospérité ma-
terielle.’ In 1836 the population appeared to have
attained its summit: *the births rarely replaced the
deaths.*"

Professor Vulliemin, in his statistical account of the
canton of Vaud, where all the land is divided into small
estates, says, that the mean ages of the persons married
in the canton of Vaud from 1837 to 1841, were as
follows : —

Years.						Yrs.	Mths.	Days.
1837	Men	-	-	-	-	30	10	12
	Women	-	-	-	-	27	11	9
1838	Men	-	-	-	-	32	1	8
	Women	-	-	-	-	28	2	29
1839	Men	-	-	-	-	30	9	14
	Women	-	-	-	-	28	4	12
1840	Men	-	-	-	-	31	6	10
	Women	-	-	-	-	28	3	17
1841	Men	-	-	-	-	31	6	2
	Women	-	-	-	-	27	3	24

As the peasants of this canton are better educated
and more prosperous than those of almost any other
country in the world, the advanced age at which they
marry is peculiarly significant.

One of the manufacturers of Argovie, in speaking
to me of the effects of the subdivision of property upon
the prudential habits of the town and country poor,

said, " the men never marry before the age of twenty-
five, and often later ; and it is a curious fact, that they
generally choose for their wives, women who have attained the age of thirty, in preference to younger ones,
because they imagine the women of thirty will be more
thrifty and better managers."

In 1843, 4680 marriages were celebrated in Prussia,
between persons, of whom, either the man or the woman
was more than 45 years old.   In the same year, 26,836
marriages were celebrated, where the man was more
than 45 and the woman less than 45 years of age, or
where the woman was more than 30 and the man less
than 60; 21,138 men were married, each of whom was
more than 30 and less than 35 years of age, and 25,123
women, each of whom was more than 30 years of age.

Of all the persons married in Prussia in 1843, there
were, —

  131,737 men under 45 years of age.
   7,273 men between 45 and 60 years of age
   1,444 men above 60 years of age.

  111,396 women under 30 years of age.
   25,123 women between 30 and 45 years of age.
   3,935 women above 45 years of age.

We are not told the ages of the men, who married
under 45 years of age, but it appears, that the majority
of them married later in life, than their ancestors used
to do, and that the customary age for marriage is gradually becoming later than it was formerly.   I believe
I am about right, when I state 35 to be the average
age of marriage in Prussia.

In England, where there is so little intelligence, and,
therefore, so little prudence or foresight, and so much

misery among the labourers, and where there are so
few reasons to induce the peasants to postpone their
marriage, the state of things is singularly different.

In England, in 1846, out of 24,356 men married to
24,356 women, —

> 596 men were under 20 years of age.
> 11,790 men were just 20 years of age.
> 6,467 men were just 25 years of age.
> 2,464 men were just 30 years of age.
> 1,180 men were just 35 years of age.
> 708 men were just 40 years of age.
> 455 men were just 45 years of age.
> 696 men were more than 45 years of age.
>
> 2,812 women were under 20 years of age.
> 12,470 women were just 20 years of age.
> 5,079 women were just 25 years of age.
> 1,849 women were just 30 years of age.
> 897 women were just 35 years of age.
> 596 women were just 40 years of age.
> 328 women were just 45 years of age.
> 425 women were more than 45 years of age.

These statistics show, that in Prussia, one man in
every sixteen, who marry, is 45 years old, while in
England, only one man in every twenty-one, who marry,
is 45 years old, and nearly half of all the men married
every year are not older than 20 years.

We thus see how much later the age of marriage is
in Prussia than in England.   This alone is an un-
answerable proof of the greater prudence and prosperity
of the people of Prussia ; for it is always found, that,
the greater the ignorance of the people, and the less the
chance of their improving their condition by present
self-denial, the earlier will be the age, at which they will
enter into the married life.

Counsellor Reichensperger, writing in the midst of peasant proprietors, and comparing the results of the two systems, — the English system of great estates in few hands, with laws tending to prevent the peasants and small shopkeepers from obtaining land, and the German system of subdivision of land, and its freedom from all restraints upon its sale, — says* : —

" By the latter system it is possible for each person to obtain a plot of land of a size corresponding to his ability; and under it, the position of even a day-labourer is by no means one, without hope or capability of improvement ; but it is rather one, which leads to the acquirement of property and independence, since the labourer, by economy and credit, may easily, under this system, manage to work his way to prosperity and comfort. Where the land is free from all shackles preventing its sale, this result may be seen daily ; and it is by means of this system, that an approximate realisation is obtained, by indirect means, of the socialist idea of the division of goods according to the skill and deserts of the individual.

The possibility of increasing the size of their little properties stimulates in the highest degree the activity and the progress of the prosperity of the peasants; for the landowner knows no more enviable possession than that of land, and *no stronger inducement to economy than the hope to purchase another acre and to increase his farm ;* for he feels that the savings, which are put out at interest, are much less secure than those invested in land.

" But, for the peasant and day-labourer, this possi-

* Die Agrarfrage, 315.

bility of purchasing land, and of thus acquiring independence, is the *only possible inducement in his case to exertion and economy;* and this inducement urges him on much more surely, than all the alms and poor-rates of Great Britain can ever do. . . . .

" The contrary system of restriction of the subdivision of land renders the condition of the peasant labourers a hopeless one, while it destroys the natural freedom of both owners and peasants. The freedom of the land from these restrictions, and the industrious spirit which it stimulates, raise the moral character of the people, and, by so doing, exercise the most beneficial influence upon their health, their manners, and their whole mental habits. . . . . . Where the land is divided into great estates, and kept out of the market by intricate settlements, we never see the prosperous and growing little proprietors, but only day-labourers, or, at best, small tenants at will, who never can feel any real or positive interest in the progressive improvement of the land, or in the prosperity of the state, but who dislike all labour which does not promise to themselves some immediate recompense. The hope, by industry and economy, and by the exercise of all their powers, to prepare a future independence for themselves and their families — this powerful inducement to the improvement of their own and of the public well-being — is unknown to the peasants, where the lands are consolidated in the hands of a few great proprietors, because they see no hope of ever acquiring an acre, or, by so doing, of making a step towards an independent position, which they might afterwards hope gradually to improve by adding bit by bit to the first acquired possession.

" A population condemned in this way to eternal poverty and dependence on others, and deprived of all hope of a happier future, will know scarcely any other happiness than to devote to mere animal gratifications some few passing moments of their unhappy lifetime; and, by means of spirituous drinks, to forget the gnawing cares of the coming days, from the impending misery of which they cannot, by the greatest industry, save themselves. . . . These peasants are degraded in mind by their utter dependence upon the landlords. . . . . They are uncivilised, and scarcely capable of receiving any mental improvement, because this only goes hand in hand with the improvement of their physical condition; their bodies exhibit the effects of privations, and of the too frequent resort to their only solace of drinking, of which fact Ireland, and many parts of Great Britain, afford most lamentable instances.

" This peasant class, on account of its great poverty, is deprived of all comforts, and, as it consumes very few and very common articles of manufacture, offers no encouragement to the industry of the towns, and scarcely any market for their products."

Nor does the habit of marrying at a later period of life seem to necessarily increase the amount of immorality among the peasants. The statistics collected by the governments of Germany, Austria, Belgium, and France, show, that fewer illegitimate children are born in Prussia than in any other of the European countries.

From the statistics published by Mr. Porter, and by
Herr Dieterici, it appears that there is, —

Illegitimate birth.		Legitimate births.
1 to every	-	$9\frac{2}{3}$ in Denmark,
1 ,,	-	8 in Austria,
1 ,,	-	4 in Bavaria,
1 ,,	-	9 in Mecklenburgh,
1 .,	-	7 in Saxony,
1 ,,	-	$7\frac{1}{10}$ in Wirtemburg,
while there is only 1 to every		13 in Prussia.

There may be, doubtless, much immorality which
these statistics do not show; but there is no sign
which discloses its existence, to any great extent, to a
traveller in the country.

The carefulness and eagerness to amass of the Swiss
peasantry has become proverbial throughout Europe.
Englishmen accuse them of sordid penuriousness, yet
this is but the natural and healthy effect of that subdivision of land, which renders it possible for a saving
and prudent peasant to make himself a proprietor. The
gains of a Swiss, French, Prussian, Saxon, and Dutch
labourer, instead of being expended in the ale-house,
are added to the stock, which is one day to purchase the
garden or the farm.

Mr. Mill says * : — " It is not to the intelligence
alone, that the situation of a peasant proprietor is full of
improving influences. *It is no less propitious to the moral
virtues of prudence, temperance, and self-control.* The
labourer who possesses property, whether he can read and
write or not, has, as Mr. Laing remarks †, ' an educated

* Principles of Political Economy, vol. i. p. 332.
† Residence in Norway, p. 20.

mind; he has *forethought, caution,* and *reflection* guiding every action; he knows the value of restraint, and is in the constant habitual exercise of it.' It is remarkable how this general proposition is borne out, by the character of the rural population in almost every civilised country, where peasant properties are frequent. Day-labourers, where the labouring class mainly consists of them, are usually improvident; they spend carelessly to the full extent of their means, and let the future shift for itself. This is so notorious, that many persons, otherwise well affected to the labouring classes, hold it as a fixed opinion, that an increase of wages would do them little good, unless accompanied by at least a corresponding improvement in their tastes and habits. The tendency of peasant proprietors, and of those who hope to become proprietors, is to the contrary extreme, — to take even too much thought for the morrow. They are oftener accused of penuriousness than of prodigality. They deny themselves reasonable indulgences, and live wretchedly in order to economise. In Switzerland almost every one saves, who has any means of saving. The case of the Flemish farmers I have already mentioned" (see below). " Among the French, though a pleasure-loving and reputed to be a self-indulgent people, the spirit of thrift is diffused through the rural population" (all peasant proprietors) " in a manner most gratifying as a whole, and which, in individual instances, errs rather on the side of excess than defect. Among those who, from the hovels in which they live, and the herbs and roots which constitute their diet, are mistaken by travellers for proofs and specimens of general indi-

gence, there are numbers, who have hoards in leather
bags, consisting of sums in five-franc pieces, which they
keep by them a whole generation, unless brought out to
be expended in their most cherished gratification — *the*
purchase of land. If there is a moral inconvenience
attached to a state of society in which the peasantry
have land, it is the danger of their being too careful of
their pecuniary concerns, — of its making them crafty
and 'calculating' in the objectionable sense." . . . . . .
" But some excess in this direction is a small and a passing
evil, compared with recklessness and improvidence in
the labouring classes, and a cheap price to pay for the
inestimable worth of the virtue of self-dependence,
as the general characteristic of a people, — a virtue
which is one of the first conditions of excellence in a
human character — the stock on which, if the other
virtues are not grafted, they have seldom any firm root
—a quality indispensable, in the case of a labouring class,
even to any tolerable degree of physical comfort, and
by which the peasantry of France and of most European
countries of peasant proprietors are distinguished beyond any other labouring population.

" Is it likely that a state of economical relations, so con-
ducive to frugality and prudence in every other respect,
should be prejudicial to it in the cardinal point of increase of population ? . . . . . . The true question is, supposing a peasantry to possess land not insufficient, but
sufficient for their comfortable support, are they more
or less likely to fall from this state of comfort through
improvident multiplication, than if they were living in
an equally comfortable manner as hired labourers ? All

à priori considerations are in favour of their being less likely. The dependence of wages on population is a matter of speculation and discussion. That wages would fall if population were much increased, is often a matter of real doubt, and always a thing which requires some exercise of the reflecting faculty for its intelligent recognition. But every peasant can satisfy himself, from evidence which he can fully appreciate, whether his piece of land can be made to support several families in the same comfort in which it supports one. Few people like to leave to their children a worse lot in life than their own. The parent, who has land to leave, is perfectly able to judge whether the children can live upon it or not; but people who are supported by wages see no reason, why their sons should be unable to support themselves in the same way, and trust accordingly to chance. 'In even the most useful and necessary arts and manufactures,' says Mr. Laing*, ' the demand for labourers is not a seen, known, steady, and appreciable demand; but it is so in husbandry,' under small properties. .' The labour to be done, the subsistence which that labour will produce out of his portion of land, are seen and known elements in man's calculations upon his means of subsistence. Can his square of land, or can it not, subsist a family ? can he marry or can he not ? are questions which every man can answer without delay, doubt, or speculation.' " †

It is the having no hope and no opportunity of rising in the world, however provident and self-denying a man

* Notes of a Traveller, p. 46.
† Mill's Political Economy, i. p. 336.

may be, — it is the feeling that saving can do no good whatever, and that the workhouse will keep them from actual starvation, which is demoralising and pauperising our peasants, which is increasing the numbers of our population so considerably, and which is laying such a heavy poor-rate upon the backs of the already too heavily taxed middle classes.

No writer has ever been more keenly sensible of the injurious effects of over-population upon the labouring classes than Sismondi. It is one of the grounds of his earnest advocacy of peasant properties. He had ample opportunities, in more countries than one, for judging of their effect on population. Let us see his testimony * : " In the countries in which cultivation by small proprietors still continues, population increases regularly and rapidly, until it has attained its natural limits ; that is to say, inheritances continue to be divided and subdivided among several sons, as long as by an increase of labour each family can extract an equal income from an equal portion of land. A father who possessed a vast extent of natural pasture, divides it among his sons, and they turn it into fields and meadows ; his sons divide it among their sons, who abolish fallows. Each improvement in agricultural knowledge admits of another step in the subdivision of property. But there is no danger lest the proprietor should bring up his children to make beggars of them. He knows exactly what inheritance he has to leave them ; he sees the limit beyond which this division would make them descend from the rank which he has himself filled ; and

* Mill's Political Economy, vol. i. p. 338.

a just family pride, common to the peasant" proprietor " and to the nobleman, makes him abstain from summoning into life children for whom he cannot provide. If more are born, at least they do not marry, or they agree among themselves which of several brothers shall perpetuate the family. It is not found that, in the Swiss cantons, the patrimonies of the peasants are ever so divided, as to reduce them below what will afford an honourable competence, although the habit of foreign service, by opening to the children a career indefinite and incalculable, sometimes calls forth a superabundant population."*

Mr. Laing's testimony respecting the peasant proprietors of Norway is to the same effect. Though there is no law or custom of primogeniture in this country, and no manufactures to take off a surplus population, the subdivision of property is not carried to an injurious extent, and consequently the growth of population, beyond the number which the subdivided land will maintain, is checked. " ' The division of the land among children,' says Mr. Laing †, 'appears, during the thousand years it has been in operation, not to have had the effect of reducing the landed properties to the minimum size that will barely support human existence. I have counted from five-and-twenty to forty cows upon farms, and that in a country in which the farmer must, for at least seven months in the year, have winter provender, and houses provided for all the cattle. It is evident that some cause or other, operating on the aggregation of

---

* Sismondi, Nouv. Princ., book iii. ch. 3.
† Residence in Norway, p. 18., quoted by Mr. Mill.

landed property, counteracts the dividing effects of partition among children. That cause can be no other
than what I have long conjectured would be effective in
such a social arrangement, viz. that in a country where
land is held, not in *tenancy* merely, as in Ireland, but in
full *ownership*, its aggregation, by the death of co-heirs,
and by the marriage of female heirs among the body of
landholders, will balance its subdivision by the equal
succession of children. The whole mass of property
will, I conceive, be found, in such a state of society, to
consist of as many estates of the class of 1000*l.*, as
many of 100*l.*, as many of 10*l.* a-year at one period as
at another.' That this should happen, supposes diffused
through society a very efficacious prudential check to
population; and it is reasonable to give part of the
credit of this prudential restraint to the peculiar adap-
tation of the peasant proprietary system for fostering it.

" But the experience, which most decidedly contra-
dicts the asserted tendency of peasant-proprietorship to
produce excess of population, is the case of France. In
that country, the experiment is not tried in the most
favourable circumstances, a large proportion of the properties being too small." (In France, the law com-
pulsorily *divides* the greatest part of the estate of each
proprietor at the time of his death. In the greatest
part of Germany, I believe, the law simply prevents the
proprietor entailing or tying up his property after his
death, or making any disposition of it, which would
prevent its being sold after his own death. The difference between these two systems is worthy of note.)

" The number of landed proprietors in France is not

exactly ascertained, but on no estimate does it fall much short of five millions; which, on the lowest calculation of the number of persons to a family (and for France it ought to be a low calculation), shows much more than half the population as either possessing, or entitled to inherit, landed property. A majority of the properties are so small as not to afford a subsistence to the proprietors, of whom, according to some computations, as many as three millions are obliged to eke out their means of support, either by working for hire, or by taking additional land, generally on metayer tenure. When the property possessed is not sufficient to relieve the possessor from dependence on wages, the condition of a proprietor loses much of its characteristic efficacy as a check to over-population; and if the prediction, so often made in England, had been realised, and France had become a ' pauper warren,' the experiment would even then have proved nothing, against the tendencies of the same system of agricultural economy in other circumstances. But what is the fact ? That *the rate of increase of the French population is the slowest in Europe.*"

During the thirty years, which immediately followed the division of the enormous estates of the old French noblesse among the people, a great increase of population took place. But the rapidity of that increase was soon lessened, and a generation has now grown up which, having been born in improved circumstances, has acquired the habits and tastes of prosperity, and upon them the spirit of thrift operates most conspicuously, *in keeping the increase of population within the increase of national wealth.*

In the following tables, extracted from the work of Mr. Mill, from which I have been quoting, the rate of annual increase of population in several countries is given.

The first table is that taken from Professor Rau's work on the agriculture of the Palatinate.

	Years.	Per Cent.	
United States -	1820–30	- 2.92	
Hungary (according to Rohrer)		- 2.40	
England - -	1811–21	- 1.78	
Ditto - -	1821–31	- 1.60	
Austria (Rohrer) -	-	- 1.30	
Prussia - -	1816–27	- 1.54	This was immediately after the system of peasant proprietors was first introduced into Prussia.
Ditto - -	1820–30	- 1.37 ⎰	These two numbers show,
Ditto - -	1821–31	- 1.27 ⎱	that the annual rate of increase began to diminish, as soon as the subdivision of land had proceeded so far as to enable the peasants to acquire land.
Netherlands -	1821–28	- 1.28	
Scotland - -	1821–31	- 1.30	
Saxony - -	1815–30	- 1.15	
Baden - -	1820–30	- 1.13	
Bavaria - -	1814–28	- 1.08	
Naples - -	1814–24	- 0.83	
France - -	1817–27	- 0.63	According to Mathien.
		0. 5	According to Moreau de Jonnès.

The very slow rate of increase in France so early as 1817, *i. e.* only about seventeen years after the French peasants had begun to acquire land, is very remarkable.

The second table is given by M. Quetelet*, and differs, as Mr. Mill observes, in some items, from the

* Sur l'Homme et le Développement de ses Facultés, tome i. c. 7.

preceding, probably from the author's having taken in those cases an average of different years.

Increase of Population.
Per Cent.

Ireland	-	-	- 2.45
Hungary	-	-	- 2.40
Spain	-	-	1.66
England	-	-	- 1.65
Rhenish Russia	-	-	- 1.33
Austria	-	-	- 1.30
Bavaria	-	-	- 1.08
Netherlands -	-	-	- 0.94
Naples	-	-	- 0.83
France	-	-	- 0.63
Sweden	-	-	- 0.58
Lombardy	-	-	- 0.45 Here all the land is divided among the peasants.

The third table is from M. Legoyt[*], and brings up the results for France to the census of the year 1846.

Increase of Population.
Per Cent.

Great Britain (exclusive of Ireland)			- 1.95
Prussia	-	-	- 1.84
Saxony	-	-	- 1.45
Norway	-	-	- 1.36
Sardinia	-	-	- 1.08
Holland	-	-	- 0.90
Austria	-	-	- 0.85
Sweden	-	-	- 0.83
France	-	-	- 0.68
Wirtemburg -	-	-	- 0.01

It will be seen, in all these tables, that France, where the law not only allows, but actually to a certain extent *forces*, the subdivision of property, *the increase of population is slower than that of almost every other country in Europe.* Nor is this result caused by any excess of

[*] Journal des Economistes for May, 1847.

deaths in France, for in another table, given by M. Legoyt, it is shown, that the excess per cent. of births over deaths is annually *twice as great in Great Britain*, even exclusive of Ireland, as it is in France !

Mr. Mill says, " I am not aware of a single authentic instance which supports the assertion, that rapid multiplication is promoted by peasant properties." *

Wherever I travelled in North Germany and Switzerland, I was assured by all, that the desire to obtain land, which was felt by all the peasants, was acting as the strongest possible check upon the undue increase of population.

" In England," as Mr. Mill most truly observes, " where the labourer has no investment for his savings but the savings' bank, and no position to which he can rise by any exercise of economy, except, perhaps, that of a petty shopkeeper, with its chances of bankruptcy, there is nothing at all resembling the intense spirit of thrift, which takes possession of one who, being a day-labourer, can raise himself, by saving, to the condition of a landed proprietor." . . . . . The hope of buying a piece of land, he continues to observe, " is the most powerful of inducements, to those who are without land, to practise the industry, frugality, and self-restraint, on which their success in this object of rational ambition is dependent. In Flanders, according to Mr. Fauché, the British consul at Ostend, ' farmers' sons, and those who have the means to become farmers, will delay their marriage until they get possession of a farm.' Once a farmer, the next object

* Principles of Economy, vol. i.

is to become a proprietor.   ' The first thing a Dane
does with his savings,' says Mr. Browne, the consul at
Copenhagen, ' is to purchase a clock, then a horse and
cow, which he hires out, and which pay good interest.
Then his ambition is to become a petty proprietor; and
this class of persons is better off than any in Denmark.
Indeed, I know no people in any country, who have
more easily within their reach all that is really necessary
for life than this class, which is very large in comparison
with that of labourers.'

  " As the result of this inquiry into the direct operation, and indirect influences, of peasant properties, I conceive it to be established, that there is no necessary
connection between this form of landed property, and an
imperfect state of the arts of production; that it is
favourable in quite as many respects as it is unfavourable to the most effective use of the powers of the soil;
that no other existing state of agricultural *economy has
so beneficial an effect on the industry, the intelligence, the
frugality, and prudence of the population, nor tends, on
the whole, so much to discourage an improvident increase
of their numbers;* and that no other, therefore, is, on the
whole, so favourable, in the present state of their education, both to their moral and their physical welfare." *

It was by introducing the system of small properties,
that the great ministers of Prussia, Stein and Hardenburg, raised the peasants of Prussia and Prussian Poland,
from a state precisely analogous to that of the Irish
peasantry in the present day, to their present happy and
flourishing condition.   It is this system which, as I have

  * Principles of Political Economy, vol. i. p. 346.

before shown, has raised the condition of the Saxon peasants so much above that of their neighbours, the Bohemians; which has raised the French *peasants* from that wretched condition in which all writers of the time of Louis XV. declare them to have been then sunk, to their present prosperous, tranquil, and conservative status in society; and which has made the Dutch and Swiss Protestant peasants what all writers represent them now to be, viz., intensely industrious, self-denying, and prosperous. It is the existence of a precisely opposite system, which is the principal cause of the miseries, turbulence, and bad cultivation of Ireland; and, in the opinion of all continental thinkers, it is to the repeal of all laws preventing the sale and division of land in Ireland, that we can alone look for any radical improvement in the condition of the peasants of that country. The character of a people is dependent only upon surrounding institutions and circumstances. No people are naturally depraved. If we wish to raise the character of Irishmen, we must change, and that radically, the institutions of Ireland.

The description of the parish of Montreux, near Vevay, on the Lake of Geneva, given by Mr. Laing*, is a fair illustration of the manner, in which small farms and diffused intelligence tend to foster the prudential habits of the peasants of Holland, Germany, and Switzerland. That intelligent writer says, " the parish of Montreux is divided into three communes or administrations. In that in which I am lodged, Veytaux, there is not a single pauper, although there is an accu-

* See his Notes of a Traveller.

mulated poor-fund; and the village thinks itself sufficiently important to have its post-office, its fire-engine,
and its watchman; and it has a landed population
around. . . . .

"The parish is one of the best-cultivated and most
productive vineyards in Europe, and is divided in very
small portions among a great body of small proprietors.
What is too high up the hill for vines is in orchard,
hay, and pasture-land. There is no manufacture, and
no chance work going on in the parish. These small
proprietors, with their sons and daughters, work on their
own land, know exactly what it produces, what it costs
them to live, and whether the land can support two
families or not. Their standard of living is high, as
they are proprietors. They are well lodged, their houses
well furnished, and they live well, although they are
working men. I lived with one of them two summers
successively. This class of the inhabitants would no
more *think of marrying without means to live in a decent
way*, than any gentleman's sons or daughters in England; and indeed less, because there is no variety of
means of living, as in England. It must be altogether
out of the land. The class below them, again, the mere
labourers or village tradesmen, are under a similar
economical restraint, — which it is an abuse of words to
call a moral restraint. The quantity of work, which
each of the small proprietors must hire, is a known and
filled-up demand, not very variable. There is no corn-
farming, little or no horse-work, and the number of
labourers and tradesmen, who can live by the work and
custom of the other class, is as fixed and known as the

means of living of the landowners themselves. There
is no chance living — no room for an additional house,
even, for this class, because the land is too valuable and
minutely divided to be planted with a labourer's house,
if his labour be not necessary. All that is wanted, is
supplied; and until a vacancy naturally opens, in which
a labourer and his wife could find work and house-room,
he cannot marry. The economical restraint is thus
quite as strong among the labourers, as among the class
of proprietors. Their standard of living, also, is necessarily raised by living and working all day along with a
higher class. They are clad as well, females and males,
as the peasant proprietors. The costume of the canton
is used by all. This very parish might be cited as an
instance of the restraining powers of property, and of
the habits, tastes, and standard of living, which attend
a wide diffusion of property among a people, on their
own over-multiplication. It is a proof that a division
of property by a law of succession different in principle
from the feudal, *is the true check upon over-population.*"

This is a fair picture of three fourths of the parishes
of Holland, Prussia, Saxony, and the Protestant cantons of Switzerland. There can be no doubt whatever,
that the great intelligence of the lower orders, joined to
the system of small estates, which puts it within the
power of a peasant, who can exercise present self-denial,
to become a proprietor, conduce in forming the strongest
of all possible checks upon improvident marriages, and
upon the too rapid growth of population. The following account of the Belgian peasant farmers, by
Mr. Nicholls, late one of the Poor Law Commissioners,

and now one of the two secretaries of the Poor Law
Board, applies with equal truth to the educated peasant
farmers of Holland, Switzerland, and Germany. "The
labour of the field, the management of the cattle, the
preparation of manure, the regulàting the rotation of
crops, and the necessity of carrying a certain portion of
the produce to market, call for the constant exercise of
industry, skill, and foresight among the Belgian peasant farmers; and to these qualities they add a rigid
economy, habitual sobriety, and a contented spirit,
which finds its chief gratification beneath the domestic
roof, from which the father of the family rarely wanders
in search of excitement abroad.   It was most gratifying
to observe the comfort displayed in the whole economy
of the households of these small cultivators, and the
respectability in which they lived.   As far as I could
learn, there was no tendency to the subdivision of the
small holdings.   I heard of none under five acres held
by the class of peasant farmers; and six, seven, or eight
acres is the more common size. *The provident habits
of these small farmers enable them to maintain a high
standard of comfort, and are necessarily opposed to such
subdivision.   Their marriages are not contracted so early
as in Ireland*, and the consequent struggle for subsistence among their offspring does not exist.   The
proprietors of the soil retain the free and unrestricted
disposal of their property, whether divided into smaller
or larger holdings."*

The effects of this system are also visible in the

* Inquiry into the Condition of the Poor in Holland and Belgium,
p. 166.

small number of beggars to be seen in most parts of North Germany, and of the Protestant cantons of Switzerland. In Saxony and the Protestant provinces of Prussia this is particularly remarkable. It is very rarely indeed that a traveller in these countries ever sees a badly clothed person, or is ever accosted by a mendicant. Even Mr. M'Culloch, the able and decided opponent of the system of peasant proprietors, in speaking of the state of the poor of Switzerland, says*, " In most instances the communes have poor-funds administered independently of the cantonal government" (*i. e.* funds which are generally the collections of private charity); " but if these are not sufficient a poor-rate is levied. *This rate is always limited, being, in Zurich, no more than* $2\frac{1}{2}d.$ *a-year from each individual.* The number of poor *appears to be on the decrease; and it is only in Uri, Tessin, Valais, and one or two other cantons, that pauperism is at all common.*"

In the canton of Berne about 250,000*l.*† was paid in the year 1840 in relief of the poorer classes; but this sum included all that the canton disbursed in the same year in the cantonal hospitals, in some of the schools for poor children, and in grants to assist those peasants, who had lost property by inundations and sudden accidents. When this is deducted, it is apparent that no great sum was expended in that year in the relief of actual pauperism, even in the canton of Berne with its 400,000 inhabitants. The following facts will give some further idea of the small amount of pauperism in

* Geog. Dict., title Switzerland.
† I believe this is about the average yearly expenditure in this canton.

those parts of Switzerland, where the land is subdivided, and where the people are well educated ; as compared with the amount of pauperism in England.

In 1834 the population of the canton of Vaud was about 180,000.   In that year about 1s. 3d. a head, upon the whole population of the canton, was expended in the relief of the poor, whilst in England, in the same year, without reckoning all the enormous sums expended in the same way from private sources, more than 6,000,000l. raised by the poor-rates, were expended in relieving the poor, or about 9s. a-head on the whole population !   In that year, therefore, in a given number of people, there was about seven times more pauperism in England than in the same number of people in the canton of Vaud.

In 1834, in the canton of Vaud, each person in the receipt of public funds received upon the average 1l. In five parishes of the canton, there was no person in receipt of public assistance.   More than half of the families, who were assisted, received less than 13s. each, so that, as Professor Vulliemin says, these families, with a very small increase of earnings, or with a very small decrease of expenditure, were able to support themselves.

Herr Pupikofer, in speaking of pauperism in the canton of Thurgovie, says * :—" One finds scarcely anywhere in this canton great poverty.   The number of paupers is very small.   Whoever will work may find employment.   The wages of labourers rise.   The occu-

* Gemälde der Schweitz. Thurgau.

pations and industry of the people increase. Agriculture is becoming more productive and profitable. The people are well clothed. They build better houses. They have more food and drink than they require."

In the canton of Argau, in 1839, the funds expended in the relief of paupers amounted to about *eight-pence* per head, on the whole population of the canton. In 1841, in England, when there was less pauperism, than in almost any preceding year, the expenditure per head in Wiltshire, Berkshire, Buckinghamshire, Sussex, Essex, and Dorsetshire amounted to between 9s. 6d. and 10s. per head upon the population of those counties; while the expenditure of the kingdom upon pauperism, in 1841, amounted to 6s. 2d. per head upon the whole population, and this, be it remembered, exclusive of all the immense sums expended by private charity, for the relief of the destitution of our labourers. In truth, there is no country in Europe, which expends a tithe of the enormous sums, which are sunk by the unions and by private charity in England, in the vain endeavour to stop the increase of a pauperism, which our own legislation is fostering.

3. *The Education of the Poor and the Division of the Land encourage virtuous and temperate Habits among the People*

The peasants of Western Europe know, that it is possible to rise in the social scale by industry, economy, and self-denial. Their life, even during the period of self-denial, is a life of exciting, hopeful exertion. The consciousness that it is possible to succeed, keeps their eyes fixed upon the future, makes them forget the privations of the present, and saves them from the necessity of resorting to many of those immoral excesses, to which hopeless men too often resort, in order therewith to drown their sorrow, or to supply an excitement, which their daily life does not afford.

A German, Swiss, Dutch, or French peasant, who has not yet purchased a farm, feels that every farthing, which is expended in sensual gratification, is so much deducted from the accumulating fund which is one day to procure the coveted garden or farm; and when he has purchased his piece of land, he feels so strongly interested in improving his own property, that he spends upon it every thing, which is not absolutely required for the support of himself or his family. He knows it is a safe investment, and that he must reap the fruits of the outlay if he lives, as he stands in no risk of being made to quit his property, unless he himself voluntarily sells, in which case his outlay, if a wise one, will increase the price of the land. So that, in any case, he feels safe and interested in expending all his spare savings upon the land; and many are the mere sensual gratifications, which such a man denies himself, in order to be able to improve his estate. It is impossible to over-estimate the moral benefits of a system, which offers land to the peasants, if they will but be prudent, self-denying, and industrious. Instances of drunkenness are, comparatively speaking, rare in Germany. I was often assured by the teachers and members of the middle classes in Germany, that their poorer classes were seldom guilty of intoxication. During the whole of my travels through Germany, I never saw more than one drunken man, and he was considered such a singular spectacle, that a German, whom I did not know, came up to me and pointed him out, as a curious sight that I might not soon witness again.

The effect of the school discipline upon the people of the towns is little less remarkable, than the effect of education and the small estate system upon the people of the rural districts. The educational systems of Western Europe have, for the last twenty-five years, successively removed all the juvenile population from the street life, which thousands of the poor children of our towns lead; have accustomed them from their earliest years to habits of cleanliness, of neat dressing, and of politeness; and have secured their training in various kinds of manly exercises, and their instruction in religion and in useful knowledge. They grow up under influences so strangely different to those, under which the juvenile population of our towns grow up, that the results in the two cases could not but be strangely different also. In cleanliness, dress, manners, mode of speaking, and dialect, the inhabitants of the towns of North Germany, Holland, and the Protestant cantons of Switzerland, are greatly superior to our town poor. I will not say that in the towns abroad, there are no men and women, who are as rude and uncultivated as the majority of our town labourers are; but that such instances are comparatively rare in the countries of which I am writing.

The great majority of the town workmen are such as I have described; and when the old class of workmen have died, and when the present systems of education have been at work some few years longer, even these exceptions to the description I have given will disappear; while it will be then possible to draw the description itself in still brighter colours than at present. Everything is progressing towards this result.

The difference between the condition of the juvenile population of these countries and of our own may be imagined, when I inform my readers, that many of the boys and girls of the higher classes of society in these countries are educated at the same desks, with the boys and girls of the poorest of the people, and that children comparable with the class, which attends our " ragged schools" are scarcely ever to be found. How impossible it would be to induce our gentry to let their children be educated with such children, as frequent the " ragged schools," I need not remind my readers.

4. *The Education of the People and the Division of the Land foster Respect for Property.*

This is curiously proved in several ways. A traveller in these countries will never see anywhere trespass sign-boards, or high orchard-walls, or chained yard-dogs, but he will see the road-side hedges in Germany and Switzerland planted thickly, and for miles along, with rich fruit-trees, the property of those, who own the adjoining lands. I have driven for miles between rows of cherry and apple-trees, laden with fruit, which any passer-by could have gathered with the greatest ease, but which flourished there untouched even by a school-boy. In the immediate vicinity of Zurick, Zug, and other large towns throughout Switzerland and Germany, the rich apple, pear, and cherry-trees grow in this manner within a mile of the commencement of the streets. Within the same distance of the towns I have seen the orchards unfenced and totally unprotected; without even a railing round them, close by the public road, and filled with fruit-trees laden with fruit, which was ripening in perfect security.

To be able to cultivate orchards in the hedges in this manner is a very great advantage, inasmuch as it is a great economy of space. The farmers of these countries are thus able to turn even the hedges to a very good account, wherever hedges exist. Moreover, fruit-trees flourish remarkably well in such situations, as they get a good deal of rich soil about their roots, and as they do not keep the sun and dry air from one another so much as they do when crowded together in an orchard.

It is very seldom, however, that hedges are to be seen in foreign countries separating the fields from one another. The small proprietors are much too economical of space, and much too hostile to vermin, to leave from three to four yards in breadth, along each side of a field, occupied by a high bank of the richest soil, and filled with rats, mice, rabbits, and game.

But where hedges are necessary to divide the fields from the road, there they are generally used as I have described.

Another curious proof of the respect of the people for one another's property, is to be found in the condition of the gardens of the poor near the towns. These gardens are cultivated very richly, and are always full of produce, and are as near to the entrances of the towns as land can be purchased. They are often close to the public roads, and lie undefended, except by a wooden railing, sufficient to keep out stray cattle. Any one could easily enter them at night, and carry off what he wanted; but they lie there perfectly secure, because all the poor are interested in protecting one another's property, as each one feels, that he or his relations have property which require protection.

When a man has once become a proprietor himself, or when one of his relations has become a proprietor, he speedily finds out, how necessary it is to defend the rights of property. When a man has once acquired this feeling, he has made a great step in civilisation; and the division of land teaches the lower classes this truth, better than any other method can do.

The small estates of the different peasant proprietors are only marked out by stones, or by a deeply-ploughed furrow. Each peasant respects his neighbour's land-marks, because he wishes to have his own respected. This reason, or the expectation of becoming a proprietor some day, restrains every one from trampling upon, stealing from, or injuring in any manner his neighbour's property.

Mr. Howitt, writing of Germany, says*, "Long rows of trees on each side of the roads are all that divide them from the fields; and in the South these are generally fruit-trees."

* Rural Life in Germany, p. 7.

Speaking of the country between Mannheim and Heidelberg, he says, "far and wide, the country, without a single fence, and covered with corn and vegetables, presented, as seen from the heights which bounded it, a most singular appearance to an English eye. Its predominating colour, at that time of the year, was that of ripening corn, but of different hues, according to its different degrees of richness, and the different kinds of grain. This is not planted in those vast expanses, which you see in the corn-farms of Northumberland and Lincolnshire, but in innumerable small patches and narrow stripes, because belonging to many different proprietors. Some is also sown in one direction, and some in another, with patches of potatoes, mangel-wurzel, kidney-beans, &c., amongst it, so that it presents to the eye the appearance of one of those straw table-mats of different colours which one has seen.

" Here and there we saw villages lying in the midst of the corn plain, and large woods, but not a hedge, and few scattered trees, the long rows of those marking out the highways being the only dividing lines of the country. As we passed these trees, we observed that they were principally apple, pear, plum, cherry, and walnut trees. One could not help feeling, how those trees would be plundered in England, being set, as it were, by the very road for that purpose; and, indeed, here thorns fastened round the boles, and stuck between the branches of the cherry trees where the fruit was ripening, spoke clearly of marauders. Fruit of all kinds was in abundance, and the heavy crops that are common here were indicated by the contrivances to prevent the branches being rent off. Some had their main branches held together by strong wooden clamps, and others were propped with various poles ; others, especially the plum-trees, had their boughs tied up and supported by ropes of chesnut bark. Some of these slips of bark were so low that mischievous urchins, if so disposed, could easily have cut them."

In France, where the land is very much divided among the peasants, and where education is very widely diffused among all classes, the feeling of respect for property seems to be very strong among the poorest of the country people. Mr. Laing says*, " The French are, I believe, a more honest people than the British. The beggar, who is evidently hungry, respects the fruit upon the road-side within his reach, although there is nobody to protect it. *Property is much respected in France ;* and, in bringing up children, this fidelity towards the property of others seems much more care-fully inculcated by parents in the lowest class, in the home education of their children, than with us."

'In England it is generally difficult, if not impossible, to protect the gardens, orchards, and fields in the neighbourhood of our towns from trespassers and thieves. In Germany and Switzerland this difficulty is scarcely known : property is much more secure, because it is much more diffused. I often remarked to my German and Swiss fellow-travellers, on passing the orchards and gardens undivided from the road by even a hedge, " If those trees were in England they would be sur-

* Notes of a Traveller, p. 54.

rounded by a high wall; why is such a defence unnecessary with you?" The answer invariably was, "With us, almost every one is either a possessor of property, or has some relation or friend who is a possessor; and, whichever is the case, he feels himself equally interested in discouraging trespasses and robberies, and in defending the rights of his neighbours, that they may likewise be induced to defend the rights of himself or his friends."

The boys and children are under such constant and such excellent surveillance, that, while every opportunity is allowed them for enjoying all the pastimes of childhood, scarce any opportunity is given them for the commission of crime; so that the depredations and trespasses, which are so often committed in our country by the idle young, are, comparatively speaking, unknown in Germany and Switzerland.

This respect for property — the distinguishing feature of countries, where the land is subdivided among the peasants — is not confined to the rural districts, or mere provincial towns of those countries; it operates quite as strongly in their manufacturing districts. I have already mentioned the case of Zurick, which, with its suburbs, forms a large manufacturing district. The beautiful order and perfect security of the unguarded orchards and gardens in the suburbs of this town, and throughout all the manufacturing districts of the canton, are very remarkable. The same may be said of the manufacturing districts of the canton of Argovie, of the suburbs of almost all the towns of Switzerland, and of the suburbs of the towns in the manufacturing districts in Prussia. Neither the broken fences and trees, nor the trodden turf, nor the broken gates and stiles, nor the ruined hedges, nor the general marks of mischief and traces of ruthless depredation, nor the high walls and defences intended to resist the ingress of depredators,—all which signs so sadly deface the country districts around most of our manufacturing towns, — are to be seen near the manufacturing towns of Prussia or Switzerland. Property is as secure in the vicinity of these towns, as it is in the more rural districts ; the farms and unfenced gardens look as neat and as orderly, the orchards are as safe, the land is in as good condition, and the general appearance of the country is as flourishing, as it is in districts which are separated by distance from the multitudes of cities.

5. *The Education of the Peasants and the Division of the Land tend very greatly to improve the Cultivation of the Land.*

It is a common error in England to confound small tenants-at-will, holding little bits of land under and at the will of a landlord, who can turn them out when it pleases him, with *owners* of small estates.

When any one in England talks of peasant proprietors being always prosperous, wherever they are to be found, people point to Ireland, and say, " Well, but look at the wretched state of the poor tenants in Ireland !"

But the poor Irish are not *proprietors*. There is the greatest possible difference between the social and moral effects of small estates, *belonging* to the persons dwelling upon them, and of small pieces of land held by tenants at the will of a landlord. The peasant proprietor knows that every penny of his family's earnings, which he expends upon his land, is safely invested. He is not scared from laying out money on improvements, by the fear lest a landlord — or the agent or bailiff of a landlord — should step in and turn him out of possession, before he has reaped the return for his expenditure. On the contrary, he knows that his land is his own, until he chooses to sell it, and that, consequently, every hour's labour, and every extra penny spent upon his little plot of land, will benefit either himself or his children.

This is the great distinction between peasants like the Irish, renting small plots of land as tenants, dependent upon the will of a landlord, or, still oftener, of the sub-agent of a landlord, and uncertain how long they will be allowed to hold the land, and small proprietors like the German, Dutch, Norwegian, Danish, Swiss, and French peasantry, who own their little plots, who are certain of continuing in possession and enjoyment of them, as long as they live, or until they choose to sell them, and who know, that either they themselves or their children will derive the benefits and returns of every improvement and outlay, which they make upon their estates.

The Irish tenant is not willing to spend time or money in the improvement of his holding, for he does not feel sure, that he will derive the benefit of such improvement. He is not much interested in the good cultivation of his land, for he knows that it is quite uncertain how long he will be allowed to retain it in his possession. The land is not his own, and does not inspire him with that interest in its improvement which the feeling of *ownership* always conveys. He does not know how soon the rent may be raised so as to compel him to abandon his possession. If the present agent is a kind and just man, the peasant lessee does not know how soon another agent may be appointed in his place of a different character, who would compel him to desert his improvements and outlay by unfairness or exaction. The Irish peasant's feeling is: The land is not mine; it may not be in my possession long; it is quite uncertain how soon some unforeseen accident may deprive me of it; I do not care to improve it and take care of it for the sake of my landlord; I feel no further interest in it than just to get every pennyworth out of it I can, at the smallest outlay possible.

A small *proprietor's* situation is altogether different. He feels the same kind of interest in his little property which a gentleman does in his park, but in a higher degree, because the peasant proprietor feels more acutely than the other that the subsistence of himself and his family depends entirely upon the produce of the land. He is urged to improve the condition of his farm to the uttermost, because he knows that the more he improves it, the better will be his means of supporting his family, and the greater the comfort, happiness, and respectability of his wife and children. He knows that he or his children are *certain* to reap the benefit of every extra hour's labour, and of every extra pound spent upon the farm. He feels, too, a kind of pride in making his land look better than, or at least as well cultivated as, his neighbour's, and in thus showing off his own skill and science. He is better acquainted with every square yard of his estate, and with all its wants and requirements, than a great proprietor is with each field on his estate. He turns every square yard to some use or other, knowing that the greater his produce the more comfortable will be his position. While the great proprietor would laugh at being so particular as to grumble at the waste of square yards of territory, as the rich man laughs at the economy of a penny, the peasant proprietor endeavours to turn every morsel of his property to some account. He looks with interest on each little portion of his estate, and devotes to its cultivation as much energy and care as is spread, so to speak, over a tenfold greater surface by the great proprietor. This is one of the reasons why, as I shall show in the sequel, the *gross* produce of a piece of land cultivated by a number of peasant proprietors is found to be always much greater, than the *gross* produce of an equal quantity of land cultivated by one great proprietor.

Reichensperger, in his " Die Agrarfrage," has devoted a great part of one chapter to explain the great difference between the situations of the Irish labourer, and the German peasant proprietor. He shows very powerfully, that while the latter has every possible motive for exercising economy, and for deferring his marriage, in order first to save funds for the purchase of his farm, and afterwards to save time and funds for its cultivation; while he is intensely interested in the improvement of the farm which *belongs* to himself, and does not hesitate to expend his savings and labour upon it; while his dress, food, and house are all good and im-

proving; and while his position is one of comfort, independence, and security; the Irish labourer is entirely
dependent upon the will of an agent or a landlord; that
he feels no temptation to save, or to expend his savings
upon his land, as he does not know how long it may be
in his possession; that he has no inducement to defer
marriage, as he knows that he cannot attain a better
social position by so doing, as all he can hope for is to
become the tenant-at-will of some small plot of ground;
that his house, his dress, and his manner of living,
are utterly wretched and barbarous, owing almost entirely to that demoralising sense of the hopelessness
of his situation, which has reduced him to this condition; that he lives on the lowest and poorest kind of
food; and that the next step below him is famine and
death!

Kraus, another German writer on the subject of agriculture, says *, " The small proprietor, who knows
intimately every spot and corner of his little estate, who
regards it with all that interest, which property in land,
and especially in a small piece of land, always inspires,
and who finds an actual pleasure and enjoyment in not
only cultivating but in beautifying it; he it is, who of
all farmers and landowners, is the most industrious, the
most intelligent, and the most successful in improving
the cultivation of his estate."

I do not wish to insinuate by anything that I say in
this work, that great estates are *necessarily* evils, and
the effects of bad legislation. Nothing could be further

---

* Quoted by Reichensperger in his " Die Agrarfrage," p. 79.

from my thoughts.   What I hope to prove is ; 1st, that
it is a very great evil, that the small shopkeepers and
peasants of any country should be *prevented* by the laws
from acquiring land; and that such is the result of our
legislation in Great Britain and Ireland ; and 2ndly, that
to free land from all regulations preventing its sale or
transmission from man to man, is to enable the peasants and small shopkeepers to acquire, and by enabling
them to do this, to stimulate their habits of prudence
and economy, to strengthen their conservative feelings,
to make their life more hopeful and healthy, to reduce
very considerably the amount of pauperism and immorality, among the lower classes of society, *and to increase very considerably the productiveness of the land
itself.*

To prevent the upper classes of society acquiring
more than a certain fixed quantity of land, or wealth of
any kind, would be to destroy one of the most powerful
inducements to energy, industry, intelligence, and conservative circumspection, and to introduce a system of
fraud and chicanery, — for any such attempt would be
often evaded by one of those latter methods.   But
although this is true, still it must be confessed, that
there is a mean, between the extreme measure of preventing the upper classes acquiring more than a certain
quantity of land, and the other extreme, of preventing
the small shopkeepers and peasants acquiring any land
at all.   It is this mean which I am going to consider, such
as it exists in Germany.

I do not deny that a greater amount of produce may
be obtained, in proportion to the capital and labour em-

ployed in production, upon a large than upon a small *leasehold* farm.

But there can be no doubt that five acres, the *property* of an intelligent peasant, who farms it himself, in a country, where the peasants have learned to farm, will always produce much more per acre, than an equal number of acres will do when farmed by a mere *leasehold* tenant. In the case of the peasant proprietor, the increased activity and energy of the farmer, and the deep interest he feels in the improvement of his land, which are always caused by the fact of *ownership*, more than compensate the advantage arising from the fact, that the capital required to work the large farm is less in proportion to the quantity of land cultivated, than the capital required to work the small farm. In the cases of a large farm and of a small farm, the occupiers of which are both tenants of another person, and not owners themselves, it may be true, that the produce of the large farm will be greater in proportion to the capital employed in cultivation, than that of the small farm ; and that, therefore, the farming of the larger farm will be the most economical, and will render the largest rent to the landlord.

But even in this case, viz., where the occupiers are both tenants and not owners, it is too often forgotten, that the want of small farms deprives the peasants of all hope of improving their condition in life, cuts away the next step in the social ladder, deprives them of all inducement to exercise self-denial, habits of saving and foresight, or active exertion, exceedingly pauperises and demoralises them, very greatly increases the local poor-rates and the county-rates, and in this way very often deprives the farmers of more than all the extra gains, which they would otherwise derive from the more economical system of large farms.

So that, even in the case of *tenant* farmers, I am certain, — and the reports upon Flemish husbandry bear me out in this assertion, — that the system of small farming is the most moral and civilising, if it is not also the most economical system, for a country to pursue.

Reichensperger, himself an inhabitant of that part of Prussia, where the land is the most subdivided, has published a long and very elaborate work to show the admirable consequences of a system of freeholds in land. He expresses a very decided opinion, that not only are the *gross* products of any given number of acres, held and cultivated by small or peasant proprietors, greater, than the *gross* products of an equal number of acres, held by a few great proprietors, and cultivated by tenant farmers, but that the *net* products of the former, after deducting all the expenses of cultivation, are also greater than the *net* products of the latter. He thinks that this result is to be attributed to the following causes : —

1. The extraordinary interest, which the small proprietor feels in his little estate. It is this which makes himself and every member of his family not only willing, but desirous, to devote every leisure moment, and every hour of day-light, to the improvement and cultivation of his plot of ground, and which urges him to avail himself of every little circumstance, which can by any possibility increase the productiveness of his land, and

which, in minute care, in cleanliness, in economy of ground, and of contrivances, and in beauty of appearance, raises his farming to the perfection of garden cultivation.

2. The extraordinary pains which are always taken by peasant proprietors to collect, prepare, and employ manures.

3. The much greater quantity of small products, such as eggs, butter, milk, honey, vegetables, and fruit, which are obtained from a given quantity of land cultivated by small proprietors, than from an equal quantity of land cultivated by large proprietors, or by the tenants of such proprietors.

4. That while, on the estates of great proprietors, acres of land often lie totally unemployed and uncultivated from want of capital, or from neglect, or from wasteful farming ; not a single square yard of ground is neglected or uncultivated upon the estate of the small proprietor, but every *smallest* piece of ground is turned to some account, and, if capable of any cultivation, is forced to produce all that industry can possibly win from it.

5. That even the hedges and the sides of the public roads are made available for the purposes of production, and are planted thickly with fruit-trees, which richly requite the labours of the farmers ; while in countries, where the land is in the hands of few and great proprietors — our own for example — the thousands and millions of hedgerows are filled with useless brambles and underwood, and are made the breeding-places of quantities of destructive vermin.

6. To the above-mentioned causes, enumerated by Reichensperger, may be added another:—That the particular kind of tillage, viz., spade-labour, often pursued by peasant proprietors, of itself greatly increases the productiveness of the ground. The spade breaks and pulverises the soil much more finely than the plough and harrow do, and mixes the manure or lime with it much better. Fewer seeds are, therefore, choked or smothered, the grain shoots better and grows stronger, and the produce of any given number of acres is very considerably increased.

After having enumerated the above-mentioned advantages of the subdivision of land among the cultivators themselves, Reichensperger says *, — " The beautiful valley of the Rhine, with the greatest part of its neighbouring provinces, is there, fully to bear out and prove what I have said. Wirtemburg, Switzerland, Belgium, Lombardy, and, above all, the luxuriant fields of Tuscany and Lucca, all show that the above description of the blessings and happiness resulting from a wise and intelligent system of small proprietors is far behind the prosperous reality."

He mentions one fact, which seems to prove that the fertility of the land in countries, where the properties are small, must be rapidly increasing. He says, that the price of land which is divided into small properties, in the Prussian Rhine provinces, is much higher, and has been rising much more rapidly, than the price of land on the great estates. He and Professor Rau both say that this rise in the price of the small estates would

* Die Agrarfrage, p. 46.

have ruined the more recent purchasers, unless the productiveness of the small estates had increased in at least an equal proportion; and as the small proprietors have been gradually becoming more and more prosperous, notwithstanding the increasing prices they have paid for their land, he argues, with apparent justness, that this would seem to show that, not only the *gross* profits of the small estates, but the *net* profits also, have been gradually increasing, and that, the *net* profits per acre, of land, when farmed by small proprietors, are greater than the net profits per acre, of land farmed by great proprietors. He says, with seeming truth, that the increasing price of land in the small estates cannot be the mere effect of competition, or it would have diminished the profits and the prosperity of the small proprietors, and that this result has not followed the rise.

Albrecht Thaer, another celebrated German writer on the different systems of agriculture, in one of his later works*, expresses his decided conviction, that the *net produce* of land is greater, when farmed by small proprietors, than when farmed by great proprietors or their tenants. He says, " where real industry and moderate means are found among small proprietors, and where these latter are not fettered by unwise legislation or overburdened with taxation, there the land cultivated by the hands or under the immediate supervision of the small proprietor himself, will not only produce *more, as every one is willing to concede,* but will also yield a *greater net profit,* than land cultivated by great proprietors or their tenants."

* Grundsätze der rationellen Landwirthshaft.

This opinion of Thaer is all the more remarkable, as during the early part of his life he was very strongly in favour of the English system of great estates and great farms.

But whether the *net* produce of land cultivated by peasant proprietors be greater than its *net* produce when cultivated by great proprietors, or not, all accounts agree in showing that the cultivation and productiveness of the land has very much improved, and is in a state progressive improvement, wherever trade in land has been rendered free, and wherever the peasants have been enabled to acquire.

The peasant farming of Prussia, Saxony, Holland, and Switzerland is the most perfect and economical farming I have ever witnessed in any country. No pains, no means, are spared to make the ground produce as much as possible. Not a square yard of land is uncultivated or unused. No stones are left mingled with the soil. The ground is cleared of weeds and rubbish, and the lumps of earth are broken up with as much care as in an English garden. If it is meadow land, it is cleaned of noxious herbs and weeds. Only the sweet grasses, which are good for the cattle, are allowed to grow. All the manure from the house, farm, and yard is carefully collected and scientifically prepared. The liquid manure is then carried in hand-carts like our road watering carts into the fields, and is watered over the meadows in equal proportions. The solid manures are broken up, cleared of stones and rubbish, and are then properly mixed and spread over the lands which require them. No room is lost in hedges or ditches, and no breeding-places are left for the vermin, which in many parts of England do so much injury to the farmers' crops. The character of the soil of each district is carefully examined, and a suitable rotation of crops is chosen, so as to obtain the greatest possible return without injuring the land; and the cattle are well housed, are kept beautifully clean, and are groomed and tended like the horses of our huntsmen.

All authorities upon the subject of agriculture in Prussia agree, that the cultivation of the land, before the creation of the peasant proprietor class, was very much inferior in its results to its state at the present day. Much more is obtained from the land now than formerly, and the land is less impoverished, owing to the more skilful rotation of the crops.

Before the Prussian Government was induced to try the great experiment of enabling the peasants to obtain land, and of creating a great class of peasant proprietors, it endeavoured to improve the condition of agriculture throughout the kingdom by advancing great sums of money to the great landed proprietors, with the view of enabling them to introduce better systems of farming upon their lands. Reichensperger says,* — "Frederic II. gave away very considerable sums of money for the encouragement of agriculture. According to the minister, Von Stertzberg, between the years 1763 to 1786, the sums advanced in this manner amounted to 24,399,838 thalers. The pro-

* Die Agrarfrage, p. 306.

vince of Pomerania alone received 5,500,000 thalers; and the aristocracy of that province alone received 4,500,000 thalers. 'And yet these sums of money given by Frederic to the Pomeranian nobles, to enable them to improve the cultivation of their lands, have in reality done no good; but have often, indeed, been most injurious in their effects.'"*

Professor and Regierungsrath Dr. Shubert, in his admirable work†, says, — " Prussia has excited throughout all her provinces a singular and increasing interest in agriculture, and in the breeding of cattle; and if in some localities, on account of peculiar circumstances, or of a less degree of intelligence, certain branches of the science of agriculture are less developed than in other localities, it is, nevertheless, undeniable, that an almost universal progress has been made, in the cultivation of the soil and in the breeding of cattle. No one can any longer, as was the custom thirty years ago, describe the Prussian system of agriculture by the single appellation of the three-year-course system; no one can, as formerly, confine his enumeration of richly cultivated districts to a few localities. In the present day there is no district of Prussia in which intelligence, persevering energy, and an ungrudged expenditure of capital has not immensely improved a considerable part of the country for the purposes of agriculture and of the breeding of cattle."

* Vgl. Möglin'she Jahrbücher der Landwirthshaft von A. Thaer.
† Handbuch der Allgemeinen Staatskunde des Preussischen Staats, vol. ii. p. 5.

Dr. Shubert shows what is being done at the present day to improve the system of agriculture still more. Several large agricultural colleges, and a great number of agricultural schools, have been founded and endowed in different parts of Prussia, where the sons of the farmers study the sciences of agriculture and of agricultural chemistry. A great number of agricultural societies have been formed also; and, by means of the funds of these societies, lecturers and practical farmers are retained to travel about the country, to give lectures in farming, and to aid the farmers with information and advice.

It appears from Dr. Dieterici's " Statistics of Prussia," that the arable land of Prussia

Produced in 1805 44,000,000 scheffels of grain.
—   in 1831 55,000,000   ditto.
—   in 1841 68,000,000   ditto.

This alone proves that the land of Prussia has produced much more since a great part of it has been divided among the peasants, than it did when it was all held by a few great proprietors; and this fact is still more significant, when we consider, that the increase in the amount of grain produced by the land is much greater, than the increase in the numbers of the population.

The increase in the numbers of the Prussian population, since 1805, may be thus represented —

Years	-	-	-	1805	1831	1843
Population	-	-	1	$1\frac{3}{10}$	$1\frac{1}{2}$

while the increase in the quantity of grain produced in Prussia, since 1805, may be thus represented —

Years	-	-	-	1805	1831	1841
Grain produced		-		1	$1\frac{1}{2}$	$1\frac{3}{4}$

from which it is evident that the increase, since 1805, in the quantity of grain produced in Prussia is much greater, than the increase during the same period in the numbers of the population.

Professor Rau, of Heidelberg, has published a small work on the agriculture and on the social condition of the peasant proprietors of that part of Germany, which lies upon the Rhine and Neckar, and which we know by the name of the Palatinate. I would strongly advise every one to read this little book. It contains a striking corroboration of the account, which I am giving of the German peasants. Professor Rau says, that the land of the Palatinate is so much subdivided, that many of the plots are not more than *one* acre, while the majority of the little estates vary between twenty acres and one acre in size. Yet, with this excessive subdivision, how does he describe the state of agriculture and the condition of the people ?

After saying *, that this part of Germany has long been celebrated for its skilful and scientific farming, he continues thus : " Whoever travels hastily through this part of the country must have been agreeably surprised with the luxuriant vegetation of the fields, with the orchards and vineyards, which cover the hill-sides, with the size of the villages, with the breadth of their streets, with the beauty of their official buildings, with the cleanliness and stateliness of their houses, with the good clothing in which the people appear at their festivities, and with the universal proofs of a prosperity, which has

* Landwirthshaft der Rheinpfalz.

been caused by industry and skill, and which has survived all the political changes of the times."

" There can be no doubt of the excellence of the system of agriculture pursued there."

" Of the labour bestowed upon the land, it may be said, that it is generally expended with a high degree of industry and skill. The unwearied assiduity of the peasants,—who are to be seen actively employed the whole of every year and of every day, and who are never idle, because they understand how to arrange their work, and how to set apart for every time and season its appropriate duties,—is as remarkable, as their eagerness to avail themselves of every circumstance and of every new invention which can aid them, and their ingenuity in improving their resources, are praiseworthy. It is easy to perceive that the peasant of this district really understands his business. He can give reasons for the occasional failures of his operations; he knows and remembers clearly his pecuniary resources; he arranges his choice of fruits according to their prices; and he makes his calculations by the general signs and tidings of the weather."

According to Professor Rau, the position of even the daily labourers has improved since 1817, as the price of the necessaries of life has, since that time, fallen more than the wages of the labourers. He says, that even the labourers live more comfortably, take better care of their children, and are better able to save than they were formerly; that they eat more meat and puddings and more cheese than they did forty years ago; and that their manner of living is generally much better than it was then.

He gives a curious and minute account of the way in which the peasants collect the dung of the stables, cow-sheds, and houses; and he shows how scientifically they prepare the different kinds of manures, and apply them to the different descriptions of lands.

Speaking of their economical manner of collecting and preparing manure, Professor Rau says, "As the cows are not generally fed in the meadows, but in the sheds, none of their dung is lost."

"The bedding of the cattle generally lies under them from one to two days, but not longer. It is then carried out to the dung-heap, and, after lying there about six weeks, is carried out upon the lands."

These peasant proprietors know exactly how much manure each acre of their land requires for its good cultivation. They know also how much manure they can obtain annually from each head of cattle. If the number of cattle, which one of the small farmers possesses, is not large enough to furnish sufficient manure for the whole of his land, he reckons how much he shall require, and purchases so much from those of his neighbours who have more than they require.

All the waste water of the house, the stables, the cow-sheds, the pig-sties, and the farm-yards is collected in conduits made on purpose upon every farm, and is carried along these conduits, sometimes to a well made on purpose to receive it, and sometimes to the dung-heap. It is, however, generally, and in Switzerland always, collected in a well which is made in the farm-yard for its reception. A small pump is put down into this well, and by its means the liquid manure is pumped up into small watering-carts, and is carried in these on to the land, and regularly scattered over the well-broken soil.

In England and Wales millions of pounds' worth of manure are lost every year in our farm-yards, from the lack of science among our farmers, and from the little interest, which the greater part of even our greater leasehold farmers feel in agricultural improvements.

One objection, which has been always urged with great eagerness and apparent force against the system of subdivision of land and small farms is, that the small farmers are too poor to possess themselves of the expensive machines, which science has invented and will invent, and which enable their possessors to economise labour and time, to carry out great agricultural improvements at a small expense, and to perform many important agricultural operations which cannot be performed without them.

This objection, however, is more specious than true. The more intelligence advances among the small proprietors, by means of the agricultural colleges and of the schools of agricultural chemistry, which are being founded throughout Germany, Switzerland, France, Belgium, and Holland, for the express purpose of training the children of the peasant farmers in the science of agriculture, and which are raising up a class of small proprietor farmers, who, for the knowledge of agriculture, put to shame the majority of our large tenant farmers — the more, I repeat, intelligence advances by these means among the small proprietors, the better will they understand how to combine among themselves, so as to help one another to carry out those particular operations, which require an accumulation of capital for their successful prosecution.

As Counsellor Reichensperger says, "there is nothing to prevent small proprietors availing themselves of the more costly agricultural machines, if several of them unite in the purchase of them, and keep them for common use. It is always a very easy matter, so to arrange the agricultural operations of several farms, that one machine may perform them all without putting any of the proprietors to any inconvenience."

This opinion of Reichensperger is worthy of all the more consideration, as he is living among a nation of small proprietors, and as he has devoted a considerable period of time to the study of their condition and of its capabilities of improvement.

He further says, that the parts of Europe where the most extensive and costly plans for watering the meadows and lands have been carried out in the greatest perfection, are those where the lands are very much subdivided, and are in the hands of small proprietors. He instances the plain round Valencia, several of the southern departments of France, particularly those of Vaucluse and Bouches du Rhone, Lombardy, Tuscany, the districts of Sienna, Lucca, and Bergamo, Piedmont, many parts of Germany, and the district of Siegenshen, in all which parts of Europe the land is very much subdivided among small proprietors. In all these parts great and expensive systems and plans of general irrigation have been carried out, and are now being supported, by the small proprietors themselves; thus showing how they are able to accomplish, by means of combination, work requiring the expenditure of great quantities of capital.

The following interesting account of the character of farming in the Prussian Rhine Provinces is given by Mr. Banfield * : —

" The first study of every good farmer in Germany is the local part of his task, the influence of soil and climate. In the uplands of Cleves the climate is dry, and the sun hot in summer; the soil is strongly charged with limestone; cow-dung is found to answer better for winter crops, or at least cow-dung mixed with horse-dung better than the latter alone : for this reason, oxen are kept as draught cattle all along the Rhine. The dung-heap in the centre of the farm-yard is the point, on which the greatest care is concentrated for good farming establishments. It usually lies in a deep sloped pit, enclosed by stone walls on three sides, the bottom rising gradually to the level of the yard on the fourth side, to allow of the approach of the dung-cart. Into this pit the drains from all the offices are led, and waste of all kinds is thrown upon it. The plan of stall-feeding, but especially the care taken to keep the beasts clean (they are rubbed down every day like horses), prevents their being allowed to tread the heap down. Straw is likewise much economised, as it is used to mix with the oats during the winter. The mixture of cow and horse-dung, with the flow of cold moistening matter, prevents the fermentation that would otherwise arise in

* Agriculture on the Rhine, p. 16.

the heap, and cause much of its value to evaporate.
After the fallow-ploughing, the manure is only just
ploughed in sufficiently deep to cover it. Top-dressings
are a good deal in use amongst good farmers for grain
crops.

" At Goch, as well as in other well-managed farms in
this district, compost heaps are to be seen in all yards ;
the substances used for one resembled a mixture we
have seen in some parts of Ireland. A heap of quick-
lime is covered all over with turf-ashes, or with wood-
ashes, from the house-stoves. Water is thrown over the
heap, and, after a few days, the lime, in fermenting,
shows itself through the ashes ; the heap is then turned
over, again covered with ashes, and watered ; and this
process is repeated until the lime is thoroughly slaked ;
the mass is then mixed with sand or earth, or other
compost heaps, and forms an excellent top-dressing.

. . . . " The number of stock kept is large, even
on those uplands, where there is little grazing. One horse
for twenty acres is the proportion of the best farmers ; but
then fifteen to twenty-five oxen and cows would be the
smallest number of horned cattle on one hundred acres,
with one to two hundred sheep. On a *peasant's farm
of fifty acres, we have found four horses, fifteen head of
horned cattle, and seventy to eighty sheep.*

" In following the use to which the farmer puts this
manure, we come to the distinguishing feature of
Rhenish agriculture. No peculiar crop is here prescribed by legislative enactment, and the climate admits of a sufficient variety to allow the landowner to
draw all the help he can from the nature of his soil.

The uplands of Cleves are particularly well suited to grow barley. In the autumn, the land of this description is well ploughed and manured, and, in the following spring, barley and clover are sown; the grain obtains the highest price in the Dutch market. It is not unusual to turn the cows on the stubble; but each is fastened by the stable-chain to an iron stake driven into the ground, to prevent straying, as the lots are small in these parts, and no fences are to be found. . . . .

" The second year gives a rich clover crop, partly for stall-feeding, in part to be saved as hay, and the third (sometimes the second) cutting gives the seed known in England as Dutch clover seed, from the circumstance of its passing through Holland on its way to London and Hull. When the seed has ripened and been housed, the clover is broken up, and, after several ploughings, wheat is sown, which is followed by rye. Turnips are sown in the rye stubble; and the fifth year begins the rotation again with potatoes, followed by barley and clover in the highly manured soil. In soils less peculiarly suited to barley (which recommends itself as a profitable article of exportation), wheat and rye follow potatoes or flax, and are followed by oats. Cabbages and carrots often alternate with potatoes as fallow crops, and are richly manured; and in most large farms the two rotations go on side by side on lands of differing qualities. Perhaps the absence of expensive farming favours the study of the peculiar nature of the soil, which is evidently severely tried by the rotations we have described. Where composts with marl or lime are used as top-dressings, the rotation is usually prolonged, and the rye crop is repeated and followed by oats. It is common to top-dress the barley, after it has germinated, with compost or with liquids. . . . .

" The land is made to bear the utmost that nature without forcing admits. Horned cattle are used in abundance, but are not forced in fattening, and the average weight of an ox does not exceed forty stone."

Again, the same writer says *, " In the great occupation of turning to the best account the soil and climate given to them by Providence, the peasant of the Rhine stands untutored, except by experience. And could the tourist hear these men in their blouses and thick gaiters converse on the subject, he would be surprised at the mass of practical knowledge they possess, and at the caution and yet the keenness with which they study these advantages. Of this all may rest assured, that from the commencement of the offsets of the Eifel, where the village cultivation assumes an individual and strictly local character, good reason can be given for the manner in which every inch of ground is laid out, as for every balm, root, or tree, that covers it."

Reichensperger also bears testimony to the great prosperity of the small proprietors of the Rhine Provinces of Bavaria. He says †, " the condition of the agriculture and of the agricultural classes of the Rhine Provinces of Bavaria is in most respects analogous to that of the Rhine Province of Prussia, and most strongly attests the good results of the system of small pro-

* Agriculture of the Rhine, p. 81.
† Die Agrarfrage, p. 419.

prietors in the former provinces. Even a superficial observation of this populous, flourishing land, which, under the industrious hands of its numerous small proprietors, and under the influence of a system of free-trade in land, produces all the products of Middle Europe in the richest abundance, proves the truth of this statement."

The same writer, residing among the peasant proprietors of the Rhine Provinces of Prussia, describes the state of the farms before the subdivision of the land, and the effect of this subdivision in those provinces, in the following manner.* This account is worthy the greatest consideration.

" If we observe the effect of the subdivision of land in the Rhine Province, a merely hasty glance at the handsome and well-built villages, and the luxuriant orchards and fields, will suffice to show, that the new agrarian regulations have by no means, as their opponents have alleged, plunged the land into poverty and suffering, but that they have, on the contrary, exercised the most beneficial influence upon the cultivation of the land and upon the condition of the people.

" The indivisibility of the estates was never formally established in this province by any laws or customs; but large estates became consolidated and tied up either in aristocratic families or in spiritual or temporal corporations. These great estates were generally let out for short periods of time to farmers, *and were almost without exception wretchedly cultivated.* Although the rents of

* Reichensperger, Die Agrarfrage, p. 403.

the farms were very small and were seldom increased, yet the farmers' families, upon even the largest farms, were scarcely ever in a prosperous condition, but existed in great deprivation of even the necessaries of life, and without being able to lay by any thing. They were not able to bear the least adversity; and it was necessary, that even a dead horse should be replaced by the assistance of their landlords, if the farmer was not to be ruined by his loss, as he could not save enough to buy another himself. The land was burdened with many dues, partly feudal and partly in form of rents to private individuals, which, together with the tithes, prevented all improvement of the land.

" To this miserable, almost stationary state of things, followed, in the beginning of the present century, the subdivision of the land, which was originated by the French Revolution, and was principally caused by the sale of the so-called national property. Out of a single farm, which formerly secured to the farmer only a miserable existence, were formed very quickly, by means of speculation and division, small estates for four or more families, who, notwithstanding that the price of the land now much exceeded the value of the former farm, as calculated by the rent it paid, attained in a short time a prosperous condition. The handsome dwelling-houses and farm buildings, which arose on all sides on the sites of the old farm-houses—the enlarged villages, and their improved internal arrangement, proved that the succeeding and more numerous proprietors of the land obtained from it much more produce than the prior tenant farmers had been able to do. . . . . The cattle-breeding was now improved from year to year, and, by means of the great number of small but intelligent and active landowners possessed generally of sufficient capital, the old agricultural system gradually gave place to a clearer, more intelligent, and more rational system of husbandry. A tolerably equally divided prosperity, equally removed from the suffering of pauperism and from the superfluity of wealth, was the consequence of these changes; and if the prosperity of the larger towns has increased still more rapidly, the country districts have experienced the influence of this improvement in the increasing consumption of raw products. . . . The country people of the Rhine Province and the people of the neighbouring provinces, who enjoy a system of free proprietorship of land, may, in the face of the world, be proud among their hills and valleys, which they have made so happy in appearance, and in their clean and comfortable villages; they may point with pride to the men, whom they furnish to the yearly military levies; they may boast themselves of the propriety of their social life; nor need they fear comparison with any other race, if we except the incomparably prosperous inhabitants of Styria, the Tyrol, and Switzerland " (in all which countries the peasants are proprietors), " who, in activity, happiness, and freedom, have no equals. The inhabitants of the Rhine Provinces feel themselves to be the proprietors of the soil which they cultivate. This fact distinguishes them greatly, in every intellectual and physical respect, from the peasant labourers, who possess nothing of their own, and who at this day, in the same manner as hundreds of years ago, cultivate and labour for the great proprietors without any hope of improvement."

The inhabitants of the Rhine Province are themselves so convinced of the benefits, which they derive from the subdivision of the land among the peasants, that, in 1841, the representative assembly of the province rejected, by a majority of 49 to 8 representatives, a proposition made to them by the Prussian government to restrain the subdivision of the land. The same feeling has been manifested throughout Prussia, whenever the government has attempted, as it has done on several occasions, to found a Prussian landed aristocracy, by introducing a plan like that in force in our country, whereby to accumulate great estates, and to retain them for many generations in the same family. The middle and lower classes in Prussia are so conscious of the benefits they derive from the opposite system, and have therefore always offered so strong an opposition to any hint at a change, that the government, powerful and arbitrary as it was prior to 1848, has not ventured to carry out what it had so much at heart.

Some have thought that a country, the land of which is very much subdivided, will not support so many cattle as one the land of which is cultivated in great estates. This, however, is satisfactorily disproved by many statistics, and particularly by the statistics of the numbers of horses, cows, sheep, &c., supported in Prussia in different years since the land was first subdivided.

From these statistics it appears that, notwithstanding that the quantity of grain produced in Prussia has increased so very considerably of late years, the numbers

of horses, cows, oxen, and sheep have been also increasing in a very remarkable manner since the land
was released from the laws which prevented its subdivision.   If we compare the statistics published by the
Statistical Bureau in Berlin, and quoted by Reichensperger, it appears that the numbers of horses, cows
and oxen, sheep, and pigs in the whole of Prussia in
different years were as follows —

Years.	Horses.	Cows and Oxen.	Sheep.	Pigs.
1831	1,374,594	4,446,368	11,965,675	No return.
1837	1,472,901	4,838,622	15,338,977	1,936,304
1843	1,564,554	5,042,010	16,235,880	2,115,212

while the increase, since 1816, in that part of Prussia
where the land is subdivided the most, viz., the Rhine
Province, has been greater than that of any other part
of Prussia.   The following table shows what the increase has been since 1816 in the Rhine Province : —

Years.	Horses.	Cows and Oxen.	Sheep.	Pigs.
1816	94,564	609,960	535,754	195,466
1831	109,642	711,126	490,721	214,870
1843	122,318	776,453	575,193	277,087

In 1843 the Minister of the Interior of Prussia presented to the King a report upon the condition of
agriculture in Prussia, in which it is said, that the
system of peasant proprietors, which was introduced into
Prussia by Frederic William III., has greatly improved the condition of the peasants both intellectually
and socially, and that it has not failed in its expected
effect upon the material prosperity of the country, but
has undeniably increased the activity and enterprise of

all people engaged in agriculture, and has been the
cause of the visibly growing prosperity of the people. *

" The wonderful progress which Prussian agriculture
has made, since the laws of Frederic William III. were
issued, and owing to them, in the province of Brandenburg, was forcibly described, at the third meeting
of the German Agricultural Association at Potsdam, in
1839, by Herr Koppe, a member of the National
Economical Association, and one thoroughly well acquainted with the state of agriculture in that province." †

Herr Koppe says, that the new system has produced
greater results upon the large estates of Brandenburg
than upon the small ones. As the results on the
larger estates of freeing the land from all restraints
upon its sale and transmission from a man of little
capital and intelligence to a man of more capital and
intelligence, he enumerates the following : — The aban-
donment of the old and unscientific customs ; the diffusion of a knowledge of the science of agriculture ; the
increasing observance of the results of experience ;
better arrangement of the land ; employment of better
agricultural implements and machines ; a more scientific
management and employment of manures ; an increase
in the amount of manure ; better cultivation of the
meadows ; perceptible improvement in the breeding,
feeding, and management of the cattle ; introduction of
new and useful agricultural methods ; and, as a consequence of all this, higher rents and higher price of

* Reichensperger, Die Agrarfrage, p. 397.   † Ibid.

land. The speech of Herr Koppe is too long for insertion in this work; it may be found in Reichensperger's work.

Counsellor Doenniges expresses his conviction of the happy results of this system in the most decided manner. He says*, that the so often opposed divisibility of the land has led to happy results, and has formed, so to speak, a ladder by which the peasants and small proprietors may rise in the social scale, and increase the size of their estates.

The Geh. Ob. Reg. Rath. Lette bears his testimony in like manner to the same effect. He said, at the seventh meeting of the German Agricultural Association, that they had all been reconciled to the new system of agrarian regulations; and that their admirable results had carried conviction to the minds of all. †

A ministerial paper, laid before the provincial assembly of the Rhine Province, bears witness to the same effect. It says, that the new agrarian regulations have removed all impediments to the progress of agriculture, and that they have tended to improve the cultivation of the land so much, as to have, in 1843, raised the marketable value of the land, since 1828, about 75 per cent. ‡

Geh. Ob. Reg. Raths. Bethe, who, in 1836, made a report to the government upon the condition of the Rhine Province, confirms by his testimony the truth of the former accounts. He says that the division of the

* Die Agrarfrage, p. 400.   † Ibid.
‡ Ibid. p. 409.

land in that province has been the cause of improvement and progress. This official reporter mentions one place, the district surrounding the town of Duren, which is divided into very small parcels, and in the neighbourhood of which there are some large manufactories, and he says of it, that the prosperity of this district has increased to such a degree, that no change of the present system can possibly be desired.*

In the Protestant cantons of Switzerland not a foot of waste land is to be seen. Wherever anything will grow, something useful is made to grow. It is curious to see the singular pains bestowed upon the lands. The men are often assisted by their whole households in cultivation. From early in the morning until late in the evening the peasants labour on their farms. The workmen of the towns, who possess plots, turn out in the evenings after their day's labour is over, when they may be seen weeding, digging, cleaning, and watering with all the zest and eagerness of competitors for a prize. In many of the Swiss towns, the greater part of the workmen who are forty years of age possess plots of land, which they have purchased with the savings laid by before marriage.

In Saxony it is a notorious fact, that during the last thirty years, and since the peasants became the proprietors of the land, which they formerly held as the Irish hold their little leaseholds, viz., from and at the will of owners of great estates, there has been a rapid and continual improvement in the condition of the

* Die Agrarfrage, p. 412.

houses, in the manner of living, in the dress of the peasants, and particularly in the culture of the land.   I have twice walked through that part of Saxony called Saxon-Switzerland in company with a German guide, and on purpose to see the state of the villages and of the farming, and I can safely challenge contradiction when I affirm, that there is no farming in all Europe superior to the laboriously careful cultivation of the valleys of that part of Saxony.   There, as in the cantons of Berne, Vaud, and Zurick, and in the Rhine Provinces, the farms are singularly flourishing.   They are kept in beautiful condition, and are always neat and well-managed.   The ground is cleaned as if it were a garden.   No hedges or brushwood encumber it.   Scarcely a rush or thistle or a bit of rank grass is to be seen. The meadows are well watered every spring with liquid manure, saved from the drainings of the farm-yards. The grass is so free from weeds that the Saxon meadows reminded me more of English lawns, than of anything else I had seen.   The little plots of land belonging to the peasantry lie side by side, undivided by hedge or ditch or any other kind of separation.   The peasants endeavour to outstrip one another in the quantity and quality of the produce, in the preparation of the ground, and in the general cultivation of their respective portions; and this very rivalry tends to improve all the more the system of tillage and the value of the crops.

All the little proprietors are eager to find out how to farm so as to produce the greatest results; they diligently seek after improvements; they send their children to the agricultural schools in order to fit them to assist their fathers; and each proprietor soon adopts a new improvement introduced by any of his neighbours.

A proprietor of a small plot of land does this because he feels that any improvement, which he makes, is so much gain for himself and his family. A lessee of a small plot of land acts otherwise, because he knows that it is uncertain whether he or his landlord will reap the benefit of his improvements; because he knows that his improvements will, sooner or later, be taken possession of by the landlord; and because he cannot feel the same interest in improving the condition of a plot belonging to another, as he would if the plot belonged to himself.

If any one has travelled in the mountainous parts of Scotland and Wales, where the farmers are only under-lessees of great landlords, without security of tenure, and liable to be turned out of possession with half-a-year's notice, and where the peasants are only labourers without any land of their own, and generally without even the use of a garden; if he has travelled in the mountainous parts of Switzerland, Saxony, and the hilly parts of the Prussian Rhine Provinces, where most of the farmers and peasants possess, or can, by economy and industry, obtain land of their own; and if he has paid any serious attention to the condition of the farms, peasants, and children of these several countries, he cannot fail to have observed the astonishing superiority of the condition of the peasants, children, and farms in the last-mentioned countries.

The miserable cultivation, the undrained and rush-

covered valleys, the great number of sides of hills, terraces on the rocks, sides of streams, and other places
capable of the richest cultivation, but wholly disused,
even for game preserves; the vast tracts of the richest
lands lying in moors, and bogs, and swamps, and used
only for the breeding-places of game, and deer, and
vermin, while the poor peasants are starving beside
them; the miserable huts of cottages, with their one
story, their two low rooms, their wretched and undrained floors, and their dilapidated roofs; and the
crowds of miserable, half-clad, ragged, dirty, uncombed,
and unwashed children, never blessed with any education, never trained in cleanliness, or morality, and
never taught any pure religion, are as astounding on
the one hand, as the happy condition of the peasants
in the Protestant cantons of Switzerland, in the Tyrol,
in Saxony, and in the mountainous parts of the Prussian
Rhine Provinces, is pleasing upon the other, where every
plot of land that can bear anything is brought into the
most beautiful state of cultivation; where the valleys
are richly and scientifically farmed; where the manures
are collected with the greatest care; where the houses
are generally large, roomy, well-built, and in excellent
repair, and are improving every day; where the children
are beautifully clean, comfortably dressed, and attending
excellent schools; and where the condition of the people
is one of hope, industry, and progress.

There can be no doubt that, if the mountainous
parts of Wales and Scotland were subjected to a system of laws similar to those of Norway, Germany,
France, and Switzerland; and if the peasants of Wales

and Scotland were able to purchase land, that the mountainous parts of the latter countries would yield at least *six times* as great a produce as they do at present, while the character of the people would, in the course of two generations, be greatly improved.

Those who have not travelled in hill-countries inhabited by peasant proprietors, can have no idea how mountains may be cultivated. Mr. Gleig*, when speaking of Saxony, says, "There is, perhaps, no country in the world where more is made of the land than in Saxony. Every spot of earth which seems capable of giving a return is cultivated, and the meadows are mowed twice or thrice in the course of each summer. You never meet with such a thing as a common or a waste, while the forests are all guarded with a strictness proportionate to their value." And even Mr. M'Culloch himself says, "landed properties are rather of limited size; but, in all the rural districts, the people appear to be contented, and, on the whole, comfortable: *pauperism* is rare."† The same writer, although so earnest an advocate of the system of great estates, in speaking of the famous Prussian edict of 1811, which enabled the peasants of Prussia to become proprietors, and which broke up the old great-estate system, says, "*It has given a wonderful stimulus to improvement.* The peasantry, relieved from the burdens and services to which they were previously subjected, and placed, in respect of political privileges, on a level with their lords, have begun to display a spirit of enterprise and industry that was formerly unknown. Formerly, also, there

* Germany, i. 237.   † Geog. Dict. title Saxony.

were in Prussia — as there have been in England and
in most other countries — a great extent of land belonging to towns and villages, and occupied in common
by the inhabitants.   While under this tenure, these
lands rarely produced a third or a fourth of what they
would produce were they divided into separate properties and assigned to individuals, each reaping all the
advantages resulting from superior industry and exertion.
The Prussian government, being aware of this, has succeeded in effecting the division of a vast number of
common properties, and has thus totally changed the
appearance of a large extent of country, and created
several thousand new proprietors.   The want of capital,
and the force of old habits, rendered the influence of
these changes in the outset less striking than many
anticipated ; but these retarding circumstances have
daily diminished in power, *and it may be safely affirmed
that the country has made a greater progress since* 1815
than it did during the preceding hundred years."

Once enable the peasants to purchase land, and you
triumph over sterility.   The vast arid prairie plains of
Prussia, with a deep sandy soil, bare of hedges, and
almost bare of trees, excepting where the forests grow
for the supply of fuel, have been thus forced to yield
their increase.   From the railways, as you pass along
the surface of these prairies, your eye meets cultivation
every where.   Flourishing villages, of houses as large
as those occupied by our farmers, divide the plains between them ; no trees overshadow the cornlands ; no
old tenures prevent the farmers cutting down all which
either impede the course of the plough or the rays of the

sun, or which take up ground better employed in other ways than in growing wood. The farmer, in fine, is free to do whatever will secure him the largest return from his land. In Saxony and Switzerland it is very curious to observe, how, under the influence of the division of the land and its release from the feudal tenures, cultivation, and that, too, of the most scientific kind, has forced its way up the mountain-sides on to every little ledge where a meadow could be made, into the glades of the forests, upon the little corners of land left by the streams and rivers, and over every bog and moor. You find meadows, pasturages, and gardens where, in Wales, Westmoreland, Ireland, or Scotland, there would be only a bleak hill-side or a barren moor. A traveller in these countries will not find common lands left waste or useless; or great patches left uncultivated from want of drainage; or meadows where the grass grows rank and mixed with weeds, from the want of an embankment to turn off the waters of a passing stream; or great strips wasted and encumbered by broad and vermin-filled hedges, with wide and useless ditches on each side.

Wherever there is soil there is also cultivation; and where there is no soil the peasants often bring some.

It is singular to see the odd places where meadows of the most beautiful grass are laid out in Switzerland. You may ascend the mountains for a whole day, and often, after having left behind you belt after belt of forest, growing for the supply of fuel, up above them all, as high as soil is found, you will still see green pastures, which have been brought into cultivation by the indefatigable industry of the peasants. Up, too, upon the rocky ledges, whence you would imagine it would be difficult to let down the produce, grass is grown for winter consumption in the valleys. No difficulties deter the peasant if he can make the spot his own, and if he can win anything from it by any amount of labour. Waste lands and badly cultivated spots cannot exist long, where the possessors of land are not trammelled by a system of tenures like our own, but where they are at liberty to dispose of their lands, whenever they feel it for their interest to do so, and where the peasants can, by prudence and self-denial, make themselves proprietors.

In Saxon Switzerland, the government of Saxony possessed a number of barren heath-clad hills, which had never been brought into cultivation, and which, by many persons, were supposed to be quite unfit for cultivation.   The government gave notice, a few years ago, that it would grant portions of the sides of these hills to any peasant, who would cultivate them, on the following conditions : —

For three years no rent was to be paid for it; afterwards the cultivator might either purchase the land at a certain rate fixed and specified, or he might rent it from government at a small annual payment, the amount of which was to bear a certain fixed proportion to the produce obtained from the land. The scheme has succeeded admirably. Whole hill-sides have been taken by the peasants, and brought into cultivation. The moorlands have been drained; the stones have been carried away; the land has been well trenched, and

VOL. I.

has become very valuable.   This shows how enterprising an intelligent peasantry will prove, when their efforts are not impeded by legislation or by old feudal prejudices.   Were we to enable the Irish peasant to make himself a proprietor, we should in twenty years alter the character of Ireland.   The peasants would become conservative, orderly, and industrious; the moor and waste lands would disappear; cultivation would spread its green carpet over the bogs and mountains; and that now unhappy island would become a powerful arm of Great Britain.   But so long as we subject the Irish peasantry to the present under-lessee system, so long will they be a turbulent, idle, and disaffected people, and so long will Ireland be a drain upon the imperial treasury, and a cause of weakness to the empire.

It would astonish the English people to see how intensely the peasants of France, Germany, Switzerland, and Holland labour on their fields.   The whole of the farmer's family assists.   It is not an unwilling drudgery, but a toil in which they feel pleasure; for they know, that the harder they labour, the greater will be their profits, and the better will be their means of subsistence. There is always something to be done.   When they can work on their fields, they are opening drains, breaking up lumps of earth, spreading manures, digging, cleaning, weeding, sowing, or gathering in the harvest.   When they cannot work in their fields, they are putting their farm-yards and farm-buildings into order, whitewashing (this they are very fond of doing), repairing walls, mixing or preparing manures, or doing something in preparation for some of their out-door operations.   They do all this,

be it remembered, for themselves; and they take real
pleasure in their work, and do it ten times better, and
ten times more expeditiously, than the poor, hired, and
ignorant peasants of England, who have nothing to look
forward to, but to remain peasants for ever, earning
from seven to nine shillings a-week, and without any
interest in the soil; or even than the farmers of England, who farm the land of another, having often no
lease of it, and scarcely any security for any expenditure upon it, and who seldom care anything about
either their land or their buildings, except to get as
much out of them, and with as small an outlay, as
possible.

The governments of Western Europe are doing a
great deal, to enable the peasant proprietors to acquire
a knowledge of the best systems of agriculture and
management of cattle.

The cantonal governments of Switzerland have been
earnestly engaged for several years in establishing, in
various parts of the country, great schools, where the
children of the farmers may be educated, at a very
trifling expense, in the science of agriculture. I went
over several, in company with M. de Fellenberg and
M. Vehrli. I have described them more fully in the
chapter on Swiss education.

To each of these institutions are attached, a large
farm, barns, cowsheds, farm-yards, orchards, a plentiful
supply of the best farm implements, a laboratory, and
class-rooms. The greatest portion of the expense of
maintaining them is defrayed by the cantonal governments. Many of the sons of the peasant farmers enter

these institutions after leaving the primary schools. They remain in them from one to three years. They learn there agricultural chemistry and practical farming. They are taught how to analyse earths; how to mix and manure them, so as to make them as fertile as possible; how to prepare and collect manures; how to drain land; how to tend, and fatten cattle; how to manage the dairy; how to breed cattle, so as best to improve the stock; how to vary the succession of crops, so as to make the most of particular soils; how to prune fruit-trees; and, in fact, the whole science of farming. Is it surprising that farmers educated in such a manner should be much more skilful, and should make much more out of their lands, than the farmers of our country? Similar colleges are being established throughout Germany and France.

But this is not all, that is being done in foreign countries, in order to secure a scientific system of farming among the peasant proprietors.

All the teachers of the village schools, as I shall hereafter show, are prepared for their duties in the villages, by a long and very careful preparation in the Normal colleges.

Among other things which they learn, in many of these colleges, are, botany, the art of pruning, and the art of gardening; and, in some of them, as in the Bernese Normal College, they are taught and practised in farming.

This is done for two purposes; first, in order to strengthen their sympathies for the peasants, among whom they have in after-life to labour, by accustoming them to all the habits of the peasants; and, secondly, in order to enable them to give the children in the village schools a rudimentary knowledge of pruning, gardening, and farming, so as to insure their being taught, at least, the first principles of these arts, and so as to stimulate their interest in them, and to teach them that there is a right and a wrong way of conducting them. Boys who have received these ideas in early life will not afterwards scoff at instruction, but will always be ready, not only to receive, but to seek out, advice and assistance.

Science is welcomed among the small farmers of foreign countries. Each is so anxious to emulate and surpass his neighbours, that any new invention, which benefits one, is eagerly sought out and adopted by the others.

The system of agriculture, therefore, good as it is among these intelligent peasant proprietors, is not at a stand still, but is making rapid progress. The governments, poor as they are, have ample funds to devote to the best possible education of all classes.

No one who has travelled through the Rhine Provinces of Germany, through Prussia, Saxony, Holland, the Protestant cantons of Switzerland, and some of the Catholic cantons, as Soleure, Zug, and the upper part of the valley of the Rhone, can possibly deny the excellence, or the progressive improvement of the cultivation of the soil.

The small farms round Berne, and in Saxon Switzerland, are so beautifully managed, that a traveller is tempted to believe them to be the property of rich

men, who keep them up for their own amusement, and
do not mind spending upon them in order to make them
neat and good-looking.   Not that there is really much
expended on mere beautifying, but that every thing is
carefully kept in order, as by proprietors who feel an
interest and a pride in their little properties.

In some parts of Switzerland the farm-buildings are
much plainer and much poorer than in others, as, for
instance, in the Ober Vallais; but in most parts, the
same careful and beautiful cultivation is to be seen, and
the same degree of interest is displayed by the proprietors in the condition of their little estates.   Among
these intelligent peasants, who labour on their own
lands, there is no need to get up ploughing matches, to
offer premiums for the best crops, for the largest turnips,
or for the finest potatoes; or to get up cattle shows
and prize exhibitions, in order to promote a good
system of farming.   The peasant farmers feel themselves too immediately interested in the state of their
farms, to need such inducements to exertion as these;
as they know, that all they expend upon their little
estates is a safe investment, and will be returned
tenfold to themselves or to their children.   This feeling stimulates the peasant proprietors of Germany,
Holland, Switzerland, and France to spend their earnings upon their lands, to adopt every discoverable means
of improving their systems of tillage, to send their
children to the agricultural schools, and to bring them
up in habits of industry and economy.

I have spent a great deal of time among the peasant
proprietors in different parts of Europe.   I have resided

or travelled about among them in North, South, and West Prussia, in North and South Holland, in Belgium, in the valleys of Switzerland, Styria, and the Tyrol, in Saxony, Bavaria, and upon the banks of the Rhine.

In all these countries the same evidences of progress and improvement may be seen among the peasants; viz., a laboriously careful tillage of the fields, and cultivation of the gardens; large, good, and substantial houses for the peasantry; orderly and clean villages; and great industry. I was assured, in the Rhine Provinces and in Saxony, that the face of the country had quite changed, since the laws tending to prevent the sale and division of the landed property had been altered; and that the system of farming, the character of the houses, and the condition of the peasants, had progressively improved and were still improving. Certainly, the appearance of the villages, houses, farms, and peasantry was singularly satisfactory. The cultivation of the land was as beautiful and perfect as I have ever seen. The careful manner in which the sods were broken up upon the ploughed fields, and the way, in which all the weeds, stones, and rubbish were removed from the ground, in which every disposable bit of ground was brought under cultivation, and in which the land was drained of all superabundant moisture and manured, filled me with surprise, at what Professor Rau most truly calls, the " superhuman industry," " das ubermenschliche fleis," of the peasants.*

* I only wish I could persuade my readers to go and *stay* in Saxon Switzerland, and examine for themselves the state of the peasant pro-

Owing to the care, with which the peasants constantly water their meadows with the liquid manures, which they collect and prepare in the farm-yards, and which they carry out to their lands in small hand watering-carts, and spread over the lands in equal proportions, and owing also to the care, with which they clear the ground of stones, rubbish, and noxious grasses, the meadows attain a remarkable luxuriance of verdure, and yield a peculiarly rich and innocuous hay, for the food of the well stalled cattle during the winter months.

During the summer months, in the valleys of Switzerland, the Tyrol, and Styria, as the snow gradually melts off the mountains, the cattle are driven higher and higher, to eat up the sweet grass of the mountain pasturages, while that of the valley meadows grows for the winter store of hay. The cattle leave the villages towards the end of spring, followed by two or three families, who accompany them from pasturage to pasturage, as the snow melts, and who change their

prietors of that country. If a man wishes to ascertain the effect of a country's institutions, and the condition of a people, it is ridiculous for him to satisfy himself with merely passing through the country. I met, in 1848, at a table d'hote at Ostend, an English traveller, who had just returned from Saxony; I asked him what he thought of the condition of the peasants there. " Oh," he replied, " the're a miserable and wretched people, ground to the earth by their rulers." " I am surprised," I ventured to observe, "to hear you express such an opinion of them, as I have spent some time in two several years among them, and I certainly thought I had never seen so happy or so flourishing a peasantry." " Oh very likely, very likely," he eagerly replied, " I don't know much about them. I staid only three days there, and I don't speak the language."

residence from one chalet or log-hut to another, as the cattle get higher into the mountains. Those, who attend the cattle, milk them, make the milk into butter and cheese in the mountain chalets, and send it down to the villages by the young men, who carry up at regular intervals from the village, provisions for the consumption of the guardians of the cattle. In this way, the cattle and their guardians gradually ascend the mountains, from pasturage to pasturage, until the middle of August; and then, in the [same manner, when the snow begins to descend in the higher pasturages, they gradually descend, and re-enter the village about the end of the month of September, when the cattle are housed for the winter. The day of the return of the cattle and their guardians is a grand gala-day in the villages, and is celebrated with great rejoicings. The cattle are driven in from the mountains garlanded with flowers, and with bells hung round their necks; the peasants assemble in their gayest attire; and processions are formed to welcome back again the young people, who have been so long absent, and the cattle, which are one great source of the prosperity of the village.

In speaking of peasant proprietors, Sismondi, in his "Etudes sur l'Economie Politique," says, "Wherever are found peasant proprietors, are also found that ease, that security, that independence, and that confidence in the future, which insure at the same time happiness and virtue. The peasant, who, with his family, does all the work on his little inheritance, who neither pays rent to any one above him, nor wages to any one below him,

who regulates his production by his consumption, who
eats his own corn, drinks his own wine, and is clothed
with his own flax and wool, cares little about knowing
the price of the market; for he has little to sell and
little to buy, and is never ruined by the revolutions of
commerce. Far from fearing for the future, it is em-
bellished by his hopes; for he puts out to profit, for his
children, or for ages to come, every instant which is
not required by the labour of the year. Only a few
moments, stolen from otherwise lost time, are required
to put into the ground the nut, which in a hundred
years will become a large tree; to hollow out the aque-
duct, which will drain his field for ever; to form the
conduit, which will bring him a spring of water; to
improve, by many little labours and attentions bestowed
in spare moments, all the kinds of animals and vegetables by which he is surrounded. This little patrimony is a true savings-bank, always ready to receive
his little profits, and usefully to employ his leisure
moments. The ever-acting powers of nature make
his labours fruitful, and return him a hundredfold.
The peasant has a strong sense of the happiness attached
to the condition of proprietor. Thus he is always
eager to purchase land at any price. He pays for it
more than it is worth; but what reason he has to
esteem at a high price the advantage of thenceforward
always employing his labour advantageously, without
being obliged to offer it cheap; and of always finding
his bread when he wants it, without being obliged to
buy it dear!

" The peasant proprietor is, of all cultivators, the

one who obtains most from the soil; for it is he who thinks most of the future, as it is he, who is the most enlightened by experience ; it is he also who makes the greatest profit of human labour. . . . . Of all cultivators he is the happiest. Moreover, on a given space, land never produces so much food, or employs so many inhabitants without being exhausted, as when they are proprietors. Lastly, of all cultivators, the peasant proprietor is the one who gives most encouragement to commerce and industry; for he is the richest."

The same author says again*, " When one travels through the whole of Switzerland, and through several parts of France, Italy, and Germany, it is not necessary to inquire, when looking at a piece of land, whether it belongs to a peasant proprietor, or to a farmer holding it under a landlord. The land of the peasant proprietors is marked out by the care bestowed upon it, by the growth of the vegetables and fruits useful to a peasant's family, and by the neatness and perfection of the cultivation."

Mr. Nicholls, in speaking of the small farms of Belgium, says†, " In the farms of six acres, we found no plough, horse, or cart; the only agricultural implement, besides the spade, fork, and wheelbarrow, which we observed, was a light wooden harrow which might be dragged by hand. The farmer had no assistance besides that of his wife and children, excepting some-

* Nouveaux Principes d'Economie Politique, lib. iii. ch. 3.

† Inquiry into the Condition of the Labouring Classes in Holland and Belgium.

times in harvest, when we found he occasionally obtained the aid of a neighbour, or hired a labourer at a
franc per day. The whole of the land is dug with the
spade, and trenched very deep, but as the soil is light,
the labour of digging is not great. The stock on the
small farms, which we examined, consisted of a couple
of cows, a calf or two, one or two pigs, sometimes a
goat or two, and some poultry. The cows are altogether
stall fed, on straw, turnips, clover, rye, vetches, carrots,
potatoes, and a kind of soup made by boiling up potatoes, peas, beans, bran, cut hay, &c., into one mass, and
which, being given warm, is said to be very wholesome,
and to promote the secretion of milk. . . . . . .
The small farmer collects in his stable, in a fosse lined
with brick, the dung and urine of his cattle. He buys
sufficient lime to mingle with the scouring of his ditches,
and with the decayed leaves, potato-tops, &c., which he
is careful to collect in order to enrich his compost,
which, is dug over two or three times in the course of
the winter. No portion of the farm is allowed to lie
fallow, but it is divided into six or seven small plots, on
each of which a system of rotation is adopted; and
thus, with the aid of manure, the powers of the soil are
maintained unexhausted in a state of constant activity.
. . . . The labour of the field,
the management of the cattle, the preparation of manure, the regulating the rotation of crops, and the
necessity of carrying a certain portion of the produce
to market, call for the constant exercise of industry,
skill and foresight among the Belgium peasant farmers; and to these qualities they add a rigid economy,

habitual sobriety, and a contented spirit, which finds
its chief gratification beneath the domestic roof, from
which the father of the family rarely wanders in search
of excitement abroad."

Reichensperger, speaking of Belgium, says * : —
" The small estates of this country carry away the
palm for beautiful cultivation. . . . In the districts
of Fermonde and St. Nicholas, where the soil is rich,
light, and moist, the land is divided into very small
estates of few acres in size. The cultivation of these
little properties, — which is greatly assisted by the
neighbourhood of the towns and by the abundance of
manure, — exhibits wonders of labour and industry, and
nourishes a large and flourishing population by two,
and even three, harvests a year. The beautiful cultivation of these little estates offers to every unprejudiced
mind the clearest proof, that their greater *gross* product
is not by any means totally consumed by the producers
themselves, but that it yields a rich supply of products
to the markets, while it nourishes the great population
of the numerous towns of that country in the most
excellent manner with all the necessaries of life."

In speaking of the Palatinate, Mr. Howitt, whose
habit it is, as Mr. Mill says †, " to see all English objects
and English socialities *en beau*, and who, in treating of
the Rhenish peasantry, certainly does not underrate the
rudeness of their implements and the inferiority of their
ploughing, nevertheless shows, that, under the invi-

* Die Agrarfrage, p. 126.
† Principles of Political Economy, vol. i.

gorating influence of the feelings of proprietorship, they make up for the imperfections of their apparatus by the intensity of their application." He says*: "The peasant harrows and clears his land till it is in the nicest order, and it is admirable to see the crops which he obtains." "The peasants are the great and ever-present object of country life. *They are the great population of the country,* because they themselves are the possessors. This country is, in fact, for the most part, in the hands of the people. It is parcelled out among the multitude. . . . The peasants are not, as with us, for the most part, totally cut off from property in the soil they cultivate, and totally dependent on the labour afforded by others ; they are themselves the proprietors. It is, perhaps, from this cause that they are probably the most industrious peasantry in the world. They labour busily, early and late, because they feel that they are labouring for themselves. . . . . The German peasants work hard, but they have no actual want. Every man has his house, his orchard, his roadside trees, commonly so heavy with fruit that he is obliged to prop and secure them all ways, or they would be torn to pieces. He has his corn-plot, his plot for mangel-wurzel; for hemp, and so on. He is his own master, and he and every member of his family have the strongest motives to labour. You see the effect of this in that unremitting diligence, which is beyond that of the whole world besides ; and his economy, which is still greater. The Germans, indeed, are not so active

* Rural and Domestic Life in Germany, p. 27.; Mill's Political Economy, vol. i. p. 313.

and lively as the English; you never see them in a bustle, or as though they meant to knock off a vast deal in a little time. . . . They are, on the contrary, slow, but for ever doing. They plod on from day to day, and from year to year, the most patient, untirable, and persevering of animals. The English peasant is so cut off from the idea of property that he comes habitually to look upon it as a thing from which he is warned by the laws of the great proprietors, and becomes in consequence spiritless, purposeless. . . . The German bauer, on the contrary, looks on the country as made for him and his fellow men. He feels himself a man; he has a stake in the country as good as that of the bulk of his neighbours; no man can threaten him with ejection or the workhouse so long as he is active and economical. He walks, therefore, with a bold step; he looks you in the face with the air of a free man, but of a respectful one."

This latter observation is singularly correct. The manners of the peasants in Germany and Switzerland form, as I have already said, a very singular contrast to the manners of our peasants. They are polite but independent. The manner of salutation encourages this feeling. If a German gentleman addresses a peasant, he raises his hat before' the poor man, as we do before ladies. The peasant replies by a polite " Pray be covered, Sir," and then, in good German, answers the questions put to him. Among all the men below the age of thirty-five, the good education given to them in the schools and in the army has tended to diminish, and, in some parts, altogether to get rid of, provincial dialects; so that, in almost every case, a traveller, who knows German, can easily understand a German or Swiss peasant; and he will constantly hear them speak in the purest accent of the metropolis. This adds greatly to the pleasure of travelling about among the German and Swiss villages, as a tourist can almost always make companions of the peasants. The poorer classes of these countries so strongly feel, that their situation in life depends on their own conduct, and that the richer men are only richer because they, or their immediate ancestors, have acted in life more prudently, that the mere fact of a man's having a better coat on his back and more polished manners than themselves, neither creates in their minds jealousy, nor renders the intercourse with such a person embarrassing to them. The fact of their being proprietors, or of their being able to make themselves proprietors, begets a certain gentlemanly and independent bearing in a Swiss and German peasant, which one seldom sees in any part of our own country.

Mr. Howitt continues to describe the German peasants and their industry as follows: —

" He has no ambition to be other than he is; he wears the costume which his fathers wore, — the long coat and cocked or hollow-sided hat, the bauer's costume, — and he turns everything about him to account. . . . . Nothing that can be possibly made use of is lost. The children may be seen standing in the stream in the villages carefully washing weeds before they are given to the cattle. As we meet them and the women, with large bundles of grass on their heads tied in large cloths, one cannot but call to mind the immense quantities by our highway sides and great green lanes in England, and by wood sides, which grow and wither, but which might support many a poor man's cow. But with the German peasant it is not merely grass, it is everything, which is collected and appropriated. The cuttings of his vines are dried and trussed for winter fodder; the very tops and refuse of his hemp are saved for the bedding of his cattle; nay, the rough stalks of his poppies, after the heads are gathered, serve the same purpose, and are all converted into manure. When these are not sufficient, the children gather moss in the woods; and, in summer, you constantly meet them coming down out of the hills with their great bundles of it. In autumn they gather the very fungi out of the woods to sell for poisoning flies, and the stalks of a tall species of grass to sell for cleaning out their long pipes. Nothing is lost; the leaves in the woods are raked up as they fall, and are brought home before winter for bedding cattle. The fir cones, which with us lie all scattered on the forest, are carefully collected to light their fires, or are carried in sacks and sold in the cities for that purpose. The slop from their yards and stables is all preserved, and carried to the fields in water-carts to irrigate their crops. The economy and care of the German peasant afford a striking lesson to all Europe. Time is as carefully economised as everything else. The peasants are early risers, and thus obtain hours of the day's beauty and freshness which others lose."

In Germany and Switzerland the peasants rise a little

before five.   They then take a cup of coffee and go out.
The Romanist churches and cathedrals are all open, and
services are performed at five.   Most of the Romanist
peasants go in to prayers before going to their labour.
It is a curious sight to see the women deposit their
milk-pails, and the men their farming-tools, at the doors
of the Romanist churches, go in to prayers, remain there
about a quarter of an hour, and then, taking up their
pails and tools, start for the fields and cattle.   The
priests of the canton of Friburg, in Switzerland, told
me, that they were all obliged by turn to rise between
four and five in summer, in order to perform the early
matins at five for the peasants.   At about eight, the
peasants return home for breakfast.   Before going out,
they do not take more than a little coffee and a piece of
bread.

Mr. Howitt, in another part of his work on Germany, with reference to the same subject, says*, " There
is not an hour of the year in which they do not
find unceasing occupation.   In the depth of winter,
when the weather permits them by any means to get
out of doors, they are always finding something to do.
They carry out their manure to their lands, while the
frost is in them.   If there is not frost, they are busy
cleaning ditches, and felling old fruit-trees, or such as
do not bear well.   Such of them as are too poor to lay
in a sufficient stock of wood, find plenty of work in
ascending into the mountainous woods, and bringing
thence fuel.   It would astonish the English common

* Rural and Domestic Life in Germany, p. 44.

people to see the intense labour with which the Germans earn their firewood. In the depth of frost and snow, go into any of their hills and woods, and there you find them hacking up stumps, cutting off branches, and gathering, by all means which the official wood police will allow, boughs, stakes, and pieces of wood, which they convey home with the most incredible toil and patience." After a description of their careful and laborious vineyard culture, he continues * : — " In England, with its great quantity of grass lands, and its large farms, so soon as the grain is in, and the fields are shut up for hay grass, the country seems in a comparative state of rest and quiet. But here, they are everywhere and for ever hoeing and mowing, planting and cutting, weeding and gathering. They have a succession of crops, like a market-gardener. They have their carrots, poppies, hemp, flax, saintfoin, lucerne, rape, colewort, cabbage, rotabaga, black turnips, swedish and white turnips, teazles, Jerusalem artichokes, mangel-wurzel, parsneps, kidney-beans, field beans and peas, vetches, Indian corn, buck-wheat madder for the manufacturer, potatoes, their great crop of tobacco, millet — all or the greater part under the family management, in their own family allotments. They have had these things first to sow, many of them to transplant, to hoe, to weed, to clear off insects, to top; many of them to mow and gather in successive crops. They have their water-meadows — of which kind almost all their meadows are — to flood, to mow, and reflood ; water-courses

* Rural and Domestic Life in Germany, p. 50.

to re-open and to make anew; their early fruits to gather, to bring to market, with their green crops of vegetables; their cattle, sheep, calves, fowls (most of them prisoners), and poultry to look after; their vines, as they shoot rampantly in the summer heat, to prune, and thin out the leaves when they are too thick; and any one may imagine what a scene of incessant labour it is."

Mr. Mill *, in commenting on these remarks of Mr. Howitt's, says : — " This interesting sketch, to the general truth of which any observant traveller in that highly cultivated and populous region can bear witness, accords with the more elaborate delineation by a distinguished inhabitant, Professor Rau, in his little treatise on ' The Agriculture of the Palatinate.' † "

I have already shown ‡, what decisive testimony this able writer bears to the industry, skill, and intelligence of the peasant-proprietors of these provinces; as well as to their scientific preparation and economy of manure; their excellent rotation of crops; the progressive improvement of their agriculture for generations past, and the spirit of further improvement which is still active; the indefatigableness of the country-people; their careful study of the seasons; their excellent distribution of their labours; and their zeal in turning to use every circumstance which presents itself, in seizing upon every useful novelty which offers, and even in searching out new and advantageous methods.

* Principles of Political Economy, vol. i. p. 15.

† Uber die Landwirthschaft die Rheinpfalz und insbesondere in der Heidelberger Gegend.   Von D. Karl Heinrich Rau, Heidelberg, 1830.

‡ Supra, pp. 122, 123.

The writers on the state and progress of the Swiss cantons bear similar testimony to the happy results of releasing the land in those cantons from the old feudal laws of tenure, settlement, and devises, and of enabling the peasants to acquire.

Herr Strohmeier, in describing the progress, which agriculture has made in the canton of Solothurn, since the peasants were freed from the feudal burdens, and became the proprietors of the land, says * : " In the time of the old aristocracy, the peasant behind the plough was prized scarcely any higher, than the cattle before the same. He was cramped and injured in his rights. He was weighed down by taxes, tithes, and payments. The fruit of his industry was consumed by idle priests and landlords, who kept him in dark ignorance and in wretched superstition. What was there in those times to urge the peasant or the farmer to industry and activity, or to a better cultivation of the land ? "

Herr Strohmeier then says, that since the peasants have been enabled to purchase their lands, and make themselves proprietors, and since the intellect of the people has been raised and enlightened by means of the schools and the teachers, the system of agriculture, the agricultural implements, the cultivation of the meadows, their irrigation and manuring, the cultivation of the gardens, and the industry of the people, have, with few exceptions, greatly improved. He says, that the example of the Bernese has stimulated the people of Soleure very greatly, and that the cultivation of the

* Gemälde der Schweitz, vol. x. p. 81.

greatest part of the canton has attained a very high degree of perfection.

Several of the writers on the different cantons of Switzerland are of opinion, that the subdivision in some parts is extreme, and that it is in such cases injurious to scientific and economical farming, when compared to the farming of the *freehold* estates of from fifty to twenty acres; but they all agree, that, even in the cases of the smaller farms, the industry and unwearied perseverance of the owners is quite wonderful, and none of these writers ever think of comparing the cultivation of leasehold estates to that of estates cultivated by the owners themselves.

Thus Professor Vulliemin, in describing the progress of agriculture in the canton of Vaud, after saying that the subdivision is excessive, and that a landowner who possesses fifteen acres is considered to be well off (wohlhabend), writes thus* : — " From this great subdivision of the land spring both good and evil. The land, which is cultivated by occupiers who are themselves the owners of the soil, is farmed with extraordinary (ungewohnlichen) care and industry, although often with more unscientific hands, and at greater cost, than that of the larger proprietor farmers."

Professor Vulliemin says, however, that this great subdivision is lessening, and that the smallest of the estates are being united again. As the peasants get better educated, they learn to calculate better, what quantity of land will best repay one man's or one

* Germälde der Schweitz, vol. xix. p. 305.

family's labours; and they acquire a desire to take a higher and more comfortable position in society, than that of the smallest proprietors. They are not content to settle down upon the smallest farms. They defer their marriages until they can purchase larger farms, and more respectable positions among their neighbours. The more education advances, the more will the excessive subdivision diminish.

But even where the subdivision is too great for the most economical farming, still even there all the authorities concur in asserting, that the condition of the peasantry is most prosperous, that it has been steadily and continuously improving, and that the industry of the small farmers is quite wonderful.

Herr von Knonau, in speaking of the agriculture of the canton of Zurick, says * : " With few exceptions the land is very much subdivided, one may almost say, split up. There are very few estates of 100 acres, and scarcely five of more than 200 acres in size. . . . . The canton of Zurick shows what industry is able to win from the ground. The Zurick peasant has cultivated his little plot of ground with such intense industry, that his field agriculture, in many parts of the canton, and especially on the borders of the lake, resembles the cultivation of a garden. There, too, you may find the most valuable deposits of manure, beautiful meadows, the finest orchards, and the most productive vineyard cultivation." Herr von Knonau says, in another part of the same report, that

* Germälde der Schweitz, vol. i. p. 243.

since the government has sold to the peasants lands, which formerly belonged to the state, and has in this manner created a great number of new small peasants' properties, *very often a third or a fourth of the land which formerly belonged to the state, and was let out to farmers, produces at present as much corn, and supports as many head of cattle, as the whole estate formerly did when it was cultivated by leasehold tenants.*[*]

To the same effect is the testimony of Herr Pupikofer, member of the Council of Education of the canton of Thurgovie, in his account of this canton. He says[†], the division of the great tracts of land belonging to the government, and the creation of small peasant-properties out of them, has had this effect, that often *a third or a fourth of the original estate produces now as much corn, and supports as many cattle, as the whole of the original estate did when it was cultivated by lessees.* Herr Pupikofer, however, agrees with several of the Swiss writers in thinking, that, although the division of the land among the peasants improves the productiveness of the land and the moral character of the peasants, it is injurious, to the former, when subdivided in portions of *less* than an acre in size; and he suggests that a minimum ought to be defined by law, and that no plots of land should be allowed to be sold which are in size below this minimum.

Herr von Knonau gives also a long and very interesting account of the exceeding great care bestowed by the peasant-farmers of the canton of Zurich in managing their cattle, and in collecting and preparing the manure

---

[*] Germälde der Schweitz, vol. i. p. 245.   [†] Ibid. vol. xvii. p. 73.

for their lands.* I shall give the substance of this
account, as it is another proof of the industry, intelligence, and scientific economy and management, which
always distinguish peasant proprietors. Let my readers
compare the following facts, with the waste, which they
must have observed in most of our English farms: —

The length of the shippen depends upon the number
of cattle kept by the farmer. It is divided into stalls.
Along the bottom of these stalls a space of about four
or five feet is left open as a passage. Between the stalls
and the passage an open stone-gutter is made, to carry
off the drainings of the stalls. These latter slope very
gently down to the gutter. The floor of the upper
part of the stall is generally boarded, and upon the
boards is spread some gravel or sand, in order that the
cattle may find a good hold for their fore feet, and may
be able to raise themselves easily from the ground.

The oxen and horses are fastened in the stalls nearest,
and the cows in those furthest from the door, as these
latter are not so often taken out of the shippens as the
former.

A fresh bed is laid down under each cow, at least
twice a day, generally in the mornings and in the evenings, before milking. Whoever has sufficient straw,
changes the bedding three or four times a day. Every
morning, at an early hour, each stall is cleaned out, and
all the dung and old bedding are turned out into the well
prepared for them in the farm-yard. Into this well,
the gutter, which runs down the shippen at the bottom

* Gemälde der Schweitz, vol. i. p. 249.

of the stalls, is made to empty itself, so that the liquid manure may run into the dung and old bedding, and mix with them. The contents of the well are taken out several times a week, and are thrown upon the dung-heap. The liquid manure, which remains in the well, is then mixed with water, and is carried out upon the fields and spread over them by means of hand watering-carts. All the manure from the house is also preserved and mixed with the rest upon the dung-heap. In the towns, also, the manure is carefully preserved, and is sold out to those farmers, who cannot obtain a sufficient quantity from their own farm-yards.

In different parts of the canton, the manure obtained from the farm-yards, in the manner I have above narrated, is mixed with various ingredients, in order to make it suitable for the peculiar character of the land for which it is intended.

In Switzerland, the size of the estates varies generally from one acre to one hundred and fifty. Some few estates of greater size are to be found, but they are very rare.

Most of the married peasants, and most of the inhabitants of the smaller towns, possess as their own property either a farm or at least a garden.

Herr von Knonau, the keeper of the archives of the canton of Zurick, says *, that formerly many of the houses were thatched ; but that of late years the custom of thatching houses has been given up, partly because the science of agriculture has been so much improved,

---

* Gemälde der Schweitz, vol. i. p. 235.

that the people are not willing to expend upon the covering of the houses straw and other materials, which are useful in making good manures.

These pictures of unwearied assiduity, and what may be called, affectionate interest in the land, are borne out, in regard to the more intelligent cantons of Switzerland, by English observers. " In walking anywhere in the neighbourhood of Zurick," says Mr. Inglis *, " in looking to the right or to the left, one is struck with the extraordinary industry of the inhabitants ; and if we learn that a proprietor here has a return of ten per cent. we are inclined to say, ' he deserves it.' I speak at present of country labour ; though I believe that in every kind of trade, also, the people of Zurick are remarkable for their assiduity ; but in the industry they show in the cultivation of their land, I may safely say they are unrivalled. When I used to open my casement between four and five in the morning, to look out upon the lake and the distant Alps, I saw the labourer in the fields ; and when I returned from an evening walk, long after sunset, as late perhaps as half past eight, there was the labourer mowing his grass, or tying up his vines. . . . . It is impossible to look at a field, a garden, a hedging, scarcely even a tree, a flower, or a vegetable, without perceiving proofs of the extreme care and industry, that are bestowed upon the cultivation of the soil. If, for example, a path runs through, or by the side of a field of grain, the corn is not, as in England, permitted to hang

* Quoted by Mr. Mill in his Political Economy, vol. i. p. 304.

over the path, exposed to be pulled or trodden down by every passer; it is everywhere bounded by a fence; stakes are placed at intervals of about a yard, and about two or three feet from the ground, boughs of trees are passed longitudinally along. If you look into a field towards evening, where there are large beds of cauliflower or cabbage, you will find that every single plant has been watered. In the gardens, which around Zurick are extremely large, the most punctilious care is evinced in every production that grows. The vegetables are planted with seemingly mathematical accuracy; not a *single weed is to be seen, not a single stone.* Plants are not earthed up as with us; but are planted each in a small hollow, into which a little manure is put, and each plant is watered daily. Where seeds are sown, the earth directly above is broken into the finest powder; every shrub, every flower, is tied to a stake; and where there is wall-fruit, a trellis is erected against a wall, to which the boughs are fastened; and there is not a single thing that has not its appropriate resting-place."

Of one of the remote valleys of the High Alps, the same writer thus expresses himself: — " In the whole of the Engadine, the land belongs to the peasantry, who, like the inhabitants of every other place where this state of things exists, vary greatly in the extent of their possessions. . . . . Generally speaking, an Engadine peasant lives entirely upon the produce of his land, with the exception of the few articles of foreign growth required in his family, such as coffee, sugar, and wine. Flax is grown, prepared, spun, and woven, without ever leaving his house. He has his own wool, which is converted into a blue coat, without passing through the hands of either the dyer or the tailor. The country is incapable of greater cultivation than it has received. All has been done for it, that industry and an extreme love of gain can devise. There is not a foot of waste land in the Engadine, the lowest part of which is not much lower than the top of Snowdon. Wherever grass will grow, there it is ; wherever a rock will bear a blade, verdure is seen upon it ; wherever an ear of rye will ripen, there it is to be found. Barley and oats have also their appropriate spots ; and wherever it is possible to ripen a little patch of wheat, the cultivation of it is attempted. In no country in Europe will be found so few poor as in the Engadine. In the village of Suss, which contains about six hundred inhabitants, there is not a single individual, who has not wherewithal to live comfortably ; not a single individual, who is indebted to others for one morsel that he eats."

One of the countries, in which peasant proprietors are of oldest date and most numerous in proportion to the population, is Norway. Of the social and economical condition of that country a very interesting account has been given by Mr. Laing. He describes the effects of the subdivision of land in that country, as being most satisfactory in every respect. I shall quote a few passages : —*

" If small proprietors are not good farmers, it is not from the same cause here, which we are told makes them so in Scotland — indolence and want of exertion. The

* Quoted in Mill's Political Economy, vol. i.

extent, to which irrigation is carried on in these glens
and valleys, shows a spirit *of exertion and co-operation*,
to which the latter can show nothing similar. Hay
being the principal winter support of live stock, and both
it and corn, as well as potatoes, being liable, from the
shallow soil and powerful reflection of sunshine from the
rocks, to be burnt and withered up, the greatest exertions are made to bring water from the head of each
glen, along such a level, as will give the command of it
to each farmer at the head of his fields. This is done, by
leading it in wooden troughs (the half of a tree roughly
scooped) from the highest perennial stream among the
hills, through woods, across ravines, and along the rocky,
often perpendicular, sides of the glens; and by giving from
this main trough a lateral one to each farmer in passing
the head of his farm. He distributes this supply by move-
able troughs, among his fields; and at this season waters
each rig successively with scoops, like those used by
bleachers in watering cloth, laying his trough between
every two rigs. One would not believe, without seeing it, how very large an extent of land is traversed expeditiously by these artificial showers. The extent of
the main troughs is very great. In one glen, I walked
ten miles, and found it troughed on both sides; on one,
the chain is continued down the main valley for forty
miles. Those may be bad farmers, who do such things;
but they are not indolent, nor ignorant of the principle
of working in concert, and keeping up establishments
for common benefit. They are undoubtedly, in these
respects, far in advance of any community of cotters in
our Highland glens. They feel as proprietors, who re-

ceive the advantage of their own exertions. The excellent state of the roads and bridges is another proof, that the country is inhabited by people, who have a common interest to keep it under repair. There are no tolls."

On the admirable effects of peasant proprietorship in other parts of Europe, the same writer expresses himself as follows:—*

" If we listen to the large farmer, the scientific agriculturist, the (English) political economist, good farming must perish with large farms; the very idea that good farming can exist, unless on large farms cultivated with great capital, they hold to be absurd. Draining, manuring, economical arrangement, cleaning the land, regular rotations, valuable stock and implements, all belong exclusively to large farms, worked by large capital and by hired labour. This reads very well; but if we raise our eyes from their books to their fields, and coolly compare, what we see in the best districts farmed in large farms, and what we see in the best districts farmed in small farms, we see, and there is no blinking the fact, better crops on the ground in Flanders, East Friesland, Holstein, in short, on the whole line of the arable land of equal quality of the Continent, from the Sound to Calais, than we see on the line of British coast, opposite to this line and in the same latitudes, from the Frith of Forth all round to Dover. Minute labour on small portions of arable ground gives evidently, in equal soils and climate, a *superior* productiveness, where these small portions *belong in property*,

* Quoted in Mill's Political Economy, vol. i.

as in Flanders, Holland, Friesland, and Ditmarsh in
Holstein, to the farmer. It is not pretended, by our
agricultural writers, that our large farmers, even in
Berwickshire, Roxburghshire, or the Lothians, approach
to the garden-like cultivation, attention to manures,
drainage, and clean state of the land, or in productiveness from a small space of soil, not originally rich,
which distinguish the small farmers of Flanders or
their system. In the best-farmed parish in Scotland or
England, more land is wasted in the corners and borders
of the fields of large farms; in the roads through them,
unnecessarily wide because they are bad, and bad because they are wide; in neglected commons, waste spots,
useless belts and clumps of sorry trees, and such unproductive areas; than would maintain the poor of the
parish, if they were all laid together and cultivated.
But large capital applied to farming is, of course, only
applied to the very best of the soils of a country. It
cannot touch the small unproductive spots, which require more time and labour to fertilise them, than is
consistent with a quick return of capital. But, although
hired time and labour cannot be applied beneficially to
such cultivation, the owner's own time and labour
may. He is working for no higher returns, at first, from
his land than a bare living. But, in the course of generations, fertility and value are produced; a better living,
and even very improved processes of husbandry, are
attained. Furrow draining, stall feeding all summer,
liquid manures, are universal in the husbandry of the
small farms of Flanders, Lombardy, and Switzerland.
Our most improving districts, under large farms, are but

beginning to adopt them. Dairy husbandry even, and the manufacture of the largest cheeses, by the co-operation of many small farmers — the mutual assurance of property against fire and hail-storms, by the co-operation of small farmers — the most scientific and expensive of all agricultural operations in modern times, the manufacture of beet-root sugar — the supply of the European markets with flax and hemp, by the husbandry of small farmers — the abundance of legumes, fruits, poultry, in the usual diet even of the lowest classes abroad, and the total want of such variety at the tables even of our middle classes, and this variety and abundance essentially connected with the husbandry of small farmers — all these are features in the occupation of a country by small proprietor farmers, which must make the inquirer pause, before he admits the dogma of our land doctors at home, that large farms worked by hired labour and great capital can alone bring out the greatest productiveness of the soil, and furnish the greatest supply of the necessaries and conveniences of life to the inhabitants of a country."

The scientific and economical manner in which the Swiss peasant proprietors combine to carry on cheese making by their united capital, deserves to be noted.[*] "Each parish in Switzerland hires a man, generally from the district of Gruyère, in the Canton of Friburg, to take care of the herd and make the cheese. One cheeseman, one pressman or assistant, and one cow-herd, are considered necessary for every forty cows.

* Notes of a Traveller, p. 351.; Mill's Principles of Political Economy, vol. i.

The owners of the cows get credit each of them, in a book daily, for the quantity of milk given by each cow. The cheeseman and his assistants milk the cows, put the milk all together, and make cheese of it, and at the end of the season, each owner receives the weight of cheese, proportionate to the quantity of milk his cows have delivered. By this co-operative plan, instead of the small-sized unmarketable cheeses only, which each could produce out of his three or four cows' milk, he has the same weight in large marketable cheese, superior in quality, because made by people who attend to no other business. The cheeseman and his assistants are paid so much per head of the cows, in money or in cheese ; or sometimes they hire the cows, and pay the owners in money or cheese." A similar system exists in the French Jura. One of the most remarkable points in this interesting case of combination of labour, is the confidence, which it supposes, and which experience must justify, in the integrity of the persons employed.

The admirable and scientific character of the system of farming pursued by the small farmers and peasant-proprietors of Holland, is attested by the writer of a carefully prepared, systematic treatise on Flemish husbandry, in the Farmer's Series of the Society for the Diffusion of Useful Knowledge. He observes, that the Flemish agriculturist* "seems to want nothing but a space to work upon. Whatever be the quality or texture of the soil, in time he will make it produce something. The sand in the Campine can be compared to

* Geographical Dictionary, art. " Belgium," pp. 4. 11. ; Mill's Principles of Political Economy, vol. i. p. 316.

nothing but the sands on the sea-shore, which they probably were originally. It is highly interesting to follow, step by step, the progress of improvement. Here you see a cottage and rude cow-shed erected on a spot of the most unpromising aspect. The loose white sand blown into irregular mounds, is only kept together by the roots of the heath; a small spot only is levelled and surrounded by a ditch; part of this is covered with young broom, part is planted with potatoes, and perhaps a small patch of diminutive clover may show itself; but manures, both solid and liquid, are collecting, and this is the nucleus from which, in a few years, a little farm will spread around. . . . . If there is no manure at hand, the only thing that can be sown on pure sand, at first, is broom: this grows in the most barren soils; in three years it is fit to cut, and produces some return in faggots for the bakers and brickmakers. The leaves which have fallen have somewhat enriched the soil, and the fibres of the roots have given a certain degree of compactness. It may now be sown with buck-wheat, or even with rye, without manure. By the time this is reaped, some manure may have been collected, and a regular course of cropping may begin. As soon as clover and potatoes enable the farmer to keep cows and make manure, the improvement goes on rapidly; in a few years the soil undergoes a complete change; it becomes mellow and retentive of moisture, and enriched by the vegetable matter afforded by the decomposition of the roots of clover and other plants. . . . . After the land has been gradually brought into a good state, and is cultivated in a regular manner, there ap-

pears much less difference between the soils, which have
been originally good, and those, which have been made
so by labour and industry — at least, the crops in both
appear more nearly alike at harvest, than is the case in
soils of different qualities in other countries.   This is a
great proof of the excellency of the Flemish system; for
it shows, that the land is in a constant state of improvement, and that the deficiency of the soil is compensated
by greater attention to tillage and manuring, especially the latter."

Mr. Mill, in reasoning on the preceding account of
Flemish husbandry, says * : — " The people, who labour
thus intensely, *because labouring for themselves,* have
practised for centuries those principles of rotation of
crops and economy of manures, which in England are
counted among modern discoveries; and even now, the
superiority of their agriculture, as a whole, to that of
England, is admitted by competent judges.   ' The cultivation of a poor light soil, or a moderate soil,' says the
writer last quoted †, ' is generally superior in Flanders
to that of the most improved farms of the same kind in
Britain.   We surpass the Flemish farmer greatly in
capital, in varied implements of tillage, in the choice
and breeding of cattle and sheep ' (though, according to
the same authority ‡, they are much ' before us in the
feeding of their cows'), ' and the British farmer is in
general a man of superior education to the Flemish
peasant.   But in the minute attention to the qualities
of the soil, in the management and application of

---

* See Principles of Political Economy, vol. i.
† Flemish Husbandry, p. 3.   ‡ Ibid. p. 13.

manures of different kinds, in the judicious succession of crops, and especially in the economy of land, so that every part of it shall be in a constant state of production, we have still something to learn from the Flemings,' and not from an instructed and enterprising Fleming here and there, but from the general practice.

" Much of the most highly cultivated part of the country consists of peasant properties, managed by the proprietors, always either wholly or partly by spade husbandry. ' When * the land is cultivated entirely by the spade and no horses are kept, a cow is kept for every three acres of land, and entirely fed on artificial grasses or roots. This mode of cultivation is principally adopted in the Waes district, where properties are very small. All the labour is done by the different members of the family;' children soon beginning 'to assist in various minute operations, according to their age and strength, such as weeding, hoeing, feeding the cows. If they can raise rye and wheat enough to make their bread, and potatoes, turnips, carrots, and clover for the cows, they do well; and the produce of the sale of their rape-seed, their flax, their hemp, and their butter, after deducting the expense of manure purchased, which is always considerable, gives them a very good profit. Supposing the whole extent of the land to be six acres, which is not an uncommon occupation, and which one man can manage,' then (after describing the cultivation) ' if a man with his wife and three young children are considered as equal to three and a half grown up men,

* Flemish Husbandry, pp. 73, *et seq.*

the family will require thirty-nine bushels of grain, forty-nine bushels of potatoes, a fat hog, and the butter and milk of one cow.   An acre and a half of land will produce the grain and potatoes, and allow some corn to finish the fattening of the hog, which has the extra buttermilk ; another acre in clover, carrots, and potatoes, together with the stubble turnips, will more than feed the cow ; consequently two acres and a half of land are sufficient to feed this family, and the produce of the other three and a half may be sold to pay the rent or the interest of purchase-money, wear and tear of implements, extra manure, and clothes for the family.   But these acres are the most profitable in the farm, for the hemp, flax, and colga are included ; and by having another acre in clover and roots, a second cow can be kept, and its produce sold.   We have, therefore, a solution of the problem, how a family can live and thrive on six acres of moderate land.'   After showing, by calculation, that this extent of land can be cultivated in the most perfect manner by the family, without any aid from hired labour, the writer continues, ' In a farm of *ten* acres, entirely cultivated by the spade, the addition of a man and a woman to the members of the family will render all the operations more easy ; and, with a horse and cart to carry out the manure, and bring home the produce, and occasionally draw the harrows, *fifteen* acres may be very well cultivated. . . . . Thus it will be seen' (this is the result of some pages of details and calculations *) ' that by spade husbandry, an indus-

---

* Flemish Husbandry, p. 81.

trious man with a small capital, occupying only fifteen acres of good light land, may not only live and bring up a family, *paying a good rent*, but may accumulate a considerable sum in the course of his life.' But the indefatigable industry, by which he accomplishes this, and of which so large a portion is expended, not in the mere cultivation, but in the improvement, for a distant return, of the soil itself — has that industry no connection with *not* paying the rent? Could it exist without presupposing, at least, a virtually permanent tenure?

" As to their mode of living, ' the Flemish farmers and labourers live much more economically than the same class in England; they seldom eat meat, except on Sundays and in harvest; buttermilk and potatoes, with brown bread, is their daily food.' It is on this kind of evidence that English travellers, as they hurry through Europe, pronounce the peasantry of every Continental country poor and miserable; its agricultural and social system a failure; and the English the only *régime* under which labourers are well off. It is, truly enough, the only *régime* under which labourers, whether well off or not, *never attempt to be better*. So little are English observers accustomed to consider it possible, that a labourer should not spend all he earns, that they habitually mistake the signs of *economy* for those of *poverty*. Observe the true interpretation of the phenomena.

" ' Accordingly, *they are gradually acquiring capital*, and their great ambition is to have land of their own. They eagerly seize every opportunity of purchasing a small farm, and the price is so raised by the competition, that land pays little more than two per cent. interest for the purchase-money. Large properties gradually disappear, and are divided into small portions, which sell at a high rate. But the wealth and industry of the population is continually increasing, being rather diffused through the masses, than accumulated in individuals.'

" With facts like these known and accessible *, it is not a little surprising to find the case of Flanders referred to, not in recommendation of peasant properties, but as a warning against them, on no better ground, than a presumptive excess of population, inferred from the distress, which existed among the peasantry of Brabant and East Flanders, in the disastrous years 1846, 1847. The evidence, which I have cited from a writer conversant with the subject, and having no economical theory to support, shows that the distress, whatever may have have been its severity, arose from no insufficiency in these little properties to supply abundantly, in any ordinary circumstances, the wants of all whom they have to maintain. It arose, from the essential condition, to which those are subject, who employ land of their own in growing their own food, namely, that the vicissitudes of the seasons must be borne by themselves, and cannot, as in the case of large farmers, be shifted from them to the consumer. When we remember the season of 1846, a partial failure of all kinds of grain, and an almost total one of the potatoes,

* Mr. Mill's Principles of Political Economy, vol. i. p. 321.

it is no wonder, that in so unusual a calamity, the produce of six acres, half of them sown with flax, hemp, or oil seeds, should fall short of a year's provision for a family. But we are not to contrast the distressed Flemish peasant, with an English capitalist, who farms several hundred acres of land. If the peasant were an Englishman, he would not be a capitalist, but a day-labourer under a capitalist; and is there no distress in times of dearth among day-labourers? Was there none that year, in countries where small proprietors and small farmers are unknown? Is there any reason whatever to believe, that the distress was greater in Belgium, than corresponds to the proportional extent of the failure of crops compared with other countries?

" It is from France, however, that impressions unfavourable to peasant properties are generally drawn; it is in France, that the system is so often asserted to have brought forth its fruit, in the most wretched possible agriculture, and to be rapidly reducing, if not to have already reduced, the peasantry, by subdivision of land, to the verge of starvation. *It. is difficult to account for the general prevalence of impressions so much the reverse of the truth.* The agriculture of France *was* wretched, and the peasantry in great indigence *before,* the revolution. At that time they were not, generally speaking, landed proprietors. There were, however, considerable districts of France, where the land even then was, to a great extent, the property of the peasantry, and among these, were many of the most conspicuous exceptions to the general bad agriculture and to the general poverty. An authority, on this point

not to be disputed, is ARTHUR YOUNG, the inveterate
enemy of small farms, the *Coryphæus* of the modern English school of agriculturists, who, nevertheless, while
travelling over nearly the whole of France in 1787, 1788,
and 1789, when he finds remarkable excellence of cultivation, NEVER HESITATES TO ASCRIBE IT TO PEASANT
PROPERTY. 'Leaving Sauve,' says he *, ' I was much
struck with a large tract of land, seemingly nothing but
huge rocks; yet most of it inclosed and planted with the
most industrious attention.   Every man has an olive,
a mulberry, an almond, or a peach tree, and vines scattered among them ; so that the whole ground is covered
with the oddest mixture of these plants and bulging
rocks, that can be conceived.   The inhabitants of this
village deserve encouragement for their industry ; and
if I were a French minister, they should have it.
They would soon turn all the deserts around them
into gardens.   Such a knot of active husbandmen,
who turn their rocks into scenes of fertility, because
I suppose *their own, would do the same by the wastes,
if animated by the same omnipotent principle.*'   Again †,
' Walk to Rossendal' (near Dunkirk), ' where M. le
Brun has an improvement on the dunes, which he very
obligingly showed me.   Between the town and that
place is a great number of neat little houses, built each
with its garden, and one or two fields inclosed, of most
wretched, blowing, *dune* sand, naturally as white as
snow, but improved by industry.   *The magic of property turns sand to gold.*'   And again ‡, ' Going out of

* Arthur Young's Travels in France, vol. i. p. 50.
† Ibid. p. 88.   ‡ Ibid. p. 51.

Gange, I was surprised to find by far the greatest exertion in irrigation, which I had yet seen in France; and then passed by some steep mountains highly cultivated in terraces. Much watering at St. Lawrence. The scenery very interesting to a farmer. From Gange to the mountain of rough ground, which I crossed, the ride has been the most interesting which I have taken in France; the *efforts of industry the most vigorous ; the animation the most lively. An activity has been here, that has swept away all difficulties before it, and has clothed the very rocks with verdure.* It would be a disgrace to common sense to ask the cause; *the enjoyment of property must have done it.* Give a man the secure possession of a bleak rock, and he will turn it into a garden; give him a nine years' lease of a garden, and he will convert it into a desert.'

" In his description of the country at the foot of the Western Pyrenees, he says *, ' I took the road to Moneng, and came presently to a scene, which was *so new* to me in France, that I could hardly believe my own eyes. A succession of many well-built, tight, and *comfortable* farming cottages, built of stones and covered with tiles; each having its little garden, enclosed by clipt thorn-hedges, with plenty of peach and other fruit trees, some fine oaks scattered in the hedges, and young trees nursed up with so much care, that nothing but the fostering attention of the owner could effect any thing like it. To every house belongs a farm perfectly well enclosed, with grass borders mown and neatly kept

* Young, pp. 322—324.

around the cornfields, with gates to pass from one in-
closure to another. There are some parts of England
(where small yeomen still remain) that resemble this
country of Béarn; but we have very little that is equal
to what I have seen in this ride of twelve miles from
Pau to Moneng. *It is all in the hands of little proprietors*, without the farms being so small as to occasion
a vicious and miserable population. An air of neatness,
warmth, and comfort, breathes over the whole. It is
visible in their new-built houses and stables; in their
little gardens; in their hedges; in the courts before
their doors; even in the coops for their poultry, and
the sties for their hogs. A peasant does not think of
rendering his pig comfortable, if his own happiness
hang by a thread of a nine years' lease. We are now
in Béarn, within a few miles of the cradle of Henry IV.
Do they inherit these blessings from that good prince?
The benignant genius of that good monarch seems to
reign still over the country; each peasant has the *fowl
in the pot*.' He frequently notices the excellence of the
agriculture of French Flanders where the farms ' *are
all small, and much in the hands of little proprietors*.' *
In the Pays de Caux, also a country of small proprietors, the agriculture was miserable; of which his
explanation was, that it ' is a manufacturing country,
and farming is but a secondary pursuit to the cotton
fabric, which spreads over the whole of it.' † The same
district is still a seat of manufactures, and a country of
small proprietors; *and is now, whether we judge from*

* Young, pp. 322—324.   † Ibid. p. 325.

*the appearance of the crops or from the official returns,
one of the best cultivated in France.*   In 'Flanders,
Alsace, and part of Artois, as well as on the banks of
the Garonne, France possesses a husbandry equal to
our own.'*   These countries, and a considerable part of
Meecy, '*are cultivated more like gardens, from the
smallness of properties.*'†   In those districts the admirable rotation of crops, so long practised in Italy, but
at that time generally neglected in France, was already
universal.   'The rapid succession of crops, the harvest
of one being but the signal for sowing immediately for
a second' (the same fact which must strike all observers
in the valley of the Rhine) 'can scarcely be carried to
greater perfection; and this is a point perhaps of all
others the most essential to good husbandry, when such
crops are so justly distributed as we generally find them
in the provinces ; cleaning and ameliorating ones being
made the preparation for such as foul and exhaust.'

   " It must not, however, be supposed that Arthur
Young's testimony on the subject of peasant properties
is uniformly favourable.   In Lorraine, Champagne,
and elsewhere, he finds the agriculture bad, and the
small proprietors very miserable, in consequence, as he
says, of the extreme subdivision of the land.   His
opinion is thus summed up‡ : — ' Before I travelled, I
conceived that small farms *in property* were very susceptible of good cultivation, and that the occupier of
such, having no rent to pay, might be sufficiently at his
ease to work improvements, and carry on a vigorous

* Young, vol. i. p. 357.   † Ibid. p. 364.
‡ Ibid. p. 412.

husbandry; but what I have seen in France has greatly lessened my good opinion of them. In Flanders, I saw excellent husbandry on properties of thirty to one hundred acres; but we seldom find here such small patches of property as are common in other provinces. In Alsace and on the Garonne, that is on soils of such exuberant fertility, as to demand no exertions, some small properties also are well cultivated. In Béarn I passed through a region of little farmers, whose appearance, neatness, ease, and happiness charmed me; it was what *property* alone could, on a small scale, effect; but these were by no means contemptibly small: they are, as I judged from the distance, from house to house, from forty to eighty acres. Except these, and a very few other instances, I saw nothing respectable on small properties, except a most unremitting industry. Indeed, it is necessary to impress on the reader's mind, that though the husbandry I met with, in a great variety of instances on little properties, was as bad as can well be conceived, yet the industry of the possessors was so conspicuous and so meritorious, that no commendations could be too great for it. It was sufficient to prove that property in land is, of all others, the most active instigator to severe and incessant labour, and this truth is of such force and extent, that I know no way so sure of carrying tillage to a mountain top, as by permitting the adjoining villagers to acquire it in property; in fact, we see, that in the mountains of Languedoc, &c., they have conveyed earth in baskets on their backs, to form a soil where nature had denied it.'

" The experience, therefore," Mr. Mill goes on to
say, " of this celebrated agriculturist and apostle of
la grande culture may be said to be, *that the effect of
small properties, cultivated by peasant proprietors, is
admirable, when they are not too small; so small,
namely, as not to fully occupy the time and attention
of the family :* for he often complains, with great apparent reason, of the quantity of idle time, which the
peasantry had on their hands, when the land was in
very small portions, notwithstanding the ardour with
which they toiled to improve their little patrimony, in
every way which their knowledge or ingenuity could
suggest.   He recommends, accordingly, that a limit of
subdivision should be fixed by law; and this is by no
means an indefensible proposition in countries, if such
there are, where the *morcellement* having already gone
further, than the state of capital and the nature of the
staple articles of cultivation render advisable, still continues progressive.   That each peasant should have
a patch of land, even in full property, if it is not
sufficient to support him in comfort, is a system with
all the disadvantages, and scarcely any of the benefits,
of small properties ; since he must either live in indigence on the produce of his land, or depend as habitually, as if he had no landed possessions, on the wages of
hired labour; which besides, if all the lands surrounding him are held in a similar manner, he has little
opportunity of finding.   The benefits of peasant properties are conditional upon their not being too much
subdivided; that is, upon their not being required
to maintain too many persons in proportion to the pro-

duce, that can be raised from them by those persons. The question resolves itself, like most questions respecting the condition of the labouring classes, into one of population — Are small properties a stimulus to undue multiplication, or a check to it ?"

It has been already shown, in a previous section of this chapter, and by indisputable statistics, that small properties do form one of the strongest possible checks upon the undue increase of population.

That there is no need to fear, that a repeal of the entail and settlement laws would lead to great subdivision of land, will be shown in the last section of this chapter, from the fact, that even in France, *where the law actually attempts to* FORCE *it*, the subdivision is actually *diminishing*, and the average size of the estates is progressively *increasing*.

From the authorities, facts, and statistics given in this present section, it is then clear, that independently of the vast moral benefits accruing from a system of small estates, the economical advantages arising from it are great and numerous, as it leads to a more economical use of the land; it prevents any waste of portions of it; it tends to improve its tillage, weeding, and cleaning; it provides better systems of farming, better rotations of crops, and more economical and scientific management of manures; and by these means it vastly increases the total produce of the land, while it stimulates in an extraordinary manner the science, industry, intelligence, virtue, prosperity, and happiness of the farmers and peasant classes of the country.

6. *The Education of the Poor, and the Division of the Land, tend greatly to improve the Character of their Houses and of their Villages.*

Every one with whom I conversed in Germany and Switzerland, concurred in assuring me, that a great and visible improvement had taken place in the condition of the houses of the poor since 1816, when the lands were divided, and when the education of the people was commenced.

The children are accustomed for so many years to the clean, well-ventilated, and comfortable school-rooms, and the young men, after leaving the schools, are so long accustomed to the clean and roomy bar-racks, that by the time, they have attained the age of twenty-one, when they return to their homes, they are as unable as our shopkeepers would be to live in such filthy cellars and hovels, as those in which the Irish and many of our own poor vegetate. A good roomy house becomes a positive necessity to them, just as a comfort-able parlour is a necessary luxury to an English shop-keeper. Until a peasant of these countries can afford a comfortable house and a plot of land, he defers his marriage, in the majority of instances.

The villages of Germany, Switzerland, and Holland show the truth of these assertions. The houses of the pea-santry in those parts of these countries, where the peasants are *proprietors*, are remarkably good. They are always at least two, and often three, stories high. They are very substantially built. The windows are large, and numerous, and the rooms are lofty and commodious. The villages in those parts of Prussia where the land is

VOL. I.

divided, look like groups of houses belonging to sub-stantial farmers. Accustomed as my eye had always been to the low-roofed, one-storied, and poorly built cottages of English labourers, I often found it really difficult to believe, that the substantial homesteads of these parts of Germany belonged to the peasants.

The peasant proprietors are very fond of frequently whitewashing, and are very particular about keeping the streets or roads near their houses clean. This con-duces to give the villages a very orderly and neat ap-pearance. The villagers do every thing for themselves, and feel interested in improvements, as their houses are their own property, and not that of a landlord.

The injuries occasioned by time's defacing hand are carefully repaired, and neighbours vie with one another in the comfort, neatness, and respectability of their homes.

In the Rhine provinces the exteriors of the houses are not always quite so prepossessing as in other parts of Germany. They are often built with wooden frame-works, filled up between the beams with a dirty-looking cement, as it is frequently very difficult to obtain brick or stone. This cement makes a very good wall; but, if unwhitewashed, looks poor. Travellers should not, however, judge the interiors of these houses from the look of their exteriors; their interiors are generally roomy, constantly whitewashed, well furnished, and beautifully clean.

In some parts of Prussia however, where the land is not subdivided, and where the peasants are only the day labourers upon the great estates of the rich landowners, as in some parts of the province of Posen, the condition of the peasants' cottages is very wretched. It is said by German writers, that in travelling through Prussia and other parts of Germany, a traveller can always tell, whether the peasants are proprietors, by the state of the cottages, as those of the proprietors are always so much superior to those of the mere labourers. I am convinced of the truth of this observation ; the difference between the houses and general social condition of the peasant proprietors and those of the labourers on the great estate, is much too remarkable throughout the whole of western Europe to allow of any doubt as to the cause.

Mr. Banfield, in speaking of the cottages and farm-buildings of the peasants of the Prussian Rhine provinces, says *— "The size of the offices is a remarkable feature in all German farm-houses, from the cot of the peasant to the largest castle."

And again, in another part of the same work, he says † — " The houses themselves offer a contrast to the diminutive holdings of which they are the representatives. As we have already observed, they are out of all proportion large.   .   .   .   .   .

In the villages the houses are usually built of wooden frames, whose beams and standards are mortised into each other and bound and supported by sloping stays, the mortises being fastened by pegs throughout ; where that timber abounds, the wood most in use is oak ; near the Rhine, fir and pine wood are used.   The wood is

* Agriculture of the Rhine, p. 12.   † Ibid. p. 95.

usually seven inches square, which conveniently holds a layer of bricks laid breadthwise in each compartment. The bricks are not always burnt, and the compartments are sometimes filled up with strong wickerwork, which is plastered over. When the house is coated with lime or clay and whitewashed, the wooden frame is left conspicuous all over, and is often painted in fanciful colours.

" The value of the building is indicated by the thickness of the timber shown to be employed in this framework. Formerly, while timber was abundant and cheap, this style of building was recommended by economy; now stone (which is almost always to be had) and bricks are less expensive, excepting to the owners of forests.

" The house usually contains (on the ground floor) one or two sleeping-rooms, besides a sitting-room and kitchen; sometimes the same number of rooms is found in an upper story." There is almost always a second, and often a third, story in the village houses in Germany. " The roof is invariably lofty, and serves the purpose of storehouse and barn. In its spacious cavity the threshed corn, the hay, and often the vegetable store for winter use, are kept. The housewife dries her clothes in winter on the crossbeams. A cellar is invariably found in better houses; *and, in general, when a stranger is told that these are the abodes of people little above the station, of cottiers, he finds them splendid;* when he hears that these cottiers are the landowners and masters of the soil, he scarcely knows how to estimate their position."

In Saxony the houses in the villages were so large, that I constantly inquired of my conductor where the poor of the villages resided. He said that several families often joined in taking or buying one good house, and in sharing the rooms between them. The houses of the peasant proprietors of Saxony, are quite as good, and often better, than those of many of our farmers.

They generally belong to the inhabitants, who feel a pride in keeping them in good repair, and interested in doing so, from having experienced, that it is cheaper to do so than to repair seldom and at long intervals.

The peasants of these countries, and, indeed, of most Continental countries, do not live as ours do, scattered over the face of the country, but always collected in large villages. A traveller will seldom find isolated houses. The villages are, therefore, generally much larger than ours; because they contain all the people who, in England, would live in cottages scattered along the road-sides or in the fields.

A German professor, who knows England very well, once remarked to me, that it would be a much more difficult matter for us to educate all the children of our poor than for foreign countries to do so, because so many of our poor live apart from the village where the school would naturally be placed; whilst abroad, as I have said, the people generally live close around the village school, and are, consequently, able to send their youngest children there in almost all weathers.

The majority of the German and Swiss villages and towns have scarcely any cellar dwellings, or back alleys and streets, like the foul and degraded haunts of the lowest classes of our town poor.   The majority of the German and Swiss poor are too civilised to live in such places. The towns of these countries, in the much better character of their suburbs and back streets, and in the almost total freedom from any class of children in any respect comparable to those, which swarm in the gutters and on the door-sills of our back streets and alleys, form a strange contrast to most of the towns of England; and a still stranger and more affecting contrast to the pauperism-haunted towns of Ireland.

Dr. Bruggeman, the Romanist counsellor of the Educational Bureau of Berlin, who had visited London, said to me, " *Your countrymen are unconscious of the extent of their town pauperism, and will be quite unable to believe you if you tell them the difference between the state of the English and of the Prussian poor.*"   And so it is.   I am unable to convey a clear idea; but I advise my readers to spend a few hours in any of our back streets and alleys, those nurseries of vice and feeders of the gaols; and to assure himself, that children of the same class as those he will see in haunts — dirty, rude, boisterous, playing in the mud with uncombed hair, filthy and torn garments, and skin that looks as if it had not been washed for months — are always, throughout Germany, Switzerland, Denmark, Holland, and a great part of France, either in school or in the school play-ground, clean, well-dressed, polite and civil in their manners, and healthy, intelligent, and happy in their appearance.   It is this difference in the early life of the poor of the towns of these countries, which explains the astonishing improvement which has taken place in the state of the back streets and alleys of many of their towns. The majority of their town poor are growing up with tastes which render them unfit to endure such degradation as the filth and misery of our town pauperism.*

In many parts of Switzerland, as in the cantons of Berne, Zurick, Vaud, Schaffhouse, and others, as also in Saxony, the houses of the small peasant-farmers are pictures of rural prosperity and happiness. In Switzerland the houses are generally built, more or less, in the old quaint style known by us as Swiss cottages, with the great wooden eaves, the high-pitched roofs, the open galleries outside, running round and forming an exterior passage from room to room, the quaint balustrades, the carved timbers, and the painted sentences or figures covering the walls or ornamenting the entrance. Great settles stand outside the door, on which the family sit in the fine evenings when the field-work is over, and on Sunday afternoons. The perfect neatness of every thing connected with many of these houses is very curious. The family mansion, which has, perhaps, been in the hands of the same family for some time, is preserved in the most careful state of repair, and with the fondest veneration. The wooden palings enclosing the yards, the little gardens round the house, and the yards and offices themselves, look as if the

---

* The horrible condition of the juvenile population, of the back courts and alleys, and of the lodging-houses of our English towns, will be proved in the second chapter of this work, by references and statistics of the highest possible authority.

family spent every spare minute in keeping them in order.

But even supposing it were true, which it most certainly is not, that the peasants were worse fed, worse clothed, and worse lodged in countries, where the land is so divided as to enable them to acquire a part of it, than in a country like ours, where it is in the hands of a few proprietors, still, even under such circumstances, it would be easy to prove, that the condition of the peasant proprietors of the one country was a much happier, a much more moral, and a much more satisfactory one considered on grounds of national expedience, than the condition of the dependent and helpless labourers of the other.

The consciousness, that they have their fate in their own hands; that their station in life depends upon their own exertions; that they can rise in the world, if they will only be patient and laborious enough; that they can gain an independent position by industry and economy; that they are not cut off by an insurmountable barrier from the next step in the social scale; that it is possible to purchase a house and farm of their own; and that the more industrious and prudent they are, the better will be the position of their families; gives the labourers of those countries, where the land is not tied up in the hands of a few, an elasticity of feeling, a hopefulness, an energy, a pleasure in economy and labour, a distaste for expenditure .upon gross sensual enjoyments, — which would only diminish the gradually increasing store, — and an independence of character, which the dependent and helpless labourers of the other country can never experience. In short, the life of a peasant in those countries, where the land is not kept from subdividing by the laws, is one of the highest moral education. His unfettered position stimulates him to better his condition, to economise, to be industrious, to husband his powers, to acquire moral habits, to use foresight, to gain knowledge about agriculture, and to give his children a good education, so that they may improve the patrimony and social position he will bequeath to them.

I repeat, then, that even if it were true, that peasant proprietors were worse lodged, clothed, and fed than dependent day labourers, still there would be much to say in favour of a system, which makes the peasants free, which enables the shopkeepers and peasants to acquire land, and which, by so doing, holds out a strong inducement to all the poor classes of the nation to practise self-denial, industry, and economy.

But it is not true that peasant proprietors are worse lodged, clothed, and fed than peasant labourers. Most certainly the peasant proprietors of Prussia, Saxony, and Switzerland, are better lodged, better clothed, and better fed than our labourers. Statistical writers tell us that a less quantity of animal food is consumed per head in foreign countries than in England. Even if this be true, it is easily accounted for by the great quantity consumed by our middle classes, and by the difference of climates and of national tastes. Our peasants scarcely ever eat any animal food, but our middle classes eat much more than the middle classes of foreign countries. With our cold humid atmosphere we require a more nourishing diet than they do. In many parts of those countries, and at certain parts of their seasons, it would be very injurious for the inhabitants to eat as much animal food as we do. But, however this may be, even if the peasant proprietors do not get a sufficiency of animal food, it is a very small self-denial in comparison with the immense benefits which they all feel they are deriving from *free trade* in land.

The accounts published in foreign countries fully bear out my descriptions of the houses of the peasant proprietors. Herr Meyer von Knonau, describing the peasants' houses in the Canton of Zürick, says *—— " Almost all the houses are two, few three, but still fewer only one, story in height. On the ground floor, looking towards the south, may be almost universally found the family room, two bedrooms, and the kitchen. The first story is divided into bedrooms. There is seldom any second story. Under the high-peaked roof, however, there are generally two small lofts above the upper story, where the corn and seeds, &c. are laid up.

" The rooms are generally from seven to nine feet high, are roomy and light, and are guarded against the lightning of summer by lightning-conductors, and against the cold of winter by double windows or shutters.

" There are always tables in the family rooms, and the adjoining chambers also are furnished with tables; and the floors of all the rooms are boarded; under the

* Gemälde der Schweitz, Zürick.

broad and far overhanging eaves of the houses, the wood required for the household fuel is piled up. . . . Each family room has a large stove put up in one of the walls of the room, so that it may warm both the family room itself, and also one of the adjoining bedrooms, which is devoted to the use of the husband and wife and of the young children. In many of the family rooms there is a sort of oven, warmed from the stove, and used for drying linen and for baking fruit and other edibles. There are generally from three to four windows in the room, all of them side by side. Benches are placed under the windows, and before the benches stands the old-fashioned solid table.   There is also a cupboard full of polished bowls and cups, of milk-cans, crockery of all kinds, books, towels, and brushes; and upon the cupboard, or in one corner of it, is the large folio family Bible. Over the stove, or the door of the room, hangs the militia musket. On the walls hang the bread-knife, the number of the year, a slate for the family accounts, a calendar, a looking-glass, a cover for soup, a small pair of scales, sentences learned at the time of confirmation, keepsakes and remembrances of deceased relatives and friends, the baptismal certificate of the children, and Scriptural, political, and still oftener illuminated, pictures of all kinds, generally framed and glazed.

"In a case on one side stands a carefully preserved clock. Near the stove are the table and benches where the grandfather, grandmother, uncles, and aged friends of the family generally sit. Fastened by a small chain to a leg of the bench which stands under the windows, or hanging on a nail by itself, is the shoehorn; near it stands the saucer for the cats. On one side is a stool, the cradle, and a chest which can be also used as a seat. Under the stove (the bottom of which is generally at least a foot above the floor), are placed the boots and shoes; near the window the spinning-wheel, or the straw-platting apparatus used by the girls, and near the stove that used by the mother and grand-mother. The kitchen, which generally contains a sink, where all the washing is done, is beautifully neat and clean. The older children and the servants sleep in the chambers of the upper floor, two in a bed; upon the same floor are the clothes chests, and often the fruit and lumber stores, the meal, bran, and salt-boxes, bundles of yarn, dried sausages, hams, and flitches of bacon. The generally deep cellars contain in very dif-ferent proportions beer, fruits, &c. In the cow-sheds and stables reign great order and cleanliness."

The average number of inhabitants in each house in the canton of Zürick is about nine persons; in some parts of the canton it is only seven, and in some only six persons. In the canton of Argovie, the average is eight persons in each house.

Herr Bronner, librarian of the canton of Aargau, describes the houses of the peasant farmers, as fol-lows * : —

" In the villages, the plan of the building of a good peasant house is generally much the same. Under one roof of tiles, or of straw, the following different build-

* Gemälde der Schweitz, Aargau.

ings are united:— 1. The dwelling-house of the family.   2. The threshing-floor.   3. The cow-shed.   4.
The barn.   The waggon-shed and pig-sty are detached from the building.   In general, the roof of
the house projects some distance over the walls, in
order that the overhanging eaves may afford covering
for the farming implements, the plough, &c., and for
the store of wood for the fuel.   This makes the upper
chambers very dark ; but they are accustomed to this,
and think that it is fully compensated by the extra
warmth and by the shelter afforded by these overhanging eaves."

" Connected with these houses there is generally a
garden full of flowers and vegetables, a well arranged
dung heap; and, in many cases, a constantly running
fountain with a basin of clear water before it, where
the cattle can drink."

" Near the house door there is a bench, generally
placed against the wall, where the friends and neighbours of the family sit and rest themselves after the
day's work is over, and talk over their concerns."

Speaking of the same houses, he says :—" Stone steps
ornament the entrance.   The bright roomy dwelling-
room on the ground floor, with the warm stove, with
convenient tables and benches by the walls, with the
cupboard full of crockery, &c., and with the clock; the
kitchen next to this room, and the bedrooms, show a no
small degree of comfort and prosperity.   Such houses
are not certainly the most numerous in the villages, but
neat stone-houses of less size are generally common
enough.   Even the straw-thatched houses, with their

overhanging roofs, have their own peculiar advantages. They are cheaper than the stone houses, and yet very warm. . . . They are not, perhaps, so clean as the others; but are generally, where the housewife is active, very well taken care of."

Herr Bronner says, that many of the houses of the day labourers, who do not possess farms of their own, are much poorer than the houses of peasant farmers. Among the mountains, too, the houses are much meaner and much less commodious than the houses of the valleys and plains; but all the accounts agree in stating, that since the people were freed from the old feudal burdens and restrictions, and since they have been receiving a good education, the houses have been everywhere, and even in the mountain villages, rapidly and steadily improving in size, in appearance, and in comforts.

Herr Strohmeier, after describing the old wooden, straw covered, and badly built houses, which used some years ago to be built in the canton of Solothurn, says * — " These straw-covered houses lessen in number, or are improved, year by year; houses are no longer built of wood alone and covered with straw. As the intelligence of the people becomes more and more enlightened, and education is enlightening it, so also do the dwellings of the people become more and more comfortable, commodious, and handsome. Light or dark, well ventilated or close houses have the greatest influence for good or ill upon the character of a people. At the present time, the houses of the peasants are not built

* Gemälde der Schweitz, vol. x. p. 79.

together so closely as formerly, but are situated in healthy and open situations.   Great proud buildings of a really stately appearance may be constantly met with in all the villages, and even among the mountains.   The building there consists generally of two floors.   Adjoining it are two roomy barn-floors, two stalls for cattle, and one or two sheds for carts.   Before the dwelling-house there is always a very neat flower-garden.   Such dwelling-houses prove the prosperous condition of the free Swiss proprietors."

Of course, in all the cantons there are still houses of a miserable character; but all the reports agree in representing these to be exceptions, and to be diminishing constantly in numbers.

In the canton of Thurgovie, Herr Pupikofer says *— " Generally speaking, every family dwells in its own house ; very few live in rented houses.   It is very seldom that several families are obliged to share the same family room and kitchen.

" The old style of houses is progressively giving place to better-built, more comfortable, and more roomy dwellings.   Even in the end of the last century, it had become common to cover the roofs of the houses with tiles, and to build the walls of wood and composition, or of stone.

" The floor of the ground-floor rooms, used as the family room and kitchen, is now often raised some few feet above the ground, in order to leave a greater space for the cellars beneath, where the stores are kept, and to make the ground-floor rooms dryer and healthier."

* Gemälde der Schweitz, vol. xvii. pp. 62, 63.

Professor Vulliemin, in describing the houses of the peasants in the canton of Vaud, says * — "Everywhere throughout the canton well-built and roomy peasants' houses are rising; and this is the surest proof of the *growing prosperity* of the peasants."

He says, that the dwelling-houses have cellars, a ground floor, and a second story where the sleeping-rooms are. The ground floor, he says, contains the dwelling-room of the family, a kitchen, and a children's bedroom. Over these rooms, which are of good size, are the sleeping-rooms of the rest of the family.

Herr Im-Thurm describes the peasants' houses of the canton of Schaffhouse as large buildings, containing, under one roof, dwelling-house, cow-shed, and barn. The dwelling-house, he says, is generally two, and sometimes three, stories high, with cellars beneath the ground floor. The ground floor generally consists of a dwelling-room, a kitchen, and a small room for the parents. The upper floor is divided into bedrooms for the children and farm assistants. "Few houses," he says, "have three, or even two, families, as inmates, and in still fewer do two families live together in the same dwelling-room."

Herr von Knonau, in his description of the canton of Schweitz, says †—" Four hundred years ago Gessler's anger was excited by Stauffacher's beautiful house. A few years back, jealousy would have been excited in the same way among the inhabitants of a village, if any one had built a beautiful and ornamented house; they

* Gemälde der Schweitz, vol. i. p. 303.
† Ibid., vol. v. p. 106.

would have thought it too fine.   In the canton of
Schweitz many such houses have now long existed.
There are no houses which are built of stone, and very
few which are built altogether of brick.   The walls of
the ground floor, however, are generally constructed of
these materials; while those of the upper floors are
formed of wooden frames, filled up with brick and
plaster.   There are very few slate roofs in the canton
(in the whole canton there is only one cow-shed which
is covered with slates).   The houses are roofed with
tiles, throughout the canton.   The old wooden roofs are
becoming more rare every day.

"The house rests generally upon a wall, which
rises about six feet above the ground," and forms
the cellar where the potatoes are kept.   "It is customary to build the houses higher than formerly; so
that houses *of four, and of even more than four, stories
in height are no longer uncommon.*   Sometimes the
peasant proprietors cover the wooden beams of which
the walls of the house are formed, upon the west and
north sides of the house, with small pannels of oak, in
order more effectually to protect the beams from rain
and snow."

These houses, Herr von Knonau informs us, have a
kitchen, a good-sized dwelling or sitting-room, and a
small chamber on the ground floor, and three or four
bedrooms on the second floor.   Under the ground-
floor rooms are cellars, where the potatoes are stored.
The bedrooms of the upper story are united by an
open and ornamental balcony, which runs round the

outside of the house, covered above by the overhanging eaves, and communicating with the bedrooms.

Mr. Jellinger Symons, now one of Her Majesty's Inspectors of schools, says*—" The cantons of St. Gall and Appenzel, which are, perhaps, among the first of the German manufacturing cantons, present the most enchanting picture of the happiness of the artizans. . . . The canton of Appenzel presents the *maximum* of prosperity and contentment among the peasantry of Switzerland. I had a favourable opportunity of examining them, whilst visiting my venerable friend M. Zellweger, to whose eminent philanthropy the canton chiefly owes its superior welfare, and to whom Switzerland is indebted for many of those well appreciated principles of political economy and social government, which have created the prosperity which signalises her among the nations of Europe. I visited many of the cottages of the artizans of Appenzel with M. Zellweger and was invariably *delighted* by the high degree of ease and peacefulness they exhibited.

" I confidently believe that it would require 30*s.* per week in England, in the neighbourhood of any country town, to put a man, his wife, and three children (two of whom shall be above fifteen years of age) in the same condition as, and in all physical respects on a footing with, the average of Swiss artizan peasants, having the same family."

Mr. Chambers himself says—" Switzerland in every quarter presents a spectacle of humble independence

---

* Quoted by Mr. Chambers in his " Tour in Switzerland," p. 86.

and happiness, which is exceedingly pleasing to contemplate.   .   .   .   Switzerland is unquestionably
the paradise of the working-man.   .   .   .   Both Bow-
ring and Symons are in rapture with the cottage system of the Swiss artizans; I own it is most attractive,
and, as I have said, is doubtless productive of much
happiness."

Mr. Symons says, again*— " The Swiss labourer is,
as I have stated, almost universally the proprietor, or
the son of a proprietor of land, and few householders
are there in the whole canton (Argovie), who do not
keep a pig, and generally a few sheep.   Their cottages
are strewed over the hills and dales, and exhibit in the
interior every degree of comfort and ease.

Herr Mügge, writing of the social condition of the
people of the canton of Vaud, says †—" The distinctions
of rank have been more completely abolished in this
canton than in any other; but the influence of the
nobles has not been extinguished without great sacrifices, for Vaud did not, like France, abolish all privileges
at a blow.   All feudal rights, duties, tithes, and so forth,
were purchased from the proprietors, and cost the canton a sum of three millions of dollars; and this could
not, of course, have been done had its affairs not been in
a prosperous condition; but the freedom of movement
thus acquired has been in its turn a cause of greatly
increased prosperity.   When we consider the brief
period, scarcely half a century, in which it has been in

* Chambers's " Tour in Switzerland," p. 86.
  † Switzerland in 1847, by Theodore Mügge; translated by Mrs.
Percy Sinnett.

the enjoyment of independence, and that previous to that the Bernese and the Dukes of Savoy had ruled it through satraps, who oppressed and exhausted the country in the most shameful manner, *the progress it has already made is really astonishing.*

" Wooden houses are already giving place to handsome buildings of freestone and marble; the value of the soil is extraordinarily high; no canton has more numerous herds of cows, horses, sheep, goats, and pigs; large quantities of wine are grown, the finest liquors are manufactured; and the excellent cheese of the Vaud forms, as is well known, an article of considerable trade."

Sismondi, in speaking of the Swiss peasants and their houses, says * : —

" It is Switzerland particularly that must be gone over, that must be studied, to judge of the happiness of peasant proprietors.   Switzerland has only to be known to convince us that agriculture, practised by those who enjoy the fruits of it, suffices to procure great comfort to a very numerous population, great independence of character—the fruit of an independent situation,—and great exchange of what is consumed — the consequence of the well-being of all the inhabitants, — even in a country where the climate is rude, the soil moderately fertile, and where late frosts and uncertain seasons often destroy the hopes of the labourer.   Whether we pass through the cheerful Emmenthal, or bury ourselves in the most distant valleys of the canton of Berne "

* See his " Etudes sur l'Economie Politique."

(*even in the heart of the mountains, for I have visited the most secluded valleys, and know that even there these remarks generally apply*), " we cannot see without admiration, without being affected, those wooden houses of the least peasant, so vast, so well-closed, so well constructed, so covered with carvings. In the interior every detached chamber of the numerous family opens into large corridors ; each room has only one bed, and is abundantly provided with curtains and with coverings of the whitest linen ; furniture carefully kept surrounds it ; the closets are full of linen ; the dairy is large, well-ventilated, and exquisitely neat ; under the same roof are found provisions of corn, of salt-meat, of cheese, and of wood ; in the stables are seen the most beautiful and best managed cattle in Europe ; the garden is planted with flowers ; the men, as well as the women, are warmly and properly clad ; and the latter preserve with pride their ancient costume, and bear in their countenances the marks of vigour and of health. . . . Let other nations boast of their opulence, Switzerland may always with pride place its peasantry in opposition to it."

Mr. Laing, says*:—" The peculiar feature in the condition of the Swiss population—the great charm of Switzerland, next to its natural scenery — is the air of well-being, the neatness, the sense of property imprinted on the people, their dwellings, their plots of land. They have a kind of Robinson Crusoe industry about their houses and little properties ; they are perpetually building, repairing, altering, or improving something about their

* Notes of a Traveller, p. 354.

tenements. The spirit of the proprietor is not to be mistaken in all that one sees in Switzerland. Some cottages, for instance, are adorned with long texts from Scripture, painted on, or burnt into the wood in front over the door: others, especially in the Simmenthal and the Haslethal, with the pedigree of the builder and owner; these show sometimes, that the property has been held for 200 years by the same family. The modern taste of the proprietor shows itself in new windows, or in additions to the old original picturesque dwelling, which, with its immense projecting roof sheltering or shading all these successive little additions, looks like a hen sitting with a brood of chickens under her wings. The little spots of land, each close no bigger than a garden, show the same daily care in the fencing, digging, weeding, and watering."

Mr. Nicholls, writing of the small proprietors of Belgium, says*: — " The small farms of from five to ten acres, which abound in many parts of Belgium, closely resemble the small holdings in Ireland; but the small Irish cultivator exists in a state of miser-. able privation of the common comforts and conveniences of civilised life, whilst the Belgian peasant farmer enjoys a large portion of those comforts. The houses of the small cultivators in Belgium are generally substantially built, and in good repair; they have commonly a sleeping-room in the attic, and closets for beds connected with the lower apartment, which is con-

* See his " Inquiry into the Condition of the Poor in Holland and Belgium," p. 164.

venient in size, a small cellarage for the dairy, and store for the grain, as well as an oven and an outhouse for the potatoes, with a roomy cattle-stall, piggery, and poultry-loft. The houses generally contained decent furniture; the bedding was sufficient in quantity; and although the scrupulous cleanliness of the Dutch was everywhere observable, an air of comfort and propriety pervaded the whole establishment. In the cow-houses, the cattle were supplied with straw for bedding, the dung and urine were carefully collected in the tanks; the ditches had been scoured to collect materials for manure; the dry leaves, potato-tops, &c. had been collected in moist ditches, to undergo the process of fermentation, and heaps of compost were in course of preparation. The premises were kept in neat and compact order: and a scrupulous attention to a most rigid economy was everywhere apparent. The family were decently clad; none of them were ragged or slovenly, even when their dress consisted of the coarsest materials. The men universally wore the blouse; and wooden shoes were in common use by both sexes. The diet consisted to a large extent of rye bread and milk; the dinner being usually composed of a mess of potatoes and onions, with the occasional addition of some ham or slices of bacon. The quantity of wheaten bread consumed did not appear to be considerable. *I need not point out the striking contrast of the mode of living here described with the state of the same class of persons in Ireland.*"

Reichensperger says, that, since the laws were issued in Prussia, in 1807, which, by enabling every landowner to sell his land and to effect the conveyance at a small expense, enabled the peasants to purchase land, and thus created a large class of small proprietors, *the people in Prussia are better dressed, better fed, and better housed than they used to be ;* and that this fact is the clearest proof of the excellent effects of freeing land from the trammels of the feudal regulations.

I have already mentioned the singular difference between the state of the cottages and the condition of the peasants of Saxony, and of those parts of Prussia, where they are educated proprietors of the soil ; and the state of the cottages and the condition of the peasants of Bohemia and Austria, and of those parts of Prussia where the peasants are, like the poor Irish, only the under-lessees of great proprietors, who reside and spend their incomes in a distant capital. This difference is so remarkable as to strike the most casual observer. The cottages of the peasantry in Bohemia, and in other parts of the Austrian empire, and in those parts of Prussia where the land is in the hands of great proprietors the descendants of the old feudal nobility, are very like the cottages of the peasants in Ireland and many parts of England. They are one low story in height, old and wretched in appearance ; grouped together in straggling, crowded, dirty villages ; looking as if they belonged to proprietors, who had no spare income to spend upon the repair of cottages, or upon the improvement of estates ; or as if they were under the care of agents, who were only interested in getting all they could out of the peasantry. The inhabitants of Prussia and Saxony point with pride to the different effects of the great estate and small estate systems, and to the continually increasing comfort and happiness of the peasant proprietors. The cottages of Austria generally look like the cabins of half-civilised squatters; those of Saxony, Prussia, and Switzerland, like the homesteads of flourishing and civilized farmers.

But why this difference between the results of the two systems? Why should the houses of the under-lessees of great landlords be generally so miserable, and those of tenant proprietors be generally so good and comfortable? I will endeavour to answer the question.

1. In the former case, the land has to support, not merely those who are engaged in its cultivation, but (besides these) the landlord. Now, however expedient it may be, that the landlord should have a large income, a splendid mansion, and all conceivable luxuries; yet it is quite clear, that the produce of the land, which goes to build and adorn his great house, and provide him with all his pleasures, would, were the land in the hands of small proprietors, be divided among them. It is impossible to deny, that if the *owner* of land cultivates it himself, he receives the whole of the produce; but that if he does not, all that part of the produce, which is paid to him, and is employed in enhancing his luxuries and comforts, reduces by so much the share of the produce to be divided among the actual cultivators.

In Germany, Switzerland, Belgium, and France, the houses that are enlarged and ornamented by the extra produce of the land are the cottages and farms of the small proprietors. In England, the houses thus enlarged and ornamented are the mansions of the large proprietors. Which of these arrangements conduces most to the well-being of society, is a separate question ; but it is quite clear, from the experience of every country in Europe, that where a large part of the income from the land belongs to great proprietors, their houses will be magnificent, and the cottages of the peasants generally miserable ; and that where the whole income from the land is distributed among the peasants themselves, their cottages will be more comfortable and commodious, and the mansions of great landowners fewer and less magnificent.

The *spare wealth* drawn from the land, after paying the expenses of cultivation, can clearly do only the same amount of work under either arrangement of society. It can pay for a certain amount of bricks, of chairs, of tables, of looking-glasses, of books, &c. If it is spent upon the walls of one great house, and upon stocking that one great house with splendid chairs, tables, mirrors, &c., and its great gardens with choice flowers and shrubs, then it can do no more. If, on the other hand, it is spent in building up the small walls of many small houses, and filling them with chairs, tables, crockery, &c., and their small gardens with pinks and roses, then it can do no more. In so far as it does one, it cannot do the other. Under the peasant proprietor system, the *whole* of this *spare wealth* is devoted to the latter purpose.

2. A second cause, why the cottages upon the estates of great proprietors are generally much less good and comfortable, than where they and a portion of the land

belong to their occupants, is, that the means at the command of the tenants on the great estates are diminished, not only by the division of the produce of the land between the tenant and the proprietor, but also by the unnaturally high cottage rents, which the great estate system causes.

For, where the land belongs to great proprietors, the cottage rents are always higher than their natural level, because the great landowners, from a fear of increasing the number of the miserable labourers (who are almost always the appendants of great estates), and of augmenting, by this means, the amount of their poor rates, generally keep the number of the cottages much below the number actually required by the population.   The population also, as I have already shown, increases much faster under the great estate system than under the small estate system; so that the competition for the cottages on the great estates is rendered doubly severe,— 1. by the unnatural diminution in the number of the cottages, and, 2., by the unnatural increase in the number of the population.   This competition for cottages has the effect of raising the rents considerably, as the poor peasants bid against one another, even beyond the value of the cottages, for their possession.   Every increase, however, in the rent, diminishes by so much the slender means of the cottagers, and renders them by so much the less able to spend upon the improvement of their cottages; while the small proprietors, who own the houses they inhabit, who work with greater intensity, and therefore produce more than ordinary labourers, and who receive the whole amount

of their production for their own use, are both willing
and able to improve.

3. The tenant cottager has but a languid motive to
do anything himself to better his cottage and to make it
weather-proof, roomy, and comfortable, compared with
that which excites to exertion the man, who feels that
his cottage is *his own;* that no one can turn him or his
children out of it ; that whatever he expends upon it will
be so much gain to himself during his life, and to his
family afterwards, and who, besides the bare calculation
of profit, is animated to do all he can to improve his
own home, by the exhilarating and personal interest he
feels in the well-being of that, which belongs to himself,
and which shelters, comforts, and supports his family,
and those dearest to him.

4. A fourth reason why the cottages of the peasantry
are not so good in countries where the land is divided
among a few great proprietors is this : the great proprietor is not generally able, even if he be willing, to spend
much upon the cottages of his tenantry ; and even when
he is able, he is interested in not spending on such an
object more than is absolutely necessary. A great landlord has not, generally, so much to spare in proportion to his wealth as a smaller one. Ideas of luxury
and the standard of necessary expenditure increase *at
a greater ratio* than the means of satisfying those ideas.
A great landlord often fancies, that he is obliged to keep
up a certain appearance in the world, to live as much
like his next richer neighbour as possible, and to make
as great a display as possible of wealth, in order thereby
to increase his influence.

Such a man (and how many such are there not?) needs all he has for the fancied requirements of his position. He does as little as possible to his estate and to the houses of his tenantry. He thinks, that if he keeps them weather-proof he does his duty, and that if he provides cottages, which are just large enough to let a family squeeze into them, it is all that can be expected from one, who is obliged to spend his last available farthing in keeping up a certain style in the world; for he often learns to imagine it a higher duty to do this, than to care for his tenants or his labourers.

If he hears of the complaints of his tenant at all, it is to be told that it is only his squeamishness; that the cottage gives his family two rooms; that his sons and daughters can very safely sleep in the same room with the parents; that the roof keeps out the rain, and that this is all a tenant has a right to expect. Besides, what is such a proprietor to do, if he listens to the whims and fancies of *all* his tenants. Supposing they were all to ask for houses and farmsteads like those of the German, Swiss, and Dutch peasants, where would the landlord's income and his luxuries be? The agent, therefore, keeps the cottage in repair; but he does nothing more; or when he is forced to build a new cottage, he builds it no larger than is absolutely necessary. In this way the peasant gets pinched at both ends. The division of the profits of the land between the landlord and the tenant, the fancy rents, and the uncertain tenure, prevent the peasant doing much for himself, while the landlord's own wants often prevent him improving for the peasant.

The consequence is, that partly owing to the above causes, and partly to the neglected education of the people, the peasants in Ireland are living and breeding like pigs, while in England and Wales the cottages of our peasantry are shamefully inferior to those of Germany, Switzerland, and Holland. I do not mean to say that this picture is universally true, but, unhappily, it is generally so.

Why is it that in England an *owner* of a house takes so much pleasure in improving it, and in keeping it in order? Is it not because he feels it is his own; because he knows that his own family will derive the benefit of all his improvements; because he feels a sort of attachment to the house, which he has either received from his ancestors, or purchased with the produce of his own labour? The improvements which an owner makes on his own house, and the money he spends upon it, he does willingly and as a work of love; but is it the same with a mere tenant of a house? Does the leasehold tenant, or the tenant from year to year, spend willingly upon improvements? Does either of these, and especially the latter, make additions to the house, or even repair anything, except what the terms of his lease oblige him to repair? Does a tenant, in the higher or middle ranks of life, act in this way? and if he does not, can it be expected that a poor peasant, who in our country is never any thing more than a tenant-at-will, or from year to year, will expend money on improving property in which he has not any certainty of tenure for more than a year at the outside?

Repeal all the laws which prevent the sale of landed

property in Ireland, and which keep the whole country in the hands of a few men, who are most of them deep in debt, and have not capital wherewith to cultivate their estates ; enable the landlords in *all* cases to sell the land out and out ; enable the farmers and peasants by these means to purchase, and prevent henceforward any settlement of landed property which would prevent its being sold after the death of him who settled it ; and you would soon change the face of things there, as the great statesmen of Prussia, Stein and Hardenburg, by *similar means*, renovated the face of Prussia.

The Irish, who make such good colonists when they emigrate *, would, with a system of free trade in land, make equally good citizens at home.   The enormous tracts of waste lands would be soon brought into cultivation, as the mountain sides of Saxony and Switzerland, as the sandy plains of Prussia, and as the low lands of Holland have been under the same invigorating system.   Capital would make its appearance in Ireland from a thousand unexpected sources ; a good class of yeomanry would grow up there, as in Germany, Holland, Belgium, Denmark, Switzerland, and France ; while, as has been the case in these countries, since the subdivision of the land among the peasants, the habits, manners, dress, appearance, and industry of the people would all revive and improve under the invigorating influence of a sense of ownership, and of a consciousness in the labourer's mind that he may be prosperous and happy, if he choose to be patient, self-

* That they do, see authorities collected in Edin. Rev. for Jan. 1850.

denying, and industrious. If Stein and Hardenburg had been ministers of England, depend upon it they would have endeavoured long ago to introduce into Ireland, at least, that system which has raised the Prussian, Saxon, and Swiss peasantry from a social condition, analogous to that of the Irish poor, to one which renders them worthy of being regarded as examples for the consideration of the world.

7. *The Education of the Poor and their improved Social Condition tend to give them Habits of Neatness and Cleanliness.*

No child is allowed to take his place at the school-desks in these countries, unless he is perfectly clean and neatly dressed. Rags, uncombed hair, dirty faces or hands, or unbrushed clothes, are not allowed to be brought into the school-room. If the parents of a child are too poor to clothe it well enough for appearance at a school, the parish or town where the parents live is obliged to do so; but by one means or the other the children must appear neat and clean at the school classes.

The appearance of all the children of Germany, Switzerland, and Holland is very pleasing. As they attend the schools, and remain either in the school-room or school play-ground all the mornings and afternoons, they are kept out of the dirt all day; they get their exercise in dry and well-drained play-grounds attached to the schools, and are not allowed any time to run into the streets, except for a short time before going to bed in the evenings. In this way the children spend four-

teen or sixteen years of their lives, and before this
period is over they acquire habits of cleanliness and
neatness.   These habits are still further strengthened
in the case of the men, by their three years' drill in
the army.   There they wear the good and handsome
clothes of a soldier, and are forced to keep their persons, clothes, and apartments perfectly clean.   The
tastes for respectable clothing and for cleanliness, which
they thus gain, remain during their after lives.   Although the Germans of the higher and middle ranks
of life are not so clean and neat as the English of
corresponding classes, yet the German poor are much
cleaner and much neater than the English poor.   Men
in rags or in badly patched clothes are very seldom to
be seen among the German and Swiss peasantry in those
parts of the country where the land is divided.   They
have all of them two suits of clothes — a week-day or
working suit and a Sunday suit.   The week-day or
working suit is made of strong, plain materials, but in
the case both of men and women it is generally in good
repair, and free from unseemly patches, and it is always
as clean as the nature of the work will allow it to be
kept.   The Sunday suit of the peasants in Germany,
Switzerland, and Holland rivals that of the middle
classes.   A stranger taken into the rooms where the
village dances are held, and where the young men and
young women are dressed in their best clothes, would
often be unable to tell what class of people were
around him.   Long association with gentlemanly and
intelligent teachers, the drill of the army, and the association with children of the middle and lower classes in

the same schools, are diminishing rapidly the outward difference observable in England between the middle and lower ranks of society. This is the tendency of things abroad. I do not mean to say that this result is universally attained; but it is certainly being attained in many provinces.

The children of many of the peasants, after leaving the primary schools, continue their education in the secondary schools, and even in the colleges, in most of which the German, and more especially the Swiss governments, have founded many free places, where clever and promising children of peasants, who have distinguished themselves in the primary schools, may continue their education free of all expense. The women of the lower classes of Germany have not advanced in civilisation quite so quickly as the men; but they are improving too, as women always will do where the men have improved before them. To estimate the civilisation of the generality of the peasant women of Germany, Holland, and Switzerland, a stranger ought to go to the village dances and fairs: there he would see wives and daughters of the peasants so neatly dressed, so beautifully clean, with such well-arranged hair, and so polite in demeanour, when compared to many of our peasant women, that he would be agreeably surprised. He should remember that all these women have been educated in the same schools with the men, — that they can all read, write, sing, chant, cipher, knit, and sew, — that they all know the geography and history of their own country, and the Scripture narrative and doctrines, — and that they have all been educated, until their fifteenth or sixteenth year, by learned and gentlemanly teachers, who have themselves been trained in the Normal Colleges.

The dress which the German and Swiss women wear to work in is very plain, coarse, and homely in appearance; but it is always free from rags, and is very suitable for the purpose for which it is intended. At the fairs, village merry-makings, musical promenades in the gardens and village balls, and on the Sundays, the working dress is always exchanged for another, which exhibits the taste of educated people, is often the costume of the province in which they live, and in its texture, make, and cleanliness satisfactorily proves the good taste and prosperous condition of the peasant classes.

It is very curious and interesting, at the provincial fairs, to see not only what a total absense there is of anything like the rags and filth of pauperism, but also what evidence of comfort and prosperity there is in the clean and comfortable attire of the women. Travellers ought to make a point of visiting some of the fairs upon the Rhine; it would not take them far out of their way to do so, and they would thus see one very good proof of the progress of civilisation among the German poor.

A German Doctor of Laws sat by me, a short time since, in the Crown Court at Liverpool, and saw the peasants and labourers who were put into the dock, one after another, charged with the commission of some crime. They appeared in the garb too common among our labouring classes, — with clothes dirty and patched, without regard to appearance, with bits of cloth, and with stuff of all sorts of shapes and colours, — with the lappets of the trouser pockets hanging open, greasy and torn at the corners,—and with clothes which fitted badly, and which, from their appearance, might have belonged to several generations before the wearer's time. After he had seen a good many such specimens in the dock, he said to me, " *You never see such specimens of clothing among our German poor. Are such dresses really common among your poor?*" I could have told him, that among the most flourishing of our peasantry, he would have found many worse specimens than those he saw, and that in Ireland anything which barely covered the person was considered good enough for dress.

A singular and instructive scene may be, and no doubt has been, witnessed by all who have attended our courts of assize or of quarter sessions. I refer to the mass of labourers, who crowd the parts of these courts behind the prisoners' docks. A miscellaneous assembly may be always seen gathered there, dressed, in their ordinary manner. Any one might imagine, from their appearance, that he was in a half-civilised country. The men are many of them begrimed with dirt; their faces, their necks, and the parts of their breasts which are left uncovered by their shirts, are so filthy, that the skin looks as if it had acquired the colour of the dirt which habitually covers it; their hair is uncombed, and dusty, and has that dry and light colour at the ends, which shows that it is seldom, if ever, brushed or cleaned; it is often knotted and entangled in masses from long neglect; their neck-handkerchiefs are greasy, soiled, and crumpled up into something, which looks like

an old rag picked up in the streets of a town, or in the
heaps of a rag-shop; their shirts are open at the front,
and soiled from dust, sweat, and long wear; their
clothes are patched, without regard to appearance or
to decency; their trousers are generally greasy and
torn; and their whole appearance is that of men who
are totally regardless of the decencies of life, and totally ignorant of the comfort and advantages of cleanliness.

What makes the spectacle all the sadder, is the reflection that filth and untidiness are always the signs
and accompaniments of a low moral tone, and of coarse
and depraved tastes.

During the last thirty years the dress of the peasants
of Switzerland has greatly improved, not only in appearance but also in cleanliness. More than three
times as much soap is imported annually, at the present
day, into the canton of Vaud, as was imported thirty
years ago. The peasants change their linen much more
frequently than they used to do. The chests of drawers
in the cottages are full of clean linen and clean table-
cloths. A young peasant girl often brings with her, as
part of her marriage portion, twelve dozen shirts and as
many pairs of stockings.

The men and women have generally, for Sunday and
holiday use, a good suit of clothes made of finer materials than those of which their week clothes are made.

The working dress of the labourers consists of a
shirt and trousers of thick coarse linen, and of a
woollen waistcoat and jacket. The materials of the
working clothes of both men and women in Switzerland

are very coarse; but in the Protestant cantons they are very tidy, free from unseemly patches and clean.[*]

There is one point upon which all travellers in France, and even those who are most unfriendly to its institutions, agree, and that is, in their account of the dress of the peasants. They all tell us that the peasants are well and comfortably clothed, that their dress exhibits considerable taste and refinement, and that it is in every way very much better and very much more comfortable than that of our own labourers.

The French writers, too, all agree in saying, that the dress of the people has very much improved during the last half century, both in the character of the materials of which it is made, and in the manner of wearing it.

All the younger part of the peasants, of the countries I have mentioned, have gone through so very different a training to that which our boorish peasants enjoy, that it is not a matter of surprise, that the women and men of the peasant classes of those countries should be somewhat superior in mind, manners, and appearance, to those of our own country. An Irish or a Dorsetshire peasant would, indeed, be a *rara avis* among the younger generations of the Swiss and German peasants, though he would find plenty like himself, if he crossed over the mountains into the Bohemian plains. These observations are amply borne out by the authorities quoted in former parts of this work.

---

[*] Gemälde der Schweitz, le Canton Vaud, von Professor Vulliemin.

8. *One generally true Index of the Condition of the Poor of any Country is the Character of their Amusements.*

No people exist without some kind of amusement, or some means of relaxation or excitement. In one country they frequent ale and spirit houses; in another, shooting matches; in another, dances, fairs, and village-festivals; in another, they amuse themselves with gardening; and in another, with healthy pastimes, such as cricket, foot-ball, and other games. The more hard-worked and degraded a peasantry is, the more degraded will invariably be their amusements, — the more invariably will they frequent the drinking booths, and the less able and willing will they be, to indulge in those healthier and more civilised pleasures, which require more leisure time, or a higher degree of civilisation, for their enjoyment.

In England, it may be said that the poor have now no relaxation, but the alehouse or the gin palace. It is a sad thing to say of a people; but, alas! it is too true. The good old country games of the times of our forefathers are forgotten. The class of yeomanry or small proprietors which used to keep them up have disappeared. The cricket matches, wrestling matches, running matches, shooting matches, and dances, which formed some of the healthy sports of our peasantry in former times, are now, as far as the peasantry are concerned, abandoned and forgotten; and the commons and greens, where they were once held, have been nearly all enclosed. Nor is this because our peasants have exchanged their healthy country pastimes for any of a more civilised character. They do not generally amuse themselves with gardening, for they have seldom any gardens. They do not practise music together, as they have no opportunities of learning it, and they are too poor to make it worth the while of good bands to travel among the villages, as is the case in Germany. It may, therefore, be said that, as a general rule, our peasants have no other amusement or relaxation than that unhealthy and demoralising one — the tavern. There they acquire intemperate habits; there they spend a great part of the earnings of their families; there they excite one another to rick-burnings, to poaching, and to low debauchery; and there the younger men learn all kinds of immorality from the older and more hardened frequenters.

The crowds of low pot-houses in our manufacturing districts is a sad and singular spectacle. They are to be found in every street and alley of the towns, and in almost every lane and turning of the more rural villages of those districts, if any of those villages can be called rural.

The magistrates and judges, who administer law in those parts of our island, unanimously affirm, that almost all the crime committed there originates in these taverns.

The habit of drunkenness pervades the masses of the operatives to an extent never before known in our country.

The spare hours of the Sunday, and of many of the week days, are spent in these *pleasure* houses. Chartism,

Socialism, and all the political theories of an unenlightened people are fostered and stimulated in these
places. The political clubs are held there. The political
demagogues harangue there. The public morality is destroyed there. The operatives, generally speaking, have
no other relaxation or amusement than tavern frequenting, and they are often too much demoralised to desire
any other.

In a great number of these taverns and pot-houses of
the manufacturing districts, prostitutes are kept for the
express purpose of enticing the operatives to frequent
them, thus rendering them doubly immoral and pernicious. I have been assured in Lancashire, on the
best authority, that in one of the manufacturing towns,
and that, too, about third rate in point of size and
population, there are *sixty* taverns, where prostitutes
are kept by the tavern landlords, in order to entice
customers into them. Their demoralising influence
upon the population *cannot be exaggerated;* and yet
these are almost the only resorts, which the operatives
have, when seeking amusement or relaxation.

In those taverns, where prostitutes are not actually
kept for the purpose of enticing customers, they are
always to be found in the evenings, at the time the
workmen go there to drink. In London and in Lancashire the gin palaces are the regular rendezvous for
the abandoned of both sexes, and the places where the
lowest grade of women-of-the-town resort to find customers. It is quite clear that young men, who once
begin to meet their friends at these places, cannot long

escape the moral degradation of these hot-houses of vice.

The singular and remarkable difference between the respective condition of the peasants and operatives of Germany and Switzerland, and those of England and Ireland, in this respect, is alone sufficient to prove the singular difference between their respective social condition.

The village inn in Germany is quite a different kind of place to the village inn in England. It is intended and used less for mere drinking, than as a place for meeting and conversation; it is, so to speak, the villagers' club.

Mr. Banfield, in describing the village inns of Germany, says*, — " The central point of meeting in every village is some favourite inn. At nightfall the men of any standing usually resort to it as a lounge. They meet there the officials of the magistracy, if there be any; the tax gatherer; those who, having no establishments, are boarders with the host; and those who seek the spot to exchange opinions with their neighbours. In the early part of the evening, *the pastor may be seen amongst them,* and his presence indicates, that propriety is not supposed to be violated by such meetings, as long as order is maintained. Whoever is sufficiently master of the language to follow the peculiar tone of the conversation, which is anything but wordy, if he can endure the tobacco fumes, will carry away with him, from a few sittings, the idea of a people ma-

* Agriculture on the Rhine, p. 87.

naging their own little interests with full consciousness, with an attention to economy that is most praise-worthy, *and with a regard to propriety that must call for admiration.*"

The amusements of the peasants and operatives in the greater part of Germany, Switzerland, and Holland, where they are well educated, and where they are generally proprietors of farms or gardens, are of a much higher and of a much more healthy character, than those of the most prosperous of similar classes in England. Indeed it may be safely affirmed, that the amusements of the poor in Germany are of a higher character than the amusements of the lower part of the middle classes in England. This may at first seem a rather bold assertion; but it will not be thought so, when I have shown what their amusements are.

The gardens, which belong to the town labourers and small shopkeepers afford their proprietors the healthiest possible kind of recreation after the labours of the day. But, independently of this, the mere amusements of the poor of these countries prove the civilisation, the comfort, and the prosperity of their social state.

In the first place, then, every child learns, from the age of six to the age of fifteen, to sing, to chant, to read music, and to dance. During the whole time they are at school, *i. e.* from their sixth to their fifteenth or sixteenth year, every child practises singing and chanting daily; hence has arisen that general or national taste for music, which we in England imagine a German to bring into the world with him. It is however nothing more, than the result of the musical instruction given to all the people in the primary schools. If a boy or girl in Germany has a fine voice or a good ear, or a remarkable taste for music, it is immediately discovered in the school classes; it is exercised and trained at an early age; and is carefully cultivated during the whole period of school-attendance. This is the reason, and the only reason, why Germany has produced so many great singers, composers, and musicians. Of the universality of the knowledge of music in that country, it is difficult for Englishmen to form any adequate idea. In every village and town, all the young men and women below the age of forty can sing and chant, while many of the inhabitants can play on some musical instrument; and in most small towns and large villages, there is at least one good band which practises every week, and performs at all the village festivals and dances. These bands are not like those we now and then find in our small provincial towns, untutored, harsh, without expression, and without harmony; but they are bands which are formed to please the ear of people who understand music, and who can discriminate between good and imperfect performances.

I have heard many of them at the village festivals of Germany, and can safely affirm that they would not disgrace any ball-room of London by their playing; indeed many of our military bands could not surpass them in execution.

This universal knowledge of, and cultivated taste for, music has given the peasants of Germany many innocent means of amusement in the long winter evenings, and

has put within their reach, pleasures of the most civilising and of the most gratifying kind.   It has improved
the public services in the churches and chapels, and has
given the peasants a greater interest in them, and additional motives for attending them.   The singing and
chanting in the churches and chapels of Germany, is
more beautiful than any, which can be heard in any
other country. The whole congregation joins in this part
of the service, and joins, too, as if it felt interested in
it.   The body of sound, which is produced and managed
by a German congregation, is as remarkable as it is
delightful and exhilarating.   It is more like what one
hears from Mr. Hullah's assembled classes, at his great
performances in Exeter Hall, than anything else I can
remember.   The effect is quite magical, to stand among
the people upon the floor of a large church in Germany,
and to hear the swell of the great volume of sound,
poured forth by hundreds of men, women, and children,
all singing together, without leaders, and in perfect
unison.   People, educated as these are, are not able to
find pleasure in such coarse gratifications, as those which
satisfy the frequenters of our gin-palaces.

There are, perhaps, no peasantry in the world, who
have so much healthy recreation and amusement as the
peasants of Germany, and especially as those of Prussia
and Saxony.   In the suburbs of all the towns of Prussia
and Saxony, regular garden concerts and promenades
are given.   An admittance fee of from one penny to
sixpence, admits any one to these amusements.   In the
suburbs of the larger towns, there is in summer one of
these garden-concerts almost every evening.   I will

describe one of them, as they form one of the principal amusements of the inhabitants of German towns.

In the neighbourhood of a German town, there are always a number of houses, surrounded by large gardens planted with shady trees, and intended as refreshment and pleasure-houses. They are buildings of two lofty stories; the upper one is a large saloon, intended for indoor concerts in bad weather, and for balls; the ground-floor is in part occupied, as a house for the pleasure-house keeper, and in part used, as a suite of refreshment-rooms, where coffee, tea, beer, wine, and cakes are sold; while outside in the open air, hundreds of small tables and chairs are arranged under the trees and alcoves of the gardens.

When the owner of one of these pleasure-houses intends to give a concert, he gives notice by posting placards in the neighbouring towns and villages. He then hires a first-rate band, arranges all his tables and chairs outside his pleasure-house, if it is fine weather, or in the great saloon up-stairs, if it is wet or cold, lays in a store of beer, wine, and coffee, and then awaits his company.

There are, of course, cheap pleasure-houses and dear ones; but the dearest, even in Berlin, do not charge more than sixpence for the entry ticket, while the cheapest charge only a penny. Owing to the low price of the entrance tickets, of even the most fashionable pleasure-gardens, the assemblies of people are composed of all classes of society.

The band sits on a raised kind of stage in the middle of the garden, while around it in every direction, as far as the music can be distinctly heard, sit thousands of people of all ranks and conditions, listening to the performance of the most splendid compositions of the great masters of Germany. Nobles and peasants, officers and privates, merchants and shopkeepers, old and young, rich and poor, sit there mixed up together, with their wives and daughters, smoking their cigars, drinking their coffee or beer, and listening to the music. In the intervals, they stroll up and down in the shelter of the trees, rich and poor enjoying themselves together. In these pleasure-gardens of Germany there is very little excess. The people do not meet to drink, but to hear the music, and to see and talk to one another. The rich do not feel disgusted to sit at a table next to one occupied by a poor man's family, because the poor man is too well bred, too well mannered, and too neatly dressed, to cause the rich man or his family any annoyance. Whilst the band plays, the most perfect silence is preserved by the crowds assembled, except when it is broken by a murmur of approbation at the finer passages, showing always how genuine is the pleasure, and how good the taste and appreciation of the multitudes present.

These " pleasure-gardens," as the Germans call them, are to be found in every village. In the neighbourhood of the large towns there are always very large ones, so situated, in the prettiest villages and spots around, as to command the finest views. Each of them is distinguished and known by some particular name, as the " Brühl Garden," " Kroll's Garden," &c. Every month a great garden-concert is given, and for a week beforehand, placards headed with the name of the garden in which the fête is to be held, are posted in all the towns and villages within six or seven miles. These are the great *concerts*; but bands play in these gardens one or two evenings in almost every week during the spring, summer, and autumn. At the larger gardens, and on ordinary days, the people can enter without paying entrance fee required on the great occasions, and are only expected to spend two-pence in a cup of coffee, or in a glass of beer.

I went constantly to these garden-concerts. I rejoiced to see, that it was possible for the richest and the poorest of the people to find a common meeting ground, that the poor did not live for labour only, and that the schools had taught the poor to find pleasure in such improving and civilising pleasures. I saw daily proofs at these meetings of the excellent effects of the social system of Germany. I learned there how high a civilisation the poorer classes of a nation are capable of attaining, under a well-arranged system of those laws, which affect the social condition of a people. I found proofs at these meetings of the truth of that, which I am anxious to teach my countrymen, that the poorer classes of Germany are much less pauperised, much more civilised, and much happier than our own peasantry.

Can an Englishman imagine the inhabitants of the filthy cellars, alleys, and courts of our towns, or the peasants of our villages, sitting in Kensington or any other gardens, mixed up with the gentry of our metropolis and with the officers of our army? The idea seems to us preposterous, — so low, so poor, and so uncivilised are our poor; and yet assemblies of the same classes of society may be seen by any traveller in Germany almost every summer evening.

In most of the towns of Germany and Switzerland public promenades have been made and planted with avenues of trees, under which the citizens stroll or sit on the summer evenings, chatting, listening to the bands, which play on the promenade, reading and talking over the newspapers, drinking coffee or beer at some of the many refreshment-rooms always erected near, and enjoying life and the society of their fellows. These resorts are by no means used exclusively by the wealthier classes, as almost all amusements are in England, but mingled up with the richer classes on week-days; and especially on Sunday evenings may be always seen crowds of the lower classes, with their wives and children, enjoying themselves at least as much as any of their richer neighbours.

Can it be contended that such an association as this can possibly exist, without exercising a great humanising and civilising influence over the less educated and poorer classes of society?

Besides the garden concerts, of which I have spoken, there is another kind of fête, which is in Germany peculiarly a people's festival, and which shows very clearly the difference between the social condition of the German and the English poor.

I refer to the village merry-makings. We have no word in English which would describe them. They are not at all like the wakes of former days, or the fairs of modern times. In the harvest time, these German fêtes are called *Kirmess*.

Each of the villages of Germany, through the summer and autumn months, gives several of these merry-makings. The times of holding them are arranged, so that those of villages lying near to one another do not occur at the same time; so that the peasants of one village may attend the merry-makings of their neighbours.

When the time of holding this village fête is decided, full particulars of it are placarded in the villages and towns which are within walking distance.

The pleasure-houses of the village are put in order, the gardens trimmed, and the cellars replenished. Two or three long tents are then erected, each large enough to contain 1000 persons; an orchestra is raised in each; the floors are carefully boarded with well-smoothed planks, made so as to be easily laid down when wanted, and always kept and used for the same purpose; and small tables, with seats round them, are set all down the long sides of the tents, for the fathers and mothers of the young people who come to dance.

The entrance ticket to one of these tents generally costs one penny; that to another, perhaps two-pence; and that to the third, never more than sixpence. A first-rate band is hired for each tent; a bar for refreshments, consisting of beer, Rhine wines, coffee, bread and butter, and cakes, is raised in each tent, at the end opposite to the orchestra; plentiful supplies of refreshments are laid in; and outside, over all, are hoisted the German and provincial colours.

When there are three pleasure-houses in the village, the tents are dispensed with, and all the needful preparations are made in the great saloons of these buildings.

Outside the tents, in the streets of the village, stalls are erected, where cakes, gingerbread, and various other edibles are sold; while near them swings, turnabouts, wooden horses, targets, and other amusements for the young are prepared. Tables and chairs are set out in the gardens for the visitors; and waiters are hired for the day to attend to the quiet frequenters of the gardens, and to serve them with beer, coffee, or wine, as they may desire.

In the afternoon of the appointed day, the people from the neighbouring villages begin to arrive. On the various roads leading to the village fête, may be seen old people with their children, young men and women dressed in their best attire, students in their coloured caps and surtouts, each with his pipe hanging from his mouth, and his round bag of tobacco suspended from his button-hole; young women, with their glossy hair dressed smoothly on their well-shaped heads, without bonnets or caps, but in very becoming and well-made dresses, and with neat little shawls thrown over their shoulders; musicians, with their books and instruments; soldiers and officers, merchants and shop-keepers, all wending their way to the scene of amusement. Arrived at the village, the relations of the young people take their children to the dancing-rooms or tents, pay their entrance fees, enter and take their seats at the tables placed along the sides of the tents. Those who have not brought their families with them, generally betake themselves to the gardens, and enjoy there the mingled pleasures of the scene, the music, and the refreshments.

As soon as the music has begun in the tents, the young men lead out their partners to the dance. In Germany, a young man at a ball needs no special introduction. He may walk up to any of the tables, bow to the father and mother, and ask permission to dance with their daughter. He does not, as in England, walk about with his partner after the dance; but as soon as it is over, he leads her back again to her relations, bows to them again, and seeks another.

When the weather is fine and warm, the fathers and mothers sit at tables in the gardens with their children, and the young men, who wish to dance with their daughters, come out of the ball-room and seek their partners in the gardens, bringing them back to their parents as soon as the dance is over.

The dancing itself, even in those tents frequented by the poorest peasants, is quite as good, and is conducted with quite as much decorum, as that of the first ballrooms of London. The polka, the waltz, and several dances, not known in England, are danced by the German peasants with great elegance. They dance quicker than we do, and from the training in music which they all receive from their childhood, and for many years of their lives, the poorest peasants dance in much better time than English people generally do.

There are few, if any, excesses ever committed at these fêtes. So decorously is everything conducted, that the merchants and professional men of Germany take their little daughters of six, eight, and fourteen years of age to these amusements, sitting with them in the tents, watching over them while dancing, but not hesitating for a moment to trust them among the crowd, in order to enjoy this recreation, so innocent if properly conducted.

I went to many of these fêtes during my travels in Germany. The last time I was at one of them, was in 1848, at a village a few miles distant from Cologne. I went there with an English gentleman. There were three or four large tents, each capable of containing at least a thousand people. We went into each of them in succession. At the entrance of the cheapest we paid two-pence or three-pence for our ticket. The young people of the poorest class were dancing there. The orchestra was excellent. The people present were, in dress and manners, quite equal to those of our small shopkeepers' class. The dances were conducted with the utmost zest and decorum. The parents of the young women were sitting at small tables round the tent, sipping their coffee and beer, and smoking their pipes and cigars. The whole scene was one of innocent pleasure and healthful exercise.

We afterwards went into the more expensive tents, where the richer classes were assembled. We joined a German merchant and his family. He was surrounded by three young daughters and two boys. Whilst we sat talking with him, the young men and boys who were present came by turns, and after bowing to the old gentleman requested permission to dance with his daughters. The permission was always granted. As soon as the dance was concluded, the girls were brought back to the table at which we were all sitting. The old gentleman never seemed to dream of his young daughters running any risk, by mingling with the crowd, which was enjoying itself before us. His only cause of regret seemed to be, that he could not himself join the young men in their festivities.

I have been several times with different English friends to these village fêtes, in different parts of Germany, when there was not another stranger besides ourselves present, and in villages, too, where Englishmen had most probably never been seen in the dancing-rooms before. No rude stare greeted our entry, though we were at once observed, and though we were evidently objects of curiosity to all who were assembled.

No uncourteous smile was to be seen on any countenance. The young peasants came up, and addressed us with ease, showed by their manners that they were glad to have us among them, and answered our questions with an eagerness to please us, which proved how civilised they were.

The politeness which the poorest of the German and Swiss show to strangers is one of the strongest proofs of their great civilisation. I, myself, have experienced it a hundred times upon my travels; and here it is called to my remembrance, by what I have already mentioned, the conduct of the poor when a stranger visits them in their festivities. I have seen Englishmen attend the village festivals of the poorest peasants in Highland caps, and in costumes, which would in themselves have been quite sufficient to render them the objects of remark and observation, and which, in an assembly of English poor, would have certainly rendered them the butts of a hundred rude jokes; and yet no person present even stared in an uncivil manner, still less was any remark made; but they were treated just as they would be treated in the higher circles of English society, where the great maxim is, to do nothing which would offend the feelings of any person present.

In the German and Swiss towns, there are no places to be compared to those sources of the demoralisation of our town poor — the gin palaces. There is very little drunkenness in either towns or villages, while the absence of the gin palaces removes from the young, the strong causes of degradation and corruption, which exist at the doors of the English homes, affording scenes and temptations which cannot but inflict upon our labouring classes moral injury which they would not otherwise suffer.

When we have educated our labourers as the labourers of Germany, Holland, Switzerland, Denmark, Norway, and France are being educated, and when we have annulled all that part of our present legislation, which prevents an industrious peasant improving his social position by present self-denial and exertion, and which takes from him all motive for exercising either, our peasants, and the Irish peasants, will soon regain their natural independence; will find healthy amusements and pleasures for themselves; will cease to be a burden upon the unions, and will stand in need of public assistance just as little as our middle classes.

Full confirmation of the truth of what I have said, respecting the amusements of the German peasants, may be found in Mr. Howitt's "Domestic Life in Germany," in the same writer's "German Experiences," in Murray's "Handbook of Germany," and in many other publications.

In Switzerland and the Tyrol, one great amusement of the peasants, besides their gardens and their village fêtes, is rifle practice. The Austrian and Swiss Governments give every possible encouragement to this pastime; as by it they prepare the peasants, at a small expense, for the defence of their mountain homes, in case of invasion. Rifle-shooting matches are instituted by the governments in different provinces. Prizes are offered to the best marksman. The target, which is fired at, is presented to the successful competitor, and is taken home by him, and proudly nailed outside his house, to tell all passers, that the owner is one of the best shots in the country.

In the Tyrol I have seen three and four of these targets affixed to the walls of a single house. The preparation for the great shooting matches occupies much of the leisure time of the young peasants of these countries. They meet for practice one or two evenings in every week. The precision of aim which they acquire is very remarkable. If either of these countries should again be invaded, it will be seen what terribly effective corps their rifle militia form, as means of defence among the mountains and forests. If they continue to encourage these exercises, as they have been doing of late years, it will render many parts of these countries almost impregnable to a foreign invader.

But the greatest of all advantages, which the peasants of Germany, Switzerland, France, and Holland, enjoy, in the way of amusement, is their being able, on holidays and Sundays, to walk through the fields in every direction. The land is scarcely ever enclosed. The plots belonging to the small and greater farmers lie side by side, without any other separation than a path, or a furrow to mark out the boundaries. There are no hedges, no park walls, no palings, and very few enclosed pieces of lands. Along the walks, which are made on the lands to the different farms and plots, any one may ramble, without any chance of interruption, as long as he does not tread upon the cultivated ground. In the neighbourhood of towns, the land is scarcely any more enclosed, except in the case of the small gardens, which surround the houses, than in the more rural districts. Yet this right is seldom abused. The condition of the lands near a German, or Swiss, or Dutch town, is as orderly, as neat, and as undisturbed by trespassers, as in the most secluded and most strictly preserved of our rural districts. All the poor have friends or relations, who are themselves proprietors. Every man, however poor, feels that he himself may, some day or other, become a proprietor. All are, consequently, immediately interested in the preservation of property, and in watching over the rights and interests of their neighbours.

This freedom from enclosures, and this ability to

walk anywhere, are of incalculable advantage to all the poor, and more especially to those who live in the towns, and in the manufacturing districts. They are thus enabled to enjoy, at least on Sundays, country walks, good air, and healthy recreation. They are never confined in their rambles to dusty roads or lanes, but may walk through the richly cultivated fields.

In our manufacturing districts, and in the neighbourhood of our large towns, the results of a different system of landed tenures may be seen. Where the boys of the towns can get into the fields, there devastation follows. Hedges are destroyed, the herbage is killed, and cultivation is trampled down. The land, in the neighbourhood of most of the Lancashire towns, wears a singular aspect of untidiness, trespass, and devastation. If a path crosses a field, the passengers, instead of religiously avoiding the grass on each side, as they do in Germany and Switzerland, where the peasants own the lands, is marked by three or four parallel tracts, which seem to have been made out of mere wantonness; so that I have seen cases in Lancashire, where proprietors have found it better worth their while to build, at great expense, two long parallel walls, confining the path between them, than to leave it to passers to please themselves, whether they keep to the path, or wander over the fields, destroying the herbage.

Where the people can get in, the hedges are broken through and through, the trees are stripped for sticks, and the ditches are trodden in, by lads practising jumping over them; and, what is worse, every fruit-tree, which is not strictly guarded, is soon cleared of its fruit.

All this makes the owners of land in Lancashire, and near our larger towns, necessarily and naturally anxious to keep the operatives and lads out of their lands. Enclosures of the strongest kind are therefore becoming more and more numerous, and the rural walks are being gradually stopped or spoiled by walls; so that while population is becoming denser and denser, the labourers are being shut into the high roads and lanes more and more, and the public paths through the fields are being themselves enclosed, from the absolute necessity of protecting the land from the depredations of those, who feel no interest whatever in its being kept in good condition.

One proof, among many others, that a system like that of Germany, Switzerland, France, and Holland, would in England produce, in this respect, a result similar to that produced in those countries, may be derived from the fact, that where there are any allotments, even merely *rented* by the poor, in the neighbourhood of a manufacturing town, however near to the town they lie, and however exposed and uninclosed they may be, they are quite safe, and are undisturbed, showing that the people have a great respect in general for the property which belongs to any of themselves. Instances of this kind may be seen in the neighbourhood of Birmingham, Preston, and some other towns in England.

9. *The excellent Education given to the Poor of Germany, Switzerland, and Holland, the great Subdivision of the Land, and the Amusements of the People, tend very materially to improve the Health and social Comfort of the Poorer Classes in the Towns.*

I have already said, that in the German and Swiss towns there is scarcely any degradation like that to be seen in the English towns. The poor are too civilised, and too well off, to be able or willing to live in such cellars, or in such foul courts and alleys as those which are haunted by myriads of poor creatures in the towns of England. The poor of the German, Swiss, and Dutch towns are better clothed and lodged, better fed, and much cleaner than the majority of our peasants and town labourers. All this of itself conduces very materially to the health of the poor populations of their towns. The character, cheapness, and excellence of the evening amusement tempt them out into the gardens and public promenades, to be found at no great distance from the centre of every German town, much oftener than our poor are tempted into country air and to healthy amusements. It were much to be wished that our Government would build places in all the parts of our great metropolis, where bands might play every summer evening. Good bands would soon find it worth their while to play there, especially, if the owners were allowed a small piece of ground, just around where the band would stand, where they might let chairs at two-pence or three-pence each, as in Germany, and where they might provide coffee, tea, or beer, for any one who wished to sit there. It would often tempt many of the poor, who now scarcely ever see the green lawns of our parks, from their close alleys, and from their gin palaces on the summer evenings, and would afford them a rational and civilising amusement.

The government provides bands of music for the amusement of the rich in London; but these bands play at an hour, when the poorer classes are at work, and cannot attend. The rich can afford to provide such amusements for themselves, but the poor cannot. Why should not the idle bands of our regiments be made to play for two or three hours every evening in the neighbourhood of the towns, where the regiments are quartered, so that the poor might be tempted out into fresh air to listen to the music. The regimental bands might make such hours in summer, their hours of practice, and they would thus secure two ends, — their own improvement and the healthy amusement of the poor, who would thus be able to enjoy a very great gratification at no expense.

But that which more than anything else promotes the comfort and health of the small shopkeepers, operatives, and labourers of the provincial towns of Germany, Holland, and Switzerland is the possession of gardens outside the towns. It is impossible to exaggerate the vast importance of this possession to inhabitants, and especially to the poorer workmen of the towns. The provincial towns of these countries, as I have already said, are surrounded by gardens, which *belong* to the labourers and small shopkeepers of the

towns. Here they grow vegetables, fruits, and herbs
for the use of their families, and flowers for the adorn-
ing of their houses.

In the evenings, after the day's work is over, and
when our poor would be resorting to their only amusement, — the alehouse, — the labourers and small shopkeepers of the German, French, Swiss, and Dutch
provincial towns turn out into their gardens to dig, or
sow, or weed, or water.

Father, mother, and children may be often seen there
together, assisting in the cultivation of the garden,
which is to afford many a savoury and good dish for
their table, and to add to their comforts and luxuries
during the remainder of the year.

The extraordinary neatness and beautiful cultivation
of these gardens show, how their owners prize them,
and how they enjoy their evenings' labour. If they
rented these gardens, they would not care one half so
much about them; but it is the feeling, that they are
THEIR OWN, that they have a share in the land of their
country, that no one can deprive them of it, that all
they expend upon it will increase their own comforts
and not the rents of another, and that if they die, their
children will enjoy the benefit of their expenditure;
it is this feeling, I say, which begets in them, that
attachment to their little plot, which urges them to
improve it to the most of their power. It is a beautiful
sight, on a summer evening, to see these gardens, in
the neighbourhood of the provincial towns of these
countries, full of the families to which they belong.
One feels that the people who have such pleasures as

these are much more secure than others, from the peculiar temptations, and much less injured by the peculiar occupations and pursuits of town labourers.

The parents and children get out, in the summer evenings, from their counters, their desks, their labours, and their schools into fresh air; they enjoy some vigorous exercise, they return with a healthy appetite; and, whilst they have been gaining all this good, they have also added something to the comforts and luxuries of their families.

Any one who has examined the condition of the allotments in the neighbourhood of Birmingham, or of Preston, or some other of the manufacturing towns of Lancashire, will know, how much the operatives prize, even the *uncertain* possession of these gardens, which they hold without any lease, and liable to be turned out at half an hour's notice.

The number of such allotments is, however, very small, and the character of the holding is miserably uncertain for the tenant.   Still these are better than nothing.

A poor labourer of one of the Lancashire towns said to me only a few months since, " Ah, sir, if we could only get allotments, it would do us all a great deal of good.   It would keep a good many of us from the alehouses in the evenings; it would give us a healthy occupation when we came out of the mills; and it would enable us to support our families in greater comfort; but you see, sir, that land is so monopolised, that we poor people have no chance of getting hold of any."   And yet Mr. Porter informs us, that there are nearly 11,000,000 acres in the United Kingdom, which are capable of cultivation, and which are still wholly uncultivated by any one.

Reichensperger, who lives in the neighbourhood of towns, where the German operatives possess gardens of their own, in which they and their families labour in the evenings in the cultivation of vegetables for the use of their households, says * — " The advantages of this system, *if it be only in improving the health of the operatives, are very great, and worth a great sacrifice.* But these are by no means the only good results of this system. The social and economical results cannot be rated too highly. The interchange of garden-labour with manufacturing employments, which is advantageous to the operative who works in his own house, is a real luxury and necessity for the factory operative, whose occupations are almost always necessarily prejudicial to health. After his day's labour in the factories, he experiences a physical re-invigoration from moderate labour in the open air, and moreover, he derives from it some economical advantages. He is enabled by this means to cultivate at least part of the vegetables, which his family require for their consumption, instead of having to purchase them in the market, at a considerable outlay. He can sometimes, also, keep a cow, which supplies his family with milk, and provides a healthy occupation for his wife and children when they leave the factory. . . . .

. . . . " The freedom of the land from intricate settlements, and from all restrictions pre-

* Die Agrarfrage, p. 332.

venting its sale, by enabling the operatives to purchase
or to increase the size of their gardens, is productive of
this further excellent result, — that it offers him the
means of attaining, through economy and industry, a
certain social independence, and saves him from a state
of hopelessness, — that exhaustless source of countless
vices and sufferings. . . . . Several great manufacturers, particularly the firm of Jung, in the neighbourhood of Elberfeld, have furthered this system in
the most exemplary manner, whilst the generosity, with
which they have provided their workmen with plots of
land, deserves public and honourable mention."

The daily attendance at school, the cleanliness and
the neatness of dress, which all the children are obliged
by law to observe, and the cleanly and healthy exercises provided for the children in the school play-
grounds, keep them entirely from the filthy, immoral,
and unhealthy pursuits of the tens of thousands of
poor children, who live in the streets and alleys of our
towns, and improve incalculably the physical condition of the young. From morning to night all the
children of every town of Germany, Switzerland, the
Austrian empire, Holland, and Denmark are taken care
of, watched, kept clean, and kept out of mischief from
eight o'clock every morning until five every afternoon.
Clean dry play-grounds are attached to every school.
One of the teachers always superintends the exercises
and pastimes of the children in these play-grounds.
The parents are fined if the children do not attend some
school or other regularly, and the children are not

admitted to the morning and afternoon roll call, if they
are not perfectly clean and neat.

These regulations make the parents anxious to keep
the children out of the streets, and from filthy sports,
when they are away from school; and, after a few
months' attendance at the schools, the children themselves learn that cleanliness adds to comfort and happiness. The habits which are thus acquired at school
are never afterwards shaken off; but tend to improve
the *health* of the children very much; and afterwards
to improve the physical condition of the *men* and
women.

The appearance of the poorer inhabitants of the
German, Swiss, and Dutch towns — and especially of
those of them, who have grown up under the social and
political system, which I have attempted to describe —
is singularly different to the appearance of the lower
classes of our town labourers. Not only are they, as
I have before said, more intelligent-looking, better
dressed, much cleaner, and more gentle, but they are
also much healthier-looking than our town poor. A
traveller in these countries seldom sees the marked
votaries of the gin palaces; the yellow and jaundiced
feeders on bad food; the dirty, offensive, and careworn
cellar inhabitants; the pale, thin, high cheek-boned,
and careworn-looking mechanics, which one meets at
every turn in our streets. The labourers in the German
towns are cleaner, better clothed, fatter, and altogether much more comfortable-looking, than those of
our towns. They are not so large, so muscular, or so
powerfully made as our people; they are not by nature

so active a race as we are; their climate is not so favourable to vigorous exertion as ours is; but they look healthier, happier, and less careworn.

They drink much less spirits, and weaker beer, than our labourers. If they do not eat so many pounds of meat in a year,—a fact I much doubt,—they still live much better than our peasants, and even than the majority of our town labourers, excepting it be the operatives of Lancashire. They always have plenty of coffee, milk, butter, bread, potatoes, greens, soups, and puddings.

The poor women of Germany understand very well how to cook savoury soups and dishes, and the art of making a little meat go a long way. English travellers have often been in the habit of laughing at their brown bread, because it is sour; but the truth is, this bread is eaten in Germany both by rich and poor, and is generally preferred, because it is thought more savoury than the white. The Germans are fond of many sour dishes which would not suit our tastes. The brown bread is very wholesome and nourishing food, and is to be found in the best hotels, and on the tables of the richest people. In many parts of Germany, travellers cannot get white bread at all.

The Germans and Swiss, both rich and poor, rise very early. The peasants generally get a cup of coffee and a piece of bread before they go out to their work. Between eight and nine, they return to breakfast, which generally consists of coffee, milk, brown bread and butter, with a little cheese or sausage.

In Holland, the cheese is always brought on to the

breakfast tables even of the richer classes, the only
difference being, that three or four different kinds of
cheeses are sometimes put upon the breakfast table of
the rich man, while the peasant contents himself with
less variety.

Between twelve and one, the labourers return to
dinner. In some of the mountain cantons of Switzerland they dine before twelve. The dinners consist of
soup, vegetables, bread and butter, sausages, puddings,
salad, beer, cheese, and, now and then, of a little meat,
cooked alone, and not in soup.

At about five, they take a little coffee, milk and
bread; and, at about nine, a supper of soup, vegetables,
sausages, bread, butter, and beer. This is the general
diet throughout Germany and Switzerland. The house-
wives vary it, by cooking the vegetables and meats in
many different ways. Sometimes the potatoes are boiled
in their skins; sometimes cut into slices, and baked with
butter, pepper, and salt; sometimes cut into slices and
boiled with other herbs, and afterwards dressed with
butter and other adjuncts. In like manner, the soups
are varied in every possible manner. The puddings, although plain, are excellent, and very nourishing. The
cooked meats are not nearly so good as in England, as
they are generally boiled some time to make soup, before
they are baked for the table. Roast meat is hardly
ever prepared. There are no fires in Germany or Switzerland like ours. The cooking is all performed by
baking in ovens, or by boiling in kettles, hung over
little fires of wood made on the top of stone tables.

The German, Swiss, and French peasants enjoy a

much greater variety of food and better cooked meals than the peasants of England. Simple as their meals are, they are both wholesome and savoury.

At the village festivals, the feast of the peasant families is generally a bottle of Rhine wine, or a quart of their bitter beer, or some coffee, with a great lump of currant bread. This bread is very sweet and excellent.

It is made expressly for the village autumn fêtes, and is called kermess bread. My repast at a fête was always either wine or coffee, and bread; and the poorest families ate the same food.

The total absence of intemperance and drunkenness at these, and indeed at all other fêtes in Germany, is very singular. I never saw a drunken man either in Prussia or Saxony, and I was assured by every one that such a sight was rare. I believe the temperance of the poor to be owing to the civilising effects of their education in the schools and in the army; to the saving and careful habits, which the possibility of purchasing land, and the longing to purchase it, nourish in their minds, and to their having higher and more pleasureable amusements than the alehouse and hard drinking.

The small farms and gardens add a good many little luxuries to their meals. Butter, cheese, and eggs are articles of general consumption. Fruit for puddings, herbs for seasoning, salad and vegetables are procured from the gardens or the farms, to add a relish to the cottage meals.

All these seemingly trifling little adjuncts, do more to increase the average of daily happiness in the cottage, than the inhabitant of the palace can imagine. A prince may need his champagne and claret, his pineapples and his venison, to supply a relish to his appetite; but a poor man makes a feast by the addition of a few eggs, a little fruit, a little meat, or some savoury herbs.

Counsellor Reichensperger, in his learned work " Die Agrarfrage," says * : — " In general there can be no doubt that, in those countries where the land is subdivided, and where the subdivision is not extremely small, the people are *well fed*, well clothed, highly civilised, both physically and mentally, and comfortably housed; that under the influence of the small proprietor system, the whole subdivided land exhibits, in every part, the proof of industry and of praiseworthy improvement; and that, by the happy change of different kinds of cultivation, by rich orchards and by products and manufactures of all kinds, it exhibits the significant proof of evenly divided and real prosperity."

The remarkable increase in the quantities of bread and meat consumed per head by the people of Prussia, since the division of the land, is one proof among others of the improvement in their social condition.

It appears † that the increase in the consumption of grain per head of the population, in seven large towns of Prussia, between 1831 and 1841, was as follows: —

* Die Agrarfrage, p. 43.

† See a very interesting paper published by Mr. Banfield, in the eleventh volume of the " Journal of the Statistical Society," and founded upon the reports of my friend, the Prussian Minister of Statistics.

	1831.			1841.		
	Wheaten Bread.	Rye Bread.	Total.	Wheaten Bread.	Rye Bread.	Total.
	lbs. oz.	lbs. oz.	lbs. oz.	lbs. oz.	lbs. oz.	lbs. oz.
Berlin	84 7	180 7	268 14	107 2	175 10	282 12
Breslau	52 10	256 6	309 0	150 12½	227 14½	378 11
Kœnigsberg	61 14	213 3	274 15	60 8½	215 6½	275 15
Danzig	45 5	220 12	265 15	52 14	232 1½	284 15½
Stettin	101 2	249 0	350 14	106 14	312 14	419 12
Halberstadt	65 9½	286 2	351 11½	84 11	315 8	400 3
Brandenburg	86 10½	216 7	303 1½	92 11½	266 6	359 1½

The consumption of corn in *all* the Prussian towns increased, between 1805 and 1831, 10 lbs. 12 oz. rye per head, with a diminution of only 1 lb. 10 oz. per head in wheat, and a very considerable increase per head in the consumption of potatoes!

There are, however, some towns in Prussia, as Magdeburg and Potsdam, where the consumption of bread per head since 1831 has somewhat lessened. But the consumption of all the great towns taken together, shows a considerable progress since 1831, both in the *quantity* and in the *quality* of the food eaten by the people. This increase in the great towns is represented to have been as follows: —

YEARS.	Consumption of lbs. per Head.		
	Wheaten Bread.	Rye Bread.	Total.
	lbs. oz.	lbs. oz.	lbs. oz.
1831	65 5½	240 12½	306 2
1841	78 14¼	237 13½	316 12
Increase per head of the consumption of Bread from 1831 to 1841	-	-	10 10

But what is still more remarkable, is, that since the division of the land among the peasants, the quantity of *m eat* consumed per head, by the population of the *whole* kingdom, has also greatly increased, notwithstanding the increase in the numbers of the population.

In 1805 the average quantity of meat consumed, by each
  person in Prussia, was -   -   -   -   -   -   -   33$\frac{82}{100}$ lbs.
In 1831   ditto   ditto   -   -   -   -   34$\frac{74}{100}$ lbs.
In 1842   ditto   ditto   -   -   -   -   35$\frac{14}{100}$ lbs.
Increase per head of the consumption of meat, from 1805
  to 1842, -   -   -   -   -   -   -   -   -   1$\frac{32}{100}$ lbs.

While in the following towns the increase, in the average quantity of meat eaten by each individual, had increased still more remarkably : —

	1805.		1831.		1842.	
	lbs.	oz.	lbs.	oz.	lbs.	oz.
Berlin - - - -	83	6	104	8$\frac{1}{2}$	116	13
Breslau - - -	94	1	76	12	95	2
Danzig - - -	72	31	75	9$\frac{1}{2}$	83	3$\frac{1}{2}$
Magdeburg - - -	63	25	82	8	92	9$\frac{1}{2}$
Potsdam - - -	62	22	84	0	101	12$\frac{1}{2}$
Stettin - - -	88	9	72	0	104	13$\frac{1}{2}$
Erfurt - - - -	65	23	71	11$\frac{1}{2}$	75	13$\frac{1}{2}$
Halberstadt - - -	51	1	62	13	71	15$\frac{1}{2}$
Brandenburg - -	56	2	51	3	78	14
Neisse - - -	59	26	63	11	62	14$\frac{1}{2}$

When it is considered how very greatly the population of Prussia has increased since 1804, viz., from 10,000,000 in 1804, to 15,000,000 in 1841, it will be evident to all, that this increase, in the quantity of good wholesome food eaten by the people, is an undeniable proof of the good effects of their social system, and proves incontestably that the social condition of the people is progressively improving.

A further proof of the improved social condition of the people of Prussia, since the subdivision of the land, is the increase, which has taken place since that event, in the general consumption of the whole country. The following table, taken from the able work * of the Minister of Statistics in Berlin, shows what the amount of this improvement in the social condition has been.

Food and Materials.	1805. Quantity consumed per Head.	1842. Quantity consumed per Head.
Bushels of Wheat, Corn, &c.	4	4
Pounds of Flesh - - -	33	35
— Rice - - -	$\frac{3}{10}$	$\frac{11}{16}$
— Sugar - -	$1\frac{1}{2}$	5
— Coffee - -	$\frac{2}{3}$	$2\frac{1}{2}$
— Salt - - -	17	17
— Tobacco - -	$1\frac{1}{2}$	$3\frac{1}{10}$
Ells of Cloth - - -	$\frac{3}{4}$	$1\frac{1}{3}$
— Linen - - -	4	5
— Woollen Stuffs -	$\frac{3}{4}$	13
— Silks - - -	$\frac{1}{4}$	$\frac{3}{8}$

The Prussian people, therefore, eat more bread, meat, rice, and sugar, as much wheat and corn, drink more coffee, and wear more cloth, linen, woollen stuffs, and silks, than they did, before the peasants were enabled to purchase lands.

The Prussian Minister of Statistics, after giving these remarkable statistics says † : — " The principal object of

* Der Volkswohlstand im Preuss. Staate. pp. 28. 218. and 250.
† Ibid., seite 251.

agriculture is to obtain bread and meat. As our Prussian agriculture raises so much more meat and bread on the same extent of territory, than it used to do, it follows, that agriculture must have been greatly increased both in science and industry. There are other facts which confirm the truth of this conclusion. The division of estates has, since 1831, proceeded more and more throughout the country. There are now many more small independent proprietors than formerly. Yet, however many complaints of pauperism are heard among the dependent labourers, WE NEVER HEAR IT COMPLAINED, THAT PAUPERISM IS INCREASING AMONG THE PEASANT PROPRIETORS. Nor do we hear, that the estates of the peasants in the eastern provinces are becoming too small, *or that the system of freedom of disposition leads to too great a division of the father's land among the children.* Complaints such as these are heard in a few exceptional cases from the western provinces of the kingdom, where there was freedom of disposition before 1806. They are not, therefore, the necessary consequences of the law, which regulates the rights of the possessors of land. Throughout the kingdom, wherever the small proprietor has become the *unfettered* owner, there agriculture has been delivered from all the fetters which used to impede its improvement. The owner is well acquainted with his small estate. *It is an almost universally acknowledged fact, that the gross produce of the land, in grain, potatoes, and cattle, is increased, when the land is culti-vated by those who own small portions of it ;* and, if this had not been the case, it would have been impossible to raise as much of the necessary articles of food, as has been wanted for the increasing population. Even on the larger estates, the improvement in the system of agriculture is too manifest to admit of any doubt. . . . . . Industry, and capital, and labour, are expended upon the soil. It is rendered productive by means of manuring and careful tillage. The amount of the produce is increased. . . . . . The prices of the estates, on account of their increased productiveness, have increased. The great commons, many acres of which used to lie wholly uncultivated are disappearing, and are being turned into meadows and fields. The cultivation of potatoes has increased very considerably. Greater plots of lands are now devoted to the cultivation of potatoes than ever used to be. . . . . . The old system of the three-field-system of agriculture, according to which one third of the field used to be left always fallow, in order to recruit the land, is now scarcely ever to be met with. . . . . With respect to the cattle, the farmers now labour to improve the breed. Sheep breed-ing is rationally and scientifically pursued on the great estates. . . . . . . A remarkable activity in agricultural pursuits has been raised; and, as all at-tempts to improve agriculture are encouraged and assisted by the present government, agricultural col-leges are founded, agricultural associations of scientific farmers meet in all provinces, to suggest improvements, to aid in carrying out experiments; and even the pea-sant proprietors form such associations among them-selves, and establish model farms and institutions for themselves."

The accounts of Switzerland agree with the above remarkable extract, and agree in stating that of late years the food of the people has considerably improved.

Herr Pupikofer says *, that, in the canton of Thurgovie, the *food of the people has considerably improved of late years,* — that coffee and potatoes have taken the place of the groat-gruel, which used to be eaten at breakfast; that the dinner formerly consisted, generally, of soup, dried meat, flour-cakes, and fruit; but that now fresh meat is often eaten in the stead of the flour-cakes, that potatoes are exchanged for fruit, that bread is always eaten at dinner, and that this bread is generally made of wheaten flour and potatoes.

Herr Im-Thurm says †, that in the canton of Schaffhouse the breakfast consists of coffee, together with milk and bread or potatoes. In some parts of the canton, a soup made of milk and meal or groats is eaten for breakfast. Dinner is eaten in this and in many of the more mountainous cantons at eleven o'clock; it consists of soup made of milk, meal, bread, or groats, and also frequently of a meat soup. Beef, ham, and bacon are often eaten by the peasants of this canton.

Between three and four in the afternoon, the men have some bread and wine, the women some coffee, milk, and bread. Tea is very seldom drunk: it is very expensive throughout Switzerland. About seven or eight o'clock in the evening, a soup made of milk and bread or potatoes is eaten; and at nine o'clock the people go to bed, so as to be ready for the break of day.

---

* Gemälde der Schweitz, Thurgau.
† Ibid., Schaffhousen.

" All the people of this canton drink wine at dinner, and often also at supper, and between meals beer is drunk."

Professor Vulliemin, in describing the food of the people in the canton of Vaud, in Switzerland, says*: — " Not only is it true, that there are few lands where the people live on better food than in the canton of Vaud, but it is also a *fact, that the food of the people is improving year after year.* Coarse black bread, milk, and herbs, no longer constitute the food of the people; but white wheaten bread, mixed sometimes with potatoes, or with fresh or pickled meat. The breakfast (or, as it is called with us, the dinner) consists of coffee, or of a thick porridge, with cheese and whey, and often with potatoes also. At ten o'clock the peasants eat some cheese, and drink with it sometimes a glass of wine. Soup and greens, with bacon, potatoes, cheese, salad, pickled meat, and pancakes, compose the dinner. On Sundays, however, and on holidays, fresh cooked meat is eaten at dinner.

" At four o'clock, from Easter to Lent, they take coffee with bread and cheese, and sometimes a spoonful of preserved fruits. The frugal peasant among the vineyards makes his four o'clock meal of bread, cheese, and common red wine. The supper of the peasants consists of soup and cheese. All the peasants drink wine : even the poorest labourer would be discontented, if he did not get at least a quart of wine daily. Formerly, the peasants drank wine much less frequently

* Gemälde der Schweitz, xix Band. 1 Theil. s. 283.

than they do now, but they were accustomed, every eight or fourteen days, to get intoxicated; now every family keeps its cask of wine or cider for the use of the family.

" In the towns, fresh cooked meat, soup, bread, and vegetables are the food of the inhabitants, and often even of the poorest.

" Our militia receive daily, during the time of their service, 1½ lb. of bread, 8 oz. of meat, and vegetables."

It has been the habit of English writers to presume that the peasants of Western Europe eat much less meat than our peasants, and that this is one proof of their inferior social condition. The presumption is as untrue as the inference. The peasants of Western Europe do not, it is true, eat meat every day in the week, nor do they eat much meat; but in most parts of these countries they eat meat once or twice a week at least.

Our middle classes eat so much more animal food daily than the middle classes of France, Germany, and Switzerland, that the fact of the amount of meat consumed annually per head in Great Britain being greater than the amount consumed per head in the countries I have mentioned, is quite possible, without any necessity for resorting to the hypothesis, that our peasants eat even as much animal food as the peasants of Western Europe.

Even if the peasants of England, Wales, and Ireland did eat animal food oftener than they really do, it would be but a poor compensation for the loss of all the vast advantages enjoyed by the peasants throughout Western Europe, viz., the freedom of action, and the possibility of improving their condition, of acquiring a farm and a house of their own, and of rising, by prudence, self-denial, and exertion, to a higher station in society.

But all the inquiries, which have been made in recent years, and the careful investigations made by the correspondents of the public journals, and particularly by the writers of the admirable letters on " Labour and the Poor," recently published in the " Morning Chronicle," prove, that the peasants of England seldom obtain any animal food at all.

10. *Another of the many and great Advantages arising from the cultivated Intelligence of the Peasants of Germany, Switzerland, and Holland, and from the Subdivision of the Land among them, is, that all the Peasant Proprietors of these Countries are naturally, from their Position, adverse to rash and ill-considered Political Changes, and to Political Agitation, and are all rendered strongly Conservative in Character, so that the Majority of the People, instead of the Minority, are interested in the Cause of Order and public Tranquillity.*

It will be said, " But do not the events of 1848 prove the contrary ?" I unhesitatingly answer, " No." The government of Louis Philippe fell, not because the country people rose against it, but because the government had so governed, as to alienate the affection of the peasant proprietors to such an extent, that they would not rise in its defence. Louis Philippe's government refused almost every peasant proprietor in France the right of voting at the elections; it refused to repeal several taxes, which pressed with peculiar weight upon them; it had burdened and was burdening them with an ever-increasing weight of taxation; it had annually increased, and was still annually increasing, the public debt and the public expenditure; it had increased the number of placemen to such an extent, that they were much more numerous than the electors; it had broken important national alliances, and had run the risk of war for the sake of a mere family connection, in which the people felt not the slightest interest; and it had continually and unnecessarily infringed the inestimable privilege of the free expression of opinion, whether by word of mouth or by the press.

By these means, the government of Louis Philippe had completely estranged the affections of the small landed proprietors throughout France. In the hour of necessity, therefore, although the proprietors did not rise against the government, they would not rise in its defence, and consequently it fell. Even the shopkeepers of Paris refused to fight for it. One remarkable proof of the feeling of the people with regard to M. Guizot's scheme of government, is, that in the first two Assemblies returned after the erection of the Republic, he has been unable to obtain a seat, notwithstanding all the exertions of his friends, and notwithstanding all that the people have suffered from the excitement and excesses, which necessarily attended the great political change.

Since the Revolution, however, the peasant proprietors have uniformly shown themselves the friends of order. In the insurrection of June, 1848, which I witnessed myself, the peasant proprietors flocked to

Paris by thousands, and shed their blood in the support of Cavaignac, and for the sake of public tranquillity.

M. Michelet happily and forcibly represented the tranquil and firm attitude of the peasants of France, when he said, that " the whole of the country districts of France, with their millions of peasant proprietors, formed, so to speak, the *Mount Ararat of the Revolution.*"

This is the principal cause, why the late Revolution was so different to the one of 1789. *Then* there were scarcely any peasant or small proprietors. There were only lords and oppressed tenants. When the former fled, there remained no conservative body, either in the towns or rural districts, capable of defending or upholding the governments, which successively endeavoured to check those, who were interested in turmoil and bloodshed. *Now,* all the inhabitants of the rural districts, and of the smaller towns, are allied with the shopkeepers and merchants on the side of order. This renders their ultimate triumph certain, however great the changes through which the state may be obliged to pass.

Throughout all the excitement of the revolutions of 1848, the peasant proprietors of France, Germany, Holland, and Switzerland, were almost universally found upon the side of order, and opposed to revolutionary excesses. It was only in the provinces, where the land was divided among the nobles, and where the peasants were only serfs, as in the Polish provinces, Bohemia, Austria, and some parts of South Germany, that they showed themselves rebellious. In Prussia they sent deputation after deputation to Frederic William, to assure him of their support; in one province the peasant proprietors elected his brother as their representative; and in others they declared, by petition after petition forwarded to the chamber, and by the results of the elections, how strongly they were opposed to the anarchical party in Berlin.

The insurrections, which broke out in Germany, broke out in the *large towns*, among the *middle classes*, and among those town poor, who owned no land, and who were not individually interested in the preservation of public order and tranquillity.

Hecker and Struve could find little or no support among the peasant proprietors of South Germany, though they went about from village to village, bribing and intimidating by turns: their adherents were inhabitants of the towns.

When we consider what enormous political changes were effected in those countries, within the short space of one year, and with how little bloodshed they were effected, when compared to that which our own great Revolution cost us; when we compare the fierce struggle through which England passed in our Great Rebellion, in obtaining even less results than they have obtained; when we reflect, that at the beginning of 1848, the Germans had no free press — could not assemble, even in private houses, to discuss political matters — had no public assemblies which deserved the name of Parliaments — and had no voice or influence in the levying of taxation, in the affairs of the nation, or even in the political regulations which affected their own domestic concerns; when we remember, that the acts and speeches of every individual were watched, and noted down by odious systems of espionage, supported by the governments, and that every attempt to rise against this state of things was crushed in the bud, by enormous armies and bodies of police, — we shall plainly see that some strong conservative influence must have been at work, to have kept the people so long quiet, and to have prevented the transition to universal suffrage, and to all the rights of democratic states which has taken place, from plunging those countries into ungovernable licence and confusion.

But such an influence was and is at work. That influence is the conservative feeling, or rather the fear of civil discord, which the subdivision of land among the peasantry of any country will invariably produce. A revolution, like the French Revolution of 1789, in either Germany, Switzerland, or France, is now impossible.

A great town may now and then rise in insurrection, and may indulge in the excitement of riot and street warfare, but anything like a general bloody revolution is quite impossible.

What, I would ask, has induced the governments of Prussia, Saxony, Bavaria, and, indeed, of all the German countries, as well as those of Switzerland and Sardinia, to grant universal suffrage so willingly to their people? Simply this : — That these governments knew, that the whole of the peasants were strongly conservative, by interest and disposition ; that they were the steadiest of all the supporters of public order, and of a firm government ; that the people of the towns were the most democratic, and that to grant the suffrage to

them, and not to the peasants, would be to put themselves in the hands of the anarchists, and to deprive
themselves of the powerful and certain support of the
intelligent body of the peasant proprietors.

Urged by these views, these governments have not
attempted to limit the number of the electors, by
adopting a property qualification, but have admitted the
whole people to the electoral privileges. They could
not have adopted a more conservative policy, for they
have, by this means, enabled the peasants to swell the
members of the conservative party in the Chambers, by
sending thither representatives of their own feelings
and principles.

The peasant proprietors of all the provinces of those
countries are all immediately interested in the preservation of public order. Everybody, except the labourers
of some of the largest towns, has, or expects soon to
have, something to lose by a revolution. None, but
those labourers, fancy themselves interested in public
disturbances ; and even in the large towns, the riots of
1848 often arose, more from the excitement always attendant upon sudden political change, and from the
rioting of people long unaccustomed to political liberty,
than from any strong or deep-rooted discontent, or
long-cherished anarchical feelings.

All the substratum of society, in most of the rural
districts of these countries, is conservative. It is the
minority only, who are interested in political change.
The English order of things is inverted. In England
it is the peasants and operatives, who fancy they have
nothing to lose and much to gain by a revolution of

society. It is the majority with us, who think they are deeply interested in an upturning of society. It is the majority, who hope to gain some share of the vast territorial domains of the nobles, or at least to get some part of those great tracts of land, which they observe lying uncultivated by any one; or who, without having any specific views whatever, say, we cannot lose, for we have nothing to lose, we cannot be poorer than we are, or more wretched than we are; we may possibly gain by a change; but if not, it is clear we cannot lose.

There are vast masses, not only of our town operatives, but also of our country peasants, who, in times of commotion, reason in this manner, and are at the beck of the first demagogue who arouses their slumbering feelings.

Symptoms of this under-current of passion are now and then vouchsafed us, like the warnings of a volcano. Sometimes we have Rebecca riots; sometimes, Chartists' risings; sometimes, actual insurrections, sometimes, wide-spread incendiary fires; and in Ireland, constant rebellion.

The more intelligence spreads among the poor of our country, the more will all this increase, unless we alter the laws which tend to prevent the peasants acquiring property. The classes, who are deprived of the natural means of improving their social condition, will rise more and more fiercely against the obstacles, which beset them, the more clearly they perceive those obstacles. If it be necessary or expedient that the present landed system should be continued, it would be wiser to get rid of every school in the whole country.

To give the people intelligence, and yet to tie their hands, is more dangerous than to give fire to a madman. At present our peasants are deficient in intelligence, and therefore they are quiet.

In Germany, Switzerland, Belgium, Holland, Denmark, Norway, and France, all is different to the picture I have just been attempting to draw. The *peasant proprietors*, and the inhabitants of the smaller provincial towns of those countries, will never be insurrectionary, whilst the present subdivision of land continues. Every peasant feels, that his social position and well-being depend entirely and solely on his own exertions. He knows, that if he does not acquire land of his own, and if he does not better his condition, it is entirely his own fault. He knows, that no law impedes him, or diminishes the returns of his labour; that no class is favoured more than his own; that he can ask for no social change, unless it be less taxation and improved education. He feels, therefore, that change cannot benefit him socially, and that it might possibly deprive him of some of the advantages he now possesses. He is, therefore, adverse to sudden changes of all kinds. He is naturally, and from motives of self-interest, a supporter of a strong and peaceful government. He is adverse to war, because war costs money, and entails heavy taxation. The *peasants* of France have gradually, during the last thirty years, been becoming more and more pacific, solely owing to the effect of the subdivision of property.

The people of several of the greatest towns of France are still as warlike as ever. In Germany and Switzerland the same fact is observable. The war party, and the revolutionary party, in Germany, are formed of the inhabitants of the great towns. The same may be said of Switzerland. The people of the small provincial towns, and of the rural districts, are eminently pacific and conservative in their tendencies.

I was constantly told in Germany, prior to the outbreaks of 1848, that if political changes were ever effected, they would originate with the people of the larger towns, and not with the *peasantry*. I remember, in particular, a very intelligent man at Elberfeld, in Rhenish Prussia, saying to me, " The *peasants* are so adverse to political commotion, and so interested in public tranquillity, on account of their being the owners of the land, that they will never endeavour to effect any political changes, however much they may dislike the present political thraldom. They feel, that they are well and cheaply governed, that they have no *social* advantage to gain by a change, that they have property, which might be considerably injured by public riots, and that they might themselves lose some of that freedom of labour, which they now enjoy."

This opinion has been remarkably verified by the conduct of the peasants during the political riots and struggles, which have taken place in the great towns of Germany. Nowhere have the town rioters found much countenance or support given them by the peasants. In the late barricade riots in the manufacturing district and town of Elberfeld, the peasants kept aloof; and when the rioters forsook their barricades, and attempted to make their way in a body across the Rhine Provinces, in order to join the republicans of the towns of South Germany, the peasant proprietors armed, pursued and attacked them, took them prisoners, and delivered them all into the hands of justice. Many such instances might be quoted.

This represents the universal feeling of the German peasants in all those provinces where the land is divided. Every thing I heard upon my travels in Europe, and every thing which occurred in 1848, confirmed the truth of the opinion expressed by the gentleman of Elberfeld. I travelled with a banker of Berne, just after the invasion of Lucerne, by the people of Argovie. He assured me, that nothing was to be feared from the Swiss *peasants*. He told me that, only just before, the *peasants* of the canton of Berne had sent a deputation to the Council of State of the canton to tell them, that if the radicals of the city ventured to engage in any insurrection against government, or in any unconstitutional proceeding, they would instantly arm in the defence of public order, and would assist the executive officers with their united strength.

Such also was the opinion of the head professors of the great schools in Vevay, and such, indeed, was the opinion of almost all the gentlemen connected with the cantonal governments, with whom I conversed.

It is true, that in 1847, the peasants joined with the townspeople in the greatest part of Switzerland, in invading the small mountain cantons. But I believe they were not only warranted in taking that course, but that they were *forced* to take it.

By the old constitution of Switzerland, imposed upon them by the allies on the settlement of Europe, it was necessary to have a majority of three-fourths of the cantons in order to effect any change in the constitution. Now it so happened, that all the populous cantons of Switzerland, nearly two-thirds of all the cantons, and more than *nine-tenths* of all the people desired to increase the executive power of the *Diet of Switzerland,* and to make it something more like a parliament. Until 1847, it was *almost entirely powerless,* the government of each canton being carried on almost independently of the other cantons, by means of a separate Council of State. Owing to this, Switzerland, as a nation, was almost incapable of action. It could not combine for any great object. It had no weight in the Councils of Europe. It was even weak in matters of mere defensive policy.

There were five or six of the small mountain cantons, who systematically voted against every national proposal made in the Diet, and who systematically opposed all revision of the Constitutional Chart. It was believed, by the majority of the Swiss, and it seems probable, that these little cantons were in the pay of Austria; and that Austria, by means of her gold, annulled all the votes of the Diet, and, by preventing Switzerland from combining for any object, kept her a weak and submissive neighbour. These obstructive cantons were the most thinly populated of all, but they had just enough votes to enable them to prevent the Diet from effecting any constitutional reform.

The people of all the other cantons, and more populous cantons, were unanimous in desiring these changes. A large party even in the small cantons concurred in the wish, but all their peaceable efforts were unavailing. The vast majority of all the people of Switzerland were compelled to submit to the will of a very few, and those few bribed, as it was and is now generally believed, by the gold of the ancient, traditional, and inveterate enemy of Swiss freedom — Austria.

Under such circumstances the patience of any people would have broken down. That no change was effected in Switzerland so many years, was solely owing to the conservative feelings of the peasant proprietors, and to the antipathy they felt to political commotions. But at length even these feelings gave way, and the peasants joined the townspeople in remodelling the Constitutional Chart by force of arms.

I have given this hasty sketch of Swiss politics merely to explain circumstances, which have seemed to many to prove, that the Swiss are revolutionary in their habits and interests. Such a supposition is utterly unfounded. There is not a more industrious, frugal, temperate, and conservative peasantry in Europe. The profound tranquillity of Switzerland throughout the revolutionary movements of 1848 and 1849 is a strong proof of this. It should be remembered, that every man in Switzerland is a soldier; that every man has a gun or a rifle of his own hung up on the wall of his cottage sitting-room; that every man has a vote; that every one can read and write ; and, more than all, that the police force is very small. If these facts are borne in mind, my readers will comprehend, that the perfect tranquillity of Switzerland during 1848 and 1849 was a very remarkable and significant proof of the conservatism of the peasant proprietors, who form the great majority of the people.

With Austria convulsed on the one side, with Italy, France, and Germany revolutionised on the other sides, and with her own territory deluged with political adventurers and refugees, Switzerland existed in the midst of the turmoil as tranquil and as safe as a sea-bird in a storm.

Political tranquillity is established upon a much surer basis in Switzerland than in England. A rising of the peasants in Switzerland will never take place except in defence of their liberties, or in opposition to the enemies of social order and prosperity.

The peasants of Switzerland have nothing to gain, and everything to lose, by political disturbances; and *they are intelligent enough to understand this truth.*

If the system of landed tenures in Ireland could be altered, and a class of peasant proprietors be created, instead of the present miserable class of tenants-at-will, the Irish farmers and the Irish peasantry would be rendered as strongly disposed to support government, to maintain the public tranquillity, and to preserve intact the union of the two countries, as the present Irish landed proprietors are.

The results which have universally followed the abolition of the laws, which enable proprietors to keep their lands out of the market for a great number of years, which thus tend to create and preserve great estates, and which immensely increase the difficulty and consequent expenses of transferring land from man to man, would again follow, if a similar great change were effected in the sister kingdom.

The farmers and peasants would buy land. The bogs would soon be divided, purchased, drained, and cultivated.

A great class of small yeomanry, like those who in the olden times existed in England, would rapidly spring up. A great conservative class would be thus created.

The houses and social condition of these proprietors would improve in the same ratio as their industry; and the industry of the Irishman at home would be as great, as it proverbially is on his clearings in the colonies.

Every man who spent 100*l*. in a plot of land would laugh at the demagogues. The peasant proprietors would not ask our assistance to keep them from starvation.

The Irish farmers, who now send over their savings to the English savings-banks, or hide them among the rafters of their barns in Ireland, would soon buy land. Public discontent and rebellion would gradually subside, the more the peasantry and farmers acquired a stake in the country; foreign capital would then flow into Ireland; that land which had not been bought up by the inhabitants would be purchased by new comers; manufactures would spring up; the splendid havens of the sister island would once more be crowded with the shipping of the world; and Ireland, so fertile and so admirably situated to carry on an immense trade with America, would soon become one of the most productive and prosperous islands of the sea.

This is no fanciful picture. No country has yet changed tenants-at-will for small proprietors, without being vastly benefited, and benefited, too, as I say Ireland would be.

Many countries have now tried the experiment, and in all it has signally succeeded. Before the division of land in France among the peasants, they were, according to the accounts of Arthur Young and many contemporary writers, in as bad a condition, as that of the Irish at the present day. The same may be said of the peasantry of many parts of Germany, before the great statesmen of Prussia, Stein and Hardenberg, persuaded the late King of Prussia to annul all the laws, which enabled the old proprietors to prevent their successors from selling any portion of their lands. Since those great men effected that change, the peasants of Prussia have risen from a condition analogous to that of the Irish at the present day, to the prosperous and happy one, which I have endeavoured to describe. A similar result has followed a similar change in Saxony, Baden, Bavaria, Styria, the Tyrol, Switzerland, Holland, Belgium, Denmark, Norway, and France ; and it is but reasonable to conclude, that if a change were made in the landed tenures in Ireland, similar to that brought about in Prussia by Stein and Hardenberg, an equally happy result would follow; and I am convinced that it can be effected by no other means.

In England, too, it becomes every day more and more important to decide, how we shall endeavour to introduce conservative elements into the masses of operatives, which are so rapidly and so prodigiously accumulating in our northern counties. In another twenty or thirty years the population of Lancashire and Yorkshire will be 10,000,000 people, of whom almost all will be operatives. Republican or revolutionary opinions are spreading, and will continue to spread among them. Are we prepared to let them spread without any check? Are we conscious of the dangers of a republican operative population of 10,000,000 people assembled on so small an area? Are we prepared to see the intelligence of those masses increase without some attempt to direct that intelligence by good schools, to impress a strong religious character upon that population, and to endeavour to render them more conservative by the liberality of our institutions? When we consider the dangers, which threaten us, from the enormous development which free trade will give to our commerce, and, consequently, to the augmentation of the masses of our operative population, it is but too clearly evident, that it behoves us to do all we can while we have yet time, in order to enlist as many as possible of our poorer classes on the side of order, and to increase as much as possible the conservative feelings of our people.

The more intelligence advances among the peasants of Germany and France, the more clearly will they perceive that they can gain nothing, and that they might lose much, by civil commotions, and therefore the more conservative will they become in their ideas and in their habits ; but the more intelligence advances in our country, the more plainly will the peasants see the misery of their situation, — the more clearly will they understand the difference between their own state and the state of the peasants abroad, — the better will they understand the working of the laws affecting the landed property in this country, — the more plainly will they perceive, that the effect of those laws is to take away from them any *chance* of improving their social condition, unless they leave their native parishes and homes, — and the more strongly will they be inclined to combine for the violent alteration of the system of the tenures of land.

Our situation is one of increasing pauperism and of growing danger, while that of Germany is one of growing strength and of increasing happiness.

11. *The Education of the People and the Division of the Land beget a Spirit of healthy and active Independence in the People.*

An Englishman can have scarcely any idea of the extent to which the subdivision of land, the cheapness of the modes of conveying it from man to man, and the intelligence of the peasants, tend to diminish pauperism and to stimulate the activity and enthusiasm of the peasants.

An English peasant is in this position at the present day : — He can earn, on the average, from seven to nine shillings per week. If he marries, of course he cannot lay by anything from such a pittance, more especially as his wife has not, in the rural districts, such opportunities of earning wages as the wives of the operatives possess.

If he were to defer his marriage for some time, he might, by great economy, save from his wages about 8*l.* a year; and if he were intelligent enough to avail himself of every advantage, he might, by spending his evenings in weaving, knitting, basket-making, or some other kind of handicraft, lay by at least 10*l.* per annum.

If I have not exaggerated the resources of an English peasant, it is clear that, between his seventeenth and his thirty-second year, (before which latter year the peasants in those parts of foreign countries, where land is much subdivided, never marry), he might lay by between 150*l.* and 200*l.*, and if he deferred his marriage still longer, he might lay by still more. To do this, however, would require great diligence, economy, prudence, and self-denial. To save in this laborious and self-denying manner is a high moral discipline. *It requires great intelligence and a strong inducement.*

That it is not impossible, is proved by the fact, that it has been done by millions of peasants throughout the countries of Western Europe.

Our peasants are not, however, nearly intelligent enough to undertake such a work, even if they had the inducement; and they have no inducement, even if they had the requisite intelligence. Supposing an English peasant were to put off his marriage until he was thirty-two, and to save in the meantime as I have described, what good would it do him? In many parts of this country, he could not even hire a farm, they have so lessened in numbers and so increased in size, and they so often remain for generations in the hands of the same farmer's family; while in most parts of the country the peasant would not have the slightest chance of buying a plot of land.

The effect of our present laws is, to make land generally sell in large estates, and not in small portions: and even when a small farm is for sale, to render the expenses and difficulties of the conveyance so great as to deter a peasant from purchasing.

What could he do, then, with his savings? He might either emigrate and buy land with them abroad, or he might leave the rural districts, go to some town and set up as shopkeeper, in a business of which he knows nothing — in a town, for residence in which his rural life and habits have unfitted him, and with the great risk and almost certain prospect of bankruptcy staring him in the face. Even if either of these prospects were such as to offer a strong inducement to the peasant, if put before him, yet they are too remote and too much removed from his observation and from his knowledge to ever affect him strongly. But I deny that either of them is a strong inducement. They never have and never will act as such; they never have and never will stimulate his energies or his prudence. Emigration is difficult, even for an intelligent man of the middle classes, so strong are the ties and associations of home; but it is far more difficult for a peasant, whose only consolations are his relations and his old associates. A town life offers him no inducement whatsoever; nothing but sheer necessity will ever drive him there. The

English peasant knows, therefore, that prudence and saving habits can do him little, if any, practical good. He feels, that there is no chance of his rising in the world, whatever his exertions. He is opposed by a system of laws, which nullify all his efforts; he does not, therefore, make any. He marries as soon as he can, drowns his thoughts and cares in the ale-house, gets assistance from the workhouse, and is laid in the same humble church-yard with his boorish forefathers.

Such a man has no energies, no hope, no independence. He feels himself the slave of circumstances, against which it is useless to rebel. He sinks into the stupid inanity of a serf, except when his slumbering passions now and then break forth and take revenge, by means of incendiary fires or nightly depredations, on those, who are living in a sphere so different, so sadly different from his own.

No system has ever been invented so well qualified to stupify the peasant, and to destroy all his hopes and all his virtues, as the system of landed tenures, which exists in England and Ireland, and which did exist throughout Europe, before the shock of the first great revolution of France, which crumbled the old system to pieces, and set the peasants free. It deprives him of every worldly inducement to practise self-denial, prudence, and economy; it deprives him of every hope of rising in the world; it makes him totally careless about self-improvement, about the institutions of his country, and about the security of property; it undermines all his independence of character; it makes him dependent on the workhouse, or on the charity he can obtain by begging at the hall; and it renders him the fawning follower of the all-powerful landowner.

The contrary system, as pursued in Germany, Switzerland, the Tyrol, France, Holland, Belgium, Denmark, Norway, and some parts of Italy, produces a contrary result.

A peasant, who knows that it is possible, by present self-denial and exertion, to acquire a small farm of his own, and who perceives, that many of his neighbours have so acquired farms, feels that it is his own fault, if he does not rise in the social scale. He sees the path of improvement open to him and unimpeded by legal obstructions; he sees many of his companions far advanced upon that road; he knows that they have so advanced themselves, solely by their own exertions; and that his own success depends entirely upon himself.

A man so situated will not rest contented, until he has made himself a proprietor, like his neighbours. He will not consent to lose caste, by subsisting upon public charity, while his brothers or his cousins have made themselves, by their own exertions, independent. He will resolve to be independent also.

Whilst there is a single hope before him, he will not sink into the pauper class; and, if he ever does acquire land, rest assured, such a man will be still less willing than before, to become the dependent upon charitable assistance. Before he is reduced so low as to beg, he must sell his land again; and, before he will re-sell that, which has cost him so many labours, and so much prudence to obtain, he will put up with many and with great sacrifices.

Thus, in those countries where the peasants are able to purchase land, they acquire a sense of dependence upon their own exertions, which is peculiarly their characteristic.

The peasant proprietors know, that they have nothing but their own exertions to look to for support; they are not enervated by feeling, that they have no chance of improving their condition, however great their efforts; nor by knowing, that a great landlord, or a board of guardians, will dole out charity to them in the hall or in the workhouse, if they will so far sacrifice their independence as to beg. They fear pauperism as an evil, which means loss of station, comforts, independence, and chance of acquiring property. Nothing, therefore, but extreme necessity will reduce such men to beggary.*

This position of independence of others and of dependence on himself alone, and this consciousness, that his own success is unimpeded by any restriction, ennoble the peasant in his own eyes, and give him an exhilarating resolution to succeed, which increases his virtue and his manliness, as much as it ensures his prosperity.

The fact, too, that he has, or soon will have, a share of the landed property of his country, gives him a much greater interest in the national glory and prosperity. He feels that he himself is individually concerned in the stability and honour of the government, in the

---

* How little real pauperism there is in those districts, where the land is much subdivided, I have shown in a former part of this chapter.

preservation of public order, and in the improvement of himself and the people around. He thus becomes a real patriot.

It is this characteristic of peasant proprietors, which explains the extraordinary efforts and pains, which the peasants of several of the Swiss cantons are now taking to educate and improve the children of their own class. As I shall show in a subsequent chapter, there is no country, which is doing more than some of the peasant cantons of Switzerland, to improve the village and town schools; to build agricultural colleges; to open the higher schools and colleges to the poorest of the people; to establish Sunday classes; and to induce even the older people to increase their stock of intelligence, and to fit themselves for the exercise of their great liberties.

Even in some of the Romanist cantons of that country, all the educational establishments are thrown open gratuitously to the very poorest of the people; and I myself have seen children of the poorest peasants studying in the classical colleges, at the same desks with the children of the shopkeepers, and of the richest of the people.

The burden of what every one said to me in Switzerland was, " Our peasants are perfectly free here; the land is divided among them, and they have nothing left to wish for; so we all feel, that the more intelligent they are, the better they will farm their small estates, and the better citizens they will become. Those who are rich pay for the education of those who are poor; for the rich feel, that they are, if possible, even more interested than the poor themselves in the wide diffusion of intelligence, and in fitting the people for the proper exercise of their liberties."

More is expended in Switzerland upon the education of the people than in any other department of the administration. The finest buildings in the country, after the churches, are those used as educational institutions.

The teachers of the poor are some of the most enlightened men of the community, and the work of national education is considered the first great duty of the national executive.

The peasant proprietors have something to work for, something to live for, and something to fight for, which the peasants of our country do not possess. It is not, then, surprising if the peasants of Germany, Switzerland, and France are more energetic, more independent-spirited, more intelligent, more hopeful, more self-denying, more patriotic, more conservative, and more virtuous than the poor hand-bound peasants of England.

A peasant proprietor of Western Europe is in a far more independent position than even an English farmer. He does not depend for the possession of his property upon the will of any man. His farm is *his own;* and, until he chooses to sell it, no man can deprive him of it. It is not, therefore, necessary for him to flatter, or to cringe to some rich proprietor, in order to secure his position. The consciousness of the thorough independence of his position gives the peasant proprietor a feeling and an air of dignity.

This consciousness is, in itself, an education of the highest order: *it renovates the man.*

The duties, too, which the ownership of landed property devolves upon the peasant, tend to carry out this education still further. He is forced, from his position, to understand something of the law affecting rights in land. He is obliged to look to the making out his title, and the proofs of his title, in the registration office; to study how the different taxes affect him in his position as proprietor, and to learn how he must set about defending his right to his property if it is interfered with.

His position makes him anxious to repress taxation; and it, consequently, makes him watch the proceedings of government, to see whether they will lead to an increase or a diminution of taxation. It obliges him to study the signs of the weather; the character of the soil; and the principle of agricultural chemistry; and to watch the results of experiments tried by his neighbours. All this is an education in itself, and renders the peasant proprietor a totally different kind of being to the mere peasant in knowledge, feelings, manners, and position.

When, therefore, the system of peasant proprietorship is, in addition to all this, aided by an effective educational system, and when the peasant proprietors are really *educated,* as they are in Germany and Switzerland, it may be imagined, how great and how excellent the result must be.

12. *Another most useful and important Effect of the Freedom of Landed Property from the old Feudal Restrictions, and of the Existence of an effective System of Registration, is, that it enables the small Shopkeepers to purchase Land, and renders them more Conservative in their Political Ideas.*

The more a man lives immured in a town, and shut out from the pleasures of the country, the more strongly do his thoughts revert to the healthy pursuits of a rural life, and the more strongly is he inclined to look for a means of escaping, towards the close of his life, from the din, the smoke, the exhausted atmosphere, and the crowded life of the town, and for a means of exchanging all this for the health and tranquillity of a rural retreat.

Under our present system of landed tenures it is seldom possible for a small tradesman to buy a small estate, even if he has saved money enough to enable him to do so. He may often take the lease of a house, or of a house and garden; but he is seldom able to get possession of a small farm even on lease; for small farms are becoming, in most parts of England, less and less numerous every day. And, even if he could get a small farm on lease, that does not offer nearly the same temptation to him, as the possibility of buying a farm would do. He knows that small farms are rare; that their rentals are very often — I might say generally — fancy rentals; that the leases are generally crowded with restrictive clauses, which destroy all the charm of ownership, and which fetter the operations of the active and enterprising improver; and that, by taking the lease of such a farm, he would only run the risk of

being drawn into liabilities, and being fettered by restrictions, which would soon make him a loser, and
diminish, instead of increasing, the capital he had saved
in business.   Whether these fears and doubts be true
or not, they certainly exist, and operate as I have said;
and I think that this operation is prejudicial to the best
interests of the country.

The small shopkeeper feels, that he is excluded from
the possibility of obtaining that, which his town life
would naturally lead him to long for.   He is deprived
of a great inducement to saving, economy and temperance.

He feels that if he defers marriage, and denies himself
present gratification, he can gain nothing more by self-
denial, than an enlargement of his shop and business;
and although this is an inducement to prudential habits,
it is not nearly so strong an inducement as the hope of
one day becoming an owner of a small estate, and an
inhabitant of a rural parish.   He finds himself prevented from acquiring that, which is the day-dream of
townspeople, and obliged to remain all his life in a
situation, in which the majority would not remain, if
they could escape.   It is, therefore, no wonder, that
such a man should be much more radically inclined,
should marry much earlier in life, and should burden
himself with a much larger family, than if he had some
strong inducement to support the existing institutions,
to practise self-denial and economy in his younger days,
and to put up for a time with the less pleasurable occupations of his town life, in the hope and expectation of

being able to change them at a future time for a long-coveted pleasure.

The small shopkeeper, who feels that he can invest his savings in the purchase of a farm, does not marry so soon as, and is more economical, more self-denying, more industrious, and much more conservative in general than, the one who feels that he is prevented by the laws from all hope of ever purchasing a farm.

So beneficial do I believe the system of small properties to be in its effects upon the characters, habits, and feelings of the small shopkeepers, that if I did not advocate such a system for the sake of the peasants, I should do so for the sake of the shopkeepers.

In a country like our own, where the accumulation of enormous masses of uneducated workmen is going on with such a rapidity, it is doubly important for us to consider, how we may render our small shopkeeper class as conservative as possible, in order thereby to create a counterpoise for the influence of the increasing multitudes of the labourers of our great cities.   It is impossible to attain this end more surely or more quickly than by encouraging the subdivision of the land, and by teaching the small shopkeepers to feel, that they may become proprietors, if they will only save capital enough for the purchase of a farm.   On this ground I repeat what I have said before, that if it were thought inexpedient to encourage the general subdivision of land, yet it would seem to be highly expedient to introduce, at least into the crowded manufacturing districts, some such system, in order thereby to create among the shopkeepers, and among those who would become owners of gardens or of farms, a strong conservative class, capable of counterbalancing the immensely powerful democratic class, which is now nursing in those districts, and which is increasing there every day in strength and numbers.

13. *The great Subdivision of Landed Property in Germany, Switzerland, France, Holland, and Denmark diminishes the intense Competition for Wealth, which is the singular Characteristic of Modern Society in England, and renders the People of these Countries more willing and better able than the Middle Classes of England to make Use of the innocent and healthy Enjoyments, which Providence has placed within the reach of all.*

One curious effect of the existence in a country of a great privileged class, like that of our landed proprietors, is to increase enormously the emulation and striving of the mercantile and professional classes below them.

The luxury in which the great estates enable the great proprietors to live, and the splendid entertainments and *fêtes* which their wealth enables them to give, stimulate a rivalry, which is felt more or less through every grade of the *middle* classes. If Lord A. or Squire B. gives dinners in a grand room hung with paintings, and covers his table with costly wines and viands brought from all corners of the world, Mr. C., a merchant living near, will not be content with a condition of life and fortune, which does not enable him in some degree to emulate the display of his wealthy and influential neighbour. He will, consequently, strive to make his equipage as

handsome, to dress his wife as well, to cover his table
in as sumptuous a manner, and to hang his walls with as
valuable paintings; and in order to do all this, he will
strive to make himself as wealthy as the rich proprietor
who lives near him, and who invites him to his luxurious dwelling.   Not, perhaps, that he imagines that all
this luxury really increases happiness, but because a
plain equipage, a plain house, and a plain dinner would
prove him to be so much poorer, and therefore so much
less influential in society, and therefore so much less
respectable in the eyes of his dependants, than his
wealthy and influential neighbour the landed proprietor.
The luxury of the rich merchant influences the shopkeeper in the same manner, as the luxury of the landed
proprietor influences the merchant.

Each class, down to the shopkeepers, emulates the
richer class, so that the greater the wealth and luxury of
the wealthiest class, the greater will be the competition
of the middle classes.   *This emulation cannot reach the
lower classes, partly because of their inferior intelligence,
and partly because of the utter impossibility of the peasants
of England ever rising in the world, by any exertion* or
present *self-denial, however great.*

Among the middle classes, however, each class in England struggles hard to emulate those above it.   The intensity of exertion necessary to ensure any sort of success
is very great; but the hope of success induces many
to spend the greatest part, and some to spend the whole,
of their lives in endeavouring to effect this end.

In no country in the world is so much time spent in
the mere acquisition of wealth, and so little time in the

enjoyment of life and of all the means of happiness, which God has given to man, as in England.

In no country in the world do the middle classes labour so intensely as here. One would think, to view the present state of English society, that man was created for no other purpose than to collect wealth, and that he was forbidden to gratify the beautiful tastes, with which he has been gifted for the sake of his own happiness. To be rich, with us, is the great virtue, the pass into all society, the excuse for many frailties, and the mask for numerous deformities.

People in England do not ask themselves, how great a variety of pleasure they can obtain by their present incomes; but how good an appearance they can keep up with it, how nearly they can imitate the manners and habits of the great above them, and how soon they can hope to imitate those manners and habits still more closely.

I have been making these remarks, in order the better to describe the difference of German and Swiss society. In these countries there is no *class*, and but few individuals, who are as wealthy as the class of our landed aristocracy. Their richest class is not nearly so wealthy as the wealthiest class of our manufacturers. The reason of this is, that the whole of the fortune accumulated by a man in his lifetime seldom goes on increasing in the hands of his children, and seldom indeed remains undivided in the hands of a successor. It is generally divided at his death among several persons, so that a great fortune or estate does not remain any length of time entire. But a fortune like that of one of our nobles can very rarely be built up by one person. To amass such a fortune generally requires the exertions of several generations, to each of whom the former collector has left his gains undivided and indivisible. Where, therefore, the law does not assist the collector to keep his property together after his own death, very few such immense fortunes can ever be amassed.

As the law does not in foreign countries allow such facilities for keeping accumulated, what has been once collected together, the class of really wealthy men there is consequently very much smaller and very much poorer than in England, and the general style of living is much less costly and luxurious. A man may live respectably and happily, in countries, where the law does not keep up a great model class, for one fourth of the income, which is necessary in England.

The French, the Dutch, the Germans, and the Swiss, look with wonder at the enormous fortunes, and at the enormous mass of pauperism, which accumulate in England side by side. They have little of either extreme. The petty sovereigns and a few nobles and merchants are wealthy; but they form too small a minority to exercise anything like so powerful an influence upon the society of those countries, as the numerous body of the English landlords do upon English society.

The consequence is, that the middle classes of those countries are not generally brought into contact with a class very much richer than themselves, and are not therefore so strongly urged into excessive expenditure by a desire to emulate a wealthy class, as is the case in England.

All classes in Germany, Switzerland, France, and Holland, are therefore satisfied with less income than the corresponding classes in England.   They, therefore, devote less time to labour, and more time to healthy and improving recreation.   The style of living among the mercantile classes of these countries is much simpler than in England, but their enjoyment of life is much greater.   They live not so much as we do to die rich, but to live happy.   They do not strive after appearances nearly so much as we do.   They do not spend so much upon their tables, their equipages, their dress, or the ornaments of their houses, but they spend more time in the enjoyment of life.   They go out oftener into the country, they frequent musical concerts much oftener, they attend the public assemblies much oftener, they associate with one another much more, they keep up more of the olden pastimes and exercises, and they work during fewer hours of the year than we do.

The strain of life and the competition for gain are not nearly so intense with them as with us.

A German or Swiss merchant, or a German or Swiss shopkeeper, trades until he has made enough wherewith to purchase a small estate ; and he then often retires from business to enjoy the remainder of his days in the country upon his own land, and in his own house, and to bring up his family amid the improving influences of a rural life.

The hope of obtaining a small estate of his own forms a very strong inducement to exertion and economy, and is a much more agreeable and enticing prospect than the hope of merely leasing a country house at some future day ever offers to a shopkeeper in our own country.

A man whose wealth alone would not entitle him to a third-rate place in English society, might, as far as his wealth is concerned, move in the highest ranks of German society. People who feel that the richest class of a country are not far removed above them, care less to devote their whole lives to destroy the remaining disparity, than those whom a long and almost insurmountable distance separates from the wealth and influence of the richer class.

This intense competition of our merchants and manufacturers, and of the middle classes of our country, to emulate the wealth of the superior class, who are upheld by the laws in the continued enjoyment of undiminished and accumulating riches, reacts upon the poor in a very injurious manner. The stronger the desire of the middle classes to amass wealth and to live luxuriously, the more will they endeavour to deduct from the wages, which they are obliged to pay out to those below them ; the more will they deal hardly with the poor ; and the more difficult will it be for the poor to earn their subsistence.

In a country, too, where, as in England, the social arrangements are such, as to deprive one class of the poor, viz., the peasants, of any means of improving their condition in life, excepting by leaving their homes, this competition among the middle classes of society will press and does press upon the labourers with peculiar hardship. The man, who fancies he is obliged to keep up a certain style, in order not to be much less respectable in appearances than his wealthier neighbour, will necessarily be obliged to reduce his payments to those around him as much as possible. His servants and labourers cannot expect to receive from him more than the lowest hire at which, by hard bargaining, he can procure their services. And even if the rate of money-wages in a country is high, yet a middle class so circumstanced will get more work out of their labourers in comparison with the wages given them, than any middle class not similarly circumstanced can do. Thus, in our manufacturing districts, although the rate of wages has been always on the average high, yet the labours of the operatives, as well as of the masters themselves, have been intense in the extreme. So that if we consider the work, which one of our operatives does for his week's hire, and compare it with what a foreign operative does for his week's hire, although the amount in value may be greater in the one case than in the other, yet I believe it would be found that the Englishman did not get nearly so much in proportion to his labour as the foreigner.

The objects which strike foreigners with the greatest astonishment, on visiting our country, and of which they see nothing at all similar in their own countries, are, —

1. The enormous wealth of the highest classes of English society.

2. The intense and continued labour and toil of the middle and lowest classes. And,

3. The frightful amount of absolute pauperism among the lowest classes.

The first of these singularities of English society produces the second, and contributes greatly to the production of the third, whilst it is itself occasioned almost entirely by the effect of the old feudal laws, which restrain the subdivision and circulation of the great properties, after they have once been accumulated.

This system is admirably well adapted for heaping up enormous masses of wealth in a state. I believe that no such masses as now exist in England, in the hands of some of the higher classes, could be heaped up under any other system than that now pursued ; but it should be remembered how, side by side with these heaps, pauperism goes on increasing.

Could we regard the poor as only the machines, by which we were to create our wealth, even then I should doubt, whether we should be economically prudent to be so careless as we now are, about the condition of the machines; but when we regard them as immortal beings of the same origin, and created for the same destiny as the richer and more intelligent classes of society, then such a system as the one we now maintain, appears to be, not only open to economical objections, but reprehensible and obnoxious on higher and more serious grounds.

Look at Ireland, where this system of great estates, and great ignorance, has been so long in force; what is the result in that unhappy country?

The whole of the land is in the hands of a small body of proprietors. The estates of these proprietors are so affected by the real property laws, that very few of them are able to sell any part of their lands.

The richer proprietors live in England, and upon the Continent, and spend all the produce of their estates, — except the small quantity which is paid to the cultivators of the land, — among foreign people. The trade of the provincial towns of Ireland is consequently nearly extinguished. All the people, whom that trade would employ, and all the people, who would be employed as servants, grooms, gardeners, and ministers to the wants of a resident class of landed gentry, and who would be fed and clothed with what feeds and clothes similar classes in foreign lands, find no employment in such channels, and are obliged to compete for work with the already poorly-remunerated agricultural labourers. There are consequently more labourers than there is labour or food for them. English grooms, English tailors, English shopkeepers, English servants, English workmen of all kinds are ministering in an English town to the wants of the Irish landlords, and are dividing among them the produce of the Irish estates, — which produce ought to be divided among the Irish labourers and Irish shopkeepers.

Of the poorer classes of Irish landlords, who live in Ireland, most have received their estates from their ancestors heavily burdened with mortgages and incumbrances, whilst others have burdened their estates themselves by their own too lavish expenditure.

Nearly all are in such a condition, that they have no ready capital wherewith to cultivate their lands, or to make any improvements; nearly all have quantities of waste lands upon their hands, which they cannot cultivate themselves, and which they cannot sell to the farmers to cultivate, because of the way in which former proprietors have been allowed, by our feudal laws of real property, to arrange the property, and to divide the whole estate in the land among several successors and incumbrancers.

Most of these landlords have had their hands tied so long, that they have grown, under the long continuance of this system, incapable of taking any step towards improvement, even if the law did not prevent them.

The farmers and the peasants, feeling that they cannot get leases, that they cannot buy land, or obtain any security for investment in land, owing to the expense of conveyancing, to the intricate titles of most of the estates, and to the inability of the landlords to sell, have lost all interest in the improvement of the land, all hope of ever improving their own condition, all respect or sympathy with the government, which supports this system, and are one united mass of increasing, though smouldering, disaffection. They long for Repeal ; many even of the squires, the greater mass of the shopkeepers, and nearly all the farmers of the south of Ireland, are unanimous with the peasants in wishing for Repeal. They feel, that they cannot be worse off than they are at present. They see no sign in the English horizon of a change. They would all sooner try an Irish tempest, than stagnate and suffer as at present. And I confess I think them right.

If it had not been that our manufactures and our commerce have afforded an outlet for the peasants of our villages, and have continually diminished the strain upon the labour markets of the rural districts, the con-

dition of the English peasants at the present day would
have been just as bad, as the present state of the Irish
peasantry. But in England, the peasant can always find
an opening in our commercial towns, and in our manufacturing districts. There is a constant emigration going
on in England, from the villages to the towns; and the
competition for labour in the villages is therefore always
far less than in Ireland, where it is so much more difficult than in England, for a peasant to emigrate to a place
where labour is wanted. The towns in Ireland are too
poor, and in too lifeless and stationary a condition, to
afford many openings; while England, is a long way off,
and her towns are already too full of the surplus of her
own rural districts to take off all the surplus hands of
Ireland. Besides, the Irish are so demoralised, and are
increasing, owing to their utter demoralisation, at so
rapid a rate, that it would be impossible to take off the
surplus hands, unless we could retard the present rapid
increase of the population.

Let us endeavour to describe the present state of
Ireland in as few words as possible.

Ireland itself is splendidly situated, in a commercial
point of view, commanding the direct route between
Northern Europe and America, with some of the finest
harbours in the world. Its soil is proverbially rich and
fruitful, and has won for it throughout the world the
appellation of the "Emerald Isle." Its rivers are
numerous, large, and well adapted for internal commerce. Its people are, physically and intellectually
considered, one of the most active and restless in the
world.

In every colony of our empire, and among the motley
multitudes of the United States, the Irish are distinguished by their energy, their industry, and their success. They make as good soldiers, colonists, and railway constructors as any other people. *They are industrious and successful every where but in Ireland.**

Nearly one third of this rich island is wholly uuculti-
vated, and is nothing more than bogs, moors, and waste
lands; the cultivation of the remaining part is generally
of the most miserable kind. Most of the great proprietors have no spare capital to invest in the improvement
of their estates, or in bringing any of their waste lands

* The Edinburgh Review of Jan. 1850 bears testimony to this undeniable fact, and says: " The capacity of the Irishman to make a successful
emigrant has been by some denied. On this subject, however, the direct
testimony we possess is stronger than either theory or prejudice. We nee l
only refer our readers to that so conclusively given, and with such remarkable unanimity, by witnesses from all our colonies, examined by the
recent Colonisation Committee. The efficiency and success of the Irish
emigrant in Canada is attested by Mr. Pemberton and Mr. Brydone ; in
New Brunswick, by Mr. Perley ; in Nova Scotia, by Mr. Uniacke ; in the
United States, by Mr. Mintern ; in Australia and Van Diemen's Land
by Colonel Mitchell, Colonel Macarthur, Mr. Verner, Mr. Cunningham,
Mr. Besnard, Mr. Justice Therry, and the Rev. C. D. Lang. A yet
more recent witness is Count Strzelecki, who observes, in his evidence
given before the Committee of the House of Lords on the Irish Poor
Law, — ' The Irishman improves in two or three years by emigrating to
Australia : he acquires habits of industry ; he learns to rely upon himself
more than he does in Ireland ; he has an openness in his character, and
shows all that he can do, while here he does not show it. . . . . .
I saw Irishmen in the United States, in Canada, and in Australia, living
as well as Anglo-Saxons, acquiring their grumbling habits, and thus improving continually their condition. . . . . . This difference may
perhaps be more successfully traced to the consequences of the transplant-
ation from a narrow and confined moral and physical sphere of action, to
a larger space, with more freedom and more cheerful prospects of life,
and of which they have none at home.' "

into cultivation. Few, of even those who have capital, are energetic or intelligent enough to expend it in so rational a manner. Many, if not most, of the resident landlords, in the south and west of Ireland, are a jovial, careless, hunting set of squires, who think and care ten times more about their sports than about their lands or tenants; while the farmers, and under-lessees of the farmers, will not invest capital in the cultivation of their lands, or in reclaiming the bogs, because they have no leases, and no security for the outlay, and because they do not feel sufficient interest in the land of another to induce them to expend their own savings in improving it; but instead of doing so, have often, as is well known, placed their spare capital, from the want of a better investment, in the banks of Ireland or of England. Many of the squires would willingly sell part of their lands, in order to get capital to improve the other part, while nearly all the larger farmers have spare capital, and would willingly and gladly purchase land and improve it, but both parties are prevented by the present laws relating to land.

Nor is civilisation in Ireland merely stationary. It is actually going backwards. In the last few years hundreds of thousands of acres have actually been thrown out of cultivation, owing, on the part of the landlords, to inability to sell, and to want of capital and activity; and, on the part of the farmers, to want of security, and to being prevented purchasing any part of the strictly entailed estates.

Sir Robert Peel, in his great speech in 1849, on Ireland, stated that in one barony, in the county of Cork,

extending over 80,000 acres, *all* the lands were thrown
waste; and that in another locality, the union of Clifden,
the rental of which is 19,000*l.*, there were lands of the
annual value of 9000*l.* thrown out of cultivation.

The great landlords spend most of their time in
England or in Europe, and leave their lands to the management of agents, who have their sub-agents for parts
of the estates, whilst these latter often have their sub-
agents again. Many of the great landlords know little or
nothing of the state of the peasantry or farming on their
estates; they receive as much of their rentals as possible,
in England or abroad, and leave their agents to enrich
themselves too often at the expense of the poor tenantry.

The condition of the peasantry is something which
none, but those who have actually witnessed it for themselves, can possibly realise. At the mercy of sub-agents
of agents of the landlords — with no interest in the soil —
liable to be evicted from their holdings by the agents —
totally uneducated, for the most part —a prey to priests,
who are as much interested in insurrection as themselves — they live more wretchedly, and more nearly
like the vermin of an uncultivated land, than any other
people upon the face of the earth.

Everywhere, even in the most prosperous of the
eastern counties of Ireland, a traveller, as he passes
along the roads, will see, on the roadsides and in the fields,
places which look like mounds of earth and sods, with a
higher heap of sods upon the top, out of which smoke
is curling upwards; and with two holes in the side of
the heap, next the road, one of which is used as the
door, and the other as the window, of the hovel, which

exists beneath this seeming mound of earth. These are the cottages of the peasantry! Inside, there is scarcely ever more than one room, formed by the four exterior mud walls; and in these places, upon the mud floor, the families of the peasants live, often without a single piece of furniture, excepting a kettle, in which they boil potatoes, a plate or two, a wooden bench, and a heap of straw in the corner of the hovel. In this hole, human beings — men, women, boys, and girls — all live and sleep together, and herd with the pigs they fatten. Gaunt ragged figures, whose clothes hardly hang about them so as to hide their nudity, crawl out of these sties, and plant the ground around their cabins with potatoes, which generally constitute the only food of the inmates throughout the year, or infest, as beggars, the thoroughfares, or swell the rebellious gatherings of the peasantry.

Let Sir Robert Peel describe this state of things. He is not generally given to exaggeration. Speaking of the testimony of the Irish Commission, Sir Robert says, — " They said, ' they regretted to be obliged to add, that though agricultural improvements were rapidly advancing, yet in most parts of Ireland there was not a corresponding advance in the condition of agricultural labourers; that they continued to suffer the greatest privations; that they were badly housed, badly fed, badly clothed, and badly paid.' In the second volume of a useful digest of the evidence on the occupation of land, reference is made to a very curious document, attached to the census made in 1841. Those who prepared that census divided the houses of Ireland into four different classes, and the result showed that the lowest of the four classes was composed of mud cabins, with one room only. They then ascertained what proportion of the inhabited houses of Ireland consisted of that fourth class. Observe, this report was made at a period which could have reference to no date posterior to the year 1844 ; and it states, that ' it may be assumed that the fourth class of houses are generally unfit for human habitation ; and yet it would appear that, in the best circumstanced county in this respect, the county of Down, $24\frac{7}{10}$ per cent., or one-fourth of the population, live in houses of this class; while in Kerry the proportion is $66\frac{7}{10}$ per cent., or about two-thirds of the whole ; and taking the average of the whole population, of Ireland, as given by the census commissioner, we find that in the rural districts about 43 per cent. of the families, and in the civic districts, about 36 per cent., inhabit houses of the fourth class.'

" But I should wish particularly to take the proportion of that part of Ireland, to which I more particularly refer, that part in which those distressed unions are now depending upon a few for the support of a great number of the inhabitants. I should wish to take the proportion there. In Donegal the number of the fourth class is 47 per cent. ; in Leitrim, 47 per cent. ; in Roscommon, 47 per cent. ; in Sligo, 50 per cent. ; in Galway, 52 per cent. ; in Limerick, 55 per cent. ; in Cork, 56 per cent. ; in Clare, 56 per cent. ; in Mayo, 62 per cent. ; in Kerry, 66 per cent. THE LOWEST, OR FOURTH CLASS, REMEMBER, COMPRISES ALL MUD CABINS, HAVING BUT ONE ROOM. In the three last counties, Clare, Mayo, and Kerry, the proportion of every one hundred families, who occupy houses built of mud, and having only a single room, is, 56 per cent. in Clare, 62 per cent. in Mayo, and 66 in Kerry. Now that was the state of affairs before Ireland was visited by that great calamity, the first appearance of which was in the Autumn of 1845."

But horrible and shameful as this state of things is, it is by no means the full extent of the evil. Not only are the majority of the Irish condemned to exist in such hovels, as Sir Robert Peel describes, but even their tenure of these disgusting cabins is insecure. If they do not pay their rent for them at the proper time, they are liable to be turned adrift, even in the middle of the night, into the bleak road, without a shelter, and with their helpless wives and children. No notice is necessary; no notice is given. The miserable tenants are subject to the tender mercies of a bailiff, without any remedy or appeal, except to Heaven.

More than 50,000 such evictions took place in 1849. More than 50,000 families were, in that year, turned out from their wretched dwellings, without pity and without a refuge!

Is it a wonder that fathers, and husbands, and brothers should often be driven to madness, desperation, and revenge?

A very able man, who travelled through Ireland in the autumn of 1849, says: — " In passing through some half dozen counties, Cork (especially in the western portions of it), Limerick, Clare, Galway, and Mayo, you see thousands of ruined cottages and dwellings of

the labourers, the peasants, and the small holders of
Ireland.   You see from the road-side twenty houses at
once with not a roof upon them.   I came to a village
not far from Castlebar, where the system of eviction
had been carried out only a few days before.   Five
women came about us as the car stopped, and on
making inquiry, they told us their sorrowful story.
They were not badly clad; they were cleanly in appearance; they were intelligent; they used no violent language, but in the most moderate terms told us
that on the Monday week previously those five houses
had been levelled.   They told us how many children
there were in their families : I recollect one had eight,
another had six; that the husbands of three of them
were in this country for the harvest; that they had
written to their husbands to tell them of the desolation
of their homes.   And I asked them, ' What did the
husbands say in reply?'   They said ' they had not been
able to eat any breakfast!'   It is but a simple observation, but it marks the sickness and the sorrow, which came
over the hearts of those men, who here were toiling for
their three or four pounds, denying themselves almost
rest at night, that they might make a good reaping
at the harvest, and go back that they might enjoy it in
the home which they had left.   All this is but a faint
outline of what has taken place in that unhappy country.
Thousands of individuals have died within the last two
or three years, in consequence of the evictions which
have taken place; evictions, too, which are altogether
unnecessary for the salvation of the proprietor, and
which are as likely to produce ruin to his property as

any other course, which he or his forefathers have heretofore taken with respect to it. But there have been
recent outrages committed in Ireland. A respectable
gentleman was shot in open day, on the Sunday morning at eleven o'clock, whilst on his way to church —
shot, too, while two men were within two or three
yards of him; one, in fact, with his shoulder against
his saddle. And the man who fired was seen going
through the garden and escaping; while two men were
walking rapidly over a bog, supposed to be the assassins
making their escape. Why were not these men apprehended? Because of the rottenness that there is in the
state of society in these districts; because of the sympathy, which there is on the part of the great bulk of
the population with those who, by these dreadful acts of
vengeance, are supposed to be the conservators of the
rights of the tenant, and supposed to give him that protection, which imperial legislation has denied. The first
thing that ever called my attention to the condition of
Ireland was the reading an account of one of these outrages. I thought of it for a moment, but the truth
struck me at once; and all I have seen since confirms
it. When law refuses its duty—when government denies
the right of a people—when competition is so fierce for
the little land, which the monopolists grant to cultivation in Ireland — when, in fact, for a bare potatoe, millions are scrambling, these people are driven back from
law and from the usages of civilisation to that which is
termed the law of nature, and if not of the strongest,
the law of the vindictive; and in this case the people of
Ireland believe, to my certain knowledge, that it is only

by these acts of vengeance, periodically committed, that they can hold in suspense the arm of the proprietor and the agent, who, in too many cases, if he dared, would exterminate them.   At this moment there is a state of war in Ireland. Don't let us disguise it from ourselves; there is a war between landlord and tenant; a war as fierce, as relentless, as though it were carried on by force of arms.   There is a suspicion between landlord and tenant which is not known between any class of people in this country: and there is a hatred, too, which I believe, under the present and past system, which has been pursued in Ireland, can never be healed or eradicated.   Of course, under a state of things like this, industry is destroyed, the rights of property are destroyed, and at this moment landlords in Ireland of the most excellent character, and of the most just intentions, cannot make those dispositions of their property, which are necessary even for the advantages of the tenants themselves in some cases, because of the system of terror, which prevails through many of the counties."*

Such is the frightful, the appalling result of our long government of Ireland.   We have made it — I speak it deliberately — we have made it the most degraded and the most miserable country in the world, and we wonder, that the Irish should rebel against such a system of misgovernment! All the world is crying shame upon us, but we are equally callous to our ignominy and to the results of our misgovernment.   Hitherto we have done nothing to effect a change.

A statute was passed in the past year (1849) to

* See Mr. Bright's late remarkable speech on the state of Ireland.

enable proprietors of estates in Ireland, which are burdened with mortgages and certain other charges mentioned in the act, to sell the estates, and to confer a good and indisputable title upon the purchasers.

This statute is a very good one, so far as it will affect the state of landed property in Ireland, but its effect will be a *very* limited one. It leaves the powers of entailing and settling lands untouched; it does not create any system of registration of titles; it does not attempt to simplify the conveyance of land, except in a few cases; and it will not, therefore, enable the shopkeepers, or the farmers, or the peasants of Ireland to purchase land. It will not create a class of yeomanry farmers, or a class of peasant proprietors. It will not tend to render the lower classes of Ireland either more prosperous or more conservative in their tendencies. The only effect it can have will be, to change the proprietors of some of the more heavily burdened Irish estates. This will be certainly an advantage, so far as it goes, inasmuch as it will transfer some of the land from careless, poor, and ignorant men, to persons having capital and intelligence to improve it. But this is but a drop in the ocean, as compared to what Ireland requires. Ireland requires a class of yeomanry, who would be naturally interested in the preservation of order, in the improvement of the cultivation of the soil, and in reclaiming the millions of acres of rich land, which now lie waste and uncultivated. Ireland requires a law, which would enable the peasants, by industry, prudence, and economy, to acquire land; which would thus interest in the peasantry the support of the government, and in the preservation of social tranquillity; which would dissipate that hopelessness and despair, which now drives the fine peasantry of that noble island into disaffection and rebellion; which would make the Irish peasant as active and as successful in Ireland, as he is throughout our colonies and the United States; which would induce him to settle on the waste lands at home, in order to cultivate them, instead of escaping to distant wilds to effect there what is so much wanted at home; and which would offer him the same inducements to exert himself, and to practise sobriety, economy, self-denial, and industry, as present themselves to him as soon as he lands in North America. And we want a law, which would bring capital to the land and land to the capitalist.

This can only be effected in the same way, as the same result was effected in Prussia and throughout Germany and Switzerland, viz. by freeing the land of Ireland from the action of the entail laws; by forbidding all settlements, entails, and devises, which would withdraw land from the market beyond the life of the person making such settlement, entail, or devise, or which would prevent any proprietor of land having a life-interest therein to sell the land; and by creating a system of registration of all conveyances, deeds, leases, mortgages, and writings affecting any piece of land, which would render the investigation of the titles of estates perfectly simple, and which, combined with the diminished power of entailing, settling, or otherwise affecting land, would render the transfer of land as cheap and secure, as the sale of a piece of furniture, cloth, or other article.

This would soon lead to the following results : —

1. Proprietors of heavily mortgaged estates would sell at least part of their lands.

2. Careless and extravagant owners would sell part of their estates to supply means for the gratification of their tastes, or for the payment of their debts.

3. Many landowners, who prefer to live in England, would sell their estates.

4. All landowners, who possess waste lands capable of cultivation, would sell at least part of their waste lands.

5. Merchants, farmers, and peasants would purchase farms or gardens ; and in this way, land would get into the hands of persons, willing and able to spend capital or labour upon its improvement, and a large class of small proprietors would immediately spring up throughout every county, all interested in social order, in the improvement of the land, and in the prosperity of the country ; and in this way, the face of Ireland, and the character of the Irish, would, in the course of a few years, be entirely changed.

Until we can find an Irish Stein or an Irish Hardenburg, who will grant the Irish people free trade in land, by *preventing* its being tied up by settlements, and who will interest the peasants and farmers of Ireland in preserving the public tranquillity and in improving the agriculture of the country, by enabling them to purchase land, we shall have done *nothing*, positively *nothing*, for Ireland.

The expenses of procedure under this new statute will be so great, owing to the intricacy of the titles of

the Irish estates, (an intricacy which can never be
diminished, so long as the law confers such extraordinary powers of disposition on landed proprietors), and
the cases, in which relief is granted by the act are, comparatively speaking, so very few, that the effect of the
statute will never be felt by those classes, who most
stand in need of relief, viz., the farmers, the shopkeepers,
and the peasants of Ireland.

Now there are three facts, of which there can be no
doubt: the *first* is, that the peasants of France and
Germany were, fifty years ago, subjected to a social
system precisely similar to that now in force in Ireland;
the *second* is, that at that time, the condition of the
peasants of France and Germany was, according to the
testimony of Arthur Young, and many other eye-
witnesses, at least as bad, as the condition of the Irish
people in the present day; and the *third* fact is, that
since the old system of great estates and great ignorance
has been changed, and since the system, which I have
described has been put into force, the condition of the
peasants of these countries has changed most undeniably,
and, according to the unanimous testimony of all
writers, immensely for the better.

There can be no doubt that in Germany, the Tyrol,
Switzerland, France, Denmark, Belgium, and Holland,
where a system diametrically contrary to our own
has been now for forty years maintained; where all
the peasants and labourers are well educated; where
good schools and thoroughly efficient and well trained
teachers are to be found in every village and town;
where no laws prevent the natural subdivision and

sale of land, or promote its unnatural and extremely
unhealthy accumulation in a few hands; and where
every peasant and small shopkeeper knows, that, if he
is prudent and economical, he may purchase a farm; I
say there can be no doubt that in these countries the
peasants are less pauperised, more intelligent, more
hopeful, prudent, prosperous, and happy, more conservative, and more virtuous than they are in our own
country.

I have always felt convinced, and I repeat my conviction here again, that if we wish to make an Irish
labourer as prosperous, prudent, independent, conservative, and virtuous, as a German, Swiss, or Dutch
peasant-proprietor is, we must legislate for the one, as
the German, Swiss, and Dutch governments have long
since legislated for the other. We must deprive every
Irish proprietor henceforward of the power of preventing the sale of the fee-simple of his estates at any
time after his death; we must introduce a good system
of registration into that country, and render every
future conveyance, which is not registered immediately
after the making, entirely ineffectual and worthless;
we must facilitate the sale of estates, which are now
kept out of the market by old mortgages, settlements,
and wills; we must greatly increase the efficiency of
the Irish system of national education, by building
good colleges for the education of the teachers, and by
facilitating the erection of schools and the support of
teachers in poor districts unable to raise local funds;
and until these measures have begun to take effect, we

must maintain public tranquillity and order by the
continued presence of a strong military force.

By these means, we should enable and induce the
farmers, and many of the peasants, to buy land; we
should thus create a class of conservative yeomanry, interested in the preservation of public peace and public
order; we should soon bring all the bogs and moors
into cultivation; we should stimulate the people to
labour, in order to make themselves proprietors; we
should induce habits of prudence, self-denial, and industry; we should improve the system of farming; we
should make capital flow into Ireland, and we should
clothe it with a new and with a progressive civilisation.

Before closing this chapter, I shall show, as briefly
as possible, —

14. *What several of the greatest Writers of France think,*
    of the Results of the Subdivision of Land in that
    Country.

In France a system exactly opposite to our own is
in force. The law endeavours to force the subdivision
of the land. It gives every child of a deceased parent
a *right* to a certain share of all the land, of which the
father dies possessed, and that, too, even if the father
wishes to devise it in a different manner.

An owner of land in France may sell it as he pleases,
or give it to whomsoever he chooses, or do what he
likes with it, *during his own life,* but he cannot devise
it as he pleases.   On his death, the law gives each child

a right to a certain portion of the property of which his father dies possessed, whether the father has made a will or not.

While in England the law gives the proprietors of land such extraordinary powers of restraining the sale of their estates, long after their own deaths, as to cause the accumulation of great estates in few hands, and to prevent the shopkeepers and peasants buying land excepting in a few instances; in France, on the other hand, the law forces, *as far as it can,* the subdivision of the estates.

Each of these extremes is objectionable in an economical point of view, although I believe the English system to be the most injurious of the two, in its effects upon the majority of the people.

The great problem to solve is, to devise a middle system, viz., a code of laws, which would prevent any land being rendered unsaleable for any period, except while held in trust for an infant; which would allow a parent to devise his land *in fee**, but only *in fee*, to any person or persons he pleases ; which would prevent the owner leaving different interests in the same piece of land to different persons, to come into possession at successive periods; and which would also, by means of an effective and cheap system of registration, render the conveyance of a piece of land simple, cheap, and secure. This could be easily effected.

I have said that the French law *forces* subdivision *as far as it can do so.*

It cannot do so in reality, for it is found that where

---

* *i. e.* so as to give the devisee full powers of sale and disposition.

an estate is too small to be divided further with advantage, one of the children buys the whole, and pays the other children an equivalent in money for their shares ; or the whole estate is sold to a stranger, and the proceeds are divided among the children, in the proportion in which the estate would have been divided.

From statistics given by our great economist Mr. Mill, in the Appendix to the first volume of his " Principles of Political Economy," it would seem, that the average size of the holdings of the 3,900,000 *smallest* proprietors of France is between *five* and *eight and a half* acres.   And as Mr. Mill says, " suppose as bad an agriculture as exists anywhere in Western Europe, and judge whether a single family, industrious and economical as the French of the poorer classes are, and enjoying the entire produce of from five to eight and a half acres, subject to a payment of only ten-pence an acre to the government, can be otherwise than in a very desirable condition ;" and Mr. Mill then goes on to show, from a series of very interesting statistics, *" that there is every reason to infer, from these general data, that the morcellement (or subdivision of the estates) is making no progress," while in many parts of France it is actually diminishing.*

As one proof, among others, of the truth of this conclusion, Mr. Mill gives the following interesting facts.   He says, " A new cadastre, or survey and valuation of lands, has been in progress for some years past. In *thirty-seven* cantons, taken indiscriminately through France, the operation has been completed; in *twenty-one* it is nearly complete.   In the *thirty-seven,* the côtes

foncières *, which were 154,266 at the last cadastre (in
1809 and 1810), have only increased by 9,011, being less
than six per cent., in considerably more than thirty
years, while in many of the cantons *they have considerably diminished.* From this increase is to be subtracted
all which is due to the progress of building, during the
period, as well as to the sale of public and communal
lands. In the other twenty-one cantons, the number of
côtes foncières is not yet published, but the number of
parcelles, or separate bits of land, has *diminished* in the
same period; and among these districts, is included the
greater part of the banlieue of Paris, one of the most
minutely divided districts in France, in which the morcellement has actually *diminished* by no less than sixteen
per cent."

This system was embodied by Napoleon and his
ministers in the Code Napoleon; and in whatever country the supremacy of the great Emperor was established,
there he and his ministers immediately introduced this
law; so convinced were they of the enormous benefits,
which would accrue to the peasants from such a system,
and of the popularity to be gained by the introduction
of this change. Several countries, and, among others,
the Prussian Rhine Provinces, have retained these laws
ever since; and the peasants of those lands still bless
the Emperor's memory, for the vast boon he conferred
upon them. It was, indeed, a great, bold, and ably-
devised measure. Napoleon knew, how these laws would
reinvigorate the people; he knew, how the peasants were

* *Two* côtes foncières, or separate accounts with the land-tax, cor-
respond to a *single proprietor.*

shackled and demoralised by the feudal laws; he knew
how thankful the peasants, and even the lower part of the
middle classes, would be, to be enabled to obtain land;
and he therefore adopted the best possible plan for rendering himself and France popular with those countries
which they conquered: he freed the people from the
feudal laws, and enabled the peasants to become proprietors of the soil, on which they laboured. It is the
recollection of this fact, that accounts, in a great measure, for the singular esteem, with which Napoleon's
memory is cherished by the people, in many parts of
Europe. He was their deliverer.

Reichensperger says, " All have acknowledged, that
the wonderful manner, in which the prosperity of France
has increased since 1790, notwithstanding the tremendous wars and revolutions they have passed through, is
entirely owing to the laws, which now regulate landed
property in that country; that it is entirely owing
to this cause, that the land of France nourishes at the
present day thirty-four millions of people, IN A BETTER
MANNER than it used to nourish twenty-five millions;
and that its people, by the increase of their wealth, pay,
with less imposed taxation, 1300 millions of francs annually, when the old monarchy fell, because it attempted
to raise 500 millions of francs annually."

It is worthy of remark, what a great array of cele-
brated politicians, economists, and literary men of
France, after having personally viewed the effects of the
French system, have written in its favour. After Na-
poleon, its legislator, follow as its defenders, Sismondi,
Troplong, Say, De Tracy, Droz, Chevalier, Ch. Dupin,
Count Gasparin, Count Villeneuve-Bargemont, Tissot,

Chaptal, Passy, Buret, Mathieu de Bombasle, De Carné, De Barante, Morel de Vindé, Moreau de Jonnés, and many others of less note; besides our own English writers, Mill, Laing, Howitt, and others; and the German politicians and writers, Stein, Hardenburg, Thaer, Reichensperger, Dieterici, and others.

Vauban, Mirabeau, Arthur Young, and many other writers, have severally left us very graphic descriptions of the state of the French peasantry, prior to the outbreak of the first Revolution, when the land belonged to the great nobles and the church, and when the peasants and farmers had scarcely ever any chance of acquiring any. They represent them, as reduced to the lowest grade of poverty and civilisation; as badly fed, scarcely covered with rags, wretchedly housed, and only removed one step from famine, to which crowds fell victims in times of even moderate scarcity.

The celebrated Vauban, in 1698, describes their condition as follows [*] : — " It is certain, that the mass of pauperism is now extremely great; and that if no aid is afforded, the poor, who have no means of assisting themselves, will sink into a depth of pauperism, out of which they will never again be raised. The great high roads, and the streets of the towns and villages, are full of beggars, who are driven out by hunger, and want of everything. . . . . *Almost a tenth of the population are as poor as beggars, and actually beg. Of the remaining nine-tenths, five are unable to give alms, because they are themselves reduced to almost the same plight, and of the remaining four-tenths, three are in a very miserable condition.* . . . ."

* Quoted by Reichensperger, p. 376.

And although, as Reichensperger observes, when Vauban wrote thus, the population of France amounted to only sixteen millions, while now it amounts to more, than thirty-four millions; yet, notwithstanding, the condition of the poor is now immeasurably superior to what it then was in every respect.

That this miserable state of things had not improved in 1760, we learn from Quesnay, who informs us, that at that time, of thirty-six million acres of arable land in France, thirty millions were cultivated by little farmers, so miserably poor, that their landlords were obliged to advance them oxen, seed, and even money, to be repaid at the next harvest.*

Arthur Young describes the misery of the peasants of France in his time, by comparing it to that of the Irish labourers; he says emphatically, " *It reminded me of the miseries of Ireland.*"

But since that time everything has been changed in France. The labourers have been enabled to purchase lands. The extraordinary powers of the landed proprietors have been taken away. The conveyance of land from man to man has been rendered almost as simple, as the sale of so many yards of cloth in a draper's shop. The peasants have become proprietors of the farms, on which they used to labour as tenants-at-will. The question, which all honest men ought to seek now to answer for themselves is, has this system made the people happier? I am convinced it has done so. Let us see what the French writers themselves say.

* See Reichensperger, p. 376.

SISMONDI * says, — " France underwent a Revolution, at a time when the great mass of the population was deprived of property, and consequently of the benefits of civilisation. But this Revolution has, after causing many miseries, bequeathed to posterity many blessings; and one of the greatest of these is the guarantee, that such a scourge can never again afflict the land. The Revolution has wonderfully increased the number of the landowners. There are now (1819), more than 3,000,000 families, comprising 15,000,000 individuals, who possess estates of their own, upon which they live. So that more than half the nation are interested, for their own sakes, in upholding the rights of all. . . . . The desire of the peasants to become landowners, was accomplished by a great deed of violence, viz., by the confiscation of national property of every kind. The miseries of wars, both foreign and civil, are no doubt evils which our nature dreads, as it does floods and earthquakes. But as soon as the scourge has ceased, we ought to rejoice if any good result has been effected : *and in this case, the good which was effected could not most certainly have been more valuable or more certain of duration.* The breaking up of the great estates proceeds daily ; daily are great estates sold, with advantage to the public, to persons who formerly farmed them, and who improve their cultivation. The nation is still removed from having reaped all the advantages, which it may expect from this division of the land, since habits are only slowly formed, and because the spirit of order, of economy, of cleanli-

* Sismondi, Nouv. Principes, liv. iii. c. 3., quoted by Reichensperger.

ness, and of elegance, can only follow a long enjoyment of the new order of things."

In another place he says *—" Whilst the condition of the agricultural labourers in England proceeds rapidly towards disorganisation, and is already disturbed in the country districts, *the peasants of France are improving and rising in the social scale;* they are establishing their prosperity on a sure foundation, and without giving up labouring with their own hands; they are enjoying great prosperity; they are receiving intellectual cultivation, and are beginning, although but slowly, to avail themselves of the discoveries of science. In fact, the condition of agriculture, and of the agricultural classes in France, is as prosperous as the present political circumstances of the country permit."

REICHENSPERGER says, that the comparative results of the English and French systems may be inferred from the fact, that in every 100 inhabitants, there are in France, according to Lawätz, 7, but, according to Villeneuve, only 5 paupers; in Prussia, according to Schmidt, $3\frac{1}{2}$ paupers; while in England there are from 16 to 20!

BURET, who visited England prior to laying a report on pauperism and its causes before the Institute of France, says that in France there is *poverty,* but in England there is *misery.*

TROPLONG, one of the ablest of the living lawyers of France, speaks in the highest terms of the results of freeing land from all restrictions preventing its sale,

* Nouv. Princ. liv. iii. ch. 8.

and thus enabling the peasants to acquire. " This result," he says *, "appears to me a fortunate one, when
considered politically, economically, or socially : it is
good that labour should reap its own fruits ; it is good
that the labourer should be enabled to attain a position
of independence and of certainty ; it is especially good
in a society of democratic tendencies, that firm foundations of social order and strong conservative interests
should be formed. This peasant proprietor class has the
conservative feelings of a landed aristocracy, without
their injurious luxury and extravagance ; it is equally
active and successful, but less ambitious. No other
class has so much to lose in the bloody game of revolutions. The state is always certain to find in it the
elements of order, and the spirit of industry and peace."

I have no need to observe how singularly these remarkable words have been verified in the late French
Revolution. The peasant proprietors have been animated, throughout nearly the whole of France and
Germany, with the best possible spirit. The demagogues failed to incite them to sedition by any pro-
mises. The people felt they were proprietors, and that
they had something to lose. They have universally
shown themselves in favour of the most liberal reforms
in the political regulations, but extremely adverse to
anything like disorder and strife.

LE COMTE CHAPTAL says†, — "Before the Revolution (of 1789) the land of France belonged to three

* Reichensperger, p. 379.
† Des Progrès de l'Industrie Agricole et Manufacturière en France,
v. ii. p. 168.

very different classes of *possessors*. The first, consisted of persons, who had scarcely any interest in the amelioration of the lands; the second, consisted of rich persons, who lived in the great cities or at court, and troubled themselves very little about the improvement of their estates; the third, consisted of a great number of little farmers, who rented a small farm, but received so small a part of the returns of their labour, as scarcely to supply their necessities, and who neither possessed intelligence nor money enough to undertake improvements. Now, all is changed. There are no longer any landowners, who do not themselves, either from necessity or interest, take the greatest pains to improve the cultivation of their lands. The tolerably even apportionment of the land-tax, the repeal of a great number of oppressive and injurious customs, *the division of the land among a great number of owners,* have stimulated industry throughout the country, and introduced improvements, which have raised French agriculture to a high degree of perfection." In another work, Chaptal speaks, in a yet more decided tone, of the good results of the division of the land in France. He says *, — " The wonderful change of property, which has taken place in the last thirty years, and the creation of a great number of proprietors, must necessarily have led to an improvement of agriculture. A long experience has shown, that the new proprietor of a plot of land is much more earnest about its cultivation than the former one was; he studies to increase its produce, and shuns no pains to attain this end.

* De l'Industrie Française, quoted by Reichensperger.

He cultivates every bit of land, which seems capable of producing, and does not rest, until he has perfected all possible improvements. Formerly, there were estates in France of very great size, the produce of each of which scarcely served for the nourishment of a single family ; *circumstances have caused their division, every part of them has been brought under cultivation, and their produce has increased* TENFOLD. Proofs of the truth of this assertion may be found in all parts of France. . . . When one compares the present cultivation of the land with that of 1789, one is astonished at the improvement which has taken place. Harvests of all kinds cover the land, a more numerous and stronger race of cattle labour on and manure the land. *Healthy and rich nourishment, clean and comfortable dwellings, and simple but good clothing, have been acquired by the inhabitants of the country ; misery is banished, and general prosperity has arisen, out of the power of disposing freely of the land.*"

And this, be it remembered, is said of a people who, in 1789, were described by Young, as being as miserable as the Irish.

CH. GIRAUD* finds the cause of the present wonderful prosperity of agriculture in France in the system of peasant proprietors.   He is of opinion that the division of landed property, and elevation of the peasants to the position of proprietors, has stimulated the industry of the farmers, and has proved the superiority of cultivation by small over the cultivation by great proprietors.

* Essay on the History of French Jurisprudence in the Middle Ages, published in 1846. See Reichensperger, Die Agrarfrage, p. 383.

De Barante has treated the question of peasant proprietors politically, and he shows, that every regulation, which tends to draw the population from the villages into the towns, is a great political error, as political riots are never begun in the country districts, but in the streets and squares of the towns. "Nothing *," he says, "makes a people calmer or more moral, than the great subdivision of the land, a regulation against which, persons who have more envy than intelligence, have raised a sort of opposition. By means of this division, the whole population become sharers in the public interests; all are made to love peace and order, which are so necessary to their prosperity; the poor man is made economical and saving; he works harder because he works for himself; his life becomes more regular; and he acquires respect for property, because he himself is a proprietor.

" As far as regards national prosperity and the improvement of agriculture, *one must shut one's eyes, if one would not see, how much both have gained by the new order of things.*

" In the greatest communes one finds scarcely ten persons, who do not assist; the soil is, so to speak, cultivated with the spade; it produces like a garden, AND YIELDS A TENFOLD HARVEST. The miseries of poverty are lessened, since every man is able to care for himself and for his family, and from due precaution prepares more than his own family requires. By this means the whole land is covered with small and divided stores, which to-

---

* De Barante des Communes et de l'Aristocratie, quoted by Reichensperger.

gether form a great and excellent safety dépôt. Besides, the great variety of products, which the division of property encourages, assists in diminishing the evils of an insufficient harvest."

DE CARNÉ expresses a very decided opinion, that the subdivision in France has reached its utmost limits, and that, while some of the greater estates are subdivided, many of the smaller ones are reunited; and that the tendency of things is to increase the number of those proprietors who possess middle-sized farms, and to lessen the number of both the large and the extremely small estates throughout the country.[*]

" One of the most recent of the French writers, EUGÈNE BURET, has inquired, with great acuteness, into the causes of poverty in different countries, but he does not find it in the system of small properties. He thinks the state of the agricultural classes of France — whose soil is laboriously but praiseworthily cultivated by a crowd of small proprietors — a happy one, and expresses his conviction, that one chief error in the state of Great Britain is, that a small plot of land cannot be obtained there; while, in France, the too great expense of the system of conveying land, and the too great burden of taxation on the poorer classes, are the only causes, which prevent the country reaping the full benefits of their present system of agriculture."[†]

M. EUGÈNE BURET says: " And yet, although one part of the population of each of the two countries (England and France), — viz., the manufacturing po-

---

[*] De la Democratie aux Etats-Unis et de la Bourgeoisie en France.
[†] Die Agrarfrage, p. 385.

pulation — is subjected to the same economical regulations, we are able to declare, that the majority of the French people will never sink into such distress, as that in which the English poor are plunged, and still less into that more frightful distress, towards which the English poor are rapidly advancing. Happily for us, the two people do not resemble one another, either in their present or in their future. Between them, there is the vast difference of a revolution. One-third only of our poor are employed in manufacturing operations; the other two-thirds live by the cultivation of the soil. This majority of the French population, although generally poor, is in an economical condition, to which it is not possible to compare the condition of the English people. It possesses a considerable part of the soil, upon which it labours, and it is gradually acquiring a greater share of the land, thanks to the law, which divides the lands of the deceased equally among his children. The land does not, with us, belong to a class, distinct from that of the labourers, or to certain privileged persons who are, so to speak, irremovable. The labourers upon the lands in our country are almost all of them elevated to the dignity of proprietors; and, after having lent their arms to the master, who employs them, they are still able to enrich, by their labours and by their intelligence, a small plot of land, which belongs to themselves. In France, there is some land for every one; whilst, in England, the agricultural labourers cannot obtain any, either on hire, or at a very high price. I need not again remind my readers of the peasants of Berkshire, of whom I have already said, that they beg in vain for a little land, in which to plant some potatoes. In Great Britain, the agricultural labourer works for wages, without having any interest in the land upon which he labours. The great estates, and the great farms, condemn him to that condition of dependence, which is the bane of his industry; while the competition of the day-labourers for work — which requires no apprenticeship, but only the exercise of brute force — keeps the wages much below what is necessary for the proper support of the labourers.

" For such a state of things — which is the absolute separation of capital and labour — there is no possible economical remedy. It is more difficult to liberate labourers from dependence upon a proprietor, than to free them from tyranny. In order to conquer civil liberty, force and audacity only are necessary; but to raise the labourers to a better economical position, great intelligence and great riches are necessary. It is necessary for them to become capitalists in their turn; and how can this great work be accomplished, when both the political and the social institutions of a country are opposed to it; when the law protects the feudal estates from the bad management, from the imbecility, and from the folly of the proprietors themselves? The future will show us, what will be the result of the English system.

" In France, the state of the laws relating to property is quite contrary to the state of these laws in England: it is the extreme division. It is, perhaps, the abuse of a good opposed to the extreme of an evil. The system of small proprietors, and of cultivation of small farms, in our country, is opposed to a system of great proprietors and of cultivation of great farms in England. Landed estates pass from hand to hand, and separate and unite in our country with such a strange rapidity, that economists have busied themselves about the evil effects that the extreme division of the soil produces.

" Such is the condition of man in society, that even good principles themselves may degenerate into abuses. But, happily, the inconveniences which result from a good principle badly applied may be diminished, or even destroyed, by wise reforms. Good principles carry in their natural development a remedy for abuses. It is already easy to see, whither the progressive division of the soil will conduct an intelligent nation. It is quite evident, that there is a means of combining the advantages of cultivation on a great scale, with the advantage of that division of the soil, which, in augmenting the number of proprietors, augments progressively the number of individuals directly interested in making the land produce more.

" *The means is, to associate the possessors of neighbouring lands, so as to cultivate them in common in the manner the most economical and advantageous to all the proprietors.* To arrive at this end requires neither revolution nor violence. The natural progress of men and of things must necessarily modify, in this manner, the economical management of the land in France. *En attendant, however, our peasant proprietors are poor, but they are not miserable.*" *

" M. CHEVALIER has, in his lectures upon political

* De la Misère des Classes Laborieuses en Engleterre et en France, tome première, p. 238.

economy, considered the same question, and has laid the greatest weight upon the condition of agriculture. He pleads for a better system of credit, for improvement of roads, means of watering the lands, &c., so as to increase by one-half the produce of the lands; but no complaint ever escapes him of the agriculture of France being injured by too great division; but it is, on the contrary, manifest from his whole system, that he regards this division as a great benefit."[*]

MATHIEU DE BOMBASLE says[†]: "During the last half century has the French system of agriculture been greatly improved; and if a proof of the truth of this were needed, it might be found in the fact, that the *present thirty-three millions of inhabitants obtain a richer and a better nourishment than the twenty-five millions of the old monarchy used to do.* The increase in the value of this year's agricultural products, over that of the first year of this present century, is at least 1500 million francs."

" M. C. DUPIN also rejoices in the increasing number of the small proprietors of land, and recognises it, as a great guarantee for the gradual and steady development of all the resources of the country."[‡]

The next authority upon this subject is that of LE COMTE GASPARIN. His testimony is very able, and very well worth perusal. He says[§], —" If it were really true, that nothing could prevent the progressive subdivision of landed property, that the father's plot of

* Die Agrarfrage, p. 385.
† Spectateur de Dijon, 9th Oct., 1840, quoted in Die Agrarfrage.
‡ Die Agrarfrage, 386.
§ Revue des Deux Mondes, Janvier, 1843.

land would be reduced to a ninth or a twelfth for his grandson, and that after three generations, each Frenchman would only possess $\frac{1}{243}$ of an acre, then we should be all of us obliged to share the doubts of those who oppose our present system ; and to endeavour, in spite of the principles of equality and justice, and of all opposition, to prevent the subdivision of the land. Who, however, does not perceive that the conclusions of those, who prophesy such results, are open to the same objection as the arguments of Malthus ? they are indeed mathematically true, but in practice they are very considerably modified. It is quite true that, as far as the law is concerned, it is possible that the land may go on subdividing *ad infinitum ;* but how do people avail themselves of this legal possibility ? It is true that the numbers of proprietors increase year by year, but one perceives, that this division is effected at the cost of the greater proprietors. The smaller plots do not generally subdivide any further. Although some foolish fellows here and there, when they inherit a share of a little plot, demand to have it divided, yet the generality of the people understand very well the evil of an estate of great circumference but of small contents. In these cases they generally effect an arrangement ; one man takes the whole property, or else one of the prosperous neighbours purchases it and adds it to his own estate ; so that what the system of division had formerly separated are again consolidated. I do not know what takes place in those countries, where the subdivision of land is of recent date, and where experience is wanting; but in my country, where people have gained experience, the great estate divides while small estates are again consolidated, so that the estates assume such a middling size as best suit the real interests of the people. . . . . . In France the small properties flourish, are purchased at high prices, and return a good profit."

LE COMTE VILLENEUVE-BARJEMONT, who acted as préfet in one of the French departments, and who has given great attention to, and made many researches into, the causes of pauperism and the effect of the subdivision of land, declares it to be his opinion that there is no reason to dread an excessive subdivision of the land. He says,—" If any one travels through the agricultural districts of the greatest part of France, where the land is subdivided the most, he will find *few paupers, few beggars,* and *few unemployed persons.* The population is moreover a stronger one, education is not less diffused among them, and their morality is greater."[*]

M. PASSY, in a work entitled " De la Division des Heritages et de l'Influence qu'elle exerce sur la Distribution des Richesses," which was published in 1839 in the " Memoires de l'Académie des Sciences Morales et Politiques," tome ii. 2ᵉ série, p. 183. et seq., opposes the doctrine, that the great subdivision of the land in France is likely to increase beyond its natural limits, so as to pauperise the little proprietors. He proves, that the small estates have just as great a tendency to *unite,* as the larger estates have to *divide.* He shows, that in the twenty years, which elapsed between 1815 and 1835, during which period the population had increased 14 per cent., notwithstanding the continued subdivision

[*] Economie Politique Chrétienne, 1824, v. i. p. 305.

of the greater estates in France, notwithstanding the increase of population ; notwithstanding that the same persons were often entered in many different communal registers as distinct proprietors ; notwithstanding the bringing into cultivation of many waste lands, and notwithstanding the building in the country districts of many manufactories, each of which is registered as standing on a small estate of its own ; the number of the landed proprietors of France only increased 8 per cent.

DE LA FARELLE* says, "that it is an error to suppose that the land is as much subdivided in France as some writers have represented. He says, that the error originated, from calculating all the names entered upon the different communal registers as names of different *individuals,* while in truth the names of very many proprietors are entered many times in different registers, as they possess lands in different communes. He calculates the number of proprietors in France at 5,000,000."

One, however, of the most remarkable testimonies in favour of the system of peasant proprietors is M. Passy's account† of the progress of agriculture in the department de l'Eure, in France, since 1800, when the lands began to divide, and when the peasants began to purchase farms. This department is, as Reichensperger says, singularly fitted to exemplify the results of the peasant proprietor system, inasmuch as it possesses no peculiar advantages over the other agricultural depart-

* Du Progrès Social au Profit des Classes Populaires :—quoted by Reichensperger.

† Journal des Economistes, 1842, p. 44.

ments, and inasmuch as it contains few towns and no great number of manufactories. It is, in truth, simply an agricultural department. We shall not then be acting unfairly or illogically in adopting the results of the peasant proprietor system in this department, as a fair illustration of its general results throughout France. M. Passy gives the following table, which shows that the agricultural products of this department have greatly increased, not only in value but in quantity also, since the peasants were enabled to purchase farms for themselves.

Kinds of Products.	Total Number of Hectolitres or Kilogrammes.		Value of the Products, estimated according to their Mean Price at the Time.	
	1800.	1837.	1800.	1837.
			Francs.	Francs.
Wheat -	1,475,173 Hect.	1,742,729 Hect.	23,502,768	27,883,664
Mixed Grain	289,000 —	419,451 —	3,757,000	5,442,863
Rye - -	136,000 —	211,221 —	1,369,800	2,112,210
Barley -	73,000 —	108,269 —	730,000	1,082,690
Oats - -	578,760 —	1,324,878 —	4,051,320	9,274,146
Buckwheat -	2,350 —	2,914 —	7,050	8,742
Potatoes -	224,000 —	1,221,130 —	672,000	3,663,293
Beetroot -	12,250 —	166,925 —	24,500	332,850
Vineyards -	34,338 —	18,651 —	686,760	373,020
Artificial Meadows -	3,042,025 Kil.	170,130,100 Kil.	91,261	5,108,903
Natural Meadows -	62,729,500 —	96,971,300 —	1,884,785	2,909,139
Gardens -	- -	- -	1,671,000	3,828,400
Cabbages -	6,940 Hect.	33,758 Hect.	152,680	742,676
Wood -	146,640 Kil.	133,200 Kil.	65,988	59,941
Flax - -	1,456,150 —	1,071,760 —	2,912,300	2,143,520
Hemp -	129,600 —	261,090 —	129,600	261,690
Cider - -	733,500 Hect.	926,800 Hect.	5,134,800	6,487,600
Vegetables -	54,210 —	55,856 —	1,084,200	1,117,120
Total -	- -	- -	47,614,812	72,428,364

This table shows, as Reichensperger says, that in the thirty-seven years, which elapsed between 1800 and 1837, the value of the products of the department increased 54 PER CENT., while the population of the department only increased during the same time from 403,506 to 424,762, or little more than 5 PER CENT.; so that in 1800 there was 128 francs' worth of agricultural products per head, while in 1837 there was 162 francs' worth per head.

But it will perhaps be asked, was there not a diminution in the number of cattle fed by the department during these years, to account for this increase in the amount and value of the agricultural products? Quite the contrary; M. Passy says that there was, on the other hand, a great *increase*, as exhibited in the following table: —

Kinds of Cattle.	1800.	1837.	Increase.	Decrease
Horses - -	29,533	51,151	21,618	
Horned Cattle -	50,809	105,745	53,876	
Sheep - -	205,111	511,390	306,279	
Pigs - - -	46,646	49,191	13,545	
Goats - -	292	808	516	
Asses and Mules	6,807	5,961	- -	846

If it is fair to take this department as a sample of the progress of agricultural affairs throughout France, then indeed there can be no longer any doubt of the extraordinary benefits of the system of farming by means of small proprietors.

But whether we take it as a sample or not, it shows, at least, what amazing results it is possible to attain with a small estate system.

The Minister of the Interior to the King of Prussia, in 1843, and the Minister of Statistics in the same country, the latter of whom has lately travelled in the departments of France, to observe the progress of agriculture, — both of them bear witness to the flourishing and improving condition of agriculture in the latter country; and they show, that there are in France 823 agricultural associations, 20 model agricultural institutions, 9 chairs for agricultural professors, and 4 agricultural institutes, founded for the promotion of the study of agriculture. *

Another equally remarkable and incontrovertible testimony in favour of the small proprietor system in France, is the report of the Central Agricultural Congress at Paris, published in the "Journal des Débats," 30th March, 1847, in which the condition of agriculture in France in 1788, when the land was in the hands of a few proprietors, is compared with its present condition.

From that report it appears †, that in the year 1788, only 612 litres of wheat and corn were raised per hectre, and that from 1700 to 1788, that is, during the time when the land was consolidated in the fewest number of hands, agriculture made no progress. While in 1839, only 39 years after the land was divided, 1301 litres of wheat and corn per hectre, i. e., MORE THAN TWICE AS MUCH PER HECTRE AS IN 1788, just before the land was divided, were raised in the *whole* of France, and in many departments, as many as 1400 litres per hectre were raised!

* Reichensperger, Die Agrarfrage, p. 394.
† Die Agrarfrage, p. 395.

According to the same Report also, in 1760, only seven millions of the French people lived on wheat and corn, while in 1843, *twenty millions* of the French people lived on wheat and corn, and the remainder were much better nourished than in the former period.

Is it possible, after such facts as these, to doubt the benefits of the small proprietor system?

Another testimony in favour of this system is that of M. Bertin, sous-préfet of the arrondissement of Fougères, the most eastern district of Brittany. The report upon this arrondissement, published by M. Bertin, in 1846, is quoted by Mr. Mill, in the Appendix to the first volume of his Principles of Political Economy, as follows :—" 'It is only since the peace,' says this intelligent functionary, 'that the agriculture of the arrondissement has made much progress; but from 1815 it has improved with increasing rapidity. If from 1815 1825, the improvement was as one, it was as THREE between 1825 and 1835, and SIX since that period.' At the beginning of the century, little wheat was cultivated, and that little so ill, that in 1809 the produce per hectre was estimated at only 9 hectolitres. At present M. Bertin estimates it at 16. The cattle being better fed and crossed with more vigorous breeds, have increased in size and strength; while in number, horned cattle, between 1813 and 1844, multiplied from 33,000 to 52,000; sheep, from 6,300 to 11,000; swine, from 9,300 to 26,100; and horses, from 7,400 to 11,600! New and valuable manures have been introduced, and have come largely into use. The extent of meadow land has increased, and is increasing, and great attention has of late been paid to its improvement. This testimony comes from an enemy of the morcellement, who, however, states that it is advancing very slowly, and is not likely to advance much further, the coheirs not dividing each parcelle, but either distributing the parcelles among them, or disposing of them by private or public sale. Some farmers, he says, who are also proprietors, have the good sense to sell the few fields which belong to them, in order to increase their farming capital. M. Bertin is an enemy to stall-feeding, which, he says, is not practised in his arrondissement. The increase of live stock is therefore the more remarkable. . . . . Of the food of the inhabitants, he says, not long ago it was composed almost exclusively of milk, buck-wheat cakes, and rye bread, *but has greatly improved in quantity, quality, and variety,* especially in the last ten years, and now consists of *wheaten bread,* or bread of two-thirds wheat and one-third rye, with butter, vegetables, and, 'in good farms,' about a kilogramme (or $2\frac{1}{4}$ lbs.) of pork per week for each person. There is also some consumption of other flesh meats among the labouring people, and the arrondissement contains sixty-three butchers' shops, where fifteen years ago there were not thirty, the increase not being in the towns (or rather town) but in the villages. The clothing of the rural population is substantial, 'and different for every season, which is always a sign of general comfort;' and '*persons in rags are very rare in this arrondissement.*'"

Since this sheet went to the press, a very remarkable paper has been read before one of the scientific societies of Paris, by the well-known statistical writer, M. Moreau de Jonnés, showing in the most striking manner, from a comparison of the statistics of different periods, the remarkable and progressive improvement which has taken place in French agriculture, and in the social condition of the peasants, since the division of the land; but hitherto I have not been able to obtain a copy of it.

There are several points connected with the progress of French agriculture, and the social condition of the French peasantry, upon which all English travellers and all writers are agreed.   They are the following:—

1. It is allowed by all, that the industry of the peasant proprietors is quite marvellous, that they seem to spare no pains, which can by any possibility increase the fertility of their farms, and that it is a wonderful thing to see how enthusiastically both men and women labour on the farms.   Some travellers call this a miserable drudgery.   To me it has always seemed a labour of love and hope, inasmuch as the French peasant knows that he is working, not for a landlord or master, but for himself, and that he and his family will derive all the benefits of every improvement of the productiveness of his farm.   If they did not feel a real pleasure in their work, they would not labour as they do. Misery and the mere fear of starvation do not make men intensely industrious.   All the miseries of the Irish have failed to produce this result.

2. It is allowed by all, that the *cultivation* of the farms of France is very beautiful, and that the fields are cleaned, weeded, manured, and irrigated, as if they were so many gardens.   Each little proprietor knows inti-

mately every square yard of his estate, and is prompted
by his desire to improve the condition of his family,
and, by the interest which, as owner, he feels in his
property, to make it as fertile and productive as possible. The extraordinary manner in which the irrigation
of the land is managed in the southern provinces, and
in which the streams and rivers are made to refresh the
lands in the dry seasons, and the richness of the verdure
and green crops, which the peasants obtain by these
means, are said by all travellers to be very remarkable,
and to testify, in the strongest manner, to the enthu-
siastic industry and enterprise which the division of
property inspires.

3. It is allowed by all travellers, and by all writers
on the subject, that the clothing of the peasantry is very
good and comfortable. Even those who are the most in-
veterately hostile to the division of landed property, bear
evidence to these facts; while all French authorities
concur in stating, that the character of the clothing of the
peasantry has very considerably improved of late years.

Some persons talk of peasant proprietors, as if these
latter could not sell their estates, even if they found
that they could not cultivate them profitably. But this
is to exhibit a total ignorance of the whole system.
The system of peasant proprietors is literally a system
of *free trade in land.* If an owner of an estate under
this system has not sufficient capital to enable him to
cultivate his land profitably, he has two courses always
open to him, viz., to borrow capital by mortgaging his
land, or to sell the land to some one who has capital. A
peasant proprietor will never keep his land, if he cannot

make a fair profit from it, so as to repay him for his labour and his expenditure. If he has mortgaged it so heavily, as not to leave him any hope of raising more upon it, or of supporting his family comfortably after paying the mortgage, he can always sell his land, pay off the mortgage, and hire himself out as a daily labourer, until he and his family have saved enough wherewith to purchase another farm. *Under this system, therefore, land never remains long in the hands of those, who are not able to cultivate it profitably, or who are not interested in its cultivation.* But under the system of entails and of great estates we know, that it is constantly the case, that landlords have no capital wherewith to cultivate their land ; that they have already borrowed so much upon it, that they can borrow no more ; and that they *cannot,* owing to the terms of the settlement, sell their estate or any part of it ; so that the landlord finds his hands tied fast, while the estate is left in a state of miserable cultivation, because its owner has no spare capital to expend upon it, and because he *cannot* sell it to any one else who has spare capital, and who would feel interested in improving the land, although there may be many such purchasers in the market.

Under the German, French, and Swiss systems, a peasant proprietor never retains his land in his own possession, if he finds he cannot make a profit from it large enough to live upon. There are no regulations, no laws, no settlements, which prevent the peasant selling whenever he feels disposed to do so.

There are always great numbers of rich merchants

or small shopkeepers, who wish to invest capital in land, and who are able to bring capital to its cultivation.

It is the principal feature of the foreign systems, that land can be brought into the market just as easily and cheaply as any other commodity. It can be passed from hand to hand with the greatest facility. This feature of these systems secures their vigour and the productiveness of cultivation in those countries, where they are in force. Land and capital are not necessarily separated. They can be always easily united.

Small estates, however, under a system of strict settlements and complicated successions, such as ours, will always be ruinous; because, under such systems, the small proprietor cannot get rid of his land, when he feels it is ruining him to cultivate it. Land under such a system is often kept for years in the hands of men, who have no capital to expend upon it. So in Saxony, before the beginning of the present century, there were a number of small proprietors, who held their lands under strict settlements; and accounts published in those times represent the condition of the proprietors themselves, and that of their farms, to have been wretched, and to have been progressively deteriorating; and those old reports, with great discrimination and justice, declare, that the cause of that state of things was, not the smallness of the estates, but that the small proprietors could not dispose of their lands to men of science and capital, when they felt it to be their interest to do so.

CHAP. II.

THE CONDITION OF THE POOR IN ENGLAND.

General survey of the social condition of the poor in the towns and in
the country districts. — Channing's opinion. — Chateaubriand's opinion. — The amount of pauperism in England and Wales. — The
amount of crime in England and Wales, and the connection between
ignorance and crime. — The comparative amount of crime in the manufacturing and in the rural districts. — The condition of the children
in our towns. — The city mission. — The English Church, in its relation to the poor. — The necessity for more clergy, and for a different
order of clergy, for our towns. — The alarming increase in the number
of vagrants during the last four years. — The character and habits of
vagrants. — The lodging-houses for vagrants in the towns. — The
frightful scenes to be witnessed in these places. — The burial-clubs and
the practice of infanticide. — The cellar-houses to be found in our
towns. — The condition of the houses of the poor in our towns and in
our villages. — The causes of this miserable condition of our poor :
1. The neglect of the intellectual training of the poor — 2. The
neglect of their religious education — 3. The Game Laws — 4. The
system of laws which affect land — 5. The gin-palaces — 6. The want
of classification in our prisons.

I SHALL now endeavour to show, from reports published by the Government, and by individuals of the
highest authority on such questions, what is the present
social condition of the poorer classes in our towns and
in our country districts ; and I shall endeavour, as
briefly as possible, to point out the causes of the condition disclosed by these reports.

The laws, to which the poorer classes of our country
are subjected, are so singularly different to those, to

which the poorer classes of foreign countries are subjected, that it is most interesting to inquire, what the results of the two systems up to this period have been.

Throughout the greater part of Western Europe and North America, *all* the children of the poorest classes are educated, *gratuitously*, much better than the children of our shopkeepers; in England and Wales more than half the poor cannot read and write, while the majority of the remainder know nothing of science, history, geography, music, or drawing, and very little of the Scripture history.   Throughout the greater part of Western Europe and North America the *habits* of the children are most carefully disciplined from their sixth to their fourteenth year; in England and Wales, little or no attention is paid to this most important national duty. Throughout the greater part of Western Europe and North America there is free trade in land, and the peasants can always, by exercising industry, self-denial, and prudence, make themselves proprietors; in England and Wales it is impossible for a peasant to purchase a piece of land, and it is becoming more and more difficult every day for a peasant even to obtain the uncertain tenure of a farm.   Throughout the greater part of Western Europe and North America the governments provide admirable and exceedingly cheap schools and colleges for the sons of the shopkeepers; in England and Wales the schools for the shopkeepers' children are generally very expensive and miserably poor. Throughout the greater part of Western Europe and North America all the men, who are above twenty-one years of age, have a voice in the election of their representatives;

in England and Wales the vast majority of the poorer classes are not allowed to take any part in the election of the members of Parliament. Throughout Western Europe and North America the churches are very democratic in their constitution, and are suited to the religious necessities of the *poor;* in England and Wales the English Church is aristocratic in its constitution, and the people of many districts are suffering from the want of a class of religious ministers, who could sympathise better with their wants, and who could better understand the peculiar necessities of their position in life, than many of our clergy, educated in the habits of, and selected from, the richer classes of society, can do.

If then the poorer classes of our people are much less happy, prudent, and prosperous than the poorer classes of a great part of Western Europe, we surely ought not to marvel.

The great French Revolution of 1789, by uprooting the feudal system in the greater part of Europe, and by making it possible for any member of the poorer classes of society in that part of Europe, by the exercise of industry and temporary self-denial, to acquire land,—by introducing the system of peasant proprietors into nearly the whole of Western Europe—a system never before tried, as far as history informs us,—and by first originating the idea of educating *all* the children of the poorest classes of society, — has begun a work, which will change the whole face of society, by lessening the present disparity between the different ranks, by civilising the poorer classes, by stimulating their providence and industry,·

and by greatly diminishing the amount of pauperism, crime, and suffering. This great and new experiment has not had nearly time enough as yet, to show all that it is capable of effecting. That its results, so far, have been very good, I have shown in the previous chapter; but what its effects will be, when the schools and the system of education have been perfected, and when two or three successive generations have been successively subjected, to the combined influence of the division of property and of an efficient education, it is impossible to foretel.

But what is the actual social condition of our poorer classes? Let us first consider the social POSITION of the poor, and afterwards their condition, as resulting from the former.

In the great mercantile and manufacturing towns of our country, it is quite true that the poor man, if he be only intelligent enough to defer his marriage, and to avoid burdening himself during his youth with the expenses of a family, may improve his condition in life, and raise himself in the social scale. But we have done as little as we could possibly help doing to give him the necessary intelligence, and it is impossible for the poor to obtain it for themselves. It is impossible for the poor themselves to bear the expenses of educating their children efficiently, even if they were intelligent enough to understand the value of a sound education for their children; and it is necessary to give them intelligence, before we can make them willing to bear any part of the expense. It is impossible for the voluntary efforts of the benevolent part of a nation ever to suffice for the

immense and expensive work of educating the nation;
and it is monstrous to burden them alone with a tax,
which ought to affect the careless and selfish, at least as
much as the others. We have not one half as many
schools as we require for the children of our towns; and
of those we have established, a great number are either
managed by teachers, who are utterly unequal to the
proper discharge of their duties, or are so wretchedly
arranged, furnished, and ventilated, or so miserably conducted and supported, as to make it certain, that in
many cases, they are doing very great harm to the
children who frequent them. Of these schools, many
are nothing but poor " dame schools," conducted often
in cellars or garrets by poor women, who know how to
read, but who often know nothing else, who labour
to eke out a miserable livelihood, by undertaking
the daily management of the children of their neighbours, and who endeavour with a birch or a cane to
frighten the children into learning by rote verses of the
Scriptures. Are the doctrines so taught, likely to be
remembered afterwards with pleasure, or are they likely
to exercise any great influence upon those, who connect
them with so many unhappy remembrances and associations? Thus, even in the towns, where a poor man
might hope to better his condition in society, if he were
only intelligent enough to desire to do so, and to know
how to realise his desires, we have hitherto refused to
grant him that education, without which, except in solitary cases of remarkable natural genius, he cannot even
commence the enterprise.

But unsatisfactory as the *position* of our town labourers is, that of our peasants is still worse. Unless the farm labourer — the English peasant — will consent to tear himself from his relations, friends, and early associations, and either transplant himself into a town or into a distant colony, he has no chance of improving his condition in the world: as " The Times" newspaper has often urged with great force, and especially in some articles published in 1844, " *once a peasant in England, and the man must remain a peasant for ever.*"

Few in number and inefficient in character as the schools for our town labourers are, still fewer and still more inefficient are the schools for our peasants. Even of those, which are established, the greater part are managed by half-educated women; and even where men are employed as teachers, they are generally persons of little or no education, who, being fit for no occupation requiring skill or hard labour, were engaged or set up as schoolmasters, as if instructing youth were an employment requiring less skill and earnest application than any other. Hence it results — and I speak it with sorrow and with shame, but with not less confidence in the assertion — that our peasantry are more ignorant, more demoralised, less capable of helping themselves, and more pauperised, than those of any other country in Europe, if we except Russia, Turkey, South Italy, and some parts of the Austrian empire. I speak this with deliberation, and refer my readers to the account of the condition of the peasants in Europe which I have already given.

But even if this were an exaggeration, and if the peasantry were not so ignorant and neglected, as I have

represented them to be, they would be still utterly unable, in the majority of cases, to improve their condition,
owing to the thoroughly depressing social system to
which we have subjected them; a system, which was
first established in the feudal times, which has long
since been abolished in Norway, Sweden, France,
Prussia, Saxony, Bavaria, Nassau, Wirtemburg, Baden,
Switzerland, Belgium, Holland, Denmark, Italy, and
America, but which survives here, to keep in our remembrance the unjust, but cunningly devised institution, of which it formed one of the main supports—I
mean the system of laws regulating the descent, entailing, conveyance, purchase, and settlement of landed
property.

The peasant is deprived by these laws of all inducement to exercise present self-denial, to defer his marriage, to live within his income, or to lay by his savings,
even if he were intelligent enough, to understand the
benefit, he might derive from such a course of conduct
under a well-devised social system. For what benefit
would he derive from such a course? He could not
purchase with his savings a plot of ground, for land
very seldom sells in small quantities except for building
purposes; and even if it did, the difficulty and expense
of obtaining the necessary legal conveyances present an
almost insurmountable barrier. He has but little chance
of getting a farm. They are, in these days, generally so large, that they would require more capital
than he could ever hope to save; and even could he
save enough, the competition for them among the sons
of farmers is so great when one does fall vacant, that a

peasant generally stands no chance of success, even if he were to make an application.

What advantage, then, would the English peasant gain if he were to exercise self-denial, to defer his marriage, and to lay by his earnings? Excepting that he would have a fund in hand to use in case of unforeseen misfortune, his economy would be of no good to him, unless he either left his country life, associations, and friends, to enter a town and embark in commercial enterprise, for which his early associations, habits, and education totally unfit him, or unless he tore himself from home to seek a livelihood in some distant land. The English peasant is thus deprived of almost every motive to practise economy, and self-denial, beyond what suffices to provide his family with food and clothing. Once a peasant in England, and a man cannot hope that he, himself, or his children will ever be anything better, than a mere labourer for weekly hire.

This unhappy feature of an English peasant's life was most powerfully, and only too justly, depicted in those articles of " The Times " to which I have referred above. It was there shown that during the last half-century, everything has been done to deprive the peasant of any interest in the preservation of public order ; of any wish to maintain the existing constitution of society ; of all hope of raising himself in the world, or of improving his condition in life ; of all attachment to his country ; of all feelings of there really existing any community of interest between himself and the higher ranks of society ; and of all consciousness that he has anything to lose by political changes ; and that every-

thing has been done to render him dissatisfied with
his condition, envious of the richer classes, and discontented with the existing order of things.

The labourer has no longer any connection with
the land which he cultivates; he has no stake in the
country; he has nothing to lose, nothing to defend,
and nothing to hope for. The word "cottage" has
ceased to mean what it once meant — a small house
surrounded by its little plot of land, which the inmate might cultivate as he pleased, for the support
and gratification of his family and himself. The small
freeholds have long since been bought up and merged
in the great estates. Copyholds have become almost
extinct, or have been purchased by the great landowners. The commons, upon which the villagers once
had the right of pasturing cattle for their own use, and
on which, too, the games and pastimes of the villages
were held, have followed the same course : they are enclosed, and now form part of the possessions of the great
landowners. Small holdings of every kind have, in like
manner, almost entirely disappeared. Farms have gradually become larger and larger, and are now, in most
parts of the country, far out of the peasant's reach, on
account of their size, and of the amount of capital requisite to cultivate them. The gulf between the peasant and the next step in the social scale — the farmer
— is widening and increasing day by day. The labourer is thus left without any chance of improving his
condition. His position is one of hopeless and irre-
medial dependence. The workhouse stands near him,
pointing out his dismal fate if he falls one step lower,
and, like a grim scarecrow, warning him to betake

himself to some more hospitable region, where he will find no middle-age institutions opposing his industrious efforts.

It is no answer to all this, to tell me, that in Ireland the peasants have small plots of land, and that their state is ¦still worse than that of our own people. The poor Irish have no certainty of tenure, and may be turned out of their little plots, even into the bleak and inhospitable night, without a remedy. They feel no interest in good farming, or in the improvement of their little lands ; nor dare they expend capital upon them, even when they have any to expend; for they know not when they may be turned adrift, or when they may be deprived of their plot and their improvements. Fifty years ago it was so, in all parts of Denmark, Germany, Switzerland, and France : the peasants were mere tenants-at-will, and cared as little about their plots as tenants-at-will always have done ; and their state in those days was just as miserable, and they were just as discontented, as the peasants of Ireland now are. The governments of those countries were forced to enable the tenants to purchase their plots; and since then, the condition and character of the peasants, and of the little proprietors, have been immeasurably improved; and now, the most prudent, economical, and conservative members of those countries, are the peasants and proprietors of the soil.

To become the proprietor of a small portion of land, is the next step in the social scale, by which alone a peasant can hope to rise : to add gradually to the first acquired portion, are the after steps. But we, and we alone, of all the well-governed European nations, have deprived our peasants of all possibility of climbing the first of these steps, and of ever raising himself above the peasant class.

The social position of the peasants of England and Wales has considerably deteriorated in the last half-century.

Fifty years ago, the farms were very much smaller, and much more numerous, than at present. They did not require nearly so much capital to work them. They were not, therefore, removed, nearly so far, out of the reach of the peasants as at present. Any peasant, who was industrious and careful enough to lay by sufficient to stock a small farm, might reasonably hope to become a tenant of one.

Besides this, there were many small farms in every county of England and Wales, which were either free-holds or copyholds, and which belonged to the farmers themselves. These small proprietors were the survivors of the old English yeomanry; men who felt that they had a stake in the country, and who were filled with that old English feeling of sturdy independence and honest self-reliance, which always distinguishes a class of small proprietors, and which peculiarly distinguished our old yeomanry. The small proprietors and farmers formed a class, to which the tenant farmers and the pea-santry themselves looked up with feelings of interest and pride; knowing that the freehold farmers had sprung, in many cases, from the ranks of the peasantry themselves, and knowing, that if they exerted them-selves with equal industry, prudence, and economy, they, too, might possibly rise to the same positions in the social scale.

But all this class of yeomanry farmers have disappeared; the small tenant farmers are likewise rapidly disappearing; the smaller farms are gradually being united, so as to form large ones; and the chasm between the peasant and the next step in the social scale is every day becoming wider.

A short time since, I was travelling among the farmers of the middle of Wales. One of them, an old man, with whom I spent some time at Aberystwith, speaking to me of the state of the country fifty years ago, said, "Times are greatly changed, sir, since I was a young man. In those days, Wales was very little visited by the English. In many parts, which are now the resorts of travellers, there were then no roads at all. Many people now living can remember, when the high roads through their villages were made, and when the first coach was started upon them.

"In those days, there were, all over the centre and north of Wales, great numbers of freehold farmers, who owned their own farms and cultivated them themselves. I can remember, that Aberystwith was in those days the summer resort and bathing-place of these yeomanry farmers. Great numbers used to come up to Aberystwith in the summer, each of them bringing his horse with him. I can show you the fields, where their horses used to be turned out to grass in the evenings. Many of the farmers used to spend a few weeks every year in this manner, in order to meet one another and to converse together.

" But since that time, all this class of yeomanry farmers has entirely disappeared. Owing to different causes, the larger landed proprietors have, on all hands, diligently bought up all the smaller farms, have united them to their great estates, and have included them in their settlements.

" All the farmers at the present day hold their farms, at the will of their landlords, or rather at the will of the agents of their landlords, for it is very seldom, that a farmer is allowed to treat directly with his landlord. There are often, as many as three and four subagents, with one of the latter of whom the farmer is often obliged to treat, and on whose will the farmer depends for the continuance of his possession.

" The agents are almost absolute; for they know that nothing is easier, than to let a farm, when it falls vacant. There are always plenty of applicants, who will bid against one another, until one wonders, how the last bidder can expect to make a profit from his bargain. Indeed, the agents are often obliged to choose a lower bidder, rather than one of the higher; because they know that the highest bidder could not make it pay, and would soon be in the workhouse, after having, most probably, defrauded his landlord of part of his rental.

" You may imagine, what the powers of an agent in this country are, and what the extortion, they sometimes practise, is, and how helpless the farmers are, when I assure you, that I know, that a gentleman, who owns a great estate near Aberystwith, and who has always been an excellent landlord, and has managed his estates himself, was only a short time since offered, for the agency and direction of his estates, 2000*l.* a-year, and guarantees, in addition, for the receipt of as great a rental as his present one!

" The farmers are the creatures of the agents, are at their mercy absolutely, seldom transact directly with the landlords, and have very seldom any security of tenure."

This account was corroborated by other Welsh farmers, with whom I conversed. One told me, that he knew a case, where the landlord had a steward, A, who had a subagent, B, who had a subagent, C, and that the farmers on the part of the estate, which was managed by C, were entirely at his beck, and subjected absolutely to his management.

Another told me, that the competition for vacant farms was disastrous and ridiculous in the extreme. He said, that whenever one fell vacant, the peasants, feeling that it was their only chance of rising in the world, and that they could not be much worse off than at present, were willing to offer any rent for it, so that they might but try to farm it.

Such is the system, for which they have exchanged the old one of small farms and yeomanry farmers.

In Westmoreland and Cumberland there have been, from ancient times to within the last few years, a great number of small estates, varying in size from five to forty acres, and belonging to peasants and small farmers. These little estates and the houses upon them have always been distinguished by their neatness, good cultivation, and general prosperity. The peasantry of these parts of our island have always been remarkable for their intelligence, their sobriety, their activity, and their contentment.

I was in Westmoreland for some time, during the autumn of 1849, and I took great pains to discover the present condition of the last survivors of these small proprietors. I cannot describe it better, than by giving the words of a gentleman of great intelligence and of Conservative principles, who is engaged in the management of some of the largest estates in Westmoreland and Cumberland. He resides in that part of the country, and is interested in opposing the system of peasant proprietors. There are obvious reasons, why I cannot mention this gentleman's name. He said to me : —

" The greater proprietors in this part of the country are buying up all the land they can get hold of, and including it in their settlements. Whenever one of the small estates is put up for sale, the great proprietors outbid the peasants, and purchase it at all costs. The consequence is, that for some time past, the number of the small estates held by the peasants, has been rapidly diminishing in all parts of the country. In a short time, none of them will remain, but all will be merged in the great estates. While this has been going on, the great landowners have been also increasing very considerably the size of the farms. The smaller farms have been united, in order to form great farms out of them. So that, not only is it becoming more and more difficult every day for a peasant to *buy* land in this part of the country, but it is also gradually becoming impossible for him to obtain even a leasehold farm. The consequence is, that the peasant's position, instead of being what it once was, one of hope, is gradually becoming one of despair. Unless a peasant emigrates, there is now no chance for him. It is impossible for him to rise above the peasant class.

" All this I believe to be a great evil. I have lived all my life among these people, and I believe, that the old system of small estates was one, which did the greatest possible good to the peasants. It stimulated them to exertion, self-denial, and sobriety, by affording them a chance of obtaining a farm of their own ; and when they had obtained one, it made them interested in the careful cultivation of the soil, in the preservation of public order, and in the general prosperity of the country.

" Besides all this, the situation and duties of a small landowner were in themselves an excellent education to the small proprietor. He had many things to do and think of, with reference to county rates, poor-rates, police, markets, agriculture, the effects of national proceedings on prices and on taxation, and the seasons. All this was as interesting to the peasants, and as improving to them, as it is to our country gentlemen, and it made up, in great measure, for the want of good schools and good instruction. But all the effect of this education of circumstances is now being done away. The situation of the peasant is becoming one void of hope, and of all improving influences whatever."

The rapidity, with which the small freeholds have been merged in the larger throughout the country, is very singular, and is a very decisive proof of the deterioration of the social position of the farmers and peasants, especially when it is borne in mind, that, whilst the numbers of the small freeholds and farms have so much diminished, the numbers of the population have much more than doubled. In order that the peasant class should be in even as good a social condition now, as they were in some seventy years ago, the numbers of small freeholds, which were within their reach in those days, ought to have doubled, as the number of the peasants has done. But what has been the course of events?

In the year 1770, there were, it is said, in England alone, 250,000 freehold estates in the hands of 250,000 different families. In the year 1815, at the close of the revolutionary war, the whole of the lands of England were concentrated in the hands of only 32,000 proprietors.* So that, in fact, since 1770, the numbers of the freeholds have been diminishing, at a much greater ratio, than that at which the numbers of the population have been during the same time increasing.

As the Rev. Henry Worsley says, " the labourer's hope of rising in the world is a forlorn one. There is no graduated ascent up which the hardy aspirant may toil step by step with patient drudgery. Several rounds in the ladder are broken away and gone. A farm of some hundred acres, requiring for their due cultivation a large capital, would be a day-dream too gaudy ever to mix itself with the visions of the most ambitious labourer, earning, on an average, probably less than nine shillings a-week. The agricultural workman's horizon is bounded by the high red-brick walls of

* The Rev. H. Worsley's Essay on Juvenile Depravity, p. 53.

the union house: his virtual marriage settlement can only point to such a refuge if troubles arise: his old age may there have to seek its last shelter."*

And yet, notwithstanding that the peasants are deprived of any chance of obtaining land or a leasehold farm, it appears, from the statistics given by Mr. Porter, that in 1827, there were about 15,000,000 of statute acres of land in the British islands, which were capable of being cultivated, but which were lying uncultivated.

In 1847 it appears, according to the same well known writer, that there were still remaining about 11,300,000 acres wholly uncultivated, all of which were capable of cultivation.   Now, when we consider this fact in conjunction with the wretched state of our peasantry, it does appear somewhat unreasonable, that such a system should be suffered to exist.

What is the effect of all this?   Why, that the millions in England and Wales fancy that they have nothing to lose and everything to gain by political changes, and that, instead of our institutions being based upon the conservatism of the masses, they are only based upon the conservatism of the few.   So that we have really much more reason than any other country to dread the growth of democracy.

Besides the depressing and demoralising effect of our system of monopoly of land upon the peasants; another great evil, which results from our English system of great and few farms, and great and few estates, is, that

* Essay on Juvenile Depravity, p. 54.

it drives vast numbers of the young peasants, and of the younger sons of farmers, into the manufacturing towns, and by overstocking their labour markets, renders it more and more difficult every year, for the small shop-keepers and labourers of these towns, to make a livelihood amid the ever-increasing competition around them.

Let us look this evil more fully in the face. An active and enterprising son of a farmer or peasant sees, that there is no chance of his ever getting a farm in his native parish, or of his ever purchasing or even renting a small plot of land, or of his ever rising above the rank of a farm labourer earning eight or nine shillings a-week. The only opening left for such a young man, if he would climb above the lowest rank in the social scale — the peasant's position — is, either to go and seek his fortune in one of our colonies, or in one of our towns. There are many such young men, who cannot persuade themselves to break off the ties of home and kindred, and to leave their native country, but who feel compelled to leave their native villages. All such crowd to the great manufacturing towns of England. The peasants go, to seek labour as operatives or artisans; the sons of the farmers go, to endeavour to establish shops or taverns. What is the result? The labour market in the manufacturing towns is constantly overstocked; the labourers and shopkeepers find new and eager competitors constantly added to the list; competition in the towns is rendered unnaturally intense, profits and wages are both unnaturally reduced; the town work-houses and the town gaols are crowded with inmates;

the inhabitants are overburdened with rates, and the towns swarm with paupers and misery.

I know not what others may think, but to me it is a sad and grievous spectacle, to see the enormous amount of vice and degraded misery which our towns exhibit, and then to think, that we are doing all we can to foster and stimulate the growth and extension of this state of things, by that system of laws, which drives so many of the peasants of both England and Ireland to the towns, and increases the already vast mass of misery by so doing.

I speak with deliberation when I say, that I know no spectacle so degraded, and if I may be allowed to use a strong word, so horrible, as the back streets and sub-urbs of English and Irish towns, with their filthy inhabitants; with their crowds of half-clad, filthy, and degraded children, playing in the dirty kennels; with their numerous gin-palaces, filled with people, whose hands and faces show how their flesh is, so to speak, impregnated with spirituous liquors — the only so-laces, poor creatures, that they have! — and with poor young girls, whom a want of a religious training in their infancy, and misery, has driven to the most degraded and pitiful of all pursuits.

Go to London, reader, or to Manchester, or Liver-pool, or Preston, or Norwich, or Nottingham, or York, or Chester, or to any other of our large and increasing manufacturing or commercial towns, and see if my description is exaggerated. An hour's walk in any one will suffice to convince you of its sad truth. And are you then willing to aid in stimulating this system?

Greater evils never threatened civilisation and religion, than the great cities which have been springing into existence within the last one hundred years. If we would save civilisation, religion, and the morality and happiness of our people, we must reform our towns. And one great step towards that end will be to do away with those causes, which drive so many of our agricultural population into them.

Dr. Channing, in his "Duty of Free States," says : —
" To a man who looks with sympathy and brotherly regard on the mass of the people, who is chiefly interested in the ' lower classes,' England must present much that is repulsive. . . . . The condition of the lower classes at the present moment is a mournful comment on English institutions and civilisation. The multitude are depressed in that country to a degree of ignorance, want, and misery, which must touch every heart not made of stone. In the civilised world there are few sadder spectacles than the present contrast in Great Britain of unbounded wealth and luxury, with the starvation of thousands and tens of thousands, crowded into cellars and dens, without ventilation or light, compared with which the wigwam of the Indian is a palace. Misery, famine, brutal degradation, in the neighbourhood and presence of stately mansions, which ring with gaiety, and dazzle with pomp and unbounded profusion, shock us as no other wretchedness does. . . . . It is a striking fact, that the private charity of England, though almost incredible, makes little impression on this mass of misery ; thus teaching the rich and titled, ' to be just before they are generous,' and

not to look to private munificence as a remedy for the evils of selfish institutions."

Listen to what the great French writer, the Viscount Chateaubriand, says in his " Essays on English Literature," Paris, 1838. "Society such as it now is in England will not continue to endure. According as education makes its way among the people, the cancerous sore which has gnawed social order since the beginning of the world, a sore that causes all the suffering and popular discontent that we see, will be detected. The too great inequality of ranks and fortunes was borne with so long as it was concealed, on the one hand by ignorance, and, on the other, by the factitious organisation of large towns; but, so soon as that inequality becomes generally apparent, it will receive its death-blow. Reconstruct if you can aristocratic fictions. Try to persuade the poor man, when he shall be able to read — him to whom knowledge is daily supplied by the press, scattering its lights in every town and village, — try to persuade the individual possessing the same information and intelligence as yourselves, that he ought to submit to all sorts of privations, while some one, his neighbour, enjoys, without labour, all the superfluities of life, and your efforts will be fruitless. Do not expect from the masses, virtues, which are beyond the force of humanity."

But let us examine the statistics and facts which show the condition of our poor.

First, with respect to their *pauperism*.

Before the enactment of the new poor law, we were expending *annually* between 6,000,000*l*. and 7,000,000*l*.

for the relief of abject pauperism in England and Wales alone. Since the enacting of the new poor law, we have been expending in the same cause between 4,000,000*l.* and 5,000,000*l*, per annum; and, from Lady-Day, 1835, to Lady-Day, 1848 — or, in 17 years—we expended on the same object, 87,505,826*l.*, without reckoning the vast sums, which have been sunk in the administration of the poor law in the different unions, or the immense sums, which have been given away annually by charitable individuals and charitable societies. All this, be it remembered, has been required to alleviate the miserable condition of our labouring population, and to keep crowds from actual starvation. Their independence is destroyed: they cannot live unless they depend upon the charity of the higher classes.

The enormous sums which — exclusive of all charitable donations — have been annually expended by the union boards, in alleviating the sufferings of our labourers since 1832, are given in the accompanying table.

Amount expended in the Relief and Maintenance of the Poor in England and Wales, exclusive of all the immense Expenditure of Poor Law Administration in the Unions and Parishes.

Years.				£
1832	-	-	-	7,036,969
1833	-	-	-	6,790,800
1834	-	-	-	6,317,255
1835	-	-	-	5,526,418
1836	-	-	-	4,717,630
1837	-	-	-	4,044,741
1838	-	-	-	4,123,604
1839	-	-	-	4,406,907
1840	-	-	-	4,576,965
1841	-	-	-	4,760,929

Years.				£
1842	-	-	-	4,911,498
1843	-	-	-	5,208,027
1844	-	-	-	4,976,093
1845	-	-	-	5,039,703
1846	-	-	-	4,954,204
1847	-	-	-	4,678,110
1848	-	-	-	5,435,973

Now, without proceeding further, it surely cannot, and will not, be contended, that a labouring population, which requires such an expenditure as this, — and that, too, in addition to the vast amount of charitable donations devoted annually to the same purpose, — to keep part of it from actual starvation, can be in a very happy, prosperous, or satisfactory condition! What country is there in Europe, or in the world, where such an expenditure is found to be necessary to save the labourers from starvation? What other country in Europe, or in the world, is obliged to keep up such a poor-law system, and for such a purpose? What other country in the world is there, where private individuals are obliged to dole out so many charitable donations for the same unhappy purpose? Why should not our peasants be at least as well able to depend on their own exertions for subsistence, as the peasants of Germany, Switzerland, Italy, or the provinces of France? Why should not our peasants be as well able to dispense with charitable donations, and as much above receiving them, as our middle classes?

Why is it that the Prussian, Saxon, Swiss, and French peasantry do not require nearly so much public relief like this? Because they have been taught and enabled to help themselves, and because they are assisted, and not hindered, by legislation in their efforts to work out their own independence.

In 1848, in addition to the hundreds of thousands assisted by charitable individuals, 1,876,541 paupers were relieved by boards of guardians, or about one person out of every EIGHT of the population was a pauper in 1848. Let every one consider the astounding nature of this fact, and let him remember, that nothing like it exists in Germany, Switzerland, or France.

The numbers of paupers relieved each year since 1840, by the boards of guardians, in England and Wales, have been as follows :—

Years.			Number of Paupers relieved in England and Wales.
1840	-	-	-	1,199,529
1841	-	-	-	1,299,048
1842	-	-	-	1,427,187
1843	-	-	-	1,539,490
1844	-	-	-	1,477,561
1845	-	-	-	1,470,970
1846	-	-	-	1,332,089
1847	-	-	-	1,721,350
1848	-	-	-	1,876,541

In each of the above years there have been the above-mentioned vast numbers of paupers, who, *exclusive of all those assisted by charitable individuals,* have been unable to exist in England and Wales, without begging assistance from the guardians. And to these have to be added also, all the beggars and vagrants, who crowd our streets and roads, and of whom I shall say more hereafter, and all those, who are in the receipt of alms from their richer neighbours, but who do not like to apply to boards of guardians for relief.

More than 2,000,000 of people were kept from starvation in England and Wales in the year 1848 by

relief doled out to them from public or from private
sources; so vast is the amount of misery and social
degradation among the poor of England and Wales,
and so great the destitution to which they are reduced!

Look, too, at the statistics, which show the frightfully low moral condition of our labouring classes, and
the connection which is found to exist between the
ignorance of the labourers and their criminality.

The following table shows the number and the cha-
racter of the education of all those, who were committed
for crime in England and Wales, from 1836 to 1847.
It shows how fearfully crime is increasing among our
poor, and how clear and undeniable it is, THAT THE
GREATEST PART OF THEIR IMMORALITY IS THE DI-
RECT AND IMMEDIATE EFFECT OF THE UTTER NEG-
LECT OF THEIR EDUCATION.

Years.	Total No. of Persons committed for Crime.	No. who could neither read nor write.		No. who could read only, or read and write imperfectly.		No. who could read and write well.		No. who had received superior Education.		No. whose Instruction was not ascertained.	
		Males.	Females.	Males.	Fem.	Males.	Fem.	Males.	Fem.	Males.	Fem.
1836	20,984	5598	1435	8,968	2015	2016	199	176	15	490	72
1837	23,672	6684	1780	10,147	2151	2057	177	98	3	421	94
1838	23,094	6342	1601	10,008	2326	2051	206	74	5	430	51
1839	24,443	6487	1709	10,523	2548	2201	261	74	4	546	90
1840	27,187	7145	1913	12,151	2958	2038	215	100	1	541	125
1841	27,760	7312	1908	12,742	2990	1839	214	126	0	541	88
1842	31,309	8162	1959	14,983	3277	1890	231	65	4	633	98
1843	29,591	7344	1829	13,892	3153	2127	244	134	6	754	108
1844	26,542	6266	1635	12,745	2990	1892	264	109	2	537	102
1845	24,303	5698	1740	11,215	2964	1859	178	86	3	483	77
*1846	25,107	7698		14,941		1936		85		446	
*1847	28,833	9501		16,980		2246		81		475	
1848	30,349	7530	2161	13,950	3161	2634	350	76	5	396	86

* I have not by me the full analysis of the returns of these two years.

Mr. Porter, from whose admirable work, " The Progress of the Nation," I have extracted this table, in commenting upon it, says : —

" The most cursory glance at these figures must carry conviction to every mind, that instruction has power to restrain men from the commission of crimes—of such a nature, at least, as will bring them before a bar of justice. If we class together those, who can neither read nor write, and those, who have acquired only an imperfect acquaintance with those elementary branches of knowledge — the scaffolding merely for the erection of the moral edifice — we find, that in the ten years comprised in the returns, there were, out of 252,544 persons committed, and whose degrees of instruction were ascertained, the great proportion of 229,300, or more than 90 in 100, *uninstructed* persons; while *only* 1085 *persons had enjoyed the advantages of instruction beyond the elementary degree*, and only 22,159 had mastered, without advancing beyond, the acts of reading and writing.

" These numbers embrace both males and females. If we examine the returns, with the view of determining the moral influence of instruction upon females, we find that among the 252,544 persons above described, there were 47,113 females, 18·65 per cent. of the whole; but when we inquire, in what proportions females are divided among the different classes as respects instruction, we see, that among the 229,300 uninstructed persons, there were 44,881 females, or 19·57 per cent. ; while among 22,159 who could read and write well, there were but 2,189 females, or 9·88 per cent. ; and among the better

instructed 1085 persons, there were only 43 females, or
3·96 per cent. The proportions in each 10,000 persons
accused that were furnished by the males and females of
the social classes, were as follows: —

" In each 10,000 persons committed for crime there
were —

Of—	Males.	Females.	Total.
Those wholly uninstructed, and those who could read only, or read and write imperfectly -	7303	1776	[9079
Those who could read and write well - - - - -	791	86	877
Those superiorly instructed -	42	2	44
	8136	1864	10,000

" Of the 43 instructed females accused of crimes throughout England and Wales in ten years, the large proportion of 15 belong to the first year of the series. Of
these, 12 were accused of simple larceny, 1 for receiving stolen goods, 1 for fraud, and 1 for perjury.
*There were, consequently, in nine years, only twenty-
eight educated females brought to the bar of criminal
justice ;* viz. 3 in 1837, 5 in 1838, 4 in 1839, only 1 in
1840, and in 1841, not one educated female was committed for trial among 7,673,633 females then living in
that part of the United Kingdom. In the remaining
four years the numbers were; in 1842, 4; 1843, 6;
1844, 2; and in 1845, 3.

" How much the internal peace of the country may
be affected, by the prevalence of ignorance or the spread
of knowledge, may be reasonably inferred from the

state of instruction of persons tried at the special commission in October, 1842, arising out of the then recent rising in the manufacturing districts.   This is shown by the following table : —

	Cheshire.	Lancashire.	Staffordshire.	Total.	Centesimal Proportion
Neither read nor write - -	26	47	81	154	27·16
Read only - -	30	26	99	155	27·34
Read and write imperfectly - -	28	97	59	184	32·45
Read and write well	9	28	36	73	12·87
Superior Instruction	- -	- -	1	1	0·18
	93	198	276	567	100·00

" In 1840, there were 100 males and 1 female who had received instruction beyond reading and writing, committed for trial in the various counties of England and Wales.   Of this number, only 59 (58 males and *one* female) were convicted, being under 59 per cent. of the number accused, while the *convictions* generally in that year exceeded 73 per cent. of the *accused.*

" In twenty counties of England and Wales, with a population of 8,724,338 persons, there were convicted *fifty-nine* instructed persons, or 1 to every 147,870 inhabitants ; while the remaining thirty-two counties, with a population of 7,182,491, *had not furnished one convict who had received more than the earliest elements of instruction.*   It is even more worthy of remark, that Middlesex, the metropolitan county, with its 1,576,616 inhabitants, among whom the proportion of instructed persons is at least equal to that in any other county, *did not furnish one educated convict,* a fact which, considering the diversity, conditions, and occupations, and the amount of temptations that assail its inhabitants, would be most difficult to believe upon any testimony less certain than that of official returns.

" In 1841, in fifteen English counties, with a population of 9,569,064, there were convicted 74 instructed persons, or 1 to every 129,311 inhabitants; while the twenty-five remaining counties of England, and the whole of Wales, with a population of 6,342,661, *did not among them furnish one conviction of a person who had received more than the mere elements of education.* It will be remembered, as a most interesting fact, one which speaks irresistibly in favour of a general system of education, *that not one of the* 100 *was a female !"*

One remarkable fact, which singularly illustrates the evil effects of our rural system, is, that notwithstanding the extraordinary numbers of workmen crowded together in the manufacturing towns of Lancashire, and notwithstanding the moral injury, which those towns suffer from the continual influx of wretched beings driven thither by want from our rural districts and from Ireland, *the annual proportion of criminals to population is very considerably less in the manufacturing towns of Lancashire, than in many of our agricultural counties !*

The supposition that the proportion of crime to population is greater in the manufacturing than in the rural districts, is one which has been taken for granted by many writers, but which is totally unfounded. The reverse of this proposition is the truth. The error has

arisen from calculating the annual amount of crime in
Liverpool, as forming part of the crime committed in the
manufacturing districts; forgetting that Liverpool is not
a manufacturing town, but a *sea-port;* that it is the
nearest English *sea-port* to Ireland; and that the greatest
amount of the crime annually committed in Liverpool,
is committed, either by vagrant Irish, by the constantly changing sailor population, or by the labourers
in the docks, who are demoralised by association with
the sailors.*

Let us shortly examine the extraordinary criminality
of Liverpool.

It appears that in the eleven months ending 30th
November, 1849, 6194 persons were brought before the
magistrates of Liverpool charged with felony, *of whom
only* 1489 *were natives of Liverpool; all the remainder,*
viz. 4705, *were strangers!*

As Mr. Clay says, in his report for 1849:—" It is the
GREAT SEA-PORT of the southern division, which throws
its own dark aspect over the moral reputation of the
entire county; and I now beg to submit evidence to
demonstrate, how much the COMBINED criminality of
Manchester, Salford, Bolton, and Preston — the great
' manufacturing centres '—falls below that of Liverpool
alone, which scarcely, if at all, subjects to the action of
machinery a single fibre of all the cotton landed from
its magnificent docks. ˙Having been obligingly furnished by Captain Willis, Mr. Dowling, Mr. Neale,
Mr. Harris, and Mr. Banister with their respective

---

* See the Rev. J. Clay's admirable Report on the Preston Gaol for 1849.

reports on the state of crime in the several towns which they superintend, I am enabled to give the following concise summary of crime and disorder in those towns:—

Comparative View of Criminality and Disorder in the manufacturing Towns of Manchester, Salford, Bolton, and Preston, and the Seaport of Liverpool, founded on the Police Returns of the respective Places.

	Man-chester.	Salford.	Bolton.	Preston.	Total.	Per Cent. to Pop.	Liver-pool.	Per Cent. to Pop.
	1848.	1849.	848-9.	1848.			1848.	
Estimated Population -	300,000	62,000	69,000	68,000	499,000		390,000	
Total of apprehensions	6,277	1,624	1,950	1,626	11,477	2·3	22,036	5·64
Committed for trial -	825	149	127	81	1,182	0·24	937	0·24
Summary convictions for robberies - -	126	11	65	41	243	0·05	3,440	0·88
Total of summary convictions - -	2,885	900	997	546	5,328	1·07	13,849	3·55
Total of *females* taken into custody - -	1,842	433	387	299	2,961	0·6	6,274	1·6
Young persons taken into custody on charges of felony - - -	under 20 838	under 20 175	under 20 64	under 19 121	1,098	0·22	under 19 2,342	0·6

" The very striking results appearing from the above statement are, that, comparing Liverpool with the *four* manufacturing towns *collectively*, and bearing in mind that its population is *one fifth less*, —

1. Its committals for trial are - - equal.
2. Its numbers taken into custody - 2½ times greater.
3. Its females taken into custody - nearly 3 times greater.
4. Its juveniles charged with felony - nearly 3 times greater.
5. Its summary convictions for all offences 3½ times greater.
6. Its summary convictions for *robberies* - more than 17 *times greater!* "

. . . .

* " If I have succeeded in removing from the manufacturing population of Lancashire the charge of excessive criminality, it has been at the expense of our great

* The Rev. J. Clay's Report on the Preston Gaol for 1849.

sea-port; and it is right that, having gone so far, I should proceed yet further, and shortly state the causes which have given to Liverpool its lamentable pre-eminence. It is scarcely necessary to say, that in every large sea-port, there exists a dissolute class, maintaining itself by preying on careless and drunken seamen, and by pilfering property lying exposed on the landing places. But this is not all, as affects Liverpool. It is her peculiar misfortune, that her harbour is too easily gained by a race of persons who, whatever may have been their habits at home, no sooner reach Liverpool, than such of them as are in a destitute state, either give way to the temptation to plunder round the docks, or become an oppressive and demoralising burden to the town. I am indebted to Mr. Rushton for much information on this subject, and for carefully prepared statistics, which should be taken into account, whenever the crime of Lancashire or Liverpool is adverted to. The Irish in Liverpool are estimated by Mr. Rushton at *one-fourth* of the entire population; *but they supply more than* ONE HALF *the number of criminals!* I have now before me a return, from which it appears, that in the eleven months ending 30th November last, 6194 persons were brought before the magistrates of Liverpool, charged with felony,—of whom 1489 were natives of Liverpool, 946 were from other parts of England, 338 from Scotland, Wales, and the Isle of Man, while 3266 *were natives of Ireland!* It also appears from the return, that, as regards the English, females are to the males in the proportion of 1 to 2; but as regards the Irish, they are in the proportion of 14 to 17.   This constant influx of Irish misery and crime it is almost impossible to restrain. The open docks of Liverpool, where the quays are covered with costly articles of commerce, swarm with thieves, whose cunning and rapacity are in continual action. When apprehended, the process of committal to assizes or sessions would not promote the ends of justice, and it becomes an unavoidable necessity that ' crimes which, in other places, would be punished by long terms of imprisonment, are punished, here, by repeated summary convictions, under the powers of various local acts of parliament; and this must be, or the criminal would go without punishment altogether. For instance, a sailor is the necessary witness; his ship is going to sea; you cannot detain him, and therefore you enforce your summary powers. This happens in hundreds of cases in Liverpool.'* Thus, again, in cases of robbery from the person by prostitutes, or by *pickpockets*, seamen being the injured parties, it is necessary to dispose of the cases at once. According to the report of the Liverpool police, robberies from the person by 67 male and 20 female pickpockets, and 198 robberies from the person by prostitutes, were *summarily* punished in 1848.

" It is obvious from all this, that Liverpool, from its unfortunate proximity to Ireland, is undergoing an aggravation of moral and social evils of the severest character, — even to the extent of clogging and embarrassing the free action with which justice should deal with delinquents. From such evils North Lancashire enjoys an almost complete immunity. At the Preston

* Mr. Rushton.

sessions, known pickpockets seldom appear, and indictments against ' unfortunate women ' for robberies from the person, are comparatively rare; but persons of either class, when convicted—former convictions being proved — have almost always been sentenced to transportation." *

From the above facts and extracts it is clear that, in estimating the criminality of the *manufacturing* districts, we ought to omit the amount of crime committed in Liverpool; first, because it is not a *manufacturing* town ; and, secondly, because the majority of its criminals are not natives, or even permanent inhabitants of the town.

But, if we reckon the criminality of Liverpool as part of the criminality of the manufacturing districts of Lancashire, what is the result even then ?   Mr. Redgrave, in his valuable tables for 1848, shows † that, even *without* excluding Liverpool, Lancashire, *as a whole*, stands ELEVENTH on the list of counties arranged in the order of their criminality, and that there are TEN *agricultural* counties, where the proportion of criminals to population is greater than in the whole of Lancashire, including Liverpool !   Mr. Clay exhibits this fact very clearly in the following table, extracted from his very able report for 1849 : —

* Such offences as those now adverted to are never disposed of *summarily* in North Lancashire.

See Mr. Clay's Report for 1849.

Order in which the Ten Counties would stand, supposing Criminality proportioned to *Density* of Population.		Order in which the Ten Counties would stand, supposing Crime to depend on the Excess of Manufacturing over Agricultural Population.		Actual Order, in Ratio of Criminals to Population. (1848.)	
Counties.	Inhabitants to 100 Acres.	Counties.	Persons in Manufactures to 1 in Agriculture.	Counties.	Criminals to Population.
1. Lancaster	147·5	Lancaster -	9·3	Warwick -	1 to 358
2. Surrey -	120·	Surrey -	4·	Worcester -	„ 364
3. Warwick -	70·	Chester -	3·8	Chester -	„ 411
4. Chester -	59·	Warwick -	3·5	Hereford -	„ 428
5. Gloucester	53·6	Gloucester -	2·1	Rutland -	„ 439
6. Worcester	50·4	Worcester -	1·6	Gloucester -	„ 443
7. Hertford	39·	Hertford -	1·	Berks -	„ 477
8. Berks -	33·5	Berks -	0·8	Hertford -	„ 480
9. Rutland -	22·3	Hereford -	0·7	Surrey -	„ 504
10. Hereford	20·6	Rutland -	0·6	Lancaster -	„ 509

But if we consider the populous manufacturing districts of North Lancashire *separately*, without considering the southern division of Lancashire, with its great sea-port, Liverpool, we shall arrive at still more remarkable results, showing how much more demoralised many of our rural districts are than the crowded cities of the north.

It appears, as shown by Mr. Clay, that there are 34 *counties whose proportion of crime to population is greater than that of North Lancashire;* that in regard to *juvenile* crime, *North Lancashire is very greatly surpassed by 22 counties*, most of which are agricultural; and that in *female* criminality *it is surpassed by* 17 *counties*, almost all of which are also agricultural!

Mr. Clay says, in Kent the ratio of criminals to the population is as 1 to 668 ; in Suffolk the ratio is greater than in Kent, being 1 to 647 ; while in North Lancashire it is only 1 to 999! In Suffolk, too, the extent of depravity among the female sex is in a greater ratio than in North Lancashire. In the former, it is 1 to 4,633, while in the latter it is only 1 to 5,441! " And as to juvenile offenders — taking the data from Captain Williams's 12th Report — *those of Suffolk are* THRICE *as numerous as those of North Lancashire ! !* "

The following table shows the aggregate criminality for each of the English counties in the five years ending 1847 ; the increase or decrease which has taken place between those periods ; and the *order* in the criminality of the counties—as evinced in 1841 and 1847 ; those counties being placed *first* in order, which furnish the greatest number of criminals in proportion to their population. It is extracted from Mr. Clay's report for 1848.

Counties : in the Order of their Criminality (1847).	Population in 1841.	Estimated Population in 1847.*	Criminals in 1847.	Aggregate of Criminals in the Five Years ending		Per-centage of Increase or Decrease in the Quinquennial Periods.		Consecutive Order in Criminality as compared to Population.	
				1842.	1847.	Incr.	Decr.	1847.	1841.
Middlesex - -	1,576,636	1,728,700	5175	18,394	22,543	22·5	- -	1	7
Worcester - -	233,336	247,800	620	2,689	3,000	11·6	- -	2	5
Gloucester -	431,383	460,700	1092	5,489	5,162	- -	5·9	3	1
Warwick - -	401,715	448,300	998	4,712	4,505	- -	4·4	4	4
South Lancashire, including Liverpool - -	1,264,383	1,471,740	3011	14,569	13,698	- -	6·0	5	3
Surrey - -	582,678	652,000	1315	4,842	5,023	3·7	- -	6	27
Chester - -	395,660	439,200	871	4,491	4,121	- -	8·2	7	6
Bucks - -	155,983	160,400	315	1,298	1,477	13·8	- -	8	18
Berks - -	161,147	171,600	335	1,600	1,460	- -	8·8	9	16
Southampton -	355,004	382,300	737	3,388	3,157	- -	6·8	10	15
Wilts - -	258,733	270,600	502	2,351	2,213	- -	5·9	11	14
Hereford - -	113,878	115,400	212	1,145	1,064	- -	7·1	12	10
Rutland - -	21,302	22,600	41	97	157	61·9	- -	13	40
Oxford - -	161,643	167,600	299	1,611	1,460	- -	9·4	14	13
Stafford - -	510,504	584,500	1028	5,165	4,656	- -	9·8	15	11
Norfolk - -	412,664	426,700	751	3,487	3,683	5·6	- -	16	25
Hertford - -	157,207	166,300	291	1,561	1,314	- -	15·8	17	12
Monmouth -	134,355	163,800	282	1,385	1,234	- -	10·9	18	2
Devon - -	533,460	558,600	949	3,356	3,845	14·6	- -	19	31
Somerset - -	435,982	456,500	774	4,968	4,354	- -	12·3	20	8
Essex - -	344,979	362,900	603	3,266	3,065	- -	6·2	21	17
Dorset - -	175,043	185,300	307	1,348	1,205	- -	10·6	22	24
Sussex - -	299,753	317,800	522	2,665	2,301	- -	13·6	23	19
Suffolk - -	315,073	327,100	505	2,525	2,598	2·9	- -	24	28
Bedford - -	107,936	116,300	178	837	908	8·5	- -	25	20
Kent - -	548,337	594,900	889	5,000	4,423	- -	11·5	26	21
Leicester - -	215,867	228,200	335	2,201	2,011	- -	8·6	27	9
Huntingdon -	58,549	62,000	89	363	405	11·6	- -	28	33
Cambridge -	164,459	177,800	255	1,157	1,324	14·4	- -	29	29
Nottingham -	249,910	266,300	343	1,623	1,597	- -	1·6	30	30
Lincoln - -	362,602	393,400	506	2,036	2,419	18·8	- -	31	35
Northampton -	199,228	212,300	243	1,496	1,379	- -	7·8	32	23
Salop - -	239,048	249,300	267	1,854	1,785	- -	3·7	33	22
York - -	1,591,480	1,745,600	1794	9,305	8,766	- -	5·8	34	32
N. Lancashire -	402,672	444,550	445	2,907	2,252	- -	22·6	35	26
Cornwall - -	341,279	368,600	341	1,469	1,463	- -	0·4	36	37
Durham - -	324,284	378,100	279	1,022	1,407	37·7	- -	37	39
Derby - -	272,217	296,200	214	1,347	1,278	- -	5·1	38	34
Northumberland	250,278	268,600	189	965	1,131	17·2	- -	39	36
Cumberland -	178,038	183,200	120	698	632	- -	9·4	40	38
Westmoreland -	56,454	57,300	33	183	221	20·8	- -	41	41

* " The estimated population in 1847 is only a rough approximation to the probable truth. It has been derived from the known increase of the respective counties in the ten years between 1831 and 1841."

This table well deserves study. It shows, that the proportional amount of crime to population, calculated in two years, 1841 and 1847, was greater, in both years, in almost all the *agricultural* counties of England, than it was in the *manufacturing* and mining districts of North Lancashire, Yorkshire, Derbyshire, Northumberland, and Durham. It also shows, how fearfully the amount of crime is increasing in the agricultural districts of Westmoreland, Lincoln, Cambridge, Huntingdon, Leicestershire, Rutland, Bedfordshire, Buckinghamshire, Worcestershire, and Devonshire ; whilst, in almost all the mining and manufacturing districts — *even reckoning South Lancashire, with its demoralised sea-port, Liverpool* — the amount of crime has been, during the same period, actually decreasing !

With what terrible significance do these statistics plead the cause of the poor of our rural districts ! Notwithstanding, that a town life *necessarily* presents so many more opportunities for, and temptations to, vice than a rural life ; notwithstanding, that the associations of the latter are naturally so much purer and so much more moral than those of the former ; notwithstanding, the wonderfully crowded state of the great manufacturing cities of Lancashire ; notwithstanding, the constant influx of Irish, sailors, vagrants, beggars, and starving natives of the agricultural districts of England and Wales ; and notwithstanding, the miserable state of most of the primary schools of those districts, and the great ignorance of the majority of the inhabitants ; still, in face of all these, and other equally significant facts, the criminality of the *manufacturing* districts of Lancashire is LESS in proportion to the population, than that of most of the rural districts of England and Wales!

Does not this show, that the peasants of England must be subjected to a singularly demoralising system, to produce so strange, so almost incredible, a result?

But let us consider the condition of the juvenile poor of our towns. The chief source and cause of the criminality of the poorer classes of our towns, is the neglected and frightfully wretched condition of a great part of their juvenile population. The children are not obliged by law to go to any school. The parents are often too vicious, or too ignorant, or too poor to care to send them, if not compelled and *enabled* to do so; and so a great part of the children are left in the streets to be educated and brought up in crime. This will always be the case, while the law does not at the same time oblige and enable poor, vicious, and ignorant parents to send their children to school. But in our country, the evil is worse than it otherwise would be, because we have not a sufficient number of schools in our towns, and because the greatest part of the schools we have, are so wretchedly insufficient in character.

The following account is quoted almost verbatim, but somewhat abridged, from Lord Ashley's admirable speech on juvenile destitution, delivered in the House of Commons on the 6th of June, 1848, clearly showing the awfully wretched condition of a great part of the children of London. But although this singular account refers to London alone, it does, in reality, give a very correct picture of the condition of a great part of the children of all the larger towns of England.

In the towns of Lancashire, and in all the larger of
the manufacturing and provincial towns, the life and
character of an equal proportion of the whole number
of the children is precisely similar to that of the juvenile population of the back streets of London.

Any one may convince himself of the truth of Lord
Ashley's account, and may learn how a great part of
the juvenile population of every one of our larger
towns is being bred in filth, immorality, and degradation, if he will only take the trouble to walk into the
back streets, and observe what is going on around
him.   He will there see one of the principal nurseries
of our criminals and paupers, and one of the numerous
overwhelming proofs of the insane folly of supposing,
that the unaided, voluntary efforts of charitable individuals will ever be able to reclaim and civilise the
rapidly increasing masses of our juvenile poor.

Careful inquiries by Lord Ashley, and by the excellent
men connected with that admirable society, the City
Mission, have shown, that in the midst of London, there
is a large and continually increasing number of lawless
persons, forming a separate class, having pursuits, interests, manners, and customs of their own, and that
the filthy, deserted, roaming, and lawless children, who
may be called the source of 19-20ths of the crime, which
desolates the metropolis, are not fewer in number
than THIRTY THOUSAND!

These 30,000 are quite independent of the number
of mere pauper children, who crowd the streets of London, and who never enter a school : but of these latter
nothing will be said here.

Now, what are the pursuits, the dwelling-houses, and the habits of these poor wretches? Of 1,600, who were examined, 162 confessed, that they had been in prison, not merely once, or even twice, but some of them several times; 116 had ran away from their homes; 170 slept in the "lodging houses;" 253 had lived altogether by beggary; 216 had neither shoes nor stockings; 280 had no hat or cap, or covering for the head; 101 had no linen; 249 had never slept in a bed; many had no recollection of ever having been in a bed; 68 were the children of convicts.

In 1847, it was found that of 4,000 examined, 400 confessed that they had been in prison, 660 lived by beggary, 178 were the children of convicts, and 800 had lost one or both their parents. Now, what was the employment of these people? They might be classed as street-sweepers; vendors of lucifer matches, oranges, cigars, tapes, and ballads; they held horses, ran errands, jobbed for " dealers in marine stores," that being the euphonious term for receivers of stolen goods, — an influential race in the metropolis, but for whose agency, a very large proportion of juvenile crime would be extinguished. It might be asked, how did the large number who never slept in bed pass the night? In all manner of places: under dry arches of bridges and viaducts, under porticoes, sheds, carts in out-houses, saw-pits, or staircases, or in the open air, and some in lodging-houses. Curious, indeed, was their mode of life. One boy, during the inclement period of 1847, passed the greater part of his nights in the large iron roller in the Regent's Park. He climbed over the rail-

ings, and crept to the roller, where he lay in comparative security.

Lord Ashley says, " many of them were living in the
dry arches of houses not finished, inaccessible except
by an aperture, only large enough to admit the body of a
man.   When a lantern was thrust in, six or eight, ten or
twelve people might be found lying together.   Of those,
whom we found thus lodged, we invited a great number
to come the following day, and there an examination was
instituted.   The number examined was 33.   Their ages
varied from 12 to 18, and some were younger.   24 had
no parents, 6 had one, 3 had step-mothers, 20 had no
shirts, 9 no shoes, 12 had been once in prison, 3 twice,
3 four times, 1 eight times, and 1 (only 14 years old)
twelve times.   The physical condition of these children
was exceedingly bad; they were a prey to vermin, they
were troubled with itch, they were begrimed with dirt,
not a few were suffering from sickness, and two or three
days afterwards several died from disease and the effects
of starvation.   I privately examined eight or ten.   I was
anxious to obtain from them the truth.   I examined
them separately, taking them into a room alone.   I
said, ' I am going to ask you a variety of questions, to
which I trust you will give me true answers, and I will
undertake to answer any question you may put.'   They
thought that a fair bargain.   I put to several of them
the question, ' How often have you slept in a bed during the last three years?'   One said, perhaps twelve
times, another three times, another could not remember
that he ever had.   I asked them, how they passed the
night in winter.   They said, ' We lie eight or ten

together, to keep ourselves warm.' I entered on the subject of their employments and modes of living. They fairly confessed, they had no means of subsistence but begging and stealing. The only way of earning a penny in a legitimate way was by picking up old bones. But they fairly acknowledged for themselves and others scattered over the town, with whom they professed themselves acquainted, that they had not and could not have any other means of subsistence, than by begging and stealing. A large proportion of these young persons were at a most dangerous age for society. I met one very remarkable instance of a boy, past 17. I was struck at discovering, that the boy knew the French language, and I asked an account of his life. He said, he had been in France at the time of the Revolution, and had fought at the barricades. He and his mother had gone to Paris some four or five years ago. He there got into some employment, but, as the political atmosphere became warm, he yielded to its influence, and being enticed by French boys, his companions, he joined in the general warfare, fought at the barricades, was taken prisoner, tried, and sentenced to punishment. There were hundreds and thousands of others, as capable of being employed for the worst purposes, as the Garde Mobile of Paris. And therefore for the peace of society, I would direct the attention of the House to the subject. What was the moral condition of those persons? A large proportion of them, (it was no fault of theirs,) did not recognise the distinctive rights of *meum* and *tuum*. Property appeared to them to be only the aggregate of plunder. They held that everything

which was possessed, was common stock; that he who
got most was [the cleverest fellow, and that every one
had a right to abstract from that stock, what he could
by his own ingenuity. Was it matter of surprise, that
they entertained those notions, which were instilled into
their minds, from the time they were able to creep on
all fours, — that not only did they disregard all the
rights of property, but gloried in doing so, unless they
thought the avowal would bring them within the grasp
of the law. To illustrate their low state of morality,
and to show how utterly shameless they were, in speaking on these subjects, I would mention, what had
passed at a ragged school, to which fourteen or fifteen
boys, having presented themselves on a Sunday evening,
were admitted as they came. They sat down, and the
lesson proceeded. The clock struck eight. They all
rose with the exception of one little boy. The master
took him by the arm and said, 'You must remain; the
lesson is not over.' The reply was, 'We must go to
business.' The master inquired what business? 'We
must all go to catch them, as they come out of the
chapels.' It was necessary for them, according to the
remark of this boy, to go at a certain time in pursuit
of their calling. They had no remorse or shame, in
making the avowal; because they believed, that there
were no other means of saving themselves from starvation. I recollect a very graphic remark, made by one
of those children in perfect simplicity, but which yet
showed the horrors of their position. The master had
been pointing out to him the terrors of punishment in
after-life. The remark of the boy was, 'That may

be so, but I don't think it can be any worse than this world has been to me.' Such was the condition of hundreds and thousands!"

Great numbers of these wretched beings live in the " *lodging-houses*." These horrible dens will be described more fully hereafter; but I shall quote Lord Ashley's account of them here, in order to show, where and how a great part of the juvenile population of our towns are lodged and *educated*. Until the poor children are rescued from these hells, how can we hope to raise them from their present degraded condition? But how can we rescue them, unless the municipalities interfere, and at their own expense clothe and send all the poor children of their towns to good and religious schools, as they do in Germany and Switzerland? But listen to Lord Ashley's description given in his own words : —

" I will read a description of the lodging-houses. Many of them, which I have seen, were abominable ; but the statement, I will lay before the House, was given on the authority of a city missionary, who had been appointed to inspect and report on the subject. It is not an exaggerated description of those places, where hundreds and thousands of the human race are congregated. The city missionary, speaking of a lodging-house, and referring to the ' parlour,' — for there were many euphonious terms to be applied, — said, —

" The parlour measures 18 feet by 10. Beds are arranged on each side of it, composed of straw, rags, and shavings. Here are 27 male and female adults, and 31 children, with several dogs; in all, 58 human beings, in a contracted den, from which light and air are systematically excluded. It is impossible,' he says, ' to convey a just idea of their state, — the quantities of vermin are amazing! I have entered a room, and in a few minutes, I have felt them dropping on my hat from the ceiling like peas.' ' They may be gathered by handfuls,' observed one of the inmates. ' I could fill a pail in a few minutes. I have been so tormented with the itch, that on two occasions I filled my pockets with stones, and waited till a policeman came up, and then broke a lamp, that I might be sent to prison, and there be cleansed, as is required before new comers are admitted.' ' Ah! ' said another, standing by, ' you can get a comfortable snooze and scrub there ! '

" A vast number of boys of tender years resort to these houses. I wish to show, what a variety of circumstances stand in the way of their moral or physical improvement. The existence of these houses is one of those circumstances. I have given a sample of the houses these children are compelled to inhabit. It would be found true on inquiry, *not only of the metropolis, but of the smaller as well as of the great towns throughout the country, that seven-tenths of the crime perpetrated in the different localities are concocted by the society, which meet in those lodging-houses.* The Warwick magistrates say, — and it is applicable to London, — ' such houses are the general receptacle of offenders. Here the common vagrants assemble in great numbers at nightfall, and, making the lodging-houses the common centre, traverse their several beats.' ' I have no hesitation,' says a public officer, ' in declaring my belief, that the principal robberies have been concocted in vagrant lodging-houses, and rendered effectual through the agency of the keepers.' That is not all. When a boy leaves the lodging-house, he is exposed to influences quite as deleterious to his moral and physical well-being. I shall read a description of a court, which I have witnessed myself. It is in such places that a large mass of the community dwell. In one of those courts there are three privies to 300 people; in another, two to 200 people. Here is a statement made by a medical man: — ' In a place, where these public privies exist, scenes of the most shocking character are of daily occurrence. It will scarcely be believed, that these public privies often stand *opposite* the doors of the houses: modesty and decency are therefore altogether impossible.' But, in a private house, is the boy exposed to better influences than in the lodging-house? Very often several families are found in one room. It is a fortunate family which has one room for itself. Everything is transacted in that room. Cleanliness is impossible; it is a scene of filth, misery, and vice. The House will permit me to give a description of a locality, which affords a fair sample of the class; for those children are a peculiar race, to be found in almost all instances, in the most filthy, destitute, unknown parts of the metropolis — places seldom trodden by persons of decent habits. These courts and alleys are in the immediate neighbourhood of uncovered sewers, of gutters full of putrified matter, nightmen's yards, and privies, the soil of which is openly exposed, and never or seldom removed. It is impossible to convey an idea of the poisonous condition, in which these places remain during winter and summer, in dry weather and wet, from the masses of putrifying matter which are allowed to accumulate. These statements are by no means exaggerations. I would not assert what I do, if I did not do so on my own personal knowledge, having gone over many parts of those districts, and having devoted a certain portion of my time to the prosecution of investigations on the subject, when, in 1846, I lost my seat in Parliament, being curious to find my way in those parts of the metropolis, which had hitherto been unexplored. In company with a medical man and a city missionary, I ventured to go over many of those places, and I am able to say, that the description, I have now given, is below the truth. I shall next advert to the physical condition of the children. They are thus described in a report by Dr. Aldis : —

" ' They are emaciated, pale, and thin, and in a low condition. They complain of sinking, depression of the strength, loss of spirits, loss of appetite accompanied by pains in different parts of the body, with disturbed sleep.' ' The depressed and low condition of health, in which these people are always found, induces habits of intemperance, unfortunately so common among them.' ' The children,' says another, ' are diminutive, pale, squalid, sickly, irritable ; I rarely saw a child in a really healthy state.'

" The report from one school says : —

" ' The boys have been sent out daily by drunken parents to beg and steal, being often cruelly treated if

unsuccessful; others are employed in vending and assisting in the manufacture of base coin. . . . .
Of 74 admitted this year between 8 and 14, 16 are known thieves, 27 are beggars and hawkers.' There is a most remarkable statement made on the authority of a city missionary in a district in the east of London. His house was the open resort of all, who chose to come to pay him a visit and ask his advice. From January to December he received from these children 2,343 visits, averaging 334 per month. Of these, under 10 years of age, there were 2 per cent. ; under 12, 9 per cent. ; above 12 and under 15, 44 per cent. ; above 15 and under 18, 36 per cent. ; above 18 and under 22, 8 per cent. Of these, 39 per cent. voluntarily acknowledged that they had been in prison ; 11 per cent. had been in once ; 4 per cent., *twice* ; 5 per cent., *thrice* ; 2 per cent. *four* times ; 1 per cent., *six* times ; 3 per cent., *seven* times ; 1 per cent., *eight* times ; 2 per cent., *ten* times ; and there were 10 per cent. *uncertain as to the number of times !* This state of matters arises in a great measure, either from desertion, or from the bad example of parents. In many instances, it is good for the children that they are deserted ; in many instances, it is good that they have no parents. But in many instances, they are misled by the bad example of their parents — in many instances, tempted by necessity. There are hundreds and thousands in this great city who, from their earliest years, have never obtained, what they do obtain, except by begging, or by stealing, or by some avocation of a questionable kind. Children are encouraged by their parents in that course of life. Even in those instances,

where parents do not bring their children up to steal, they take very good care, when property is brought in of a suspicious character, to ask no questions, and to bestow praise for adroitness in such transactions. But a very great deal of the evil, which surrounds the parents, arises from the sanitary condition, in which they are left. The same causes, which operate on the parents, operate on the children; and hundreds are found utterly reckless of decency, of comfort, of regard for the spiritual or temporal welfare of their children — reckless even of almost life itself."

What are the consequences of this terrible state of things? Hear what Lord Ashley says : —

" I wish to show the condition of the metropolis; and for that purpose, will state the number taken into custody by the metropolitan police in 1847, as contrasted with the number taken into custody in 1848. In 1847, 41,479 males were taken into custody ; OF WHOM 8,405 WERE UNDER 20 YEARS OF AGE, 3,228 BETWEEN 10 AND 15, AND 306 UNDER 10. In 1848, 42,933 males were taken into custody ; OF WHOM 8,776 WERE UNDER 20 YEARS OF AGE, 3,604 BETWEEN 10 AND 15, AND 312 UNDER 10. The total increase in 1848 of males taken into custody was 1,454, of whom one half, was under 20 years of age. But of those, who had been taken into custody under 10 years of age — the class which chiefly attended school — there had been an increase of only six. THE WHOLE NUMBER OF MALES TAKEN INTO CUSTODY BETWEEN 10 AND 20, A PERIOD OF 10 YEARS, WAS 12,692 ; between 25 and 50, a period of 25 years, 18,591 ; only one-third more. But looking at the number of those tried and convicted, there ap⁻

pears a great disproportion. BETWEEN 10 AND 20 THE MALES TRIED AND CONVICTED WERE 1,237, *whereas the males tried and convicted between 25 and 50 were only* 1,059. The same rule prevails in Manchester, to which I refer as a very large town, the returns being characterised by the same accuracy as those for the metropolis. There were taken into custody in Manchester 1,037 *males between* 10 *and* 20, *and* 2,157 *between* 25 *and* 50. But there were tried and convicted 165 between 10 and 20, 193 between 25 and 50. *These returns show the preponderating amount of* JUVENILE *delinquency*. They show also the possibility of applying the preventive system. The crimes are perpetrated, at a period of life, when the parties are open to the best influences, and are most capable of receiving permanent impressions. It is also clear that the seeds of crime are sown in early life, and would not, if they were then rooted out, grow up into rank maturity. Being anxious to ascertain the opinions of persons best acquainted with the subject, I circulated among persons having the charge of ragged schools, missionaries, and others, the question, ' Do many adult males become criminals for the first time after 20 years of age?' From 43 committees I received the answer, ' Very few.' One said, ' A small proportion, and these chiefly through drunkenness, and want of employment. In London, many country people, and the Irish, become criminals after 20 years of age, and those chiefly from the above-mentioned causes.' Another said, ' I should say not one in fifty.' Another, ' I believe that among the lowest classes of society, hardly any become criminal for the first time after 20 years of age.' That large class roaming over the streets of London, of habits, manners, feelings, and pursuits totally unlike anything, with which people are acquainted in ordinary life, forms a seed-plot for three-fourths of the crime, which prevails in this metropolis; *and what I say of the metropolis, I say of every great city in the empire.*

" The records of the tribunals and of the police courts, show only, what are the numbers of those, whom the police are adroit and quick enough to apprehend. But there is a vast amount of unseen crime ; there are breaches of the public peace, which are undetected ; there is a great deal of that training, which formed those children to a character dangerous to society. I believe the majority of criminals, in and about London, arises out of that class. If you greatly improve, or even extinguish that class as such, I do not mean to say, that crime will be removed; but the amount will be considerably abated, because I have no doubt, the greater part of the crime perpetrated within this metropolis and the neighbourhood, is perpetrated by individuals, who are formed and trained in the class, to which I have alluded. A city missionary wrote to me, that he looked on several parts of his district, as breeding places for prisons. It is the concurring testimony of those persons, who are best acquainted with the class in question, that from that class, the major part of the crimes, which are perpetrated, take their rise. The House will recollect, how I have described the children, their necessities, moral and physical, the manner in which they are trained, the state in which they remain, believing that they have a right to prey on the whole world, having no knowledge of right and wrong, except that which arises in some way or other out of their fears. I have now to call your attention to the temptations to which these children were exposed. I beg you to recollect that we have in this city a mass of THIRTY THOUSAND children, such as I have dèscribed, in a state of great necessity, living entirely by their wits, and not knowing from one hour to another whether they will obtain anything for their sustenance during the day. I ask the House, then, just to look at the temptations to which these children are exposed—temptations which are often commented on in the police court—from the want of care on the part of owners of property. I find that, of the felonies, which have been perpetrated last year, within the jurisdiction of the metropolitan police, there were 814 cases of stealing tools, &c., from unfinished houses, where they had been left by workmen, without any care or supervision whatever; that the number of cases of stealing from carts and carriages, which have been left without any one to look after them, is 298; that the number of cases of theft from houses, in consequence of the doors being left open by the most wanton neglect on the part of servants and masters, is 2,208; and that the number of cases of theft of goods exposed for sale at shop-doors—and honourable gentlemen will recollect, how freely goods of all descriptions are so exposed, especially of all kinds of provisions, calculated to tempt the appetite of poor children—of these cases the number is 2,299. Now, every one of these felonies has increased in number, with the exception, — and this is a very curious fact, — with the exception of felonies of linen exposed to dry. These have considerably abated; and I do not hesitate to assert, that this has arisen, from the establishment of public baths and washhouses; which enable poor people to wash and dry their clothes by a short and speedy process, and keep them under proper care and supervision. Now, I wish to draw the attention of the House to the result of this system of things, of the total neglect and want of care, in which these children are left, because I am pressing upon you, the necessity of doing something to extricate them from their hopeless condition. I therefore wish to show the House, that the children are of that extraordinary description that they cannot be dealt with by means of ordinary agency, that they are utterly dissimilar in their habits from other children, and that they are in nothing more remarkable than in their insubordination. I cannot give a better proof of this than by relating the kind of scenes which take place whenever a school is opened in a new locality. I have heard teachers who have undertaken to open such schools as a sort of speculation — I do not mean a money speculation, but a kind of experiment — I have heard them describe the roaring and whistling with which their ears have been assailed, and the actual onslaughts they have had to resist, on first opening these schools. There is a school over the water well known to my honourable friend the member for Kinsale (Mr. Hawes), whom I have frequently met there, to which, when it was first opened, in 1846, there came twenty-four boys, all with tobacco-pipes, who kept possession of the school, and would neither learn nor dislodge; and, as it was necessary that they should be invited, and not coerced, the teachers had to wait with patience in the hope, that they would get tired of their "lark," and go away, and let those remain who desired to do better. They did go away at last. Others came who were more anxious to be taught; and now the school is in active operation, and producing, I thank God, good effects. Another similar school has been got up in the neighbourhood of Camden Town, the teachers of which had at first their hats knocked off, and stones thrown at them. This is the history of almost every such school I have known; tumults invariably take place at the opening, and you may always calculate upon a fortnight or three weeks passing, before getting the children into habits of attention and order. It requires the highest exercise of patience to encounter obstacles so formidable and risks so peculiar."

The "Quarterly Review," not given to exaggerate on such subjects as these, describes the *juvenile population of the metropolis* as follows *: — "Every one, who walks the streets of the metropolis, must daily observe several members of the tribe—bold, and pert, and dirty as London sparrows, but pale, feeble, and sadly inferior to them in plumpness of outline. Their business, or pretended business, seems to vary with the locality. At the West-end they deal in lucifer-matches, audaciously beg, or tell a touching tale of woe. Pass on to the central parts of the town—to Holborn or the Strand, and the regions adjacent to them—and you will

* See the volume for 1847.

find the numbers very greatly increased: a few are pursuing the avocations above mentioned of their more Corinthian fellows; many are spanning the gutters with their legs, and dabbling with earnestness in the latest accumulation of nastiness; while others, in squalid and half-naked groups, squat at the entrances of the narrow fetid courts and alleys, that lie concealed behind the deceptive frontages of our larger thoroughfares. Whitechapel and Spitalfields teem with them like an ant's nest; but it is in Lambeth and Westminster, that we find the most flagrant traces of their swarming activity. There the foul and dismal passages are thronged with children of both sexes, and of every age from three to thirteen. Though wan and haggard, they are singularly vivacious, and engaged in every sort of occupation but that, which would be beneficial to themselves and creditable to the neighbourhood. Their appearance is wild; the matted hair, the disgusting filth, that renders necessary a closer inspection, before the flesh can be discerned between the rags, which hang about it, and the barbarian freedom from all superintendence and restraint, fill the mind of a novice in these things with perplexity and dismay. Visit these regions in the summer, and you are overwhelmed by the exhalations; visit them in the winter, and you are shocked by the spectacle of hundreds shivering in apparel, that would be scanty in the tropics; many are all but naked; those that are clothed are grotesque; the trousers, where they have them, seldom pass the knee; the tail coats very frequently trail below the heels. In this guise, they run about the streets and line the banks of the river at low water, seeking coals, sticks, corks, for nothing comes amiss as treasure trove. Screams of delight burst occasionally from the crowds, and leave the passer by, if he be in a contemplative mood, to wonder and rejoice that moral and physical degradation has not yet broken every spring of their youthful energies. . . . . .

" A large proportion of those who dwell in the capital" (and the writer might have added, in all the larger towns) " of the British empire, are crammed into regions of filth and darkness, the ancient but not solitary reign of the newts and toads.

" Here are the receptacles of the species we investigate ; here they are spawned, and here they perish ! Can their state be a matter of wonder ! We have penetrated alleys terminating in a *cul-de-sac*, long and narrow, like a tobacco-pipe, where air and sunshine were never known. On one side rose walls several feet in height, blackened with damp and slime ; on the other side stood the dwellings still more revolting, while the breadth of the wet and bestrewed passage would by no means allow us the full expansion of our arms ! We have waited at the entrance of another of similar character and dimensions, but forbidden by the force and pungency of the odours to examine its recesses. The novelty of a visit from persons clad like gentlemen, gave the hope, that we were official ; and several women, haggard, rough, and exasperated, surrounded us at once, imploring us to order the removal of the filth, which had poisoned their tenements, and to grant them a supply of water, from which they had been debarred for many days. Pass to another district ; you may find it less confined, but there you will see flowing before each hovel, and within a few feet of it, a broad, black, uncovered drain, exhaling at every point the most unwholesome vapours. If there be not a drain, there is a stagnant pool: touch either with your stick, and the mephitic mass will yield up its poisonous gas like the coruscations of soda water.

" The children sit along these depositories of death, or roam through the retired courts, in which the abomination of years has been suffered to accumulate. Here reigns a melancholy silence, seldom broken, but by an irritated scold or a pugnacious drunkard. The pale, discoloured faces of the inhabitants, their shrivelled forms, their abandoned exterior, recall the living skeletons of the Pontine Marshes, and sufficiently attest the presence of a secret agency, hostile to every physical and moral improvement of the human race.

" The interior of the dwellings is in strict keeping; the smaller space of the apartments increasing, of course, the evils that prevail without—damp, darkness, dirt, and foul air. Many are wholly destitute of furniture; many contain nothing except a table and a chair; some few have a common bed for all ages and both sexes; but a large proportion of the denizens of these regions lie on a heap of rags more nasty than the floor itself. Happy is the family that can boast of a single room to itself, and in that room, of a dry corner.   .   .   .

" The children that survive the noxious influences and awful neglect, are thrown, as soon as they can crawl, to scramble in the gutter, and leave their parents to amusement or business.   .   .   .   .   .

" The ' duris urgens in rebus egestas' stimulates these independent urchins; and at an age, when the children of the wealthy would still be in leading strings, they are off, singly or in parties, to beg, borrow, steal, and exercise all the cunning that want and a love of evil can stir up in a reckless race.   .   .   .   .

" They receive no education, religious or secular; they are subjected to no restraint of any sort; never do they hear the word of advice or the accent of kindness; the notions that exist in the minds of ordinary persons have no place in theirs; having nothing exclusively of their own, they seem to think such, in fact, the true position of society; and helping themselves, without scruple, to the goods of others, they can never recognise, when convicted before a magistrate, the justice of a sentence, which punishes them for having done little more than was indispensable to their existence."

This is a fair picture of the state of things in all our larger towns.   In the Lancashire towns, a great part of the juvenile poor are in, at least, as wretched a state, while the democratic tendencies of society in Lancashire, and the crowds of poor, who are congregated on a small area, add immeasurably to the dangers of this state of things.

How far this state of things conduces to the increase of vice may be gathered from the fact, that —

Out of the total of 59,123 persons taken into custody
in 1845,

15,263 could neither read nor write
39,659 could read only, and write
very imperfectly,

while in the year 1845, 14,887 persons of both sexes

UNDER TWENTY YEARS OF AGE, were taken into custody *by the police in the metropolis alone !*

It is scarcely necessary for me again to remind my readers, that in none of the towns of Germany, or Switzerland, or Holland does any thing at all comparable to this state of things exist. Throughout Germany, Switzerland, Denmark, and the Austrian empire, every parent is *obliged* to send his children to school, while each municipality is *obliged* to pay the school fees for the poor children, and to provide them all with decent and comfortable clothing. The consequence is, that all the children between the ages of six and fifteen, in the German and Swiss towns, and nearly all the children in the French, Dutch, Danish, and Norwegian towns, spend *every day* in airy, roomy, clean, and well-furnished class-rooms, or in dry exercise grounds, and often in the company of children of the middle classes, and in the society of men who are fit to be the teachers of the children of the rich.

And yet, notwithstanding that such is the state of things in the English towns, and that such vast numbers of children are uncared for and uneducated in 1850, there are good and earnest men to be found, who tell us that the *laissez faire* system has been, and is, equal to the work of reforming the condition of our poor !

I have mentioned the London City Mission. Some of my readers may not know what this society is. It is an association supported by voluntary contributions, and formed for the purpose of supporting a body of intelligent and religious men, — selected from members of the English Church and of the Christian dissenting bodies, and of a lower grade of society, than that to which our clergymen belong,—as visitors and advisers of the poor in the more densely populated districts of London.

The funds of the society amount, at the present time, to between 15,000*l*. and 20,000*l*. a-year. Between 100 and 200 visitors have been appointed, each of whom receives a salary of 70*l*. per annum. The society is under the patronage of many excellent men, and is sanctioned by several of our bishops.

Each of the visitors or missionaries has a district allotted him. He acts under the direction of some clergyman, layman, or dissenting minister, and is required to give regular accounts of his daily work, of the houses and families he has visited, of the state in which he has found them, and of the advice and assistance which he has rendered them.

The results of the labours of this excellent society have been very admirable. They have disclosed the state of the poor of London — they have rescued hundreds from degradation and misery — they have shed rays of happiness in dens of wretchedness, and have made the poor feel that good men pity them. The civilising influence of all this cannot be exaggerated.

The English clergy throughout the whole country stand in need of such assistants as the visitors of the "City Mission." Personal intercourse, and personal advice have very much greater effect upon the poor than sermons, or than the public services of the Church, even when those services are attended by the poor; but the truth is, that where there is not a constant intercourse between the clergyman and his people, the poor do not go to church. Of the operatives in Lancashire, and of the workmen in our great towns, there is not—and I speak after considerable experience and numerous inquiries—there is not one out of every ten who ever enters a church, and still fewer who attend regularly.

Let any one go into nine out of every ten of the churches in the densest parts of the metropolis, or into nine out of every ten of the Lancashire churches, and count the labourers present, and then compare them with the numbers, who live in the district, which appertains to the church, and he will soon satisfy himself of the sad truth of these assertions.

Take, for instance, the case of the parish of St. Pancras in London. The London City Mission have made the most careful inquiries into the state of church and chapel attendance in this district. It was not under the charge of a careless clergyman at the time of the inquiry. On the contrary, one of the most earnest and philanthropic of our clergy, viz. the Rev. Thomas Dale, was labouring there. From what we all know of Mr. Dale, we may be sure, that he had done all that lay in his power to foster religion among the inhabitants of his parish. And yet what was the state of things in January, 1848? In the number of the "City Mission Magazine" published in that month, I find it stated:—

1. That more than 100,000 inhabitants of the parish had NO sittings in either church or chapel.

2. That in 1841 the churches and chapels, which were opened on Sundays in the parish, were only HALF

filled, small as was their size in comparison to the population of the parish.

3. That nearly one poor family in every six in the parish was without the Scriptures.

4. That the *majority* of all the poor children in the parish were growing up without receiving daily instruction.

I do not quote this instance of St. Pancras as that of a peculiarly neglected parish. I believe, that it is well off, when compared to many others both in London and in other towns. I only quote it, as a fair instance of the state of things throughout the country.

Now, what are the causes of this state of things? There are several. In the first place, the religion of the English Church is too much above the comprehension of the *uneducated* masses; or, perhaps, I should say, that the intelligence of the masses is too little developed, to enable them to join in so intellectual and so unimaginative a form of worship, as that of the English Church, or as that of many of the sections of Dissenters. A Romanist service, or a Ranter's service, will attract crowds of poor, where the service of the English Church, or of the Independents, or of the Methodists, or of the Baptists will not attract fifty. But it will be said, that the Presbyterian churches of Scotland are filled, although the service is even less imaginative, than that of the English Church. It is so, because the Scotch poor are much better educated, and much more intelligent than our poor; because the Presbyterian clergymen are not nearly so far separated from the poor

in their social origin, habits and education, as our
clergy; and because they visit their people in their
cottages very much more than our English clergy
can do.

A second cause of the small numbers of the poor who
attend our churches, is the want of a much greater
system of parochial visitation.

In the great towns, and especially in the metropolis
and manufacturing districts of England, each poor
family *ought* to be visited at least once a week, if their
religious teachers are to have due influence upon them,
and if the doctrines and precepts of religion are to be
taught them, so as to be remembered. Of course, it is
physically impossible for the clergy in the towns, however zealous they may be, to visit the families of their
respective parishes nearly so often as this. In very
many parishes and town districts, it would be utterly
impossible for them, with the greatest efforts, to visit all
the poor in their districts, *at the most,* more than once or
twice a-year. The consequence is, that vast numbers
are never visited at all by their religious ministers,
whilst others are visited so seldom, that they cease to
feel, that they are in any way connected with the
clergyman of the district, and discontinue, or never
begin, to attend the public services of his church.

But there is another cause, of still more potent influence, which prevents a vast majority of the clergy,
from ever visiting the lowest haunts of the poor in their
districts, — and that is their education and associations. They are educated gentlemen; brought up in
comfortable homes, and in luxurious Universities;

trained in the most splendid halls of learning in the
world, in company with the sons of the highest, richest,
and most influential people of the country; and accustomed to associate with the most literary, refined, and
luxurious classes in the land. Now, however well
their origin, education, and manners, fit them to be
the patterns and advisers of the middle classes, to be
the foci of a high order of civilisation in their respective
districts, and to carry the politeness of the metropolis
into the most remote corners and into the most secluded
nooks of the island; it undoubtedly often unfits them
for the difficult task of visiting the poor in the low
haunts of our crowded towns. No one, but those who
have actually tried the experiment, can imagine, how
revolting it is to the senses of a refined man, to spend
hours, or even minutes, in the foul retreats of the most
degraded of our town poor. The atmosphere of the
rooms, where two, three, and four families often live
together in unwashed filth, and with scarce any ventilation; the manners, habits, food, and conversation
of these people; the effluvia from their beds, where
often as many as six individuals, parents and children,
crowd in together, render these dens of misery intolerable to a man of refined habits.

When to all this are added the great number of inhabitants in many of these districts, and the little assistance, which the clergyman receives; it is very easy to
understand why, even the most devoted of them find it
often impossible, ever to see anything of a vast number of the inhabitants of their districts.

It is a common remark of the operatives of Lan-

cashire, and one which is only too true, " Your Church
is a Church for the rich, but not for the poor.   It was
not intended for such people as we are."

The Roman Church is much wiser than the English
in this respect.   It selects a great part of its priests
from the poorest classes of society, and educates them
gratuitously in great simplicity of habits.   The consequence is, that they feel no difficulty in mingling with
the poor.   Many of them are not men of refined habits
themselves, and are not therefore disgusted at want of
refinement in others.   They understand perfectly what
are the thoughts, feelings, and habits of the poor.
They know, how to suit their demeanour, conversation,
teaching, and actions, so as to make the poor quite at
ease with them.   They do not feel the disgust, which
a more refined man cannot help feeling, in being obliged
to enter the low haunts of the back streets and alleys.

It is singular to observe how the priests of Romanist
countries abroad associate with the poor.   I have often
seen them riding with the peasants in their carts along
the roads, eating with them in their houses, sitting
with them in the village inns, mingling with them in
their village festivals, and yet always preserving their
authority.   Besides this, the spectacles of the Romanist
worship are much more attractive to the less educated
masses, than the less imaginative forms of Protestant
worship, and the services of the Roman Church are
shorter and much more numerous than those of the
English.   These causes fill the Romanist churches, both
abroad, and in our manufacturing districts, on the Sundays, and at the early matins of the weekdays, with

crowds of poor, who go there to receive the blessing of their priests, to hear prayers put up, which they believe to be for blessings, although they do not understand them, and to see the glittering spectacles of the Romanist worship exhibited before them.

It behoves us to consider these things, if the English Church is not willing to give up the poor to the care of the Romanist priests. There are significant facts before us, if we would but see them. Within the last few years, splendid Romanist churches, full of free sittings, have been springing up in all the crowded districts of England, and especially in the manufacturing towns of the north. In Manchester alone, three beautiful Romanist churches, and one magnificent Romanist cathedral, — now by far the finest building in the town, — have been erected within the last twelve years. The priests seem to be able to obtain as much money as they require; and to spare no pains to attract the people. Their exertions among the poorest of the operatives, and in the lowest of their haunts, are praiseworthy in the extreme. They know that it is infinitely more important to have priests than churches. When they build a church, therefore, they generally attach to it, not one, but several, and often many priests, some of them chosen from the lowest classes of the community, and educated expressly for their labours. In the manufacturing districts of England, a large handsome building, of the same style of architecture as the church, and capable of serving as the dwelling-house of ten or twelve priests, is generally attached to each of the churches.

These churches and priest-houses are situated in the districts most densely populated with the poorest of the operative classes, and near their lowest haunts. The church and its servants, both arrayed and surrounded with all the ornaments and ceremonials of a very richly and beautifully adorned form of worship, are placed close to the doors of the worst and most degraded of the population. The churches are built with the greatest possible taste, both as regards their exteriors and their interiors, and are as splendidly ornamented, as beautifully painted, as well warmed and cleaned, and as comfortable, as they could be, if they had been intended for the use of the richest classes in the land; while nearly all the sittings in them are free to the humblest of the people.

When the poor enter, they find themselves treated in the Temple of their God, with the same respect as the richest; while all their senses are gratified in the highest degree. When to all this is added the fact, that the priests carry out an indefatigable and unostentatious system of visitation, it is not a matter of surprise, that they should be making many converts among our people.

I have been assured by clergymen of Lancashire, who are equally removed above bigotry and indifference, and who are themselves the most earnest labourers among the poor, that the progress of Romanism throughout the manufacturing districts is very extraordinary.

They attribute it to the following causes: —

1st. The astounding ignorance of the great mass of

the operatives, which renders them unfit for the un-imaginative and intellectual worship of the English Church.

2dly. The too great length of the services of the English Church, and the small number of services in the week, and on the Sunday.

3dly. The small number of clergy in the most thickly populated districts.

4thly. The want of an inferior order of clergy.

If, in addition to all this, we remember, that vast num-bers of the poor of our towns cannot read or write a word, have never entered one of our churches, and have never heard the doctrines of Christianity; and that of the thousands of criminals who are convicted at our sessions and assizes, very few have ever received any instruction whatever, it certainly does behove us to stir ourselves.

The only way, by which we can hope to render the labours of our town clergy really efficient among the poor, is, to give them, as assistants, religious and intelli-gent men, chosen from among the poor themselves. Each clergyman ought to have two or three such assist-ants, whom he might employ, as the city missionaries are employed, in constantly visiting all the poor in his trict, even in the most loathsome of their dwellings; in rendering him weekly accounts of their labours; in advising, instructing, and admonishing the poor; in getting their children sent to school; in seeing that they were regular in attendance there; in urging the parents to attend a place of worship; and, in fine, in acting as their friends and religious instructors.

If the English Church does not soon adopt some such scheme, the poor of many of our towns will be entirely lost to her.

But to resume our description of the English poor.

Another very singular and very melancholy proof of the degradation and pauperism of a great part of our labouring population, is to be found, in the alarming magnitude of the numbers of vagrants, or wandering beggars, who now infest all parts of the country. This evil has become so enormous in the last six years, that the attention of the poor-law board, and of the government, has been attracted to it. An elaborate and very able Report upon the frightful extent of this growing evil has been drawn up, under the direction of the poor-law board, by Mr. Boase, and has been laid before the Houses of Parliament. From this Report, I have derived all the materials of the short sketch of this horrible phenomenon, which I now offer to my readers.

Large and ever-increasing hordes of vagrants, or wandering beggars, infest all the highways of England and Wales. These poor wretches are miserably clothed, filthily dirty, covered with vermin, and, generally, very much diseased; sometimes from debauchery, and sometimes — though this would appear to be the exceptional case — from the want of food. These vagrants consist, in some parts of the country, of nearly equal parts of Irish and English; while, in other parts, two-thirds of them are Irish, and the other third English. They are composed of persons of both sexes, and of all ages. Very few are married. The women, of whom there are great numbers, are nearly all prostitutes. Each man is generally attended by one or two such companions in misery and crime.

They clothe badly, and keep themselves as filthy as possible, in order the better to excite the compassion of those, to whom they apply for alms in the course of each day's march.

The manner of life of these creatures is singular. They beg, during the day, in the towns, or along the roads; and they so arrange their day's tramp, as to arrive, most nights, in the neighbourhood of some one of our workhouses. They then hide the money they have collected by begging, and present themselves, after sunset, at the gates of the workhouse, to beg a night's lodging. This, it appears, the guardians are obliged — or conceive they are obliged — to grant to all applicants.

To nearly every workhouse there are attached, what are called vagrant-wards, or buildings, which are specially set apart for the reception of tramps, such as those I have described. These wards are generally brick buildings, of one story in height. They have brick floors, and guard-room beds, with loose straw and rugs for the males, and iron bedsteads, with straw, for the females. They are badly ventilated, and unprovided with any means of producing warmth. It is, indeed, useless to attempt to keep them ventilated, as all holes for ventilation are sure to be stuffed up at night, by the occupants, with rags or straw, so that the stench of these sleeping-places is disgusting in the extreme. In some places, such is the filthy state of the poor wretches who are admitted at night, that it is necessary to have the framework of the beds whitewashed every day. In many places it is found impossible to give them beds, because the tramps swarm so horribly with vermin. In these cases, a rug is allowed to each, and the rug is washed in the morning.

Men are kept, in order to guard these foul receptacles every night; but it is needless to observe, that nothing can prevent scenes, which I may not attempt to describe.

The tramps are admitted from six to ten in the evenings. Those who arrive before nine are provided with a supper of milk and bread, and with a breakfast of the same kind, on condition, that they will remain in the workhouse, and perform from two to three hours' work, in breaking stones, picking oakum, or some other such employment, before they receive their breakfast.

Very often the poor wretches, and their women, prefer leaving early, without breakfast, to remaining, and obtaining breakfast on such terms as these.

Union workhouses are generally not more than ten miles apart, so that the vagrants can afford to spend time upon the road, or to make a detour, in order to beg in some town or village lying out of the direct route. If they start from the workhouse about nine in the morning, they have time to do a great deal of business before they cram into the next vagrant den for the night.

They often make as much as from five to ten shillings a day by begging, from charitable and inconsiderate people. They often carry about with them large sums of money. Before entering into a workhouse — where they would be searched — they deposit this money in shops, or hide it, or leave one of their party out of the house, with the charge of the money, while the others crowd into the ward free of expense.

The cost of receiving the crowds of these tramps, who swarm on all the great roads, is become so heavy already, and is so rapidly increasing, that the boards of guardians find it absolutely impossible to attempt any-thing like classification or separation of the sexes. The expense is already so great, that the unions are beginning, in all directions, to cry to government to be delivered from this frightful plague by some means or another. It is quite certain that the present system is aggravating the evil every day.

The degradation of these poor wretches is hardly conceivable. Mr. Boase says, that it is quite incom-prehensible how they can themselves endure the air and condition of the wards, unless it be explained, by the fact, that their senses have become dulled, and incapable of fulfilling their functions. Night-stools, or privies, are generally provided in connection with the wards; the wretched beings, however, will not use them, but defile the sleeping wards. It is found necessary to have the floors of the wards washed down every morning with buckets of water.

The conduct of the poor wretches is reported to be bad in the extreme. They are described as being noisy and turbulent; as making the wards resound with the vilest songs and language; as being ungrateful and refractory towards the ward-officers; and as having habits too filthy and indecent to be named.

This evil is rapidly increasing, and is a strange and melancholy commentary upon the state of our poorer classes, especially as compared with the improving state of the same classes in Germany and Switzerland, where no such phenomenon exists at all.

The following selections from the returns, will show the rapid increase of the numbers of tramps relieved in different unions during the last few years. These are only instances of a state of things which is almost universal.

	Year.			No. of Vagrants relieved.
Watford Union	1844	-	-	627
	1845	-	-	918
	1846	-	-	953
	1847	-	-	2,486
	1848	-	-	3,487
Derby Union	1845	-	-	2,442
	1846	-	-	2,960
	1847	-	-	6,293
Newport House of Refuge	1846	-	-	3,953
	1847	-	-	25,120

Year ending March,

	Year.			No. of Vagrants relieved.
Chepstow Union	1846	-	-	1,141
	1847	-	-	1,640
	1848	-	-	4,525

Year ending 25th March,

	Year.			No. of Vagrants relieved.
Brentford Union	1841	-	-	1,368
	1842	-	-	3,000
	1843	-	-	5,444
	1844	-	-	6,865
	1845	-	-	5,267
	1846	-	-	4,530
	1847	-	-	5,857
	1848	-	-	14,368

	Year ending 25th March,			No. of Vagrants relieved.
Uxbridge Union	1845	-	-	2,835
	1846	-	-	2,965
	1847	-	-	6,322

	Year ending Lady-day,			
Windsor Union	1846	-	-	1,708
	1847	-	-	2,033
	1848	-	-	5,368

	Year ending Michaelmas,			
Eton Union	1844	-	-	2,666
	1845	-	-	2,924
	1846	-	-	2,903
	1847	-	-	4,375

	Year ending Lady-day,			
Newcastle-under-Lyne Union	1846	-	-	1,953
	1847	-	-	2,736
	1848	-	-	4,967

	Year ending 25th March,			
Stafford Union	1845	-	-	3,126
	1846	-	-	3,047
	1847	-	-	5,264
	1848	-	-	11,108

	Year ending Midsummer,			
Aylesbury Union	1845	-	-	1,344
	1846	-	-	1,430
	1847	-	-	2,077
	1848	-	-	2,847

	Years.			
City of London Union	1840	-	-	2,403
	1844	-	-	24,574
	1845	-	-	26,003
	1846	-	-	33,655
	1847	-	-	41,743

These returns will suffice to show the alarming extent of this evil, and the way in which it is growing in almost all parts of the island. This will be made all the more apparent by the following table : —

Average number of vagrants relieved in one night in 603 unions in England and Wales, in the week ending 20th of Dec. 1845 - - - -	1,791
Average number relieved in one night in 603 unions, in the week ending 19th of Dec. 1846 - - -	2,224
Average number relieved in one night in 596 unions, in the week ending 18th Dec. 1847 - - -	4,508
Number relieved in 626 unions on 25th of March, 1848 -	16,086

If, however, I were only to state that 16,086 of such poor wretches as I have described were wandering about our roads begging alms in March, 1848, I should give no idea of the magnitude of this plague. Hitherto, I have only spoken of those, who seek shelter for the night in the workhouse vagrant-wards. But, besides these, there are vast numbers, who sleep every night in the vagrant- lodging-houses in the towns.* These lodging-houses, which are to be found in most of our towns, consist of long low rooms, filled with beds or mattresses, upon which the vagrants of all ages and of both sexes, sleep, two or three in one bed or upon one mattress. These rooms are unventilated, seldom cleaned, filthy and close beyond comprehension, to those who have not been into them. In these dens, the vagrants, pickpockets, beggars, and, in fine, all the homeless wanderers of our streets, sleep crowded together. Old men and young men, old women and young women, and, worst of all, children of all ages, from the infant at the breast to the boy, who is just ripening into the felon, are crowded together. The scenes, which take place in these places, are horri-

* For a description of these horrid dens, see Mr. Chadwick's sanitary Reports, the reports of the City Mission, the Police Reports, and Lord Ashley's speeches.

ble. In one bed sleeps a man with two women; in another, a woman with two men; in another, two or three women or men; in another, a poor mother and her children. Drunkards, pickpockets, prostitutes, and beggars, covered with vermin, are packed in together. Foul songs, oaths, drunken yells, and groans, mingle every night in one sad chorus, until sleep closes the eyes of all.

In such scenes as these, and surrounded by such companions as these, the women are often delivered of children, thus adding to the foul indelicacy and barbarity of the scene.

The sleep of the poor wretches is often broken by the entrance of the police to seek some offender, whom they are ordered to find out and give up to justice; for the police, who know all these haunts, regard them as the general rendezvous of the offscouring of the towns.

One of the city missionaries, describing the state of the Mint district in the city of London, says, "it is utterly impossible to describe the scenes, which are to be witnessed here, or to set forth in its naked deformity the awful characters sin here assumes . . . . . . *In Mint Street, alone, there are nineteen lodging-houses.* The majority of these latter are awful sinks of iniquity, and are used as houses of accommodation. In some of them, both sexes sleep together indiscriminately, and such acts are practised and witnessed, that married persons, who are in other respects awfully depraved, have been so shocked, as to be compelled to get up in the night and leave the house. Many of the half-naked impostors, who perambulate the streets of London in the day-time, and obtain a livelihood by their deceptions, after having thrown off their bandages, crutches, &c., may be found here in their true character; some regaling themselves in the most extravagant manner; others gambling or playing at cards, while the worst of language proceeds from their lips. Quarrels and fights are very common, and the cry of murder is frequently heard. The public houses in this street are crowded to excess, especially on the Sabbath evening." *

In the Police Reports published in the " Sun" newspaper of the 11th of October, 1849, the following account is given of *" a penny lodging-house "* in Blue Anchor Yard, Rosemary Lane. One of the policemen examined, thus describes a room in this lodging-house : — " It was a very small one, extremely filthy, and there was no furniture of any description in it. *There were sixteen men, women, and children, lying on the floor, without covering. Some of them were half-naked.* For this miserable shelter, each lodger paid a penny. The stench was intolerable, and the place had not been cleaned out for some time."

If the nightly inmates of these dens are added to the tramps who seek lodging in the vagrant-wards of the workhouses, we shall find that there are at least between 40,000 and 50,000 tramps who are daily infesting our roads and streets !

I might crowd my pages with such accounts.

And yet with this plague-spot spreading in this horrible manner, and distinguishing us from all the other nations of Europe, we are still wrangling and disputing

* City Mission Magazine, Oct. 1847.

HOW and WHO are to educate the poor.   And with such
facts as these staring them in the face, there are men
who tell us, that it is better that the poor should not be
educated, than that the government should be allowed
to aid in carrying out this great national undertaking.

Another sad symptom of the condition of the poor of
our towns is the use they make of the " burial clubs."
In some of our towns the degradation of many of the
poor is such, that parents often cause the death of their
children, in order to obtain the premiums from the
societies.

The accounts of these " burial clubs," and of the extent to which infanticide is practised in some parts of
this country, may be found in Mr. Chadwick's able
Reports upon the sanitary condition of the poor.

It appears, that in our larger provincial towns the
poor are in the habit of entering their children in
what are called " burial clubs."   A small sum is paid
every year by the parent, and this entitles him to receive from 3l. to 5l. from the club, on the death of the
child.   Many parents enter their children in several
clubs.   One man in Manchester has been known to
enter his child in *nineteen* different clubs.   On the death
of such a child, the parent becomes entitled to receive
a large sum of money ; and as the burial of the child
does not necessarily cost more than 1l., or, at the most,
1l. 10s., the parent realises a considerable sum after
all the expenses are paid !

It has been clearly ascertained, that it is a common
practice among the more degraded classes of poor in
many of our towns, to enter their infants in these clubs,

and then to cause their death either by starvation, ill-usage, or poison! What more horrible symptom of moral degradation can be conceived ? One's mind revolts against it, and would fain reject it as a monstrous fiction. But, alas! it seems to be but too true.

Mr. Chadwick says *, " officers of these burial societies, relieving officers, and others, whose administrative duties put them in communication with the lowest classes in these districts " (the manufacturing districts), " express their moral conviction of the operation of such bounties to produce instances of the visible neglect of children of which they are witnesses. They often say, ' You are not treating that child properly ; it will not live : *is it in the club ?*' And the answer corresponds with the impression produced by the sight.

" Mr. Gardiner, the clerk to the Manchester union, while registering the causes of death, deemed the cause assigned by a labouring man for the death of a child unsatisfactory, and staying to inquire, found that popular rumour assigned the death to wilful starvation. The child (according to a statement of the case) had been entered in at least *ten* burial clubs; *and its parents had had six other children, who only lived from nine to eighteen months respectively.* They had received from several burial clubs 20*l.* for *one* of these children, and they expected at least as much on account of this child. An inquest was held at Mr. Gardiner's instance, when several persons, who had known the deceased stated, that she was a fine fat child shortly after her birth, but that

* Sanitary Inquiry Report, 1843, p. 64.

she soon became quite thin, was badly clothed, and seemed as if she did not get a sufficiency of food. . . . . The jury, having expressed it as their opinion, that the evidence of the parents was made up for the occasion, and entitled to no credit, returned the following verdict: —' Died through want of nourishment, but whether occasioned by a deficiency of food, or by disease of the liver and spine, brought on by improper food and drink, or otherwise, does not appear.'

" Two similar cases came before Mr. Coppock, the clerk and superintendent-registrar of the Stockport union, in both of which he prosecuted the parties for murder.   In one case, where three children had been poisoned with arsenic, the father was tried with the mother, and convicted, at Chester, and sentenced to be transported for life, but the mother was acquitted. In the other case, where the judge summed up for a conviction, the accused, the father, was, to the astonishment of every one, acquitted.   In this case the body was exhumed after interment, and *arsenic was detected in the stomach.*   In consequence of the suspicion raised upon the death, on which the accusation was made in the first case, the bodies of two other children were taken up and examined, when *arsenic was found in their stomachs.*   In all these cases payments on the deaths of the children were insured from the burial clubs; the cost of the coffin and burial dues would not be more than about 1*l.*, and the allowance from the club is 3*l.*

" It is remarked on these dreadful cases by the superintendent-registrar, *that the children who were boys, and therefore likely to be useful to the parents, were not poisoned;* the female children were the victims. It was the clear opinion of the medical officers that infanticides have been committed in Stockport to obtain the burial money."

The town clerk of Stockport says [*], " *I have no doubt that infanticide, to a considerable extent, has been committed in the borough of Stockport.*

" I know it to be the opinion of some of the respectable medical practitioners in Stockport, that infanticides have been commonly influenced by various motives — to obtain the burial moneys from the societies in question, and to be relieved from the burden of the child's support. The parties generally resort to a mineral poison, which, causing sickness, and sometimes purging, assumes the appearance of the diseases, to which children are subject; and as they then take the child to a surgeon, who prescribes after a very cursory examination, they thus escape any suspicion on the part of their neighbours."

Mr. Chadwick says again[†], " At the Liverpool assizes in 1843, a woman named Eccles was convicted of the murder of one child, and was under the charge of poisoning two others with arsenic. Immediately the murders were committed, it appeared she went to demand a stated allowance of burial money from the employers of the children. The collector of a burial society, one of the most respectable in Manchester, stated to me strong grounds for believing, that it had become a prac-

[*] Sanitary Inquiry Report, 1843, p. 235.'
[†] Ibid., p. 65.

tice to neglect children for the sake of the money allowed."

The able author of the " Letters on Labour and the Poor in the Rural Districts," lately published in the " Morning Chronicle," writing of the " burial clubs " in the eastern counties, says, " The suspicion that a great deal of ' foul play ' exists with respect to these clubs is supported, not only by a comparison of the different rates of mortality, but it is considerably strengthened, by the facts proved upon the trial of Mary May.   The Rev. Mr. Wilkins, the vicar of Wickes, who was mainly in- strumental in bringing the case before a court of justice, stated to me, that from the time of Mary May coming to live in his parish, he was determined to keep a very strict watch upon her movements, as he had heard that *fourteen of her children had previously died suddenly.* A few weeks after her arrival in his parish, she called upon him to request him to bury one of her children. Upon his asking her which of the children it was, she told him that it was ' Eliza,' a fine healthy-looking child of ten years old.   Upon his expressing some sur- prise, that she should have died so suddenly, she said, ' Oh, sir, she went off like a snuff; all my other children did so, too.'   A short time elapsed, and she again waited upon the vicar, to request him to bury her brother as soon as he could.   His suspicions were aroused, and he endeavoured to postpone the funeral for a few days, in order to enable him to make some inquiries.   Not suc- ceeding in obtaining any information, which would war- rant further delay in burying the corpse, he most re- luctantly proceeded in the discharge of his duty.   About a week after the funeral Mary May again waited upon him, to request him to sign a certificate to the effect that her brother was in perfect health a fortnight before he died,—that being the time at which, as it subsequently appeared, she had entered him as nominee in the Harwich Burial Club. Upon inquiring as to the reason of her desiring this certificate, she told him, that unless she got it, she could not get the money for him from the club. This at once supplied the vicar with what appeared to be a motive for ' foul play ' on the part of the woman. He accordingly obtained permission to have the body of her brother exhumed ; doses of arsenic were detected, and the woman was arrested. With the evidence given upon the trial, the reader is, no doubt, perfectly conversant, and it will be unnecessary for me to detail it. She was convicted. Previously to her execution, she refused to make any confession, but said, ' *If I were to tell all I know, it would give the hangman work for the next twelve months.*' Undue weight ought not to be attached to the declaration of such a woman as Mary May, but coupled with the disclosures, that took place upon the trial, with respect to some of her neighbours and accomplices, and with the extraordinary rate of mortality among the clubs, it certainly does appear, that the general opinion with respect to the mischievous effects of these societies is not altogether without foundation.

"Although there are not in Essex, at present, any burial clubs, in which children are admitted under fourteen years of age, as members or nominees, still, as illustrating the evils arising from these clubs, I may state that many persons who are fully conversant with the working of such institutions, have stated, that they have frequently been shocked by hearing women of the lower classes, when speaking of a neighbour's child, make use of such expressions as, ' *Oh, depend upon it, the child 'll not live; it's in the burial club.*' When speaking to the parents of a child who may be unwell, it is not unfrequently that they say, ' You should do so and so,' or ' you should not do so and so ;' ' *you should not treat it in that way; is it in the burial club ?*' Instances of the most culpable neglect, if not of graver offences, are continually occurring in districts, where clubs exist, in which children are admitted. A collector of one of the most extensive burial societies gave it as his opinion, founded upon his experience, that it had become a constant practice to neglect the children for the sake of the allowance from the clubs, and he supported his opinion by several cases, which had come under his own observation."

From a very remarkable letter published in " The Times " of the 18th of January, A. D. 1849, by that indefatigable and earnest man, the Rev. J. Clay, chaplain of the Preston House of Correction, I collect the following particulars, still further illustrating this horrible symptom of our social state.

Mr. Clay says, — " Let me recall to your recollection *some* of the murders for burial money perpetrated since the publication of Mr. Chadwick's admirable Report on interment in towns. 1. A Liverpool paper of April, 1846, gives the details of an inquiry before the coroner in a case of 'infanticide, at Runcorn, to obtain funeral money.' It appeared, in evidence, that James Pimlet, aged ten months, died on the 6th of March, and that on the 21st of the same month died Richard Pimlet, aged four years and a half. On the 27th of the same month a *third* child was taken ill. The medical man's suspicions were roused. The authorities caused the bodies of the two dead infants to be exhumed. It was found, that the *mother* had purchased arsenic before the children's illness. Dr. Brett showed the presence of arsenic in the bodies ' in quantities more than sufficient to cause death.' The collector of the Liverpool Victoria Legal Burial Society proved, that the three children were all enrolled members ; that he had paid 1*l.* 5*s.* on the death of one child, and 5*l.* on the death of the other. The steward of another society proved the payment of 1*l.* 5*s.* and 1*l.* 15*s.* on the two deaths. Verdict, ' wilful murder ' against the mother.

2. " At York assizes, in July, 1846, John Rodda was convicted of the wilful murder of his own child, aged one year. The evidence proved, that the wretch poured a spoonful of sulphuric acid down his helpless infant's throat. It was proved that he had said, he did not care how soon the child died, for whenever it died, he should have 2*l.* 10*s.*, as it was in a ' dead list.' He said he had another that would have the same when it died, and two others that would have 5*l.* a piece when they died.

3. "In June, 1847, Mary Ann Milner was charged with the wilful murder — by arsenic — of her mother-in-law, her sister-in-law, and her niece; her father-in-law had also well nigh become her victim, and was reduced to imbecility from the effects of the poison. The only imaginable motive for the conduct of the prisoner, as

suggested by the counsel for the prosecution, and as supported by the evidence, was the obtaining moneys from a burial society.

4. " In July, 1848, Mary May took her trial for the murder of Spratty Watts, by the favourite means —arsenic. This horrible case will be still in the recollection of your readers. The woman had put her victim into a ' death list,' which lured her to her crime, by promising 9*l.* or 10*l.* on its perpetration. ' The private confession of Mrs. May afforded '—I quote from ' The Times' of September 21, — ' a clue to a system, *which it is feared is capable of most extensive proof, and will result in the conviction of a large number of women,* who have adopted the practice of poisoning their husbands and children for the purpose of obtaining the fees which are granted by what are, in this part of the country, termed *death lists.*'

5. " I must add to this imperfect, but too full catalogue, the name of Ann Mather, against whom, in August, 1847, a coroner's jury, at Warrington, returned a verdict of ' wilful murder.' Her husband's name being in three separate *'death lists,'* the usual means—arsenic —was resorted to, and the desperate gamestress won 20*l.* I shall merely name the ' Essex poisonings;' their horrible notoriety has not yet subsided. Let it be remembered, that we have here only a portion of the positive murders resulting from the temptations offered by burial clubs. No one can guess how many more victims — infants especially — have been poisoned, or otherwise destroyed, for the sake of the coveted burial money, though neither inquiry nor suspicion may have been

excited; nor, how many children, entered by their parents in burial clubs, are, when attacked by sickness, suffered to die without any effort being made to save their lives.

"My report on the sanitary condition of Preston, given in the 'First Report of the Health of Towns Commission,' furnishes startling evidence of the wide prevalence of this feeling. A collector of cottage rents states, that '*almost all the children of the families where he collects are members of burial societies. . . . . The children of the poor when sick are greatly neglected; the poor seldom seek medical assistance for sick children, except when they are at the point of death.*' Another collector states '*the poor people have often told me that they were unable to pay at that time; but when a certain member of the family — generally a child — died, they would be able to pay.*' . . . . A lady states, that a young woman, whose services she required as wet nurse, having a child ill, she offered to send her own medical friend to attend it; the reply of the nurse was, '*Oh! never mind, ma'am, it's in two burial clubs.*' It also appears, on the unimpeachable authority of a burial-club official, that '*hired nurses speculate on the lives of infants committed to their care, by entering them in burial clubs*;' that 'two young women proposed to enter a child into his club, and to pay the weekly premium alternately. Upon inquiring as to the relation subsisting between the two young women and the child, he learned that the infant was placed at nurse with the mother of one of these young women.' The wife of a clergyman told me that, visiting a poor district just when a child's

death had occurred, instead of hearing from the neighbours the language of sympathy for the bereaved parent,
she was shocked by such observations as — ' Ah! it's a
fine thing for the mother, the child's in two clubs!'
. . . . As regards one town, I possess some evidence of the amount of burial-club membership, and of
infant mortality, which I beg to lay before you. . . .
The reports of this town refer to 1846, when the population of the town amounted to about 61,000. I do not
name the town, because, as no actual burial-club murders are known to have been committed in it, and as
such clubs are not more patronised there, than in other
places, it is, perhaps, not fair to hold it up to particular
animadversion ; indeed, as to its general character, this
very town need not fear comparison with any other.
Now, this place, with its 61,000 people of all classes
and ages, maintains at least eleven burial clubs, the
members of which amount in the aggregate to nearly
52,000 ; nor are these all. Sick clubs, remember,
act as burial clubs. Of these there are twelve or
fourteen in the town, mustering altogether, probably,
2000 members. Here, then, we have good data for
comparing population with ' death lists ;' but it will be
necessary, in making the comparison, to deduct from
the population all that part of it, which has nothing to
do with these clubs ; viz., all infants under two months
old, and all persons of unsound health (both of these
classes being excluded by the club rules); all those
also of the working classes, whose sound intelligence
and feeling lead them to abhor burial-club temptations ;
and all the better classes, to whom 5l. or 20l. offer no

consolation for the death of a child. On the hypothesis
that these deductions will amount to one-sixth of the
entire population, it results, that the *death lists* are more
numerous by far than the entire mass — old, young,
and infants — which support them; and according to
the statement of a leading death-list officer, THREE-
FOURTHS of the names on these catalogues of the
doomed are the names of children. Now, if this be
the truth — and I believe it is — hundreds, if not thousands, *of children must be entered each into* FOUR, FIVE,
or even TWELVE *clubs,* their chances of life diminishing,
of course, in proportion to the frequency with which
they are entered. Lest you should imagine, that such
excessive addiction to burial clubs is only to be found
in one place, I furnish you with a report for 1846, *of a*
single club, which then boasted 34,100 *members — the en-*
tire population of the town to which it belongs having
been in 1841 *little more than* 36,000 ! ! !

" I would now bespeak your attention to the infantile
mortality in places where burial clubs flourish. In Dr.
Lyon Playfair's 'Report on the Sanitary Condition of
large Towns in Lancashire,' p. 53., it is stated, that
among the poor of Manchester, out of 100 *deaths,* 60 *to*
65 *are of infants under five years old. One man*
put his children into nineteen clubs! . . . . . Dr.
Lyon Playfair again shows (p. 54.) that children die in
Manchester, when wages are high, at a rate more than
that, at which they die among the poverty-stricken labourers of Dorsetshire. . . . .

" I have now before me communications from five
medical gentlemen, resident in the town of 61,000 inha-

bitants above alluded to (four of them surgeons to the union, and the fifth the medical officer of an institution furnishing gratuitous medical aid to the poor), showing their attendance on poor children under five years old, contrasted with their attendance on the poor above that age.   The older patients, for whom medical aid was sought, constitute 87 per cent., the younger ones 13 per cent.   Poor little creatures! 56 per cent. die, but only 13 per cent. of them have the doctor's help, though it may be had for asking.   I extract the following from the communications alluded to: —

" 1. ' The above numbers (247 patients above five years of age, and 26 under five years of age,) very strikingly illustrate what I have frequently remarked otherwise, — the great indifference displayed by parents and others in the lower ranks of life with regard to infant life.'

" 2. ' With respect to the attendance which the poorer classes give to their children in sickness, I am sorry to say it is generally anything but what it ought to be. . . . . If they seek medical aid at all, it is too often when there is not the slightest chance of recovery.'

" 3. ' My impression is, that very few of the children of the operative class, in sickness, fall under the notice of the medical men of the town.   But latterly there has been a disposition to call us in, in the last stage of disease, *for the purpose of obtaining a certificate of death,* for the registrar.'

" 4. ' My general impression, derived from three years' experience at this institution, compels me to admit, what is very painful to acknowledge, that there is *among the poorer classes a manifest* and cold indifference to the health of infants, and especially so when suffering from disease.'

" The above extracts are from letters written in 1846. Since then, the medical certificate necessary to the registration of death has been more stringently required, and it was hoped would produce better attention to sick children. How far that hope has been realised, is shown in the following extract from a letter, written by the present medical officer of the charitable institution adverted to, a gentleman of distinguished zeal and ability : — ' The return rather understates the mortality of infantile life ; for in several instances, where very gross neglect has been apparent, and where our aid has only been requested in extremes, I have declined to give certificates, and such cases do not appear in the list. The whole number of patients admitted during the year 1847, was 3052 : of these 341 were under five years of age, 2711 were above five years of age. It would thus appear, that although one half of all the deaths in the town consists of children under five years of age, the proportion of those who become patients of the only charitable medical institution in the place is only one-eighth of that above five years ! Of the cases under five years, 1 in 6 proved fatal ; of those above five years, 1 in $19\frac{1}{4}$. . . . . The difference between a mortality of 1 in 6 and 1 in $19\frac{1}{4}$ is too great to be accounted for on any other supposition, than that of the existence of great neglect on the part of the parents."

These accounts are really almost too horrible to be

believed at all; and were they not given us on the authority of men of such great experience and benevolence, we should totally discredit them.

But, alas, they are only too true! There can be no doubt, that a great part of the poorer classes of this country are sunk into such a frightful depth of hopelessness, misery, and utter moral degradation, that even mothers forget their affection for their helpless little offspring, and kill them, as a butcher does his lambs, in order to make money by the murder, and therewith to lessen their pauperism and misery!

And yet we are sending hundreds of thousands of our savings every year to convert and comfort the heathen, who are seldom so morally degraded; while we are wrangling about the *way* in which we shall educate the poor; and are still telling Government that *voluntary* efforts will enable us to accomplish this great work.

I might greatly multiply the proofs of the universal existence of this evil; but the above quotations are, I think, sufficient to give an idea of this terrible sign of the social state of many of our poor.

Another melancholy symptom of the same fact is to be found in the great numbers and miserable condition of the inhabitants of the cellars of our towns.

In all our larger towns, and especially in those in which manufactures are carried on, there are a great number of cellars beneath the houses of the small shopkeepers and operatives, which are inhabited by crowds of poor inhabitants. Each of these cellar-houses contains at the most two, and often, and in some towns generally, only one room. These rooms measure, in Liverpool, from 10 to 12 feet square. In some other towns they are rather larger. They are generally flagged. The flags lie directly upon the earth, and are generally wretchedly damp. In wet weather they are very often not dry for weeks together. Within a few feet of the windows of these cellars, rises the wall which keeps the street from falling in upon them, darkening the gloomy rooms, and preventing the sun's rays penetrating into them.

Dr. Duncan, in describing the cellar-houses of the manufacturing districts, says *, — " The cellars are 10 or 12 feet square; generally flagged, but frequently having only the bare earth for a floor, and sometimes less than 6 feet in height. There is frequently no window, so that light and air can gain access to the cellar only by the door, the top of which is often not higher than the level of the street. In such cellars ventilation is out of the question. They are of course dark; and from the defective drainage, they are also very generally damp. There is sometimes a back cellar, used as a sleeping apartment, having no direct communication with the external atmosphere, and deriving its scanty supply of light and air solely from the front apartment."

But the character of the cellars themselves is by no means the worst feature of this miserable class of dwellings. I have already mentioned that they have never more than two, and generally only one room each, and

* Reports of the Health of Towns Commission, vol. i. 127.

that these rooms are very small; but small as they are, they are generally crowded to excess. It is no uncommon thing for two and three, and sometimes for four, families to live and sleep together in one of these rooms, without any division or separation whatever, for the different families or sexes. There are very few cellars, where at least two families do not herd together in this manner. Their beds are made sometimes of a mattress, and sometimes of straw in the corners of the cellar, and upon the damp, cold, flag floor; and on these miserable sleeping-places, the father, mother, sons, and daughters, crowd together in a state of filthy indecency, and much worse off than the horses in an ordinary stable. In these cellar-houses no distinction of sex and age is made. Sometimes a man is found sleeping with one woman, sometimes with two women, and sometimes with young girls; sometimes brothers and sisters of the age of 18, 19, and 20, are found in bed together; while at other times a husband and his wife share their bed with all their children.

The poor creatures who inhabit these miserable receptacles are of the most degraded species: they have never learned to read; have never heard of the existence of a Deity; have never been inside a church, being scared from the doors by their own filth and wretchedness; and have scarcely any sense of a distinction between right and wrong.

I have heard gentlemen, who have visited these kinds of dens in London, say, that they have found men and women sleeping together, three and four in a single bed, that they have not disturbed or ashamed them in the least, by discovering them in these situations, but that on the contrary their remonstrances have been answered only by a laugh or by a sneer.

In these places criminals are raised, and from these dens a moral pestilence creeps forth, and contaminates the moral life of even the more virtuous town-labourers. While such places exist, and continue to harbour so much immorality, it is as hopeless to expect to materially raise the character of our town poor, as it is to improve the sanitary condition of London while the Thames continues to receive the contents of all the London sewers, and to emit the gasses of its poisoned waters in the very centre of the great metropolis.

It is impossible to give anything like an exact account of the numbers of cellar-houses in the different towns of England and Wales; we are not possessed of such information; but some idea of them may be formed by the statistics, which have been collected of the numbers of these cellar-houses in some of the larger towns of England.

Dr. Duncan says *, that in the twelve wards forming the parish of Liverpool, there are 6,294 inhabited cellars, containing 20,168 inhabitants, " exclusive of the inhabited cellars in courts (of which there are 621, containing probably 2,000 inhabitants). From pretty extensive data which I have in my possession, I should be inclined to think these numbers, both of the court and cellar population, to be under the mark; but as they profess to be from actual enumeration, I am of course

* Report of the Health of Towns Commission, vol. i. 127.

obliged to take them as I find them. Of the entire number of cellars, 1,617 have a back apartment; while of 5,297, whose measurements are given, 1,771, or one third, are from 5 to 6 feet deep; 2,324 are from 4 to 5 feet, and 1,202 from 3 to 4 feet below the level of the street; 5,273, or more than five-sixths, have no windows to the front; and 2,429, or about 44 per cent., are reported as being either damp or wet.

"It may be stated, that the whole of the cellar-population of the parish (upwards of 20,000), are absolutely without any place of deposit for their refuse matter."

In some instances, Dr. Duncan says, the fluid contents of the ash-pits of the houses above ooze through into these cellar-houses, filling them with pestilential vapours, and rendering it necessary to dig wells to receive it, in order to prevent the inhabitants being inundated. One of these wells, 4 feet deep, filled with this stinking fluid, was found in one cellar under the bed where the family slept.

To give an idea of the numbers of families, who reside in cellars, in some of our towns, I may mention, that in 1844, 20 per cent. of the working classes of Liverpool, $11\frac{3}{4}$ per cent. of those of Manchester, and 8 per cent. of those of Salford inhabited cellars such as I have described.

Mr. Holme, in describing some of the cellars in Liverpool, says *, — "The melancholy facts elicited by previous inquiries, clearly show, that Liverpool contains a multitude of inhabited cellars, close and damp, with no

* Report of the Health of Towns Commission, vol. i. 277.

drain, nor any convenience ; and these pest-houses are constantly filled with fever. Some time ago I visited a poor woman in distress, the wife of a labouring man ; she had been confined only a few days, and herself and infant were lying on straw in a vault, through the outer cellar, with a clay floor, impervious to water. There was no light or ventilation in it, and the air was dreadful. I had to walk on bricks across the floor to reach her bed-side, as the floor itself was flooded with stagnant water. This is by no means an extraordinary case, for I have witnessed scenes equally wretched ; and it is only necessary to go into Crosby Street, Freemason's Row, and many cross streets out of Vauxhall Road, to find hordes of poor creatures living in cellars, which are almost as bad and offensive as charnel-houses. In Freemason's Row, I found, about two years ago, a court of houses, the floors of which were below the public street, and the area of the whole court was a floating mass of putrified animal and vegetable matter, so dreadfully offensive that I was obliged to make a precipitate retreat. Yet the whole of the houses were inhabited."

Since these accounts were first published the numbers of cellar-houses in Liverpool have, I believe, been diminished by the exertions of the municipality, but in most of our great towns they remain just as foul and just as numerous as ever.

But what is the condition of the houses of the poor in our towns and in our villages?

The further we examine, the more painful, disgusting, and incredible does the tale become.

We see on every hand, stately palaces, to which

no country in the world offers any parallel. The houses of our rich are more gorgeous and more luxurious than those of any other land. Every clime is ransacked to adorn or furnish them. The soft carpets, the heavy rich curtains, the luxuriously easy couches, the beds of down, the services of plate, the numerous servants, the splendid equipages, and all the expensive objects of literature, science, and the arts, which crowd the palaces of England, form but items in an *ensemble* of refinement and magnificence, which was never imagined or approached, in all the splendour of the ancient empires.

But look beneath all this display and luxury, and what do we see there? A pauperised and suffering people.

To maintain a show, we have degraded the masses, until we have created an evil so vast, that we now despair of ever finding a remedy. The Irish poor have drunk the dregs of the cup of misery, and are hardly kept from revolution by the strong arm of the soldiers and police ; while the English poor are only saved from despair and its dread consequences, by the annual expenditure of MANY MILLIONS in relief, which our own neglect and misgovernment have rendered necessary.

The dwellings of the poor in the back streets and alleys of our towns are as wretched as they are degrading. The inquiries made in 1849, during the spread of the cholera, and those made in late years by the City Mission, by the correspondents of the " Morning Chronicle," and by private individuals, have disclosed a state of things which would disgrace a country of bar-

barians. Even leaving out of consideration the cellar-
dwellings and the "lodging-houses," which I have
mentioned above, the state of many of the houses in
the back streets and alleys is wretched in the extreme.
The amount of dwelling room occupied by many of
the families is miserably small. Even in the manufacturing towns of the north, where the houses of the
operatives are generally much superior to the wretched
dwellings of the poor in the larger towns of the south
of England, even there the accommodation afforded in
a great part of the houses is miserable. Great numbers
have only one bed-room for the whole family, where
father, mother, brothers, and sisters, all sleep together,
often in the same bed.

Many even of the houses most recently built for operatives in Lancashire have only one bed-room. Scarcely
one family in ten has more than two; so that, in the
majority of cases, it is impossible to preserve anything
like a decent separation of the sexes in the sleeping
rooms. I have been assured on all hands in Lancashire,
— by magistrates, manufacturers, and operatives,— that
the immoral consequences of this state of things are terrible. Both in London, and in our larger provincial towns,
it is no uncommon thing for two, three, and even four
families to sleep in *one* room without any screen between the beds.

The evils resulting from this want of accommodation
are still further enhanced by the wretched state of the
back streets and alleys of our towns. In the larger of
the provincial towns of England and Wales, the condition of these streets and alleys is as bad as it can be.

They are built after no plan. They are narrow and often closed at one end. They are very badly drained. The openings of what drains there are, are generally close to the windows or doors of the houses. There is often only one privy for three, four, and sometimes as many as ten houses.

The streets and yards themselves are used for the filthiest purposes. Night-soil is spread about in the yards and on the pavements. The stench of these haunts is often insufferable.

The misery of life in these places is greatly increased by the fact, that there is often a very poor supply of water, and that the inhabitants are without the means, even if they had the will, to cleanse the streets of the filth, which accumulates upon their pavements. There is scarcely a town of any magnitude in England or Wales, which has not many quarters of this description.

What renders the demoralising effects of this state of things all the more appalling, is the fact, that most of the young children born in these places are left from morning to night for many years of their lives to grow up in the filth, amid the horrible scenes, and under the continued degrading influences of these streets,— unaccustomed to clean habits, clean dress, or to happy or healthy associations, but in the darkest ignoance; and that these poor little wretches have to creep back at night into crowded, loathsome, and immoral sleeping rooms, without having enjoyed any purer or more moral atmosphere or associations during the whole of the past day. If we reflect on the *necessary* effects of such a life as this, we shall not wonder at the vast

numbers of our criminals and paupers, or at the degraded condition of so many of our town labourers.

Thus, while throughout Western Europe the schools
are tending to improve the cleanliness, order, comfort,
and propriety of the life of the town poor, by improving
and forming the tastes and habits of the young, and by
snatching them from the degrading scenes and· associations to which the young of our towns are exposed;
in our country, the way in which the children are growing up in the streets, renders the horrible state of our
back streets even more injurious and demoralising than
they otherwise would be, to the habits and the character
of our town labourers.

The following accounts of the condition of the poor
in the back streets of London will serve to illustrate
the condition of our town poor in the back streets of
most of the larger towns of England. If my space
would permit, I could indefinitely multiply such instances. I could add similar accounts of almost every
large town in England.

But as my space will not suffice, I beg to refer my
readers to those published in Mr. Chadwick's Reports;
in the City Mission Reports; in the Statistical Journal;
and in the columns of " The Times," and " Morning
Chronicle."

The Statistical Society, in 1848, appointed a committee of members to investigate the state of the inhabitants and their dwellings in Church Lane, St.
Giles, London.

The committee represent* the state of this place as

* Journal of the Statistical Society of London, vol. xi. p. 17.

horrible. They give a minute account of the houses, and comment on their own report as follows : —

" Your committee have thus given a picture in detail of human wretchedness, filth, and brutal degradation, the chief features of which are a disgrace to a civilised country, and which your committee have reason to fear, from letters, which have appeared in the public journals, *is but the type of the miserable condition of masses of the community, whether located in the small, ill-ventilated rooms of manufacturing towns, or in many of the cottages of the agricultural peasantry.* In these wretched dwellings, all ages and all sexes, — fathers and daughters, mothers and sons, grown-up brothers and sisters, stranger adult males and females, and swarms of children, — the sick, the dying, and the dead, — are herded together *with a proximity and mutual pressure* which brutes would resist ; where it is physically impossible to preserve the ordinary decencies of life ; where all sense of propriety and self-respect must be lost, to be replaced only by a recklessness of demeanour, which necessarily results from vitiated minds. . . . ."

In 1848, Mr. Hallam and Mr. Slancy furnished funds, wherewith to defray the expense of investigating the condition of the poorer classes in the parish of *St. George's in the East of London.* This parish was fixed upon, not as being the worst of the metropolitan districts, but as affording an example of the AVERAGE condition of the poorer classes of the metropolis.

1954 families, containing a population of 7711 individuals, were visited. The report upon their condition

may be found in the eleventh volume of the Journal
of the Statistical Society of London.

Out of these 1954 families —

551 families, containing a population of 2025 persons,
have only *one* room each, where father, mother, sons,
and daughters, live and sleep together.

562 families, containing a population of 2454 persons,
have only *two* rooms each, in one of which people of
different sexes must undress and sleep together.

705 families, containing a population of 1950 persons,
have only *one bed* each, in which the whole family
sleep together.

728 families, including a population of 3455 persons,
have only *two* beds each, in one of which the parents
sleep, and in the other of which all the sons and
daughters sleep together.

In more than one-fourth of the houses, there were no
serious books, Prayer-book, or Bible, and the impression
of the agents employed in visiting the houses was, that
of all the books which they found in the houses, the
Bible was the least read.

In the number of the "City Mission Reports" for
July, 1848, a description is given of Orchard's Place
and Gray's Buildings, in the west end of London.

The report is as follows : —

" Orchard Place is (including two nooks) less than
45 yards long, and 8 broad, and contains 27 houses.
Resident in this court, in 1845, *were no less than* 217
families, consisting of 882 *persons*, of whom 582 were
above 14 years of age ! The population of a large village, or a small town, is here comprised in one court.

Kew, for instance, at the last census, had a population which exceeded it but by 41, and Abingdon exceeded it but by 38. Strathfieldsaye is less populous by 43 ; while the population of Brixton, in the Isle of Wight, is only 710; of Yarmouth, in the same island, but 567 ; and of Broxbourne, in Hertfordshire, but 643. . . . The description, which we presented to our readers of the district of St. Giles's, in the Magazine for November, 1847, showed that *each of the houses there contained* 100 *persons. . . . .*"

In 1847, however, the population of Orchard Place had considerably increased, notwithstanding the way in which the houses were crowded in 1845. It appears that, in 1847, THE 27 HOUSES CONTAINED 476 FA-MILIES, AND FROM 882 TO 1222 INDIVIDUALS, and this, too, in the month of March, when the court is much more thinly populated than at any other season of the year ! !

In the back streets of Kensington, and of Oxford Street, I know, from personal inspection, that the state of the poor is just such as I have described above. In Westminster it is even worse. In the extreme parts of the city, and in the neighbourhood of the docks, it is even more horrible. And yet nothing worth speaking of is being done to check the continued growth of this terrible social cancer. It increases with the increase, and even faster than the increase in the multitudes of London, unchecked, as if there were no social remedy, and as if it were a necessary consequence of the system of great towns. And yet nothing like this state of things exists to any extent in the capitals of Germany. Certainly we have no right to say it cannot be cured, until we have tried all possible means of curing it; and as long as at least one half of the juvenile population is left to grow up without any education, we cannot say that we have done all that is possible.

In describing the wretched state of many of the houses in the parish of St. Giles's, in London, another of the city missionaries says* that in this district "there are 5 PRIVATE HOUSES, AND 8 LODGING HOUSES, IN ALL 13 HOUSES, WHICH ARE EACH INHABITED BY 100 INDIVIDUALS, *so that* 1300 *persons, or more than half a district, is comprised in only* 13 *houses.*

"Nor let it be supposed that these houses are so enormously large; for such is not the case. But the rooms are close packed with human beings, in a manner which would hardly be believed by those who had not actually seen them. Church Lane consists of 32 houses, which contain 190 rooms, IN EACH OF WHICH ROOMS LIVE AN AVERAGE OF 9 INDIVIDUALS, MAKING A TOTAL OF 1710 PERSONS. Separate families live in separate corners of the rooms. The party who hires the entire room re-lets it in portions. And such rooms are the private and *respectable* rooms of the district, in distinction to the lodging-houses. The persons living in them profess to be respectable and virtuous members of society. But we will give a few examples of the manner in which rooms of this description were tenanted only last month. In *one* room of a house in Church Lane were found —

* City Mission Magazine, Nov., 1847.

Widow with three children -	-	-	4
Widow with one child -	-	-	2
Three single women -	-	-	3
A man and his wife -	-	-	2
A single man -	-	-	1
A man and his wife -	-	-	2
			—
			14

" These fourteen persons live by day, and sleep by night, in the same small room. The missionary put to one of the married men the question, 'Are you not ashamed?' His answer was, 'At first I was; but when I saw the other people thought nothing of it, I got to do so too.' The last enumerated couple are the landlord and his wife, who pay 3s. per week for the room. The two widows and the three single women, by dividing the four children between them, slept in two beds, and there were two other beds besides the landlord's. The landlord thus managed to use the room himself, and to let parts of it to others, from whom he received 8s. a week. He therefore lived himself rent free, and made 5s. a week profit of his furnished room, the furniture of which was only worth a few shillings. And yet this room was not reckoned as quite full!

" In a first-floor front room in Fletcher's Court were found —

A man, his wife, and three children -	-	-	5
A man, his wife, and child -	-	-	3
A widow and her two children -	-	-	3
A man and his wife -	-	-	2
A single woman, aged twenty years -	-	-	1
			—
			14

" Of the above persons, only the first party enumerated had a bed; the others sleep on straw, and their only covering by night are the clothes they take off when the day is ended.

" In a ground-floor front of the same court were found —

A woman and her five children - -	6
A woman and her two children - -	3
A man and his wife - - -	2
A man and his wife - - -	2
A single woman, sister to the above wife -	1
	14

" The ages of the above children were from four to sixteen.

" Straw was the only bed in the room, and day clothes their only covering by night. Neither of the rooms in this court exceeded 7 feet by 10, and of the twenty-eight people living in them *not one could read.*

" Many women, now living with men in an unmarried state on the district, have stated to the missionary, *that it was by such crowded rooms they were led into temptation,* and that when they entered these houses they had no idea to what they were to be exposed. Some of these were servants out of place, who thought that because the houses looked respectable outside, they were the same within. They came up to London in search of situations, found they could not obtain them so immediately as they expected, were ignorant of this great city, and fell into company with the men with whom they now reside.

" Since the new street has been made the district has become more crowded than it was ever known to be before; and since the hopping season has closed, the missionary reckons that there are 500 more persons on the district than there were previously.

"THERE ARE FORTY LODGING-HOUSES OF THE LOWEST CHARACTER ON THE DISTRICT."

Mr. Riddall Wood was examined as to the effects of over-crowded tenements on the moral habits of the inmates in the various towns he had examined.*

"In what towns did you find instances of the greatest crowding of the habitations?—In Manchester, Liverpool, Ashton-under-Lyne, and Pendleton. In a cellar in Pendleton, I recollect there were three beds in the two apartments of which the habitation consisted, but having no door between them, in one of which a man and his wife slept; in another, a man, his wife, and child; and in a third, two unmarried females. In Hull, I have met with cases somewhat similar. A mother, about fifty years of age, and her son, I should think twenty-five, at all events above twenty-one, sleeping in the same bed, and a lodger in the same room. I have known two or three instances in Hull in which a mother was sleeping with her grown-up son; and in most cases there were other persons sleeping in the same room in another bed. In a cellar in Liverpool, I found a mother and her grown-up daughters sleeping on a bed of chaff on the ground in one corner of the cellar, and in the other corner three sailors had their bed. I HAVE MET WITH UPWARDS OF FORTY PERSONS SLEEPING IN THE SAME ROOM, MARRIED AND SINGLE, INCLUDING, OF COURSE,

* See Report on the Sanitary Condition of the Labouring Population.

CHILDREN, AND SEVERAL YOUNG ADULT PERSONS OF EITHER SEX. In Manchester, I could enumerate a variety of instances in which I found such promiscuous mixture of the sexes in sleeping rooms. I may mention one — a man, his wife, and child sleeping in one bed; in another bed, two grown-up females; and in the same room, two young men unmarried.

" I have met with instances of a man, his wife, and his wife's sister sleeping in the same bed together. I have known at least half-a-dozen cases in Manchester in which that has been regularly practised, the unmarried sister being an adult.

" In the course of your own inquiry, how many instances, if you were to look over your notes, of persons of different sexes sleeping promiscuously, do you think you met with?—I think I am speaking within bounds when I say I have amongst my memoranda above 100 cases, including, of course, cases of persons of different sexes sleeping in the same room.

" Was it so common as to be in no wise deemed extraordinary or culpable among that class of persons? — It seemed not to be thought of.

" As a proof of this, I may mention one circumstance which just occurs to me. Early in my visitation of Pendleton, I called at the dwelling of a person whose sons worked with himself in a colliery. It was in the afternoon, when a young man, one of the sons, came down stairs in his shirt, and stood before the fire, where a very decently dressed young female was sitting. The son asked his mother for a clean shirt, and on it being given to him, very deliberately threw off the shirt he had on, and, after warming the clean one, put it on.

" In another dwelling in Pendleton, a young girl, eighteen years of age, sat by the fire in her chemise during the whole time of my visit. Both these were houses of working people (colliers), and not by any means of ill fame.

" During your inquiries, were you able to observe any further demoralisation attendant upon these circumstances?—I have frequently met with instances in which the parties themselves have traced their own depravity to these circumstances. As, for example, while I was following out my inquiries in Hull, I found in one room a prostitute, with whom I remonstrated on her course of life, and asked her whether she would not be in a better condition if she were an honest servant, instead of living in vice and wretchedness. She admitted she should; and, on asking the cause of her being brought to her present condition, she stated that she had lodged with a married sister, *and slept in the same bed with her and her husband ; that hence improper intercourse took place, and from that she gradually became more and more depraved, and at length was thrown upon the town,* because, having lost her character, the town was her only resource. Another female of this description admitted that her first false step was in consequence of her sleeping in the same room with a married couple. In the instance I have mentioned, of the two single women sleeping in the same room with the married people, I have good authority for believing that they were common to the men. In the case which

I have mentioned of the two daughters and the woman where I found the sailors, I learned from the mother's admission, that they were common to the lodgers. In all of these cases the sense of decency was obliterated."

Mr. Baker, in his report on the condition of the labouring classes in Leeds, corroborates this statement*: —

"*In the houses of the working classes, brothers and sisters, and lodgers of both sexes, are found occupying the same sleeping room with the parents, and consequences occur which humanity shudders to contemplate.* It is but three or four years ago since a father and daughter stood at the bar of the Leeds sessions as criminals, the one in concealing, and the other in being an accessory to concealing the birth of an illegitimate child, born on the body of the daughter by the father; and now, in November, 1841, one of the registrars of Leeds has recorded the birth of an illegitimate child, born on the body of a young girl only sixteen years of age, who lived with her mother, who cohabited with her lodger, the father of this child of which the girl had been pregnant five months when the mother died."

The over-crowding of the tenements of the labouring classes is productive of demoralisation in a mode pointed out by Mr. Barnett, the clerk to the Nottingham union, who states † : —

" That the houses are generally too small to afford a comfortable reception to the family, and the consequence is that the junior members are generally in the streets.

---

* See Report on the Sanitary Condition of the Labouring Population.
† See Ibid.

Girls and youths destitute of adequate house-room, and freed from parental control, are accustomed to gross immoralities."

Mr. Chadwick says * : —

" It would require much time, and various opportunities of observation, to attempt to make an exact analysis of the combined causes, and an estimate of the effect of each separate cause, which operates to produce the masses of moral and physical wretchedness met with in the investigation of the condition of the lowest population. But it became evident in the progress of the inquiry, that several separate circumstances had each its separate moral as well as physical influence. Thus, tenements of inferior construction had manifestly an injurious operation on the moral as well as on the sanitary condition, independently of any over-crowding. For example, it appears to be matter of common observation in the instance of migrant families of workpeople, who are obliged to occupy inferior tenements, that their habits soon became of a piece with the dwelling. A gentleman, who has observed closely the condition of the workpeople in the south of Cheshire and the north of Lancashire — men of similar race and education, working at the same description of work, namely, a cotton-spinner's mill hands, and earning nearly the same amount of wages — states that the workmen of the north of Lancashire are obviously inferior to those in the south of Cheshire in health and habits of personal cleanliness, and general condition. The difference is traced mainly to the circumstance, that the

* See Report on the Sanitary Condition of the Labouring Population.

labourers in the north of Lancashire inhabit stone houses of a description that absorb moisture, the dampness of which affects the health and causes personal uncleanliness, induced by the difficulty of keeping a clean house. The operation of the same deteriorating influences was also observable in Scotland."

Even in Windsor, the city of our monarchs, the condition of the dwellings of the poor is wretched and horrible in the extreme. The following is a description of a part of the town called Garden Court, where the cholera made such ravages in 1849. I extract it from " The Times " of the 13th of October, 1849 : —

"In the court there are twenty-one small houses, each consisting of three rooms, the whole of which are occupied ; *each room containing upon an average not less, including children, than five persons.* These rooms are generally let out to separate families. The back doors of each house open close to the privies, which are in a horribly filthy state, the stench arising from them being most offensive to the whole neighbourhood. Within 5 feet of the court there is an open stinking ditch running into the Thames, into which it carries the soil from some other houses in the neighbourhood.

" This ditch at times is most offensive, especially during the hot summer months. Into the rooms of four of the houses, the soil from the privies in Thames Street absolutely oozes, rendering these habitations unfit even for a dog, and much less for human beings. In the centre of the small yard there is a pump, from which water is supplied to all the inmates of this pestiferous court. This water is strongly impregnated with the stinking water of the ditches and drains by which the pump is surrounded."

I have lying under my hand accounts, precisely similar to those I have given of London, of the back streets of Liverpool, Manchester, Wigan, Preston, Rochdale, Durham, York, Lancaster, Carlisle, Stafford, Nottingham, Cambridge, Ely, Norwich, and of many other towns in all parts of England and Wales, but want of space prevents my publishing more than the few extracts which I have given.

Before however I dismiss this part of my subject, I would repeat that the *only* way by which we can hope to reform the habits and character of the poor, who live in the back streets and alleys of our towns, is, to snatch their children from the horrible influences of such a life as most of them now lead; and to endeavour, by means of good teachers and good schools, to keep them out of the streets during their younger years, to give them good principles, good habits, and useful knowledge; to make them *desire* to escape from their present social degradation; to enable them to act wisely and prudently; and to stimulate them to improve their own social condition. Before we can hope to civilise the poor of our back streets and alleys, we must teach them to become dissatisfied with their present miserable condition.

But so long as the greatest number of the children of the town poor are left, as at present, during the most susceptible period of their lives, to spend their days in such foul and degrading scenes as now surround the majority of them from morning to night, so long will our criminal calendars continue to increase, so long will the character of our poorer classes continue to degenerate, and so long will our towns remain hotbeds of vice, of misery.

If our poor were educated, as the German town poor are, they would not be able to endure such a life as they now lead. It would become as intolerable to them, as it would be to the richer and better educated classes of society.

Educate the habits of the poor, and the poor will soon find out a way to improve their homes. The homes will then aid the schools, by surrounding the children from their earliest years with improving instead of demoralising associations.

But miserable as the habitations of a great part of the poor of our towns are, the cottages and the cottage life of the peasants in our villages are still worse ; and what is more, they have been for some time past, and still are, rapidly deteriorating. The majority of the cottages are wretchedly built, often in very unhealthy sites; they are miserably small, and are crowded to excess ; they are very low, seldom drained, and badly roofed ; and they scarcely ever have any cellar or space under the floor of the lower rooms. The floors are formed either of flags, which rest upon the cold undrained ground, or, as is often the case, of nothing but a mixture of clay and lime. The ground receives, day after day and year after year, between the crevices of the flags, or in the composition of clay and lime, water and droppings of all kinds, and gives back from them and from its own moisture combined, pestilential vapours, injurious to the health and happiness of the inmates of the cottage.

The cottages are fit abodes for a peasantry pauperised and demoralised by the utter hopelessness of their situation.

They may be classified as follows : —

1. Small cottages built of brick, of only one story in height, with a thatched roof, and without any cellar, so that the bricks or flags of the rooms rest immediately on the earth ; with two small rooms between seven and eight feet in height, one used as the day-room and cooking-room, the other as the bed-room, where husband and wife, young men and young women, boys and girls, and very often a married son and his wife, all sleep together ; without any garden, and with only a very small yard at the back, in which the privy stands almost close to the back door, pouring its gasses into the house at all hours. This species of cottage is to be found in all parts of England and Wales. In some counties they are very numerous, as in Cambridgeshire, and especially in that part called the Isle of Ely, in Hertfordshire, in Leicestershire, in Dorsetshire, Devonshire, Somersetshire, Cornwall, Surrey, Sussex, Kent, Essex, Bedfordshire, Buckinghamshire, Berkshire, the northern counties, and in Wales.

2. Cottages which have two stories with one small kitchen room on the ground floor, and with another small room above on the first floor, in which the whole family, father, mother, and children of both sexes sleep together. These house have generally no garden, and only a small yard behind, in which the privy stands close to the back door. This class is very numerous throughout the country.

3. The third class of cottages are those, which have two stories,—the ground floor, where there is a day-room and a little scullery, and the upper floor, on which there are *two* bed-rooms, in one of which the parents sleep, and in the other of which the children, boys and girls, and young men, and young women, all sleep together. In many parts of England and Wales this class of cottages is very rare.

The accounts we receive from all parts of the country show that these miserable cottages are crowded to an extreme, and that the crowding is progressively increasing. People of both sexes, and of all ages, both married and unmarried — parents, brothers, sisters, and strangers — sleep in the same rooms and often in the same beds. One gentleman tells us of six people of different sexes and ages, two of whom were man and wife, sleeping in the same bed, three with their heads at the top and three with their heads at the foot of the bed. Another tells us of adult uncles and nieces sleeping in the same room close to each other ; another of the uncles and nieces sleeping in the same bed together; another of adult brothers and sisters sleeping in the same room with a brother and his wife just married ; many tell us of adult brothers and sisters sleeping in the same beds ; another tells us of rooms so filled with beds that there is no space between them, but that brothers, sisters, and parents crawl over each other half naked in order to get to their respective resting-places ; another of its being common for men and women, not being relations, to undress together in the same room, without any feeling of its being indelicate ; another of cases where women have been delivered in bed-rooms crowded with men, young women, and children; and others mention facts of these crowded bed-rooms much too horrible to be alluded to. Nor are these solitary instances, but similar reports are given by gentlemen writing in ALL parts of the country.

The miserable character of the houses of our peasantry is, of itself, and independently of the causes, which have made the houses so wretched, degrading and demoralising the poor of our rural districts in a fearful manner. It stimulates the unhealthy and unnatural increase of population. The young peasants from their earliest years are accustomed to sleep in the same bed-rooms with people of both sexes, and with both married and unmarried persons. They therefore lose all sense of the indelicacy of such a life. They know, too, that they can gain nothing by deferring their marriages and by saving; that it is impossible for them to obtain better houses by so doing; and that in many cases they must wait many years before they could obtain a separate house of any sort. They feel, that if they defer their marriage for ten or fifteen years, they will be at the end of that period in just the same position as before, and no better off for their waiting. Having then lost all hope of any improvement of their social situation, and all sense of the indelicacy of taking a wife home to the bed-room already occupied by parents, brothers, and sisters, they marry early in life,—often, if not generally, before the age of twenty,—and very often occupy, for the first part of their married life, another bed in the already crowded sleeping-room of their parents! In this way the morality of the peasants is destroyed; the numbers of this degraded population are unnaturally increased, and their means of subsistence are diminished by the increasing competition of their increasing numbers.

A low standard of living always tends to stimulate improvident marriages, to unduly increase the numbers of the population, and to engender pauperism, vice, degradation, and misery.

As I have said before, the landlords are unwilling to increase the number of cottages in the rural districts, because they fear to increase the numbers of the resident labouring population, and the amount of their poor-rates; and they are generally unwilling, even when they are able, to spend money in improving the size or character of the cottages, because they know, that they can easily let any of the existing cottages, no matter how wretched, owing to the great demand for house-room.

The crowding of the cottages has, therefore, of late been growing worse and worse. The promiscuous mingling of the sexes in the bed-rooms has been increasing very much, and is productive of worse consequences every year. Adultery is the very mildest form of the vast amount of crime which it is engendering. We are told by magistrates, clergymen, surgeons, and union officers, that in many parts of the country, cases of incest, and reports of other cases of the same enormity, are becoming more and more common among the poor. And there is no doubt whatsoever, — and in this all accounts and authorities agree, — that the way in which the married and unmarried people, and the different sexes, are mingled together, in the same bed-rooms, and even in the same beds, throughout the rural districts, is tending to destroy the modesty and virtue of the women, to anni- hilate the foundations, on which are based all the national and domestic virtues, and to make want of chastity before marriage, and want of delicacy and purity after marriage, common characteristics of the mothers and wives of our labouring population.

An eminent writer represents the consequences of the state of peasants' cottages in England and Wales, in the following powerful terms : — " A man and woman intermarry, and take a cottage.   In eight cases out of ten it is a cottage with but two rooms.   For a time, so far as room at least is concerned, this answers their purpose ; but they take it, not because it is at the time sufficiently spacious for them, but because they could not procure a more roomy dwelling, even if they desired it. In this they pass with tolerable comfort, considering their notions of what comfort is, the first period of married life ; but, by-and-by they have children, and the family increases, until, in the course of a few years, they number, perhaps, from eight to ten individuals. But all this time there has been no increase to their household accommodation.   As at first, so to the very last, there is but the ONE SLEEPING-ROOM. As the family increases, additional beds are crammed into this apart- ment, until at last it is so filled with them, that there is scarcely room left to move between them. *I have known instances in which they had to crawl over each other, to get to their beds.* So long as the children are very young, the only evil connected with this is the physical one arising from crowding so many people together into what is generally a dingy, frequently a damp, and invariably an ill-ventilated apartment. But years steal on, and the family continues thus bedded together. Some of its members may yet be in their infancy, but others of both sexes have crossed the line of puberty. But there they are, still together in the same room — the father and mother, the sons and the daughters — young men, young women, and children. Cousins, too, of both sexes, are often thrown together into the same room, *and not unfrequently into the same bed*. I have also known of cases in which uncles slept in the same room with their grown-up nieces, and newly-married couples occupied the same chamber with those long married, and with others marriageable but unmarried. A case also came to my notice, already alluded to in connection with another branch of the subject, in which two sisters, who were married on the same day, occupied adjoining rooms in the same hut, with nothing but a thin board partition, which did not reach the ceiling, between the two rooms, and a door in the partition which only partly filled up the doorway. For years back, in these same two rooms, have slept twelve people of both sexes and all ages. Sometimes, when there is but one room, a praiseworthy effort is made for the conservation of decency. But the hanging up of a piece of tattered cloth between the beds, which is generally all that is done in this respect, and even that but seldom, is but a poor set-off to the fact, that a family, which, in common decency, should, as regards sleeping accommodations, be separated at least into three divisions, oc-

cupy, night after night, but one and the same chamber.
This is a frightful position for them to be in when an
infectious or epidemic disease enters their abode. But
this, important though it be, is the least important consideration connected with their circumstances. That
which is most so, is the effect produced by them upon
their habits and morals. In the illicit intercourse to
which such a position frequently gives rise, *it is not
always that the tie of blood is respected.* Certain it is,
that when the relationship is even but one degree removed from that of brother and sister, that tie is frequently overlooked. And when the circumstances do
not lead to such horrible consequences, the mind, particularly of the female, is wholly divested of that sense
of delicacy and shame, which, so long as they are preserved, are the chief safeguards of her chastity. She
therefore falls an early and an easy prey to the temptations which beset her beyond the immediate circle of
her family. People in the other spheres of life are but
little aware of the extent to which this precocious demoralisation of the female amongst the lower orders in
the country has proceeded. But how could it be otherwise? The philanthropist may exert himself in their
behalf, the moralist may inculcate even the worldly
advantages of a better course of life, and the minister of
religion may warn them of the eternal penalties, which
they are incurring; but there is an instructor constantly
at work, more potent than them all, — an instructor in
mischief; of which they must ged rid ere they can make
any real progress in their laudable efforts, — and that is,
the single bed-chamber in the two-roomed cottage."

But what are the poor to do? So long as the law prevents their purchasing land; so long as they cannot obtain ground, on which to build their own cottages, as the foreign peasants do; so long, too, as the government will not interfere to educate the children of the peasants in higher tastes and better habits; and so long as they are only the tenants at the will of the agent of a landlord, one does not see how the peasant has a chance of improving the condition of his cottage, or the social position of his family.

I cannot too often repeat, that the great primary causes of the pauperism and degradation of our peasants are the utter *hopelessness* and *helplessness* of their position. We have done all we can to prevent their helping themselves; and to deprive them of every strong inducement to practise self-denial, prudence, and economy.

A man will not practise self-denial, economy, and prudence without an object. What object has an English peasant to practise them?

A peasant cannot possibly buy land as the foreign peasant does. He cannot get a farm even as a tenant-at-will of it. He cannot buy a house, or a plot of ground on which to build a house. He cannot even get the lease of a cottage. He cannot buy or get the lease of a garden. He often cannot even get the mere occupation of a cottage for himself. He is often obliged to take his wife to his father's or his brother's cottage, and to sleep with her in their bed-room.

What earthly inducement, then, has such a peasant to practise self-denial and economy? Absolutely none.

He does not, therefore, practise any. He says to himself, if I put off my marriage and save, what should I gain by such a course? I'll marry early. If I cannot get a cottage, I'll take my wife to my father's cottage; and if bad times come, I'll apply to the union.

Such is the hideous social system to which we have subjected our poor.

How different is the condition of the foreign peasant! The majority of even the French peasants, who have attained the age of thirty-five, possess houses and farms of their own, the latter averaging from five to eight acres in size. The foreign peasant feels that his fate is in his own hands. He knows, that if he postpones his marriage, he will be able to purchase a house and farm of his own, and thus to establish his own complete independence. He is not dependent on agents of landlords or on landlords for the condition of his house, or for its tenure, or for the tenure of his farm, or for the social position of his family. All this, as well as his own future success in life, depends solely and entirely on his own exertions. This stimulates his energies and exertions. This makes his life hopeful and happy. This ennobles and developes his own character. This makes him a good citizen. This makes him a successful farmer. This increases his intelligence; and, while it makes his life hopeful and happy even amid privations, it makes him a good and conservative citizen even in times of suffering and distress.

I have myself examined, during the present year, the condition of the peasants' cottages in Cambridgeshire, and particularly in that part of Cambridgeshire called the Isle of Ely, in Hertfordshire, and in Leicestershire.

These are agricultural counties, where the land is very rich and very well cultivated. The farms are generally of considerable size. The peasants have no chance of ever rising to the farmer class. The cottages have scarcely ever a garden attached to them. The land is all divided between great farms and parks.

Now, what is the condition of the majority of cottages of the peasants of these counties?

They are almost as wretched as they can be. The majority of them are small low huts of one story in height. The walls are about eight feet high. The roofs are very often thatched. The thatch is very seldom repaired. Through the top of the thatch projects the chimney. There is no cellar beneath the rooms. The floors are made of bricks or flags, which are laid upon the earth, and, as may be conceived, are damp and cold.

In the middle of one of the side walls there is a door, and on each side of the door a window, which is but too often minus several panes at least, their places being occupied with rags. One half of the interior of many of these cottages is boarded or walled off, so as to divide the house into two little rooms. One of these rooms is the living room, the other is a bed-room, in which sleep the whole family, parents, sons, and daughters. It is by no means rare for the two sexes to sleep not only in the same bed-room but in the same bed.

Many of the cottages are two stories in height, with one room on the ground floor, and one above. Some

CAMBRIDGESHIRE AND HERTFORDSHIRE. 481

have two small bed-rooms, in one of which the parents
sleep, while all the sons and daughters sleep in the
other.

Scarcely any cottages have more than two bed-rooms,
and very few have more than one.

Even of the few new cottages which are being built,
none have more than two bed-rooms, while many have
not more than one. Their walls are better built than
those of the older cottages, and their roofs are slate
instead of thatch; but these are in general the only
improvement on the old and general style of cottages.

The sites of the new cottages are at least as wretched
as those of the old.

One singular thing is, that this state of things has
existed so long, that the poor have sunk below com-
plaining, and that the landlords and richer classes are
quite surprised, if you talk to them of the miserable
condition of the peasants' cottages. They have learned
to think it a necessary state of things, and ridicule the
idea of its being the result of a system of defective
legislation. Many go much further, and boldly maintain, that it is better that the peasants should not be
educated, as education would make them thoroughly
discontented with their present position in life. I pray
God it may. When it has so done, there will be a
chance of reformation ; but at present they are below
even discontent.

Another singular thing is to hear people talk about
the *picturesque* cottages of the English peasants, forgetting, or not caring to remember, that the thatched roofs,
old, moss-covered, low, and crooked walls, and dilapidated

chimneys, may, indeed, give them an old and quaint appearance, but that they at the same time render them scarcely fit habitations for our cattle, and certainly incapable of being compared to the well-built stables of the landlord's horses.

The following remarkable extracts, selected from various sources of the highest authority, will show the miserable condition of the cottages and dwellings of the peasantry in other parts of England and Wales.

I offer these extracts only as specimens, which I could multiply indefinitely, if my space would allow, of a state of things which exists more or less in every county in England, and as proofs of the wretched way in which the cottages of our peasantry are built; of the miserable lodging and accommodation afforded by them to their poor inmates; of the wretched and unhealthy sites, which are often chosen for them by agents and persons, who do not care where or how the peasants are lodged; of the want of drainage, ventilation, water supply, and privies, which distinguishes most of them; and of the sickness and shocking moral degradation caused by this miserable and lamentable state of things.

If any one should desire to see more of such sad and disgusting details, as those collected in the following pages, I beg to refer him to the Report on the Employment of Women in Agriculture, published by Government, in 1843; to Mr. Chadwick's very able Reports on the Sanitary Condition of the Labouring Population; to the Reports of the Welsh Commissioners; to the Reports of the Poor Law Commission; to the columns of "The Times"; and to the remarkable and exceedingly able letters published in the " Morning Chronicle " in the autumn of 1849.

The first series of extracts will show the present condition of the peasants' houses in the south-western counties — Wiltshire, Dorsetshire, Devonshire, Gloucestershire, Somersetshire, and Cornwall.

Mr. Alfred Austin, Special Assistant Poor Law Commissioner, in reporting upon the condition of the peasants' cottages in the counties of Wilts, Dorset, Devon, and Somerset, says * : —

" The want of sufficient accommodation seems universal. Cottages generally have only two bed-rooms (with very rare exceptions); a great many have only one. The consequence is, that it is very often extremely difficult, if not impossible, *to divide a family, so that grown-up persons of different sexes, brothers and sisters, fathers and daughters, do not sleep in the same room. Three or four persons not unfrequently sleep in the same bed.* In a few instances I found that two families — neighbours — arranged, so that the females of both families slept together in one cottage, and the males in the other ; but such an arrangement is very rare, and in the generality of cottages, I believe, that the only attempt that is or that can be made to separate beds, with occupants of different sexes, and necessarily placed close together, from the smallness of the rooms, is an old shawl, or some article of dress, suspended as a curtain between them.

" At Stourpain, a village near Blandford, I measured

* See Report on the Employment of Women in Agriculture.

a bed-room in a cottage, consisting of two rooms, the bed-room in question upstairs, and a room on the ground floor, in which the family lived during the day. The room was 10 feet square, not reckoning the two small recesses by the sides of the chimney, about 18 inches deep. The roof was of thatch, the middle of the chamber being about 7 feet high. Opposite the fire-place was a small window, about 15 inches square, the only one in the room."

Three beds were crammed into this little room. There was no curtain or separation between the beds.

One bed contained the father and mother, a little boy, and an infant.

The second bed contained *three* daughters, the two eldest, twins, aged twenty years each, and the other rged seven.

The third bed was occupied by *four* sons, aged respectively seventeen, fifteen, fourteen, and ten.

Mr. Austin says, — " This, I was told, was not an extraordinary case; but that, more or less, every bed-room in the village was crowded with inmates of both sexes and of various ages, and that such a state of things was caused by the want of cottages.

" It is impossible not to be struck, in visiting the dwellings of the agricultural labourers, with the general want of new cottages, notwithstanding the universal increase of population. Everywhere the cottages are old, and frequently in a state of decay, and are consequently ill adapted for their increased number of inmates of late years. The floor of the room in which the family live during the day is always of stone in these counties, and wet or damp through the winter months, being frequently lower than the soil outside. The situation of the cottage is often extremely bad, no attention having been paid at the time of its building to facilities for draining. Cottages are frequently erected on a dead level, so that water cannot escape ; and sometimes on spots lower than the surrounding ground."

With reference to the subject of lodging, Mr. Phelps, an agent of the Marquis of Lansdowne, says * : —

" I was engaged in taking the late census in Bremhill parish ; and, in one case in Studley, I found twenty-nine people living under one roof ; amongst them were married men and women, and young people of nearly all ages. In Studley, it is not at all uncommon *for a whole family to sleep in the same room. The number of bastards in that place is very great ;* the number of unmarried women is greater than that in the neighbouring places. I don't think this state of things is attributable to the women working in the fields, but rather to the want of proper accommodation in the cottages."

Mr. Austin says again,—" The morality of the agricultural labourer is a subject, to which my inquiry did not extend, nor had I sufficient opportunities of making any satisfactory inquiry respecting it ; but certain things forced themselves upon my attention, and, amongst others, the consequences of the want of accommodation in their dwellings for sleeping. The sleeping of boys and girls, young men and young women, in the same room, in beds almost touching one another, *must have the effect of breaking down the great*

---

* Report on the Employment of Women in Agriculture.

barriers between the sexes, — the sense of modesty and
decency on the part of women, and respect for the other
sex on the part of men. The consequences of the
want of proper accommodation for sleeping in the cottages are seen in the early licentiousness of the rural
districts, *licentiousness which has not always respected the
family relationship.*

" It appeared to me, that, generally, the accommodation for sleeping is such as necessarily to create an early
and illicit familiarity between the sexes ; *for universally
in the villages, where the cottages are the most crowded,
there are the greatest number of illegitimate children, and
also the greatest depravity of manners generally.*"

The Rev. J. Guthrie, vicar of Colne, Wiltshire,
says * : —

" The want of good cottages, where the members of a
family can live separately, is a great cause of demoralisation. When grown up members of the same family are continually occupying the same room, modesty,
and delicacy, and sense of shame, are soon put to flight.
When these are absent, and dirt and disorder take
their place, a gradual declension in good morals and
character succeeds, and the whole family sink percep-
tibly to a lower grade in character and conduct."

The Hon. and Rev. S. Godolphin Osborne, rector
of Bryanston-cum-Durweston, Dorsetshire, says † : —

" The children of the agricultural labourer, for the
most part, sleep in the same room with his wife and
himself; and whatever attempts at decency may be made,

* Report on the Employment of Women in Agriculture.
† Ibid.

— and I have seen many most ingenious and praise-
worth attempts — still, there is the fact of the old and
young, married and unmarried, of both sexes, all herded
together in one and the same sleeping apartment.
Within this last year, I saw in a room about 13 feet
square, three beds; on the first, lay the mother, a
widow, dying of consumption; on the second, two unmarried daughters, one eighteen years of age, the other
twelve; on the third, a young married couple, whom I myself had married two days before ! A married woman, of
thorough good character, told me a few weeks ago, that
on her confinement, so crowded with children is her one
room, they are obliged to put her on the floor in the
middle of the room, that they may pay her the requisite
attention ! She spoke of this, as, to her, the most
painful part of that her hour of trial. I do not choose
to put on paper the disgusting scenes that I have known
to occur from this promiscuous mingling of the sexes
together. Seeing, however, to what the mind of the
young female is exposed from her very childhood, I
have long ceased to wonder at the otherwise seeming
precocious licentiousness of conversation, which may be
heard in every field, where many of the young are at
work together."

The Rev. H. Austen, curate of Pimperne, Dorset,
says * : —

" The poor people have to struggle with the want of
proper accommodation in their dwellings, which, I fear,
is too general in our rural districts. A man and his

* Report on the Employment of Women in Agriculture.

wife, with a large family of children, have, in most cases, only two bed-rooms."

Mr. M. Fisher, of Blandford, Dorset, says * : —

" I think, generally, the habits of the people are worse, and the manners of the women especially, where the accommodation of the cottages is bad. Milton Abbas, I think, is a place, where the character of the population is decidedly inferior. On the average at the late census, *there were thirty-six persons in each separate house.* The houses there are all built on one plan, each containing two dwellings with four rooms. In most of these dwellings there are two families, that is to say, on the average, A FAMILY OF NINE TO EVERY TWO ROOMS. Stourpain is another village, where the population is very thick, the cottages comparatively few, and in a miserable state, and the people crowded together. In that village, there are more bastard children than in any other village of the same size in the union of Winterborne. Kingston is another village, where there is a similar want of accommodation, and where you may see open stagnant drains, pools, and filth of all descriptions; and the character of the people is similar to these external appearances.

" Throughout the whole union, there appears to me to be a great want of cottages; very few have been built for many years, whilst the population has gone on increasing. The villages are overflowing, which produces great demoralisation; the surplus, and that generally the very worst characters, come to Blandford, owing to

* Report on the Employment of Women in Agriculture.

a great many new houses having been built within the last few years."

H. N. Tilsey, Esq., of North Petherton, Somersetshire, surgeon, and one of the medical officers of the Bridgewater union, says * : —

" There is a great want of cottage accommodation on many farms, so that the labourers are driven to the villages, and often congregate to the injury of their morals, many of them resorting to the beer-shop, who would, under a different system, be better members of society. What cottages there are, are generally badly arranged, badly ventilated, and badly drained ; occasionally, all ages and sexes sleeping in one common room. As a class, these labourers — men, women, and children — although, perhaps, sufficiently skilled in all matters relating to their own particular calling, manifest the most complete and perfect ignorance of all that regards school instruction."

Mr. Gilbert, formerly Assistant Poor Law Commissioner for Devonshire and Cornwall, gives the following, as an instance of the common condition of the dwellings of the labouring classes † : —

" In Tiverton, in Cornwall, there is a large district, from which I find numerous applications were made for relief to the board of guardians, in consequence of illness from fever.

" One cause of disease is to be found in the state of the cottages.

" Many are built on the ground, without flooring, or against a damp hill.

* See Report on the Employment of Women in Agriculture.
† See Report on Sanitary Condition of the Labouring Population.

" Some have neither windows nor doors sufficient to keep out the weather, or to let in the rays of the sun, or supply the means of ventilation; and in others the roof is so constructed or so worn, as not to be weather-tight.

" The thatch roof is frequently saturated with wet, rotten, and in a state of decay, giving out malaria, as other decaying vegetable matter."

The state of the dwellings of many of the agricultural labourers in Dorset, where the deaths from the four classes of disease bear a similar proportion to those in Devon, is described in the return of Mr. John Fox, the medical officer of the Cerne union in Dorsetshire, who, remarking upon some cases of disease among the poor whom he had attended, says * : —

" I have often seen the springs bursting through the mud floor of some of the cottages, and little channels cut from the centre, under the doorways, to carry off the water, whilst the door has been removed from its hinges for the children to put their feet on whilst employed in making buttons. It is not surprising that fever, and scrofula in all its forms, prevail under such circumstances.

" It is somewhat singular that seven cases of typhus occurred in one village, heretofore famed for the health and general cleanliness of its inhabitants and cottages. The first five cases occurred in one family, in a detached house on high and dry ground, and free from accumulations of vegetable and animal matter. The cottage was originally built for a school-room, and consists of one room only, about 18 feet by 10 feet, and 9 feet high.

* See Report on Sanitary Condition, &c.

About one third part was partitioned off by boards, reaching to within 3 feet of the roof; and *in this small space were three beds, in which six persons slept.* Had there been two bed-rooms attached to this one day-room, these cases of typhus would not have occurred.

" Most of the cottages are of the worst description, some mere mud hovels, and situated in low and damp places, with cesspools or accumulations of filth close to the doors.

" The mud floors of many are much below the level of the road, and in wet seasons are little better than so much clay.

" In many of the cottages, also, where synochus prevailed, the beds stood on the ground-floor, which was damp three parts of the year; scarcely one had a fire-place in the bed-room; and one had a single small pane of glass stuck in the mud wall, as its only window, with a large heap of wet and dirty potatoes in one corner. Persons living in such cottages are generally very poor, very dirty, and usually in rags, *living almost wholly on bread and potatoes, scarcely ever tasting any animal food,* and consequently highly susceptible of disease, and very unable to contend with it. I am sure, if such persons were placed in good, comfortable, clean cottages, the improvement in themselves and children would soon be visible, and the exceptions would only be found in a few of the poorest and most wretched, who perhaps have been born in a mud hovel, and had lived in one the first thirty years of their lives.

" In my district, *I do not think there is one cottage to be found consisting of a day-room, three bed-rooms, scul-*

lery, pantry, and convenient receptacles for refuse and for fuel, in the occupation of a labourer."

The tenor of much information respecting the condition of many of the labouring classes in Somerset, is exhibited in the Sanitary Report of Mr. James Gane, the medical officer of the Axbridge Union, in Somersetshire, who states * that, —

" The situation of this district, where the diseases therein-mentioned prevail, is a perfect flat called the South Marsh, in the main road between Bristol and Bridgewater. There are numerous dykes or ditches for the purpose of drainage. The cottages of the poor are mostly of a bad description. The walls are frequently made of mud. They are often situated close to the dykes, where the water, for the most part, is in a state of stagnation. *Oftentimes there is not more than one room for the whole family;* sometimes two, one above the other; with the really poor, *the latter is seldom to be met with* (unless it should happen now and then in a parish where a poor-house was built a short time before the formation of the union). A pigsty, where the inmates are capable of keeping a pig, is frequently attached to the dwelling, and in the heat of summer produces a stench quite intolerable : the want of space, however, prevents it being otherwise. The ordinary houses of the poor peasants (those mentioned above being detached cottages), in most of the parishes in this district, are of a much worse description, several large families existing under the same roof, and *each family occupying only one room*, and having but

* See Report on Sanitary Condition, &c.

one entrance door to the dwelling. Here filth and poverty go hand in hand, without any restriction, and
under no control; the accumulation of filth being
attributable to the want of proper receptacles for refuse.
Owing to the indolent and filthy disposition of the inhabitants, in no instance have such places been provided.

" The floors are seldom or never scrubbed, and the
parish authorities pay so little attention to these houses,
that the walls never get white-limed from one end of the
year to the other. The windows are kept air-tight by
the stuffing of some old garments; and every article for
use is kept in the same room. *The necessary is close to
the building,* where all have access, and produces a most
intolerable nuisance. In a locality naturally engendering malaria, the diseases with which the poor are for the
most part afflicted are fevers, such as are stated in this
Report, which sometimes run into a low typhoid state.
The neighbourhood in general is considered in as good a
state of drainage as it will admit of.

" The occurrence of disease among the poor population, is for the most part at spring and autumn. At
those times agues and fevers prevail. Smallpox and
scarlet fever are met with at all seasons of the year, but
prevail as epidemics, the former in spring and summer,
and the latter about autumn or the beginning of winter.
I attribute the prevalence of diseases of an epidemic
character, which exist so much more among the poor
than among the rich, to be owing to the want of better
accommodation as residences (their dwellings, instead of
being built of solid materials, are complete shells of mud

on a spot of waste land, the most swampy in the parish
—this is to be met with almost everywhere in rural districts); to the want of better clothing, better food, and of
more attention paid to the cleanliness of their dwellings;
and to the being so congregated together. The health
of persons, even where a large family is, and where
superior cottage accommodation is afforded to them, is
much better generally than others less advantageously
situated. The influence over their habits will also be
very beneficial; they will be less likely to run to a
beer-house with their last penny.

"The comforts of a home, after the toils of the day, keep
them by their own fireside; they become better contented,
less liable to disease, make better husbands, better fathers,
better neighbours, and better friends with each other.
There is a subject, which I wish particularly to press on
the attention of the commissioners, — *the existence
throughout the country, and in every parish, of low lodging-
houses, where persons of the lowest grade of society, beggars, thieves, and such-like, take up a temporary abode in
passing from one part of the kingdom to the other, bringing with them the seeds of infectious diseases, and oftentimes
the actual disease itself, into a neighbourhood previously in
a comparative state of health.*"

The following extract from a Report of Mr. Aaron
Little, the medical officer of the Chipperham Union,
in Wiltshire, affords a specimen of the frequent condition of rural villages which have apparently the most
advantageous sites * : " —

* Report on Sanitary Condition, &c.

" The parish of Colerne, which, upon a cursory view, any person (unacquainted with its peculiarities) would pronounce to be the most healthy village in England, is, in fact, the most unhealthy. From its commanding position, being situated upon a high hill, it has an appearance of health and cheerfulness, which delight the eye of the traveller, who commands a view of it from the great western road; but this impression is immediately removed on entering at any point of the town.

" The filth, dilapidated buildings, the squalid appearance of the majority of the lower orders, have a sickening effect upon the stranger, who first visits this place. During three years' attendance among the poor of this district, I have never known the small-pox, scarlatina, or the typhus fever to be absent. The situation is damp, and the buildings unhealthy, and the inhabitants themselves inclined to be of dirty habits. There is also a great want of drainage."

During the latter part of 1849, some very remarkable and exceedingly able letters were published in the " Morning Chronicle," describing the condition of the cottages of the peasantry in different parts of England. I might crowd my pages with extracts from these letters, all proving the truth of the description I have given above of the cottages of our peasantry. It is impossible for me to do more than make one or two extracts from them, to show how the condition of the cottages of the peasantry is *deteriorating*. I must refer my readers to those remarkable letters for further details. They will well repay the most careful study.

The correspondent of the " Morning Chronicle," de-

scribing the condition of the labourers in Devonshire,
Somersetshire, Cornwall, and Dorsetshire, says : —

" Devon and Somerset have long been classed in the
unenviable category of counties presenting the agricultural labourer in his most deplorable circumstances.
With Dorset and Wilts, they are generally regarded as
exhibiting the unfavourable, whilst Lincolnshire exhibits the favourable, extreme in the labourer's condition.

" In traversing both counties, more especially Devonshire, I was particularly struck with the utter absence
of new cottages. Along the highways and byways their
absence is observable; and not only this, but in many
places there are abundant evidences that cottages, which
a few years ago were tenanted, are now, if not altogether untenantable, going rapidly into decay. Many
are so rickety and ruined, that to inhabit them any
longer is impossible; whilst, as regards others, the process of demolition or decomposition has only commenced,
confining the wretched tenants, who had formerly two
rooms, to the only apartment which remains, and which
they can with difficulty keep together. In search of
these, one has not to go into remote and sequestered
parts, where things are done which would not be exposed in the neighbourhood of the highways. I have
seen specimens of cottages in this state along the line
from Exeter to Honiton, and in the district traversed by
the high-road to London. . . . . . .

" Not only are no new cottages being erected to meet
the exigencies of an increasing population, but old ones,
instead of being kept in repair, are suffered to crumble
to pieces, if, indeed, decay is not aided by more active

means. In a parish between Honiton and the coast, a great part of which is owned by Sir Edward Elton, this process of cottage clearing seems to be a marked feature in proprietary policy. On Sir Edward Elton's property I am told, that the average rate of decay or demolition is about six cottages per annum. As each cottage would contain a family of seven on the average, the proprietor thus clears his estate of about forty-two poor persons each year, unless they can find room in their neighbour's hovels, which can, in most cases, be but ill spared. By this means this estate, and others similarly dealt with, will, by and by, become eased of one incumbrance, at least, which presses upon them—a large and unemployed population.

"Whilst in many parts of Devon and Somerset the process of the demolition of cottages has been going on far more rapidly, than that of building new ones, the population of the two counties has been fast increasing. 'We don't find room for them,' said a farmer with whom I conversed on this subject, 'and they are drafted off to other places.' But they are not thus drafted off in all cases, and the real effect of the demolition of cottages is to reduce, if possible, to a still lower point of wretchedness the physical condition of the labourer. The clergyman of one of the parishes of Devon pointed out to me an addition which had recently been made to the parish church. As it stood, the church was but a small one, but the addition made to it was larger than the original edifice. 'Why was the addition made?' I asked. 'Because the population of the parish has increased,' was the reply. This answer was obvious, and

I had anticipated it; but I wished to obtain it, in order to base upon it another question. 'How comes it,' I inquired, 'that if the population has increased so as to require so large an addition to be made to the church, there is not a single new cottage to be found in your parish?' 'That is difficult to say,' he answered. 'It does not appear to me,' I added, 'that there is a cottage in your whole parish, which has been built within the last fifty years.' 'They all seem to be of that age, at least,' he replied, 'and many much older.' 'And when was the addition made to the church?' I inquired. 'Within the last twenty years,' said he. This simple story speaks for itself. The population of the parish in question has largely increased, but the house accommodation has not increased in the slightest degree to meet the exigencies of a growing population.

" It is evident that the new comers were not drafted off elsewhere as fast as they came, otherwise the church might have remained of its original dimensions. The truth, of course, is, that most of them stayed in the parish, every cottage in it becoming more and more crowded with inmates every year. The consequences of this, both in a moral and a physical point of view, are shocking to contemplate. And this is the process which is going on in more parishes than one in the counties of Devon and Somerset. WHILST POPULATION IS INCREASING WITHIN THEM, NOT ONLY IS HOUSE AC-COMMODATION NOT INCREASING, BUT IT IS ACTUALLY DIMINISHING.

The points in Devon, at which I more particularly inspected the dwellings of the poor, were, in the south, in the neighbourhood of Exeter, along the line between that city and Exmouth, in the direction of Totness, and throughout a great part of the union of Kingsbridge; in the vicinity of Axminster, between that town and Honiton, and between Honiton and Sidmouth; and in the north, around Barnstaple, and along the more northerly part of the Vale of the Torridge. In Somerset I examined them with some care in the neighbourhood of Minehead and Dunster in the north-west; near Bridgewater, in the centre; and about Wells, Chewton, Mendip, &c., in the north-eastern part of the county. *In the great majority of instances I found the condition of the cottages to be deplorably bad.* It is not to be denied that I encountered some, and even many, exceptions. At many points there were cottages to be found well situated and commodious, but they were exceptions to the general character of the peasants' dwellings.

" It is impossible fully to estimate the wretchedness to which the inmates of the hovels, which meet the eye at all points are exposed, without a close personal inspection of them. We are accustomed to associate with the idea of a country village, or with a cottage situated in a winding vale, or hanging upon the side of a rich and fertile slope, nothing but health, contentment, and happiness. A rural dwelling of this class, with its heavy thatch and embowering trees, makes such a nice pencil sketch, that we are naturally inclined to think it as neat and comfortable as it appears. But to know it aright, it must be turned inside out, and its realities exposed to the gaze of the observer. Could the internal be always given with the external view, it would moderate our enthusiasm for the little sketches, which work so early and

so powerfully upon our fancies, and which are suggestive
of nothing but contentment and happiness. How often
does the cot, which looks so attractive and roman-
tic upon paper, conceal an amount of wretchedness,
filth, squalor, disease, privation, and frequently of immorality, which, when exposed in their reality, are perfectly appalling! And as to health, nowhere, perhaps,
is the pure air of heaven more tainted than in the
neighbourhood of these rustic dwellings. You will encounter odours in a country village, which it would be
difficult to match in Westminster or St. Giles's. Indeed,
the most sickening and offensive, that I ever came in
contact with, had nestled themselves on the summit of
Beacon Hill, in the neighbourhood of Bath. It is high
time that people divested themselves of the false impressions too generally entertained of the character of our
rural cottages. They are chiefly drawn from descriptions which at one time may have suited the reality,
when the condition of the agricultural labourer was
much better than it is now: for that it was much
better than at present, is evident from the information
derived from a variety of valuable sources. To go a
considerable way back: We find Fortescue alluding to
their condition in his day, as one of great comfort and
happiness; inasmuch as they lived chiefly upon butcher
meat, of which they had plenty, and had abundance of
good ale, with which to accompany it at their meals. In
regard to their diet, at least, their condition now seems
the very reverse of what it was then; and as it is impossible that they could have fallen back so much in
this important element of their physical condition, with-

out having all the others deteriorated in proportion, it is
fair to infer that their house accommodation was better
formerly than now. It was better in this, if in no other
respect—that fewer people were to be found under one
and the same roof, a state of things much more favourable to health, cleanliness, and good morals than that
which now prevails. We must, therefore, judge of the
labourer's condition, not from past descriptions of it,
but from the sad realities of the present hour."

In another letter the same gentleman writes :—

" But bad as are the tenements usually occupied by
the poor, they are not, except in rare cases, quite so
revolting in their character, and in the scenes to which
they give rise, as are some tenements, which have a
claim to be regarded in the light of public buildings.
These are the parish houses, which are scattered in considerable numbers over the southern and western districts. They are the houses, in which the poor were
accommodated previously to the erection of the union
workhouses. In many cases, since the workhouses came
into use, these parish houses have been sold, and the
proceeds applied to defraying, *pro tanta,* the expense of
building the workhouses. But in others, the overseers
will not part with them, keeping them for the purpose
of letting, and thus deriving a profit from them. They
are generally let at a lower rent than ordinary cottages,
and thus become the resort of those in the most
wretched circumstances, who crowd into them by
dozens, and fill up almost every crevice of them with
lodgers. One of these I saw on the borders of Devonshire and Cornwall, and not far from Launceston. It

consisted of two houses, containing between them four
rooms. In each room was a family, who used it both
night and day. The lower rooms were about 12 feet
square. In one of them were a man, and his wife, and
five children ; in the other were a man, and his wife,
and eight children. In this latter, there were but two
beds — the father, and mother, and two children occupying one, and the other six being huddled together in the
remaining bed. They lay 'head and foot,' as they
termed it — that is to say, *three with their heads at the
top, and three with them at the foot of the bed !* The
eldest girl was between *fifteen* and *sixteen*, and the eldest
boy between *fourteen* and *fifteen*. The closeness of this
room was overpowering. The beds were necessarily
large, and occupied most of the floor ; indeed, when
the whole family was assembled, several of the children
were placed upon the beds to keep them out of the way.
In this way the beds may be said to have never been
cold. How can health be retained or morals preserved
under such circumstances as these? "

And in another letter the same gentleman describes
some of the cottages he has been visiting, thus :—

" The cabin is so rude and uncouth, that it has less
the appearance of having been built, than of having been
suddenly thrown up out of the ground. The length is
not above 15 feet, its width between 10 and 12. The
wall, which has sunk at different points, and seems be-
dewed with a cold sweat, is composed of a species of
imperfect sandstone, which is fast crumbling to decay.
It is so low, that your very face is almost on a level
with the heavy thatched roof, which covers it, and

which seems to be pressing it into the earth. The
thatch is thickly encrusted with a bright green vegetation, which, together with the appearance of the trees
and the mason-work around, well attests the prevailing
humidity of the atmosphere. In front, it presents to the
eye a door, with one window below, and another window — a smaller one — in the thatch above. The door
is awry from the sinking of the wall; the glass in the
window above is unbroken, but the lower one is here
and there stuffed with rags, which keep out both the
air and the sunshine. You approach the doorway
through the mud, over some loose stones, which rock
under your feet in using them. You have to stoop for
admission, and cautiously look around, ere you fairly
trust yourself within. There are but two rooms in the
house, one below and the other above." The sleeping
accommodations "are gained by means of a few greasy
and rickety steps, which lead through a species of hatch-
way in the ceiling. *Yes, there is but one room, and
yet we counted nine in the family!* And such a room!
The small window in the roof admits just light enough
to enable you to discern its character and dimensions.
The rafters, which are all exposed, spring from the
very floor, so that it is only in the very centre of the
apartment, that you have any chance of standing erect.
The thatch oozes through the wood-work, which supports it, the whole being begrimed with smoke and
dust, and replete with vermin. But, perhaps, the cli-
max of misery in this respect, in the district, is to be
found in the village of Taversey, about a mile distant
from Thame. One house was pointed out to me there

with four rooms; each room occupied by a separate
family, some of the families being very numerous. It
was a two-story house, covered with tiles. There was
no communication between the upper and lower stories,
the former being approached from the outside by a
flight of stone steps, which rose over the door leading
into the latter. One of the families counted eight or
ten, of both sexes, some of whom had attained maturity. The immorality to which their domestic condition
gives rise I shall have occasion hereafter to refer to."

The correspondent of "The Morning Chronicle"
traces very powerfully the enormous evils, which spring
from the present shameful condition of the cottages of
the peasants. He says, in one of his letters: —"Wherever I went, I found the uncertainty of work and the
want of cottage accommodation the two great subjects
of complaint. I was told by some of the more respectable people in Corfe, that if there were twenty new
cottages built in the town, they would be readily occupied. So great is the want of room, that many of the
labourers themselves would go to the expense of building, if the opportunity of so doing were given them.

. . . .

"But if the cottages are so much in demand, it may
be asked, why, if the landlords will not build them,
others, who are neither labourers nor landlords, do not
do so? There could not be a more profitable investment
of capital, when the rents are regularly paid, and many
would so invest, if it were in their power to do so. But
cottages cannot be built in the air, although their foundations are sometimes laid in water. Those who would

willingly invest their money in building them cannot get the land on which to build them. *All the land about Wareham is so strictly settled as scarcely to admit of this.* If one of the most respectable inhabitants of Wareham wanted to build himself a house, it is questionable if he could get the land. Not that the landlords would in all cases refuse it, but that in many cases they cannot part with it. A rather ludicrous instance of this occurred a short time ago. A firm in Wareham had negotiated with one of the neighbouring proprietors for a lease of a certain piece of land for some works, which were to be carried on upon it; but when the agreement came to be carried out, the proprietor found, that he had so strictly tied up the land, that he could not give the lease.

" This scarcity of cottages is a complicated evil. It sometimes drives families to the workhouse, who would otherwise not be there; and, at others, serves to keep them perpetually on the parish, after distress has once thrown them upon it. In the Wareham workhouse, for instance, was a woman with her six children, her husband being at the time at work, and in receipt of wages, but staying with his mother, because he could not procure a cottage for himself and family. The woman herself evidently felt her situation very much. She and the whole family would leave the workhouse if a cottage could be procured. Again, take the case of a man whose family is thrown into distress from a temporary suspension of his employment. On applying for relief, he is told by the guardians, that they can do nothing for him, unless he comes into the workhouse.

To this he has many objections, one of which is, that he has his cottage and his furniture — poor and scanty though it be, it is his own; and if he goes into the house, his little establishment will be broken up, without the least chance of his recovering it, when he comes out again. But the guardians are inflexible, and he must either starve or comply with the requirements of the law. At last he enters the house, and his little establishment is broken up. Sometimes afterwards he hears of employment, and leaves. But his cottage is now occupied by others, or it has in the meantime altogether disappeared. He cannot find another in which to shelter his family, and has to return to the workhouse. He is thus converted into what he never meant to become — a pauper; and being so, he makes up his mind to make the most of his pauperism. The chances are, that he never makes another effort to retrieve himself, but remains with his family a permanent charge upon the rates. This is not an imaginary sketch of the pauper's progress, but one drawn to me as true in but too many instances, by one who had been for years the relieving officer of a district not far from Wareham."

The "Morning Chronicle" of Nov. 30, 1849, in an exceedingly able article, after reviewing the reports of its correspondents, says, —

"In Sutton Courtney, for example, near Abingdon, (Berks), many of the houses were found by our correspondent to contain but *two* rooms, and in one instance we are told that 'ten of a family slept together,' in a room twelve feet square, and containing three beds.

The family consisted of the father and mother, young children, and girls and boys growing up to maturity, all huddled together without the smallest regard to decency. In Devonshire, on the high London road, we learn that 'many cottages are so rickety and ruined, that to inhabit them any longer is impossible.' 'One in particular,' adds our correspondent, 'struck my attention. The upper part of one of the end walls was entirely away, exposing the crazy anatomy of the roof, and laying the whole of what used to form the sleeping apartment of the family bare to every tempest that swept around their miserable house.' The family in this cottage consisted of seven. They had been obliged to sleep in the lower room, which was about sixteen feet square, and this was the sole and common dwelling place, for all purposes, of these seven persons. It had a mouldering brick floor, and the rain trickled through the rotten beams of the bulging ceiling. They had lived two years in this place and under these circumstances. At Axminster, our correspondent says, 'In one hovel with two rooms I found no fewer than eleven people; the sleeping apartment was up stairs, as usual, directly under the thatch.' This family consisted of the father, the mother, and nine children. The eldest was a girl of sixteen, the next a girl of fifteen, the third a boy of fourteen. Yet not the smallest reserve or decency could be maintained. A large tattered shawl hung between the beds of the parents and of the children in summer, was usually taken down in winter, to make an additional covering for the children. Need we speak of the demoralizing influence of such a mode of life?

" The cottages at Southleigh, in Devon, are, if possible, even worse. One house, which our correspondent visited, was almost a ruin. It had continued in that state for ten years. The floor was of mud, dipping near the fire-place into a deep hollow, which was constantly filled with water. There were five in the family,—a young man of twenty-one, a girl of eighteen, and another girl of about thirteen, with the father and mother, all sleeping together up stairs. And what a sleeping room! ' In places it seemed falling in. To ventilation it was an utter stranger. The crazy floor shook and creaked under me as I paced it.' Yet the rent was 1s. a week.; the same sum, for which apartments that may be called luxurious in comparison may be had in the model lodging-houses. And here sat a girl weaving that beautiful Honiton lace, which our peeresses wear on Court days. Cottage after cottage at Southleigh presented the same characteristics. Clay floors, low ceilings letting in the rain, no ventilation; two rooms, one above and one below; gutters running through the lower room to let off the water; unglazed window-frames, now boarded up, and now uncovered to the elements, the boarding going for fire-wood; the inmates disabled by rheumatism, ague, and typhus; broad, stagnant, open ditches close to the doors; heaps of abominations piled round the dwellings ; such are the main features of Southleigh; and it is in these worse than pig-styes that one of the most beautiful fabrics that luxury demands or art supplies is fashioned. The parish houses are still worse. ' One of these, on the borders of Devonshire and Cornwall, and not far from

Launceston, consisted of two houses containing between them four rooms. In each room lived a family night and day, the space being about twelve feet square. In one were a man and his wife and eight children; the father, mother, and two children lay in one bed, the remaining six were huddled 'head and foot' (three at the top and three at the foot) in the other bed. The eldest girl was between fifteen and sixteen, the eldest boy between fourteen and fifteen.' Is it not horrible to think of men and women being brought up in this foul, brutish manner in civilized and Christian England! The lowest of savages are not worse cared for than these children of a luxurious and refined country.

"Liskeard, in Cornwall, is no better off. 'One case,' we read, 'which may be given as an illustration of the state of things in Liskeard, was, that of a man and his wife who had a miner lodging with them, all three occupying the same bedroom at night.' A poor widow looking out for a lodger, and anxious to consult delicacy, so far as the wretched necessities of her lot permitted, placed her inmate (a miner) up-stairs to sleep, while she occupied the lower room, through which, however, the man had to pass every morning before she left her bed. In another house 'three men occupied one bed.' In general 'there were two beds in the lodgers' rooms, and sometimes both had two occupants.'

"The disclosures contained in our correspondent's letter of the 17th inst. are, perhaps, the worst of all. That letter details the condition of the labourers in the parish of St. Martin's, which for filth, immorality, and misery, surpasses every thing previously described.

To extract one specimen worse than the others would be impossible. They are all so bad, that there are no discriminating *degrees* of evil. Illegitimate children swarming about; men and women living almost indiscriminately together; unmarried women confined in the same apartment, in which nine other human beings are stowed away. Such is the moral state of things, to which physical wretchedness has reduced the population of St. Martin's. Here, as in many parts of Wiltshire and Dorsetshire, the most debasing influences seem to have been collected together in one full tide, as if to show how low a portion of a civilized and refined people can be sunk by poverty and neglect."

In some letters on the condition of the peasantry of Dorsetshire, published in the "Times" in June, 1846, by a gentleman, who was sent down, in order to obtain information, it is said,

"Another fruitful source of misery, as well as immorality, is the great inadequacy of the number and size of the houses to the number of the population, and the consequently crowded state of their habitations, which in Dorsetshire generally, and in Stourpain particularly, afford the most limited accommodation. It is by no means an uncommon thing for the whole family to sleep in the same room, without the slightest regard to age or sex, and without a curtain or the slightest attempt at separation between the beds. In one instance, which came under my notice, a family consisting of nine persons occupied three beds in the same bed-room, which was the only one the house afforded. The eldest daughter was twenty-three years of age, the eldest son twenty-one. The bedroom was ten feet square, not reckoning two small recesses by the side of the chimney, about eighteen inches deep. In some few instances, I have seen most ingenious and laudable attempts to effect a barrier between the sexes; but in general, there does not appear to exist any anxiety on the subject; and indeed, in most instances, the size and form of the rooms and the number of beds required for accommodation of the family render all such attempts futile. It will be easily imagined, that the great and promiscuous herding together of young people of both sexes is productive of the most demoralizing effects."

" In case of a death occurring in a family, should there be but one bed-room, which is, I think, generally the case, the inmates of the house are compelled to pass their nights in the same room with the corpse, until the time of burial."

" I could produce instances of the most frightful depravity, which, it must be evident, is the inevitable consequence of this disgusting and indiscriminate herding together of so many persons into one common and confined sleeping apartment; but I prefer suppressing them, more especially as they may be easily imagined."

" The atmosphere of these houses, and especially of the sleeping apartments, to an unpractised nose, is almost insupportable. It is, perhaps, worthy of remark, that dishes, plates, and other articles of crockery seem almost unknown. There is, however, the less need for them, *as grist bread forms the principal, and, I believe, the only kind of food that falls to the labourer's lot.* In no single instance did I observe meat of any kind during my progress through the parish. The furniture is such as may be expected from the description I have given of the place — a rickety table and two or three foundered chairs generally forming the extent of the upholstery."

It is said that this is the condition throughout the greater part of the counties of Dorsetshire, Wiltshire, and Gloucestershire. Another letter, inserted in the " Times" of the 29th of June 1846, and signed " A Country Rector," says, " The misery," described above, " I am afraid is not confined to that county (Dorsetshire): if you go to Devonshire, Wiltshire, and the hill country of *Gloucestershire*, you will find him (the peasant) at the point of starvation."

The Hon. and Rev. S. G. Osborne, in writing of one of the parishes of Dorsetshire, viz. that of Hilton, which he inspected personally, in company with the vicar of the parish, describes the degradation of the inhabitants and the wretchedness of the houses as something almost incredible. He says, " I despair of giving you any faint idea of the manner these people are pigged together within their dwellings ;" and yet this parish " closely adjoins the park of Milton Abbey, the beautiful seat of the Earl of Portarlington."

" In the first cottage, a man and his wife live with two children, a son of his by a former marriage, a daughter of hers by a former marriage ; this son is married ; but owing to want of room, cannot sleep with his own wife and children, who are living in another part of the parish, but sleeps in a small room, the only other bed of which is occupied by the grown girl, the daughter of the woman. They pay the parish 30s. a year rent.

" In one compartment of the large building were dwelling a man, his wife, and five children; five of them had had the fever; the man died of it. With some difficulty, we ascended to a bed-room of this cottage: no one by pen can describe it. You get into it by a sort of ladder; when in it, you find it impossible to stand upright anywhere but in the direct centre, for the roof slopes down to the floor at an acute angle; three beds are so placed as to make the base of so many triangles, of which the sides of the roof are the lateral lines; you must cross the first to get at the second, the second to reach the third; the floor is as rotten as possible, full of holes, through one of which the husband's leg had gone on one occasion. I ventured to ask how they got a corpse out of such a place. I found ' they had him down stairs to die;' there he was seven weeks, and then they took him dead to the church-yard."

" The floors of some of the down-stairs rooms are of mud, in pits or holes in many places; where mended at all, it is done with the rough stone of the country. The parish officers regularly, when they can get it, take rent even of the pauper tenants, with the exception of some few."

" Behind these buildings, is a space between them and a broad ditch, varying, perhaps, from twelve to fourteen feet in width; the said space, in the case of the first two cottages, occupied partly by some out-houses, rank grass is growing, amongst which is ample evidence of every possible abomination. The ditch is full to overflowing of black sewer filth; the first two cottages have a partitioned portion of a common privy built over this ditch; the other portion, belonging to the larger building, being the only accommodation of the sort for nearly one hundred souls." . . .

" That this accommodation is not sufficient, or that it is too repulsive for even this sort of population, we had an overpowering proof at almost every step in this back-yard. I defy contradiction to the fact, that the night-soil is overflowing in a downward direction towards the houses, and this well accounted for the sickening stench of some of the sleeping-places. In front of these parish dwellings, across the road, there is also a ditch, as might be expected, full of decaying vegetable and other matter, cast from these houses. The one well, from which for every purpose all the water used must be drawn, is so placed that it is next to impossible, but at times some of the rain must, after washing the filth in the road and ditch, pass into it. The clergyman told me at times the water was not drinkable. The stench produced from all these causes is so great, that in hot weather, he also informed me, he is obliged to close his vicarage windows, some 200 yards off; for it is un-bearable."

" I was shown two cottages belonging to the noble proprietor of the estate. The filth here accumulated was such as defies all powers of description I possess." *

* See Mr. Osborne's letter, published in the " Times" of the 26th of October, 1848.

We need not and shall not wonder, if we find that the amount of crime in counties, where the peasants are in such a horrible social condition, is alarmingly and terribly increasing. The "Times" of the 30th of November, 1849, shows the terrible increase of crime in the last few years in Dorsetshire. The "Times" says:—"We yesterday published, in a very short compass, some grave particulars of the unfortunate county of Dorset. It is not simply the old story of wages inadequate for life, hovels unfit for habitation, and misery and sin alternately claiming our pity and our disgust. This state of things is so normal, and we really believe so immemorial in that notorious county, that we should rather deaden, than excite the anxiety of the public by a thrice-told tale. What compels our attention just now is a sudden, rapid, and, we fear, a forced aggravation of these evils, measured by the infallible test of crime. Dorsetshire is fast sinking into a slough of wretchedness, which threatens the peace and morality of the kingdom at large. The total number of convictions which

"In 1846 was 798, and
"In 1847 was 821, mounted up,
"In 1848, to 950;

"and up to the special general session, last Tuesday," (Dec. 1849) "for less than eleven months of the present year, to the astonishing number of 1193, being at the rate of 1300 for the whole year! Unless something is done to stop this flood of crime, or the tide happily turns of itself, the county will have more than *doubled* its convictions within four years! Nor is it possible for us to take refuge in the thought that the increase is in petty offences. In no respect is it a light thing for a poor creature to be sent to gaol, whatever be the offence. He has broken the laws of his country, and forfeited his character. His name and his morals are alike tainted with the gaol. He is degraded and corrupted. If his spirit be not crushed, it is exasperated into perpetual hostility to wealth and power. . . . . .

"It is, then, no light affair that a rural county, the abode of an ancient and respectable aristocracy, somewhat removed from the popular influences of the age, with a population of 175,043 by the late census, should produce in four years near 4000 convictions, being at the rate of one conviction in that period for every sixty persons, or every twelve householders."

The next series of extracts will show the condition of the houses of the peasants in the south-eastern counties, viz. Kent, Surrey, and Sussex.

Mr. Vaughan, special Assistant Poor Law Commissioner for the counties of Kent, Surrey, and Sussex, says* : —

"The undivided state of the large families, acting upon the scantiness of house-room and general poverty or high rent, often crowds them together in their sleeping apartments, so as seriously to infringe on the decencies which guard female morals."

Mr. Hart, a professional gentleman at Reigate, says* : —

"The great difficulty is to say, at what age brothers

* See Report on the Employment of Women in Agriculture.

and sisters do not sleep together in the same apartment; but *generally until they leave home, be that at ever so late a period. Many cottages have but one room, and the whole family sleep in one bed.* I have often, when taking the examination of a sick man with a magistrate, an occasion, which has more often taken me into a cottage than any other, observed upon this, and I consider its effects most demoralising."

Mr. Vaughan, says: —

" In the neighbourhood of Cuckfield in Sussex, it is said to be common for children of both sexes to use the same sleeping-room and bed up to the age of twelve and even fourteen.

" The Rev. W. Sankie, curate of Farnham in Surrey, mentioned a case within his own knowledge, where two sisters and a brother, *all above fourteen,* habitually slept together. The admission of strangers, too, into the cottager's home produces an effect of a kind sometimes occasionally the same. Where a family is admitted, the same evil is increased. Where the letting of a room to a whole family is prohibited, as in some cases by the owner of the house, and a single lodger only is allowed, the danger strikes more directly at the chastity of the family."

Mr. Rammell, a farmer on a large scale, living at Sturry near Canterbury, says * : —

" Cottage rent is very high. Cottages with two rooms are sometimes let for 1*s.* 6*d.* a-week without a garden; sometimes, though not commonly, for 2*s.* ;

* See Report on the Employment of Women in Agriculture.

2*s.* 6*d.* and 3*s.* are paid for four room cottages. It is
common for persons in roomy cottages to let off a room
for a stranger. The benefit of an airy abode is thus
lost; and other evils follow from the intimacy between
a stranger and the grown-up daughters."

The next series of extracts shows the condition of
the peasants' houses in Buckinghamshire, Bedfordshire,
Hertfordshire, Norfolk, Suffolk, and Essex.

Mr. Parker observes, that the construction of the
cottages in Buckinghamshire is frequently unwholesome * : —

" The improper materials, of which cottages are built,
and their defective construction, are also the frequent
cause of the serious indisposition of the inmates. The
cottages at Waddeston, and some of the surrounding
parishes in the vale of Aylesbury, are constructed of
mud, with earth floors and thatched roofs. The vegetable substances mixed with the mud to make it bind
rapidly decompose, leaving the wall porous. The earth
of the floor is full of vegetable matter, and from there
being nothing to cut off its contact with the surrounding
mould, it is peculiarly liable to damp. The floor is frequently charged with animal matter, thrown upon it by
the inmates, and this rapidly decomposes by the alternate action of heat and moisture. Thatch placed in
contact with such walls, speedily decays, yielding a gas
of the most deleterious quality. Fever of every type
and diarrhœa are endemic diseases in the parish and
neighbourhood."

* Report on the Sanitary Condition of the Labouring Population.

Mr. William Blower, the surgeon of the Bedford union, in Bedfordshire, states * : —

" Throughout the whole of this district there is a great want of ' superior cottage accommodation.' *Most of the residences of the labourers are thickly inhabited,* and many of them are damp, low, cold, smoky, and comfortless. These circumstances occasion the inmates to be sickly in the winter season; but I have not observed them to generate typhus, the prevailing form of disease being principally catarrhal, such as colds, coughs, inflammation of the eyes, dysentery, rheumatism, &c. However, when any contagious or epidemic malaria occurs, *the cases generally are more numerous.*"

Mr. Weale reports instances of the condition of large proportions of the agricultural population in the counties of Bedford, Northampton, and Warwick. The medical officer of the Woburn union in Bedfordshire states, in respect to Toddington, that —

" In this town fever prevailed during the last year, and, from the state of the dwellings of the persons I called on, this could not be wondered at. *Very few of the cottages were furnished with privies that could be used,* and contiguous to almost every door a dung heap was raised, on which every species of filth was accumulated, either for the purpose of being used in the garden allotments of the cottagers, or to be disposed of for manure. Scarcely any cottage was provided with a pantry, and I found the provisions generally kept in the bed-rooms. *In several instances I found whole fa-*

* See Report on Sanitary Condition of Labouring Population.

milies, comprising adult and infant children with their parents, sleeping in one room.

The medical officer of the Ampthill union in Bedfordshire, states * : —

" Typhus fever has existed for the last three or four months in the parish of Flitwick, and although the number of deaths has not been considerable, as compared with the progress of the disease, new cases have occurred as those under treatment became convalescent, and several are still suffering under this malady. The cottages, in which it first appeared (and to which it has been almost exclusively confined), are of the most wretched description : a stagnant pond is in the immediate vicinity, and none of the tenements have drains ; rubbish is thrown within a few yards of the dwellings, and there is no doubt but in damp foggy weather, and also during the heat of the summer, the exhalations arising from those heaps of filth must generate disease, and the obnoxious effluvia tends to spread contagion where it always exists. It appears that *most of the cottages alluded to were erected for election purposes, and have since been allowed to decay*; the roofs are repaired with turf dug in the neighbourhood, and the walls repaired with prepared clay without the addition of lime washing. Contagious disease has not been remarkable within the union in any other spot than the one alluded to."

Messrs. Smith and Moore, the medical officers of the Bishop Stortford union, in Hertfordshire, state * : —

* See Report on the Sanitary Condition of the Labouring Population.

"We have always found the smallest and most slightly built houses the seats of the lowest forms of disease; and, although during the last year no epidemic or infectious disease here prevailed, it is but just to state, that generally speaking *the cottages of labourers in this district are small, badly protected from both extremes of weather, badly drained, and low in the ground.*"

The Rev. Henry Worsley, late Michel Scholar of Queen's College, Oxford, and rector of Easton in Suffolk, writing of the *progressive deterioration* in the character of the peasants' cottages, says, "Another important consideration is, *the alteration for the worse in the dwelling houses of the poor.* A cottage erected in the last century will be generally found to be commodious and roomy; very different in the supply of comforts and and conveniences from the hovels, which are now ordinarily appropriated to the labouring class. At the present day, the narrowness of the poor man's cabin (the fact found to be almost universally true, that however numerous the inmates may be, *one small bedroow is deemed sufficient to accommodate all,*) implies so much domestic discomfort, that the natural impulse of the mind is to fly from misery at home to the village beer-shop. Besides this effect on the father, mother, or both, ruinous in itself to family peace, the congregating of so many into one sleeping apartment, *very frequently of two whole families or even more,* is destructive of all sense of modesty. The condition of the poor in regard to house accommodation, thus described, is well nigh general; it is common to the agricultural and manufacturing parts. During the present century we have been building dwellings for the poor, as if we were running up styes for pigs." *

Mr. Twisleton, late Poor Law Commissioner for Ireland, and a gentleman of very great experience in all social questions, and in everything relating to the social condition of the poorer classes, in his Report upon the sanitary condition of the labouring population of Norfolk and Suffolk, speaks thus of these cottages. He says, " Although they may be sufficiently commodious for a man and wife and very young children, they are manifestly uncomfortable, and the having only *one* bedroom is even indecent for a man and wife and large growing family ; *but I have seen many instances where a man and his wife and six children of different sexes have slept together in one room, on three and sometimes only two beds.* The annoyance of thus herding together must be almost insufferable, and several mothers of families among the labourers have spoken to me with great propriety and feeling against the practice, saying, ' that it is not respectable or decent, and that it is hardly bearable ;' ' that such a thing is not right for a Christian body in a Christian land ;' and they have used other expressions of a similar import. In order to diminish the evil, they have recourse to various expedients, such as putting curtains to the beds, or dividing the room into two parts, by pinning old counterpanes together, and sometimes by cutting up, and sewing together, old gowns, and stretching them across the room; all of which schemes are attended with the in-

* Essay on Juvenile Depravity, 36.

convenience, that in a crowded apartment, where pure
air is a scarce luxury, they have a tendency to check
still more its healthful circulation."

In describing the condition of the agricultural la-
bourers of Norfolk and Suffolk, the able author of the
Letters on Rural Districts, published in the " Morning
Chronicle," says : —

" The food of the labourer and his family is principally bread, potatoes, and frequently, in Norfolk, the
Norfolk dumpling, which consists simply of the dough
of which the bread is made, the difference between
bread and dumpling being merely, that the one is boiled,
while the other is baked. In the neighbourhood of
Fakenham I met with a family, whose food was chiefly
bread and turnips, and I was informed, that this was a
very general diet with the people about there. *In none
of the cottages, that I have visited in either of the three
counties, have I ever seen such a thing as a piece of fresh
butcher's meat. That it may be had occasionally, there
can be no doubt, but it is certainly at very rare and long
intervals.* When meat of any kind is purchased, it is
mostly bacon or salt pork, and the labourer invariably
finds it more economical to purchase that kind of food
than fresh meat, — the high price, which they have to
pay for any little piece, that they may want, being quite
sufficient to deter them from its purchase. While at
Bury, I was informed by a butcher, who carries on a
somewhat extensive business, that the ' shins ' and
' stickings ' of beef, which he was in the habit of selling
in the town for 1½d. per pound, he could sell on Saturday to the poor for 5d., ' bone and all,' when it was cut

up in pieces of about two or three pounds weight.
About Swaffham, Yarmouth, and Lowestoft, red her-
rings and salt fish will be found occasionally to enter
into the dietary table of the labourer.   In one cottage,
which I visited, I found the woman busily employed in
chopping up some pieces of fat pork, which she was
about to mix up with some cold potatoes and flour, for
dumplings, by way of ' a treat for the children, because
it was Mary's birth-day.'   The prices, which the poor
people have to pay for their grocery, such as tea, sugar,
and coffee, are enormous.   When in Norwich, I obtained
several samples of sugar at $3\frac{1}{2}d$. and $4d$., and $5d$. per lb.,
and compared them, in several places, which I visited,
with the sugar, for which the poor people had paid at the
rate of $5d$. and $6d$. per lb., and, according to the opinion
of the poor people themselves, my sample at $3\frac{1}{2}d$. was as
good as their fivepenny, and my fourpenny better than
their sixpenny, while my fivepenny was fit for the
squire.

"The cottage accommodation of the labourer is in
many parts of Norfolk lamentably deficient.   A few
praiseworthy efforts have been made on the part of some
of the landed proprietors to remedy the evil, but their
exertions have by no means kept pace with the wants of
the population.

.   .   .   .

" *Not only is there a great amount of unwillingness, on
the part of the proprietors generally, to build cottages for
the labourers, but in too many instances there is an evident
desire to destroy or pull down numbers of those that at
present exist.*   In the neighbourhood of Norwich, the

extent to which the destruction of cottage property has been carried on was, in the words of my informant, ' fearful and disgraceful.' In Drayton parish, fourteen cottages have been pulled down within the last few years, and none have been erected in their stead. In the Horsted Hundred, twenty-five of the cottages have been ordered to be destroyed. At Long Sutton, Pulham, Wackton, and various other parishes, the destruction has also been carried on to a great extent, though I was not able to learn the exact number, which had been destroyed. I was informed of the case of a large landed proprietor in the vicinity of Norwich, some of whose property being required by the railway company, *it was expressly stipulated in the sale, that no cottages whatsoever should be built upon any portion of the ground.* In point of fact, it is impossible to obtain a piece of ground, for building purposes, in any of the villages within eight or ten miles of Norwich. *Many of the estates have been entirely cleared of tenantry.* To such an extent has the system been carried on, that there are at present in Norwich not less than 500 agricultural labourers, who have to walk to their work distances varying from three to seven miles. Every expedient to prevent the labourer obtaining a settlement in the rural parishes is resorted to by the occupiers. In Wackton parish, one of the modes of removing the paupers was, to set a number of persons, principally weavers, who had some claim on the parish, and who, in all probability, had never had a spade in their hands before, to dig up a common in the middle of January, the snow at the time lying upon the ground several inches deep.

The poor wretches were told, that they must dig a certain portion of the common before they could obtain any relief.   The first thing, which they did, was to dig in the snow what they called ' the grave' of the magistrate, who had given the order.   So far as the experiment was concerned, it was perfectly successful; for after two or three days the greater portion of the persons left their employment, and contrived to settle themselves, by one means or other, in the city of Norwich, or in some of the surrounding open parishes.   The effect of this conduct, in addition to the injury inflicted upon the paupers, has been most materially to enhance the rates of the adjoining parishes.   In Long Sutton, for instance, a number of small cottages have been built; they are crowded by the evicted of the other parishes, and the rates are 6s. in the pound, while in the parish of St. Michael, which adjoins it, and where the cottages have been pulled down, the rates are only 2s. 6d. in the pound.   This system is not, however, confined to Norwich; for it has been carried on to a great extent in the neighbourhood of Castle Acre, which is an open parish, the consequence being, that whilst Castle Acre is overstocked with inhabitants, and the cottages there are densely crowded, there are not in the surrounding parishes anything like sufficient hands to cultivate the land.   It is owing to this excess of labourers in one district, and the great want of them in the neighbouring parishes, that the custom has sprung up within the last few years, of employing the people in what are termed ' gangs,'—a system which, there can be no doubt whatever, is attended with a considerable amount of evil to the persons employed."

Speaking of the state of the cottages in Essex, the same able writer says: —

" In the rural districts of Essex, many of the cottages are exceedingly bad; but in the northern and western part of the county this is peculiarly the case. Along the whole line of country from Castle Hedingham to Clavering, there is an almost continuous succession of bad cottages. Among the worst of these might be mentioned those in the neighbourhood of Sible Heding-ham, Weathersfield, Bardfield, Wicken, and Clavering. Great numbers of these cottages are situated in low and damp situations, and their heavy and grass-covered thatches appear, as if they had almost crushed the build-ings down into the earth. Little or no light can ever find its way into the wretched little windows, many of which are more than half stopped up with rags and pieces of paper. In point of fact, there are many of them which, but for the possession of a chimney, would be nothing superior to many of the most wretched cabins, which I have witnessed in Tipperary and many other parts of Ireland. At Manningtree, there are also a con-siderable number of wretched one-room cottages, and those which are larger are generally tenanted by as many families as there are rooms. In some cases, the number of families exceeds that of the rooms. It is customary in Manningtree to rate every one of the lodgers in such a house. In one case, of a house with three rooms, the persons living in the lower room, consisting of a husband and wife, and three grown-up children, were rated at

1*l.* 5*s.* The second compartment, occupied by a man and his wife, and one son, was rated at 1*l.* The occupiers of the third room, who consisted of a man and his wife, and five children, were rated at 15*s.*, the poor-rates being 6*s.* in the pound for the year. There are also some wretched holes situated upon Back-hill, where the amount of rates enforced averages about 3*d.* to each house."

The same gentleman describes the effects of the want of more and better cottages in the following manner : —

" One species of immorality, which is peculiarly prevalent in Norfolk and Suffolk, is that of bastardy. With the exception of Hereford and Cumberland, there are no counties, in which the per centage of bastardy is so high as it is in Norfolk — being there 53·1 per cent. above the average of England and Wales; in Suffolk it is 27 per cent. above, and in Essex 19·1 per cent. below the average. In the two first-named counties, and even in the latter one, though not to the same extent, *there appears to be a perfect want of decency among the people.* ' The immorality of the young women,' said the rector of one parish to me, ' is literally horrible, and I regret to say it is on the increase in a most extraordinary degree. When I first came to the town, the mother of a bastard child used to be ashamed to show herself. The case is now quite altered; no person seems to think anything at all of it. When I first came to the town, there was no such thing as a common prostitute in it; now there is an enormous number of them. When I am called upon to see a woman confined with an illegitimate child, I endeavour to impress upon her the enor-

mity of the offence; and there are no cases, in which I
receive more insult from those I visit, than from such
persons.   They generally say they'll get on as well,
after all that's said about it; and if they never do anything worse than that, they shall get to Heaven as well
as other people.'   Another clergyman stated to me, that
he never recollected an instance of his having married a woman, who was not either pregnant at the time
of her marriage, or had had one or more children before
her marriage.   Again, a third clergyman told me, that
he went to baptize the illegitimate child of one woman,
who was thirty-five years of age, and it was absolutely
impossible for him to convince her that what she had done
was wrong.   ' There appears,' said he, ' to be among
the lower orders a perfect deadness of all moral feeling
upon this subject.'   Many of the cases of this kind, which
have come under my knowledge, evince such horrible
depravity, that I dare not attempt to lay them before
the reader.   Speaking to the wife of a respectable
labourer on the subject, who had seven children, one of
whom was then confined with an illegitimate child, she
excused her daughter's conduct by saying, ' What was
the poor girl to do; the chaps say, that they won't
marry 'em first, and then the girls give way.   I did the
same myself with my husband.'   There was one case in
Cossey, in Norfolk, in which the woman told me, without a blush crimsoning her cheek, that her daughter and
self had each had a child by a sweep, who lodged with
them, and who promised to marry the daughter.   The
cottage in which these persons slept consisted of but one
room, and there were two other lodgers who occupied

beds in the same room; in one of which ' a young woman occasionally slept with the young man she was keeping company with.' The other lodger was an old woman of seventy-four years of age. To such an extent is prostitution carried on in Norwich, that out of the 656 licensed public-houses and beer-shops in the city, there are not less than 220, which are known to the police as common brothels. And although the authorities have the power of withholding the licences, nothing is done to put a stop to the frightful vice. ' At Bury,' said one of the guardians of the poor to me, ' there is, I believe, a larger amount of prostitution, in proportion to the size of the place, than is to be found in any town or city in England.' Harwich appears to be remarkably free from this vice. ' There are not,' I was informed by the police, ' more than six prostitutes in the town, and there is not a single brothel.'

Mr. Harding, medical officer of the Epping union in Essex, says*: —

" The state of some of the dwellings of the poor is most deplorable, as it regards their health, and also in a moral point of view. As it relates to the former, *many of their cottages are neither wind nor water-tight.*

It has often fallen to my lot to be called on to attend a labour, where the wet has been running down the walls, and where light was to be distinguished through the roof; and this in the winter season, with no fire-place in the room. As it relates to the latter, in my opinion, *a great want of accommodation for bed-rooms*

* See Report on the Sanitary Condition of the Labouring Population.

*often occurs, so that you may frequently find the father,
mother, and children all sleeping in the same apartment,
and in some instances children who have attained the
age of sixteen or seventeen years, and of both sexes; and
if a death occurs in the house, let the person die of a most
contagious disease, they must either sleep in the same
room, or take their repose in the room they live in,* which
most frequently is a stone or brick floor, which must be
detrimental to the health."

Mr. Chadwick says:—

" The reports from the great majority of the new
unions present evidence of the severe over-crowding of
the cottages of the rural districts and the tenements occupied by the working classes in the towns.

" The evidence received from every part of the
country, from rural districts as well as from towns,
attest, that the dwellings of large numbers of the labouring population are over-crowded, and that the *over-
crowding in many districts is increased.*"

Mr. T. P. J. Grantham, medical officer of the Slea-
ford union, in reference to the typhus fever in the family
of an agricultural labourer, gives the following instance
of the over-crowding, which is frequent in the rural
districts:—

" The domestic economy in this house was deplorable;
*eight persons slept in one small ill-ventilated apartment,
with scarcely any bed-clothing.* The smell arising from
the want of cleanliness, and the dirty clothes of the
children being allowed to accumulate, was most intolerable. Considering the situation of the house, its filthy
state, and the vitiated air which must have been re-

spired over and over again by eight individuals sleeping
in one confined apartment, it is not surprising that this
family should have been afflicted with fever, and that
of a malignant type.   The mother and one child fell
victims to it in a very short time."

The following extract from a communication from
the clerk to the Ampthill union, Bedfordshire, pour-
trays the effects of this over-crowding on the morals of
the population * : —

" *A large proportion of the cottages in the union are
very miserable places, small and inconvenient, in which it
is impossible to keep up even the common decencies of life.*
I will refer to one instance, with which I am well acquainted.   A man, his wife, and family, consisting in
all of eleven individuals, resided in a cottage containing
only two rooms.

" The man, his wife, and four, and sometimes five,
children, slept in one of the rooms and in one bed —
some at the foot, others at the top; one, a girl about
fourteen, another, a girl about twelve, the rest younger.
The other part of the family slept in one bed in the
keeping room, that is, the room in which their cooking,
washing, and eating were performed.   How could it be
otherwise with this family, than that they should be
sunk into a most deplorable state of degradation and
depravity?   This, it may be said, is an extreme case;
but there are many similar, and *a very great number
that make near approaches to it.*   To pursue a further
account of this family, the man is reported to be a good

* See Report on the Sanitary Condition of the Labouring Population.

labourer. The cottage he held was recently pulled down, and being unable to procure another, he was forced to come into the workhouse. After being in a short time, they left again, to try to get a house, but again they failed. The man then absconded, and the family returned to the workhouse. The eldest, a female, has had a bastard child; and another younger, also a female, but grown up, has recently been sentenced to transportation for stealing in a dwelling-house. The family, when they came in were observed to be of grossly filthy habits and of disgusting behaviour. I am glad to say, however, that their general conduct and appearance is very much improved since they have become inmates of the workhouse. I, without scruple, express my opinion that their degraded moral state *is mainly attributable to the wretched way, in which they have lived and herded together, as previously described.* I have been thus particular in my account of this family, *knowing it to be a type of many others.*"

The relieving officer of the Leighton Buzzard union states that in Leighton —

" There are a number of cottages without sleeping-rooms separate from the day-rooms, and frequently *three or four families are found occupying the same bed-room, and young men and women promiscuously sleeping in the same apartment.*"

Mr. Blick, the medical officer of the Bicester union, states that —

" The residences of the poor in that part of the district are most wretched, the majority *consisting of only one room below and one above, in which a family of eight* or ten (*upon an average I should say five*) *live and sleep.* In one of these rooms I have witnessed a father and mother, three grown up-sons, a daughter, and a child, lying at the same time with typhus fever. But few of the adjacent residents escaped the infection."

Mr. L. O. Fox, the medical officer of the Romsey, union, states *—

" There is not only a great want of cottages, but also of room, in those which now stand. In the parish of Mottisfont, *I have known fourteen individuals of one family sleeping together in a small room, the mother being in labour at the time, and in the adjoining room seven other people sleeping, making twenty-one persons, in a space which ought to have been occupied by six persons at most.* Here are the young woman and young man of eighteen or twenty years of age, lying alongside of the father and mother, and the latter actually in labour! It will be asked—What is the condition of the inmates? Just such as might be expected."

The next series of extracts show the condition of the houses of the peasants in the northern counties of England. The following extracts are only a repetition of the same sad description with respect to other parts of the northern counties.

Sir F. H. Doyle, speaking of the cottages of the peasantry of Northumberland, says:—

" The ordinary cottages *contain but one room*, perhaps 17 feet by 15 feet. In point of construction and ventilation there is nothing to be said for them; but as the

---

* Report on the Sanitary Condition of the Labouring Population.

Northumbrians are, *in spite of everything,* a healthy and vigorous race of men, such inconveniences do not amount to a crying evil; but when we find that a whole family, —father and mother, and children of both sexes and of all ages—live together, *and have to sleep together in one and the same room,* any degree of indelicacy and unchastity ceases to surprise, and the only wonder is, that the women should behave as well as they do."

Mr. W. Weatherill, clerk of the Gainsborough union, says:—

" The cottages contain occasionally one room only, generally two, though it not unfrequently occurs, that there is only one bed-room; where there are two, there are two lower rooms, and two bed-rooms. Their being crowded together at night, without any reference to sex, has unquestionably an influence in weakening, if not destroying, the modesty of the female sex."

Dr. Gilly, Canon of Durham, in an appeal on behalf of the border peasantry, describes their dwellings as built of rubble and unhewn stones, loosely cemented; and from age or from badness of the materials, the walls look as if they could scarcely hold together. " The chinks gape in so many places as to admit blasts of wind:—

" The chimneys have lost half their original height, and lean on the roof with fearful gravitation. The rafters are evidently rotten and displaced; and the thatch yawning to admit the wind and wet in some parts, and in all parts utterly unfit for its original purpose of giving protection from the weather, looks more like the top of a dunghill than of a cottage.

" Such is the interior; and when the hind comes to take possession, he finds it no better than a shed. The wet, if it happens to rain, is making a puddle in the earth floor. (This earth floor, by-the-bye, is one of the causes to which Erasmus ascribed the frequent recur-rence of epdiemic sickness among the cotters of England more then 300 years ago. It is not only cold and wet, but contains the aggregate filth of years from the time of first being used, the refuse and dropping of meals, decayed animal and vegetable matter of all kinds, which has been cast upon it from the mouth and stomach ; these are all mixed together, and exude from it.) Window-frame there is none. There is neither oven, nor copper, nor grate, nor shelf, nor fixture of any kind. All these things he has to bring with him, besides his ordinary articles of furniture. Imagine the trouble, the inconvenience, and the expense, which the poor fellow and his wife have to encounter, before they can put this shell of a hut into anything like a habitable form.

" This year I saw a family of eight, — husband, wife, two sons and four daughters,—who were in utter discomfort and in despair of putting themselves in a decent condition three or four weeks after they had come into one of these hovels.

" In vain did they try to stop up the crannies, and to fill up the holes in the floor, and to arrange their furniture in tolerably decent order, and to keep out the weather. Alas ! what will they not suffer in the winter.

" There will be no fireside enjoyment for them. They may huddle together for warmth, and heap coals on the fire; but they will have chilly beds and a damp hearth stone; and the cold wind will sweep through the roof and window, and the crazy door-place, in spite of all their endeavours to exclude it.

" The general character of the best of the old-fashioned hinds' cottages is bad at the best. They have to bring everything with them, partitions, window-frames, fixtures of all kinds, grates, and a substitute for ceiling; for they are, as I have already called them, mere sheds. They have no byre for their cows, nor styes for their pigs, nor pumps, nor wells, — nothing to promote cleanliness or comfort.

" The average size of these sheds is about 24 feet by 16 feet; they are dark and unwholesome. Their windows do not open, and many of them are not larger than 20 inches by 16, and into this place are crowded eight, ten, or twelve persons.

" How they lie down to rest, how they sleep, how they can preserve common decency, how unutterable horrors are avoided, is beyond all conception. The case is aggravated, when there is a young woman to be lodged in this confined space, who is not a member of the family, but is hired to do the field-work, for which every hind is bound to provide a female. It shocks every feeling of propriety to think, that in one room, and within such a space as I have been describing, civilised beings should be herded together without the decent separation of age and sex. So long as the agricultural system in this district requires the hind to find room for a fellow-servant of the other sex in his cabin, the least that morality and decency can demand is, that he should have a second apartment, where the unmarried female, and those of a tender age, should sleep apart from him and his wife. Last Whitsuntide, when the annual lettings were taking place, a hind, who had lived one year in the hovel he was about to quit, called to say — farewell, and to thank me for some trifling kindness I had been able to show him. He was a fine, tall man, of about forty-five, a fair specimen of the frank, sensible, well-spoken, well-informed Northumbrian peasantry ; of that peasantry, of which a militia regiment was composed, which so amazed the Londoners (when it was garrisoned in the capital many years ago) by the size, the noble deportment, the soldier-like bearing, and the good conduct of the men.

" I thought this a good opportunity of asking some questions. Where was he going, and how would he dispose of his large family (eleven in number)? He told me, that they were to inhabit one of these hind's cottages, whose narrow dimensions were less than 24 feet by 15, and that the eleven would only have three beds to sleep on ; that he himself, his wife, a daughter of 6, and a boy of 4 years old, would sleep in one bed; *that a daughter 18, a son of 12, a son of 10, and a daughter of 8 have a second bed,* and a third would receive his three sons of the age of 20, 16, and 14. Pray, said I, do you not think that this is a very improper way of disposing of your family? Yes, certainly, was the answer ; it is very improper in a christian point of view ; but what can we do until they build us better houses ?"

The next series of extracts are taken from the reports

of Mr. Lingen, the Commissioner who was sent by
Government, in 1848, to examine the state of educa-
tion in the counties of Carmarthen, Glamorgan, and
Pembroke.

Mr. Lingen is a Fellow of Balliol College, Oxford,
and assistant secretary of the Privy Council on Education; he is a very able and highly accomplished man,
and his report is a very remarkable one in every respect,
and is well worthy of study.

He describes the social state, habits, and houses of
the peasants of the above-mentioned counties as follows:—

" I am about to enter on one of the most painful
subjects of my inquiry.   It is a disgusting fact, that
out of 692 schools I found 364, or 52·6 per cent. utterly
unprovided with privies.   But it is not schools that
stand alone in this respect; they are but instances of the
general neglect."

Here are facts.

(See Report, p. 233.)

" The whole row of houses (part of the main street)
in which this school is held, varying in rent from 10l.
to 15l. a year, had not a single, not even a common
privy.   The inhabitants resorted to a hedge-side in a
field adjoining at the back, wholly unsheltered from
sight."

(See Report, p. 304.)

" The vast majority of houses have no privies.   Where
there is such a thing, it is a mere hole in the ground,
with no drainage.   This is the case nearly all over
Wales; but in a dense population the consequences of

such neglect are more loathsomely and degradingly apparent. . . . . I was assured by people, whose houses look into fields or open spaces at the back of rows and streets, that persons of every age and sex are constantly to be seen exposed in them.

" And here is an expedient to supply the deficiency." (See Report, 241.)

" The school, as usual, possessed no privy, and the master informed me, that the churchyard is generally used by the poor of the town as a privy ; few of them possessing at home any convenience of that nature.

" The peasant girls proceed from homes and domestic habits like the following to service in a farm-house."

(See Report, p. 243, 4.)

" The floor was of mud ; on the right hand of the door, on entering, ran a partition of wattles so far towards the opposite wall, as just to leave room to turn round it into the other division. At the end of the passage thus formed, was an old chest, and on turning round the end of the partition a cupboard bed occupied one whole side of the inner room. Close to it was the hearth. The remaining furniture consisted of two shapeless stools, a few inches high, another of the same sort a little higher, and an old dresser, or something like one. The chimney, which descended from the roof over the hearth like a bonnet or umbrella, was made of plastered wattles. A heavy shower must have put the fire out and deluged the hut, the orifice of the chimney was so large. The floor was perfectly hard and dry, though very uneven. The cottage was smoke-dried into a feeling of comfortable warmth. The ceiling, or what came between one's head and the thatch, was some poles laid from wall to wall, and on these poles was strewed a little loose brushwood."

Appendix, p. 229. (Evidence of Rev. J. Pugh):—

" In their habits, the labouring classes are particularly dirty. This arises, in great measure, no doubt, from their poverty and the low rate of wages which, until lately, they have been in the habit of receiving, so that it was quite impossible for them to have decent clothes or convenient houses. Pigs and poultry are frequently allowed to come inside. The flooring is generally bare earth, not even prepared with lime. There are rarely any privies. Neither light nor ventilation is well provided for. There are not usually more than two rooms. Cupboard beds are those most commonly used, which are shut up as soon as the occupant quits them, and never opened again until night. The use of linen, until lately, either by day or night, was almost unknown; it is now, however, coming more into fashion among the young people.

" I also heard, from the master of the union workhouse at Haverfordwest, that the paupers were excessively filthy in their habits.

" In the farm-houses, separation and decency are not better attended to than must have been the case in such homes, *and the natural bar which consanguinity opposes to vice is removed.*"

Ibid, p. 217. — (Evidence of John Johnes, Esq.): —

" Immorality exists between the sexes to a considerable extent, chiefly among farm-servants. The main cause is, perhaps, the imperfect arrangements in the

older farm-houses, which leave the sexes too much together, and this even at night.

" Captain Napier, the superintendant of police in
Glamorganshire, to whom, by the kindness of the Marquis of Bute, I was introduced, strongly confirmed this
statement in a conversation which I had with him,
saying that he had known servants of different sexes
put to sleep in the same room.

" But it is not merely among inmates of the same
farm-houses that evil arises ; there are several other
causes producing similar effects."

Ibid, p. 394. : —

" The system of bundling, or, at any rate, something
analogous to it, prevails extensively. The unmarried
men servants in the farms range the country at night ;
and it is a known and tolerated practice, that they are
admitted by the women servants at the houses to which
they come. I heard the most revolting anecdotes of the
gross and almost bestial indelicacy, with which sexual
intercourse takes place on these occasions."

Ibid, p. 234. (Evidence of Mr. W. Rees) : —

" The farmers connive at young people meeting in
their houses after the family has retired to rest."

Appendix, p. 282. (Evidence of Messrs. Roberts,
Glantowi) : —

" The male farm-servants sleep in the out-buildings,
and keep what hours they please ; the women ask
leave to go out in the evening, and then the men meet
them at the public-houses, of which there are fourteen
in the town here (among a population of 736), and eight

between here and Llandilo, a distance of $6\frac{1}{2}$ miles.   In this way much immorality takes place."

Ibid, p. 254. (note of a conversation): —

" Such are some of the circumstances under which the early life of a Welsh peasant girl is passed.   So far from wondering at what is said of them, viz., that they are almost universally unchaste, the wonder would be if they were otherwise.   Their offences, however, arise rather from the absence of all checks, than from the deliberate infringement of them, and betoken, there-fore, much less depravity than the same conduct in per-sons more favourably situated."

Ibid, p. 217. (Evidence of John Johnes, Esq.): —

" In cases where marriage would be out of the question, from the superior rank of the man, the women would not generally listen to proposals of an immoral kind.

" The first breach of chastity with a woman in the lower class is almost always under a promise of marriage."

Ibid, p. 237. (Mr. David Owen): —

" The peasantry are generally very poor, and possess few comforts ; but they are economical, and more cleanly than a stranger would think.   The women have the entire management of the house, and this she generally does well.   She can generally sew and knit, and is very industrious.

" But families like these are ill prepared for the change of life to which the mining districts expose them on their immigration.

" At the top of a valley forming a *cul-de-sac*, suppose

some 5000 or 6000 people collected and nearly cut off
from the rest of the world. This is their domestic
economy."

Appendix, pp. 304. and 351. : —

" The works have increased faster than adequate accommodation for those employed in them could be provided. The houses are all over-crowded. They are
commonly of two stories, and comprise four or five
rooms; the fifth, however (where there is one), is seldom
more than a pantry. *The average number of the inhabitants is said to be nearly twelve to each house* I
entered upwards of a dozen at random, and found the
average to be quite as great as this. The houses are
often in the hands of middlemen: in such cases the
rents are usually higher than when they belong to the
company. Rent ranges from 8*l.* to 10*l.* per annum.

" The tenant makes it up by the payments of his
lodgers. The cottages are expensively furnished."

Evidence respecting the mining and manufacturing
populations (Rev. John Griffith, vicar of Aberdare),
p. 489. : —

" Nothing can be lower, I would say more degrading,
than the character in which the women stand relative to
the men. The men and the women, married as well as
single, live in the same house, *and sleep in the same room.*
The men do not hesitate to wash themselves naked
before the women; on the other hand, the women do
not hesitate to change their under garments before the
men. Promiscuous intercourse is most common, is
thought of as nothing, and the women do not lose caste
by it."

Mr. Symonds, another of the commissioners, says of the peasantry of Brecknockshire, Cardiganshire, and Radnorshire : —

" The people of my district are almost universally poor. In some parts of it wages are probably lower than in any part of Great Britain. The evidence of the witnesses, numbered 22, 23, 1, 47, and 48, fully confirmed by other statements, exhibits much poverty, but little amended in other parts of the counties on which I report. *The farmers themselves are very much impoverished, and live no better than English cottagers in prosperous agricultural counties.*

" The cottages in which the people dwell are miserable in the extreme in nearly every part of the country in Cardiganshire, and every part of Brecknockshire and Radnorshire, except the east. I have myself visited many of the dwellings of the poor, and my assistants have done so likewise, and the results of some of these observations is stated in the notes in the Appendix on Tregaron, Llanfihangel, Rhidithon, Bequildy, &c. *I believe the Welsh cottages to be very little, if at all, superior to the Irish huts in the country districts.*

" Brick chimneys are very unusual in these cottages ; those which exist are usually in the shape of large cones, the top being of basket-work. *In very few cottages is there more than one room*, which serves the purposes of living and sleeping. A large dresser and shelves usually form the partition between the two, and where there are separate beds for the family a curtain or low board is (if it exists) the only division with no regular partition. And this state of things very generally prevails, even where there is some little attention paid to cleanliness; but the cottages and bed are frequently filthy. The people are always very dirty. In all the counties the cottages are generally destitute of necessary outbuildings, including even those belonging to the farmers; and both in Cardiganshire and Radnorshire, except near the border of England, the pigs and poultry have free run of the joint dwelling and sleeping rooms.

" As an exemplification of this I may perhaps venture to cite a note I took of the small town of Tregaron in Cardiganshire.

" The extreme filthiness of the habits of the poor, though observable every where, is as striking in this place, if not more so, than elsewhere ; inasmuch as in a town it might be expected that a little more of the outward observances of cleanliness and decency would be met with.

" Dung heaps abound in the lanes and streets. There seemed seldom to be more than one room for living and sleeping in ; generally in a state of indescribable disorder, and dirty to an excess. The pigs and poultry form a usual part of the family. In walking down a lane, which forms one of the principal entrances to the town, I saw a huge sow go up to a door (the lower half of which was shut) and put her fore paws on the top of it, and begin shaking it. A woman with a child in her arms rushed across the road from the other side of the way, and immediately opened the door, and the animal walked into the house, grunting as if she was offended at the delay, the woman following and closing the door behind her. Even the churchyard gives evidence of the absence of necessary outbuildings in the town, and several were covered with half-washed linen hanging to dry. This church and churchyard stand on a rocky eminence in the centre of the town, forming, therefore, a very conspicuous object in the place."

" The evidence numbered 1. 22. 47, and 48, will further develop the prevalent disregard of cleanliness and domestic comfort.

" The mining population exists exclusively in the extreme south and south-east border of Brecknockshire. It is congregated chiefly at Brynmaur in the parish of Llanelly and at Beaufort in Llangattock, Llangymder, at Vainor, and at Ystrad Cynlais. The characteristics, so well known and often desribed of mining districts, prevail in the former of these places, if possible with still less than the usual attention to cleanliness and comfort.

" The evidence given me of the immoral character of the people, with a few exceptions, tells us the same tale. The Welsh are peculiarly exempt from the guilt of great crimes. There are few districts in Europe where murders, burglaries, personal violence, rapes, forgeries, or any felonies on a *large scale*, are so rare. On the other hand, there are perhaps few countries, *where the standard of minor morals is lower*. Petty thefts, lying, cozening, every species of chicanery, drunkenness (where the means exist), and idleness prevail to a great extent among the least educated part of the community, who scarcely regard them in the light of sins. There is another very painful feature in the laxity of morals, voluntarily attested by some of those who have given evidence. I refer to the alleged want of chastity in the women. If this be so, it is sufficient to account for all other immoralities; for each generation will derive its moral tone, in a great degree, from the influences imparted by the mothers who reared them. Where these influences are corrupted at their very source, it is in vain to expect virtue in the offspring. The want of chastity results frequently from the practice of bundling, or courtship on beds, during the night, — a practice still widely prevailing.

"*It results also from the revolting habit of herding married and unmarried people of both sexes, often unconnected by relationship, in the same sleeping rooms, and often in adjoining beds without partition or curtain.* Natural modesty is utterly suppressed by this vile practice, and delicacy alike in men and women is destroyed in its very germ. These practices obtain in the classes immediately above as well as among the labouring people.

" The several features in the moral condition of the people will derive illustration from the following evidence : —

" In Brecknockshire the Reverend Edward Williams, Independent minister at Builth, says, —

" ' The house accommodation is not good in the country. They often have only two rooms, one for the kitchen and one for sleeping. *The whole family sleep in one room, without any division of sexes in most cases.* I have known cases in farm-houses where the same system existed as to farm servants, but not in the better classes of farmhouses.'

" As regards morality in that district, Mr. Williams speaks more favourably than most persons; he says, —

" ' The general character of the villagers is pretty fair as to honesty and also as to chastity. Cases of bastardy are not uncommon, but promiscuous intercourse does not usually occur. These cases are chiefly among farm servants.

" ' They are tolerably fair as to truth, and they are generally industrious.

" ' This town (Builth) is very bad as to drunkenness. In the country they are pretty fair as to that.

" ' The observance of the Sabbath is better in Breconshire than in Radnorshire, and good in the former. Radnorshire is very much neglected, and attendance at places of worship not good. The clergy generally reside at their livings just in this neigbourhood.

" ' The country people are generally peaceably disposed, they are free from gambling, but they are not very cleanly in their habits.'

" The Reverend David Charles, the principal of the College at Treveca, says, —

" ' The morals of this part of the country are certainly very defective, owing to the system of drinking cyder, &c. so prevalent here. Drunkenness is the common sin of both farmers and their servants. Seldom do we meet farm servants returning from any considerable distance with their master's waggon or cart, but that we find them intoxicated, while it is quite lamentable to witness the number of drunken farmers returning from market on Saturdays. In harvest-time this practice is still more prevalent. There is also, among the class mentioned, very little attention paid to the observance of the Sabbath.'

" The Reverend R. Harrison, the incumbent of Builth, says : —

" ' The Welsh are very dirty. I found a house in Builth, where, in the bed-room down stairs, I found two pigs in one corner, and two children ill with the scarlet fever in the other. The dung-hills are placed in the front of the houses in some parts of the town.'

" The Reverend Richard Lumley, Calvinistic Methodist minister at Builth, says : —

" ' The country-people are anything but cleanly in their habits. It is not uncommon for the *whole family among labourers to sleep in the same room, without any distinction of sexes ;* and *I have lately witnessed instances of the same habit among the classes immediately above them.'*

" The Reverend James Morgan, vicar of Talgarth, says : —

" The standard of morality is certainly low. Illegitimate children are by no means rare, and pregnancy before marriage is of common occurrence. It scarcely seems to be considered a sin, or even a disgrace, for a woman to be in the family-way by the man, to whom she is engaged to be married.

" ' Drunkenness is but too prevalent, particularly on fair-days and other similar occasions.'

" Edward W. Seymour, Esq., a magistrate of Crickhowel, speaking of the mining district, says : —

" ' The vices of lying, thieving, swearing, and drunkenness, and *the vastly increasing crime of illicit inter-*

course between the sexes, prevail to a great extent, and
these are by no means confined to the uneducated. Of
their disregard of common decency, I have an instance,
among many, which have come to my knowledge, in a
case, which was brought before me only the other day,
wherein it appeared, that a young girl of sixteen, going
on a visit to her sister (a married woman), was actually
placed by her for many nights together in the same bed-
room (without even a curtain between them), in which
lay a young labouring man (a lodger and a stranger),
which man was brought before me on a charge of stealing;
the parties, with the exception of the lodger, being to all
appearances respectable, intelligent, and above the common order among the lower classes. Upon my expos-
tulating with them on the impropriety of their subjecting
a female under their protection to such indecency, the
parties seemed rather astonished at the remark than
sensible of their error.'

" The Reverend J. Hughes, curate of Llanelly, a
mining parish, says : —

" ' . . . . Their dwellings are almost universally
destitute of those conveniences, which are necessary to
the health and comfort of mankind, and from the practice of the males stripping to wash themselves in the
presence of the females, the usual barriers between the
sexes are done away with, and the result is shown in the
frequency of illicit intercourse.

" ' Drunkenness is also prevalent, although not to so
great an extent as formerly.'

" The Reverend W. L. Bevan, vicar of Hay, says:—
" ' Drunkenness and illegitimacy are the prevailing

vices of the neighbourhood. Very many of the poorer classes are ruined by indulgence in the first, while the second is considered a very venial offence. A promise of marriage on the part of a man seems to legitimatise the whole affair in the eyes of the parties themselves, as well as in the estimation of their friends.'

" The Reverend James Denning, curate of St. Mary's, Brecknock, says : —

" ' The poor seem ignorant on most subjects, except how to cheat and speak evil of each other. They appear not to have an idea what the comforts of life are. There are at least 2000 persons living in this town in a state of the greatest filth, and to all appearance they enjoy their filth and idleness, for they make no effort to get rid of it. From my experience of Ireland, I think there is a great similarity between the lower orders of Welsh and Irish, — both are dirty, indolent, bigoted, and contented.'

" ' The Reverend Mr. Griffiths, the principal of the college, says : —

" ' Generally speaking, our calendars are not remarkable for their number of gross crimes ; in fact, I believe quite the reverse. I am afraid, however, that social and domestic moralities are very low among us.

" ' The number of illegitimate children, when compared with England, is astounding.'

" The Reverend D. Parry, of Llywell, thinks that—

" ' The morals of a great number are defective in respect of chastity, truth-telling, and veneration for God's sacred name. In proof of which, suffice it to allude to the number of illegitimate children in the country, — to the little reliance that can be placed on what is often said or spoken, provided the individual have some bias or interest in the matter, — and to the frequent abuse of God's holy name in the common intercourse and transactions of life. These are facts well known to all observant minds, and loudly calling for some means of reformation.'

" In Cardiganshire, the morals and habits of the people are not much better.

" The Very Reverend the Dean of St. David's says of many of the young persons in Sunday schools, that they are —

" ' Not only grossly ignorant on every other subject, but also grossly immoral. Many of these girls have bastard children, but this generally exists without promiscuous intercourse. Drunkenness is very general, especially at the fairs. I think there cannot be a doubt that education, accompanied by religious instruction, would materially improve this state of things; and I think people would go to good schools if they existed.'

" Thomas Williams, Esq., clerk to the magistrates at Lampeter, and superintendent of the Independent Sunday school, says : —

" ' I do not think the moral state of the people low ; but for want of education, they practise a great deal of low cunning. Generally speaking, they are honest. Bastardy cases are, however, very common. The women used to be ashamed of being in the family-way, but are not now. The promiscuous intercourse is carried on to a very great degree.'

VOL. I.

" The Reverend L. H. Davies, of Troedey Raur, says : —

" ' They (the young people) often meet at evening schools in private houses, and this tends to immoralities between the young persons of both sexes, who frequently spend the night afterwards in the hay-lofts together. So prevalent is want of chastity among the females, that although I promised to return the marriage fee to all couples, whose first child should be born after nine months from the marriage, only one in six years entitled themselves to claim it. Most of them were in the family-way. It is said to be a customary matter for them to have intercourse together, on condition that they should marry if the woman becomes pregnant; but the marriage by no means always takes place. Morals are generally at a low ebb, but want of chastity is the giant sin of Wales. I believe that the best remedy for the want of morals and of education, is that of the establishment of good schools, such as I have described.'

" Richard Williams, Esq., M. D. and coroner, says : —

" ' The youth of both sexes are very unchaste, and do not consider promiscuous intercourse any disgrace, which is chiefly owing to the want of proper education; to the ancient practice of bundling or courting in bed, still prevalent; TO THE CONSTRUCTION OF THEIR DWELLINGS; and to the bad example of their parents.

" ' The morals of the poor are generally indifferent. They are not disposed to commit atrocious crimes, but are addicted to petty thefts and prevarication. In justice

I should say, that many strangers have informed me the lower classes of Wales are far superior to those of the same class in other parts of the kingdom.'

" W. O. Brigstocke, Esq., magistrate of Blaenpant, says : —

" ' Morals generally very bad, intercourse between the sexes previous to marriage being very general. Misconduct after marriage is of rare occurrence. Drunkenness is a very common vice, especially on market or fair days.'

" In Radnorshire, the morals of the people are of a very low standard.

" The Archdeacon Venables, chairman of quarter sessions, says : —

" ' Their morals are at a very low ebb. An acknowledged thief is almost as well thought of, and as much employed, as better characters, by the lower orders.'

" The Reverend W. D. West, curate of Presteigne, says :—

" ' There is a great laxity in the prevalent notions on the subject of sexual intercourse.' And he cites an instance which will be found in his evidence. He adds —

" ' Sexual lusts and drunkenness (which last I omitted above) being the popular vices, education, not mere instruction, might counteract them by creating other tastes.'

" Sir William Cockburn, Bart., of New Radnor, a magistrate, says :—

" ' In one crime, of bastardy, I fear that the people of

this country are pre-eminent. As magistrates and individuals we have done our best to discourage this vice, but the remedy is yet to be found.'

" The Reverend R. Lister Venables, vicar of Clyro, and a magistrate, says:—

" ' Crimes of violence are almost unknown, such as Lurglary, forcible robbery, or the use of the knife. Common assaults are frequent, usually arising from drunken quarrels. Petty thefts are not particularly numerous. Poultry stealing and sheep stealing prevail to a considerable extent. There is no rural police, and the parish constables are for the most part utterly useless, except for serving summonses, &c. Sheep and poultry stealers therefore very frequently escape with impunity.

" ' Drunkenness prevails to a lamentable extent, not so much among the lower class, who are restrained by their poverty, as among those who are in better circumstances. Every market or fair day affords too much proof of this assertion. Unchastity in the woman is, I am sorry to say, a great stain upon our people. The number of bastard children is very great, as is shown by the application of young women for admission into the workhouse to be confined, and by the application to magistrates in petty sessions for orders of affiliation. In hearing these cases, it is impossible not to remark how unconscious of shame both the young woman and her parents often appear to be. In the majority of cases where an order of affiliation is sought, marriage was promised, or the expectation of it held out. The cases are usually cases of bonâ fide seduction. Those who enter the workhouse to be confined are generally girls of known bad character. I believe that in the rural districts few professed prostitutes would be found.'

"The Rev. John Price, rector of Bledfa, and a magistrate, says:—

"Drunkenness is rare in this neighbourhood, and the poorer classes are really honest, quiet, and industrious; the prevailing vice of the country is a disregard for chastity, a breach of which is considered neither a sin nor a crime. Apparently there is no disgrace attached to it; the women who have had two or three illegitimate children are as frequently selected by the young men for their wives as those of virtuous conduct. But after marriage the women are generally well conducted.

"'Probably the chief causes of this disregard to modesty and chastity *may be referred, first, to the want of room in small farm-houses and cottages. Grown-up sons and daughters, and men and female servants, commonly sleep in the same room.* Secondly, to the bad habit of holding meetings at dissenting chapels and farm-houses after night, where the youth of both sexes attend from a distance for the purpose of walking home together. As a magistrate, I can safely report that, in the investigation of numerous cases of bastardy, I have found most of them to be referred to the opportunities of meeting above mentioned.'

"Francis Phillips, Esq., of Abbey-cum-hir, Radnorshire, says:—

"'Crime of a serious character is not of frequent occurrence; but bastardy, which is scarcely considered a crime or disgrace, is very prevalent with young women. Those who afterwards marry generally become industrious and domestic, but they have little idea of cleanliness and comfort. The very high price of coal leads to pilfering of wood, &c.'

" Such appear to be the prevailing vices throughout my district, with the exception of the town of Breck-nock, and the hill district in the hundred of Crickhowel, where the mining district commences, and of which I shall presently have occasion to speak.

" In Brecknock and Builth a graver character of vice prevails than in the country.

" Mr. Thomas Davies, of Llangattock, for many years the agent of the Duke of Beaufort, says :—

" I fear in too many instances they have not much idea of the obligation of an oath when examined as witnesses. Such I know was the opinion of the late Mr. Baron Gurney, which he attributed to the want of religious education. The morals of the people are of a very low standard. In fact, immorality prevails rather from the want of a sense of moral obligation than from a forgetfulness or violation of recognised duties. I am confident that, as regards mendacity, there is frequently no real consciousness that it is sinful, so habitual is dis-regard for truth whenever interest prompts falsehood.

" ' The whole people are kept back by their immo-ralities and low tone of principle. A Bristol merchant, who endeavours to deal with the Welsh to some extent in a line of business, which throws him into communica-tion with many of the country people, told me that his efforts to continue a commerce with them, which would be mutually profitable, were they even commonly trust-

worthy, are wholly frustrated by their inveterate faith-
lessness to their bargains, the moment they see the possibility of gaining a penny by breaking them. The
astute ingenuity exercised in obtaining a minute advantage, or excusing themselves from an error, and escaping the effects of it, is remarkably great. Their want of
morality is, *however, entirely owing to their total want of
mental cultivation, and the very great deficiency of all
means of moral training.* They are not taught better,
and have at present little means of improvement.'

" The morals of the population congregated at and
near Byrnmaur and Beaufort are deplorably low.
Drunkenness, blasphemy, indecency, sexual vices, and
lawlessnes widely prevail there. This district was one of
the chief sources of Chartism. One of the main bodies
of the mob who marched upon Newport congregated at,
and issued from thence : they took the chapels by storm,
and forced many reluctant men to join them. Byrnmaur contains 5000 people, nearly all of whom are of
the lowest class, and with the exception of one or two
shopkeepers exclusively so. Nearly every family in it
is in the employment of Mr. Baily, the iron master,
whose works are at Nant-y-glo, in the adjoining parish,
in Monmouthshire.

" The town reeks with dirt; there are no lamps or
effective drainage; and although so many years have
elapsed since the Chartist outbreak, not the slightest
step has been taken to improve the mental or moral
condition of the violent and vicious community. Neither
church nor school have been established by those, who
employ the people or own the land; and the only step

that has been taken for their benefit is that of establishing within a week or two of this time a police station. It is exclusively owing to the Dissenters that instruction of any kind is given to the place. By their unaided efforts, an inferior school and six chapels have been built, and imperfect as their means of ameliorating the morals of the people are, their efforts have not been unattended with benefit. There is a visible improvement in the conduct of the people, according to the statement of Mr. Kershaw (No. 6.), but it is still lamentably bad, and their neglected state cannot be deemed otherwise than perilous to the tranquillity of the neighbourhood. I ought to state that the people of this place are not wholly Welsh.

' A large portion of them are strangers, and not unfrequently outcasts from distant places, in England, Ireland, and Scotland.

" I felt it my duty to take especial means of verifying the statements, which poured in upon me, with respect to this dangerous and degraded population ; and in addition to the evidence already cited of Mr. Seymour (an active magistrate of this district), I beg to present to your lordships the following evidence from the Reverend Richard Davies, of Courty Gollen, a beneficed clergyman and magistrate of the highest respectability, who, in answer to my request that he would as a magistrate of the district state facts, which would illustrate the condition of Byrnmaur, favoured me with the following evidence respecting it : —

" ' It has long been a matter of deep regret and sorrow to those who are responsible for the peace,

good conduct, and well-being of society, to witness
the degraded and corrupt state of what is generally
termed the hilly district, more especially the locality
designated as Byrnmaur. It has been the painful
duty of the furnisher of this information, to bring
the sad and lamentable state of this district more immediately before the view of the magistracy of the
county. It afforded a frightful picture of the consequences, that a want of education necessarily entails,
and the fearful result of masses being brought together,
without an adequate provision made for leading their
minds to higher and better things, to subject them to
the guidance of religious tuition, and thus pave the way
for their becoming loyal subjects, peaceable citizens, a
contented, well disposed, and orderly community. The
elements necessary to produce this wished for result
are not in Byrnmaur. Let us refer to statistical details as our guide and index. There are 5000 inhabitants in Byrnmaur, and fifty new houses are added at a
moderate computation yearly.

" ' There are already nineteen licensed public-
houses and thirty-eight beer houses. No church or
chapel of the established religion nearer than two miles.
Six meeting houses, of comparatively small dimensions,
with some schools attached to them, but far from affording an antidote to the great amount of evil, that a vast
increasing population, without responsible guides and
pastors, must inevitably give rise to. One half of the
criminal cases, that are entered upon the pages of our
petty sessions record, come from and may be traced to
the densely populated Byrnmaur. The scenes that the

magistrates are compelled to witness, and which I can
personally vouch for, baffle all description and outrage
every feeling of propriety.   Oaths and profane language
are apparently familiar to persons of all ages; even children lisp out the foul expressions they hear, and seem
perfectly accustomed to every epithet that the most evil
mind could suggest.'"

Speaking of the mining population of Monmouthshire, Mr. Symons says : —

" Evil in every shape is rampant in this district;
demoralisation is everywhere dominant, and all good
influences are comparatively powerless.   They drink to
the most brutal excess, especially on occasions, which I
will endeavour presently to describe, which are designed
for the purpose.   They have little regard to modesty
or the truth ; and even the young children in the streets,
who can scarcely articulate, give utterance to impreca-
tions.   The bodies and habits of the people are almost
as dirty, as the towns and houses of the swarthy region,
in which they swarm.   The whole district, with the
exception of Newport, teems with crime, and all the
slatternly accompaniments of animal power and moral
disorder, with scarcely a ray of mental or spiritual intelligence.   The people are savage in their manner, and
mimic the repulsive rudeness of those in authority over
them.   The whole district and population partake of
the iron character of its produce ; every thing centres in
and ministers to the idolatry of profit; physical strength
is the object of esteem, and gain their chief god.   There
are, of course, even in this black domain, some individual exceptions, but the general picture can only be

drawn with truth in the colours I am constrained to use.

"Even the physical condition of the people seems almost as if contrived, for the double purpose of their degradation and the employers' profit. Some of the works are surrounded by houses built by the companies, without the slightest attention to comfort, health, or decency, or any other consideration, than that of realising the largest amount of rent from the smallest amount of outlay. I went into several of this class of houses in the north part of my district, and examined them from top to bottom. *Men, women, and children, of all sexes and ages, are stowed away in the bed-rooms without any curtains or partitions, it being no uncommon thing for nine or ten people, not belonging to the same family, to sleep together in this manner in one room.* In one instance, I found three men sleeping in a sort of a dungeon, which was about 9 feet by 6 in dimensions, without any light or air except through a hole in the wall not a foot square, which opened into another room occupied by some women. The houses are many of them so constructed, that each story is let off to different tenants. The necessary out-buildings in most cases do not exist at all. An immense rent, in comparison to the accommodation, is paid to the company or master for these miserable places. Heaps of rubbish lie about in the streets, although coal is close at hand. Tram-roads intersect and run along the streets of these places, which contain about 30,000 inhabitants. Nevertheless, these places are little worse than others, and in some respects superior to Byrnmaur, which I described in my last report. In many cases, the iron companies have merely a lease of the estate, and have no other interest, than that of making the most they can out of it. In some places I heard of beds being so scarce, that they were perpetually occupied, one gang or set of men turning in as the others turned out; they work every eight hours consecutively, and the beds have never time to cool. I need hardly say that fever ensued, and the practice was then forbidden by the employers."

I select the next series of extracts from the Report of Mr. Johnson, a barrister, who was sent by Government into *North Wales*, in 1847, to examine the state of the schools there. He gives a lamentable description of the social condition of the people of that part of our island.

I visited and inspected a great part of North Wales and the Isle of Anglesey myself, in the summer of 1849. Nothing can be more miserable and disgraceful, than the condition of the greater part of the cottages in those parts. They are low hovels of one story in height, divided into one or at most two rooms. These have generally only two windows, often only little apertures in the walls, filled up with glass. The roofs are so low, that I was not able to stand upright in them, if I kept my hat upon my head. Many of them have no grate or fire-place, but only a hearth with an open chimney above it. They are generally miserably built, the lumps of stone of which the walls are formed being often merely piled one upon another, the interstices being filled up with mortar. Many of the cottages have only one little window, measuring about eight inches square.

I have seen quantities of such hovels within a few yards of the park gates of great landowners in that country; and, as a general rule, I should say, that the larger the estate in North Wales or the island of Anglesey, the worse invariably is the condition of the peasantry. I do not wish to draw attention to individuals, nor to appear to be personal in my remarks, or I could specify particular parts of the country, where any one might obtain as much evidence of the truth of this statement as he could desire. The contrast between the condition of the Welsh and Swiss or Saxon peasantry is very remarkable.

Mr. Johnson says : —

" The social defects of the agricultural districts of the counties of Merioneth, Montgomery, and a considerable portion of those of Carnarvon and Denbigh is illustrated by the following evidence, relating to the parishes of Talyllyn and Llanfihangel, in the county of Merioneth : —

" I visited many cottages in Talyllyn, and the adjoining parish of Llanfihangel. The house accommodation is wretched. The cottages are formed of a few loose fragments of rock and shale piled together, without mortar or whitewash. The floors are of earth, the roofs are wattled, and *many of these hovels have no window.* They comprise one room, in which all the family sleep. This is in some cases separated from the rest of the hut by wisps of straw, forming an imperfect screen.

" The social and moral depravity of the pauper population in the towns is illustrated by the following evidence of Mr. William Williams, Chemist, of Carnarvon : —

" ' There is a great amount of extreme poverty, filth, and misery in Carnarvon, for the most part owing to immorality and ignorance. I can mention three places in particular in this town, of Glanymor, Tanallt, and Smithfield, *where many families have only one room to live in, 9 feet square, with an earthen floor, and the ventilation dreadfully bad.*

" ' These rooms have but one window of a foot square, which is always closed. With the exception of some who are aged, sick, or widows, the poverty in Carnarvon is generally owing to the depravity of the people. Wages are good here. Owing to the railways, 2s. 6d. is now paid where 1s. 6d. would formerly have been paid. Able-bodied men can always get work, if they are disposed, and at good wages. *But the people crowd into the towns from the country round*, in order to be lodged in these filthy houses, and to beg. Carnarvon is full of such people. Rates are now 1s. where they used to be but 4d.

" ' The chief vice in this town is drunkenness. Many who earn 20s., some of them 26s. a week, bring home 5s., some only 3s., to their families ; the rest is spent in the public-house. Their families cannot attend a place of worship or a school, either on Sunday or week-day. They have no clothes. Ragged schools would do great good among these people. The two which have been set on foot by the Methodists have already done a great deal of good ; the children attend them with very little clothing.' "

" Upon the same subject, the Rev. William Williams, Independent minister, said : —

" ' In Carnarvon, if you go beyond the different religious circles, you will find scarcely a single young man, who does not devote himself to smoking and drinking, and things that are worse. They are beastly in their habits in this town.'

" Evidence to the same effect might be adduced respecting Bangor, and other large towns in North Wales.

" Mr. Joshua Williams, schoolmaster, Llandwrog, stated : —

" ' There are a great many all around the schools who are of an age for instruction. They are anxious for it, both parents and children. But they are very poor ; the majority are labourers with very large families, many of them eight or nine children. A great many are too poor to pay for instruction—too poor to pay for clothes, and shoes, or clogs for their feet, in order to send them to school. I have to teach many for nothing.

" ' The cottages are very, very poor. *One bed-room for three or four beds, and the beds of straw very bare. Very often all the family sleep in the same room. Grown up children among them of both sexes. This has a bad effect; very bad on their health and morals.*'

" But the lowest form of social degradation and moral depravity is met with in the mining districts, and is found to grow worse in approaching the English border. These districts extend from Llangollen through the parishes of Ruabon and Wrexham to the point of Air, at the north-eastern extremity of Flintshire.

" The following evidence was taken from personal
inspection of the district : —

" I visited Rhosllanerchrugog, Sunday, January 13.
It is situated midway between Ruabon and Wrexham,
and is a place of great importance, owing to the vast
number of operatives, who are employed upon the extensive coal mines, with which the district abounds.   I
visited the Sunday schools of several religious denomi-
nations, which were filled with persons of all ages, respectably dressed and well-conducted.   I then visited
many cottages in different parts of the village.

" Some of these consist of a single room, from 9
to 12 feet square; others have, in addition, a sort
of a lean-to, forming a separate place to sleep in.   They
are in general void of furniture ; but in some I *found a
bed, which is made to accommodate double numbers, by
arranging the occupants feet to feet.*   The roofs are
wattled, sometimes plastered over with mortar, sometimes bare ; others are of straw, and full of large holes
open to the sky, which are frequently the only means
for admitting light.   Each of these hovels contains, on
an average, a family of six children, with their parents.
If they comprise two rooms, the parents sleep in one,
and the children in the other ; if there is but one room,
all sleep together.   In either case, the young people
sleep together in the same confined room, regardless of
age and sex.   I observed one cottage unusually neat
and clean ; it contained a father and mother, well and
neatly dressed, a son eighteen years old, and a daughter
aged twenty : *all these sleep together in the same room,*
which is about 9 or 10 feet square.   Next door live

two idiots, a brother and sister.   In several other cottages I observed the inmates well, and even expensively, clothed, and the tables were supplied with food — bacon, &c.

" Yet in these, the families were crowded in the same unseemly manner, *the father, mother, and six children all sleeping together.*

" The existence of the evils above mentioned was less surprising than the remonstrances addressed to me by persons of high religious profession in the neighbourhood, representing the injustice of apprehending immoral results from habits of promiscuous intercourse. Nothing could more forcibly illustrate the imperfect nature of indigenous civilisation, when it is isolated and unaided.

" The following is a Report of Mr. John James, assistant : —

" ' January 20. — I went, in company with the Rev. P. M. Richards, the officiating minister of the district, to visit some of the houses of the colliers at Rhosllanerchrugog; and though I have seen St. Giles's, Cow Cross, Wapping, and other places in the metropolis, where the houses of the poor are unfit to live in, I never beheld anything to equal some of the cottages at Rhosllanerchrugog, as regards confinement, filth, and utter unfitness for human abode.

" ' Cottage No. 1. consists of one low room, about 12 feet square, containing an old man, perfectly black with dirt, lying on a bed of rags and filth.   In the same cottage lives his son, who is in a consumption.

" ' No. 2. consists of one small room, dirty, and so

close that the atmosphere was insupportable. The floor was alternately of mud and stone. In the centre an idiot was seated on a stool; her mother, an old woman, seventy or eighty years of age, was lying on a filthy bed beside her, reduced to a skeleton by disease. The room was without an article of what would be called furniture.

" ' No. 3. contains only one room, in which live a man and his two idiot children, both about twenty years old.

" ' No. 4., a cottage of one room, contains a father and mother, their daughter and her husband, occupying two beds placed close together, the room being very small. The beds were filthy, the furniture miserable, and the ventilation bad.

" ' No. 5., a cottage of one room, inhabited by two adult sisters and their two adult brothers. All occupy the same bed, which may be enlarged a little, but is still the same bed. The room is low-roofed and ill-ventilated.

" ' None of these houses had a necessary, anywhere near them, nor did I see such a thing in the whole village.

" ' The Rev. Mr. Richards and Mr. William Jones, of Llanerchrugog, informed me, that houses of this description are frequent in this place; that they are for the most part built by the poor people themselves, an acknowledgment of from 7s. to 15s. per annum being paid to the landlord as ground-rent; that fever is very common in this district, although the village is well situated, and naturally very salubrious; that morals are exceedingly low; that there is a man in the district who notoriously lives in a state of incest with his own daughter, and that this is not an isolated case.

" ' Superstition is said to be very common among the poor of this neighbourhood. There was recently a woman in the village, who gained her livelihood by conjuring, and there is now a pretended conjuror at Wrexham, to whom scores of people are said to go annually from Rhosllanerchrugog. — John James, Assistant.'

" As the influence of the Welsh Sunday-schools decreases, the moral degradation of the inhabitants is more apparent. This is observable on approaching the English border.

" The following evidence relates to the town of Flint : —

" The streets of the town are filthy ; the houses are wretchedly built, and in worse repair ; and the people are squalid and in rags. I visited several cottages in the town. A small house, 10 or 12 feet square, with a chamber above, accommodates, on an average, two parents, six children, and six lodgers. The floors are of earth, and in wretched condition. There is no room for furniture, and the interiors are filthy and unwholesome. I saw other cottages of 9 feet square, with no other room adjoining. These generally contain a husband and wife, with infants and a lodger. I visited a parish almshouse of this description, containing nine people, a father, mother, and seven children.

" There was one bed for the parents, and another for the seven children, both placed in the only room which the house contained. The eldest boy was sixteen years old, the eldest girl fifteen. The character of the inhabitants is degraded in respect of turbulence, intemperance, and debauchery.

" The prevailing vice of the neighbourhood is drunkenness, which is rendered more flagrant and pernicious from the prevalence of the old Welsh custom of keeping merry nights. A week previous to my visit, a murder had been committed by a party (as was supposed) who had been thus engaged in revelry. The clergyman informed me that fornication also is common in the town and neighbourhood; but that in Flintshire, as in England, it assumes the form of promiscuous debauchery, and is not a recognised systematic institution as in other counties of North Wales. The female population are ignorant of economy and of all kinds of domestic industry; in consequence of which, and of the general improvidence and intemperance of the men, the social condition of Flint is almost as degraded as at Rhosllanerchrugog (Ruabon).

" In the adjoining district of Bagillt, in some of the colleries the men are paid every other Saturday, and do not return to their work until the following Tuesday or Wednesday.

" In Bagillt, and in the adjoining town of Flint, the old Welsh custom of keeping a merry night (noswaith-lawen) is still prevalent, and, being generally reserved for a Saturday, is protracted to the following Sunday, during which drinking never ceases. This custom is represented by the clergy and others as involving the most pernicious consequences.

" I saw two men stripped and fighting in the main street of Bagillt, with a ring of men, women, and children around them. There are no policemen in the township. The women are represented as being, for the most part, ignorant of housewifery and domestic economy. The girls are very early sent to service, but marry as early as eighteen, and have large families. Women are not employed in or about the mines, but spend most of their time in cockling, or gathering cockles on the beach. They have low ideas of domestic comfort, living in small cottages, dirty and ill-ventilated, and at night are crowded together in the same room, and sometimes in the same bed, without regard to age or sex.

" In the district of St. Matthew, in the parish of Hawarden, where the inhabitants are exclusively English, the Rev. J. P. Foulkes, the officiating minister, states that —

" ' The state of morals is degraded in respect of drunkenness, profanity, dishonesty, and incontinence; that the latter vice is increasing so rapidly as to render it difficult to find a cottage where some female of the family has not been *enceinte* before marriage.'

" But there is one vice which is fragrant throughout North Wales, and remains unchecked by any instruments of civilisation.

" It has obtained for a long time as the peculiar vice of the principality, but its existence has almost ceased to be considered as an evil; and the custom of Wales is said to justify the barbarous practices which precede the right of marriage. Upon this subject it is unnecessary to add more than the following evidence.

" The Rev. William Jones, vicar of Nevin : —

" ' Want of chastity is fragrant. This vice is not confined to the poor.

" ' In England, farmers' daughters are respectable; in Wales, they are in the constant habit of being courted in bed. In the case of domestic servants, the vice is universal. I have had the greatest difficulty in keeping my own servants from practising it. It became necessary to secure their chamber windows with bars to prevent them from admitting men. I am told by my parishioners, that unless I allow the practice, I shall very soon have no servants at all, and that it will be impossible to get any.'

" The Rev. St. George Armstrong Williams, incumbent of Demo, states: —

" ' The want of chastity is the besetting evil of this country, but especially of this district of Lleyn. In the relieving officer's books, out of twenty-nine births, I counted twelve illegitimate. This was in one quarter of a year. Our workhouse is completely filled with the mothers of illegitimate children, and the children themselves. What is worse, the parents do not see the evil of it. They say their daughters have been unfortunate, and maintain their illegitimate grandchildren as if they were legitimate. In my parish, Llannor, in one house, there is a-woman with five illegitimate children, and these by different fathers; her sister had four children, all illegitimate. Another in the same village had four, also by different fathers. In this parish of Llannor, there are no means of education for the female children of the poor. These low morals I attribute entirely to the want of education.'

" The fullest evidence on this subject was given by the Reverend J. W. Trevor, chaplain to the Lord Bishop of Bangor : —

" ' It is difficult as it is mortifying, to describe in proper terms the disgraceful state of the common people in Wales in the intercourse of the sexes, but it is important that the truth should be known. I believe the proportion of illegitimate children to the population in Anglesey (with only one exception, and that is in Wales), exceeds that in any other county in the kingdom. The fact is enough to prove the moral degradation of our common people. But I must draw your notice more particularly to some details on this subject, which will show you at once, what I want to make known, that the moral principles of the Welsh people are totally corrupt and abandoned in this respect,—that no restraints or penalties of law can cure or even check the evil, until by appliances of better education and more general civilisation, they are taught to regard their present custom with a sense of shame and decency. I put out of consideration now any higher motives, for they are not to be looked for at present. *While the sexes continue to herd like beasts, it were idle to expect they can be restrained by religion or conscience.* I assert with confidence, as an undeniable fact, that fornication is not regarded as a vice, scarcely as a frailty, by the common people in Wales. It is considered as a matter of course, as the regular conventional process towards marriage.

" ' It is avowed, defended, and laughed at, without scruple, or shame, or concealment by both sexes alike.

And what, if, as it often happens, the man prove faithless, and marriage does not ensue, and yet a child is to be born. Then comes the affair of affiliation, and with it, as the law now requires, all the filthy disclosure in open court of the obscenities which preceded it. I will state some facts, as they came under my own cognisance as a magistrate; and you will bear in mind, they are heard by the public of all ages and both sexes. A young girl was brought to swear that she sat by the fire, while her widowed mother was in bed with her paramour in the same room, and this she did on several occasions. Another swears, that she stood by in open day-light, and in the open air, while the deed was perpetrated, which made her friend the mother of a bastard. A man lay in bed with two women, night after night for months together; and one of the women swore to the required fact.

" ' Both parents, or either of them, came forward to prove the parentage of their daughter's bastard—witnesses often to the very act. I might multiply such instances to prove the utter disregard of common natural decency and shame among the people. This evidence was given (with but few exceptions it is always given) without the slightest reluctance or modesty, and with a levity and confidence of manner, which prove the parties to be quite callous and lost to all sense of shame. When I have attempted at the union board to persuade the guardians to build a workhouse (we have none in Anglesey), and used as an argument, that it would check the increase of bastardy, which is a monstrous charge on our poor-rates, as well as a disgrace to our community; they quite scouted the notion of its being any disgrace, and they maintained that the custom of Wales justified the practice. In fact, the guardians, who are almost all country farmers, are so familiarised to this iniquity, and have so long partaken in it, that they are totally incapable of any right feeling on the subject. They absolutely encourage the practice : they hire their servants agreeing to their stipulation for freedom of access for this purpose at stated times, or, it may be, whenever they please. The boys and girls in farm-houses are brought up from childhood with these filthy practices ever before their eyes and ears, and, of course, on the first temptation, they fall into the same course themselves. In short, in this matter, even in a greater degree than the other which I have noticed, the minds of our common people are become thoroughly and universally depraved and brutalised. To meet this appalling evil, *the present system of education in Wales is utterly powerless.*' "

I have endeavoured, in the preceding pages, to represent, as dispassionately as possible, the social condition of a great part of the poor of England and Wales in this the *nineteenth* century. I have quoted the statements and statistics of government officers or eminent individuals on every branch of my inquiry. From those statements and statistics it is only too evident that the social degradation and misery of our labouring classes is appalling.

We have become so accustomed to this sad and disgraceful social state, that people talk in England of

VOL. I.

" pauperism being a *necessity ;*" of " the Bible teaching us so ;" of its being " the dream of enthusiasts to hope to change this order of things ;" and of the " necessity of submitting to the dispensations of Providence." Impious assertions ! Happily, each year since 1820 has been more and more belying this insane reasoning, and every year henceforward will still further belie it.

Since the foreign governments began to educate all the children of their poor, and since they first enabled the peasants to purchase land, *by refusing to allow proprietors to tie up their estates after their deaths, or to prevent their successors selling the fee,* the poor of many of the European countries have been steadily emerging from pauperism. The more their intelligence is developed by means of the liberal systems of education, which are in force in those countries, the higher will they henceforward rise in the scale of humanity and of social prosperity.

Not much more than a quarter of a century has elapsed, since the governments of modern Europe commenced anything like an effective effort to educate the children of their poor; not half a century has elapsed, since the peasants of foreign countries first found themselves enabled, after the long continuance of the feudal system, to purchase land; and yet, in the short time, which has elapsed, since these great changes in the middle-age system of legislation, great results, as I have already shown, have been obtained. When the present system of general education and division of land among the peasants has worked for another half century, the world will look back with astonishment on the degrada-

tion to which the poorer classes have been so long subjected, by imperfect legislation.

But what are the principal causes of the pauperism,
misery, and crime, which distinguish so unhappily the
condition of a great part of our poor? They are the
following : —

1. The great and continued neglect of the intellectual
training of the poorer classes.

2. The neglect of their religious education.

3. The game laws.

4. The system of laws which affect land.

5. The gin-palaces.

6. The want of classification in our prisons.

Let us briefly consider each of them.

1. *The Neglect of the Intellectual Training of the poorer*
Classes. *

About ONE HALF of our poor can neither read nor
write, have never been in any school, and know little,
or positively nothing, of the doctrines of the Christian
religion, of moral duties, or of any higher pleasures, than
beer or spirit drinking and the grossest sensual indulgence. Even of the small shopkeeping and farmer
classes, there are great numbers, who can neither read
nor write, and who have never entered even a Sunday
school. It is a very common thing for even farmers, who
are members of the union boards of guardians in the

* These statements are the results of an examination of the Reports
published by the Committee of Council on Education, of those of the
Welsh Commissioners, of the Journals of the Statistical Society, and of
personal inquiry in various parts of England.

midland and eastern counties of England, to sign their names with a cross, from being unable to write.

None of all this class can ever search the Scriptures for themselves; few of them care to give their children any instruction, as they have never experienced the benefits of instruction themselves; scarcely any of them are sensible enough to even desire to improve their condition in life; scarcely any of them ever enter into a place of public worship, or ever come into contact with a religious minister; none of them understand anything of the phenomena of nature around them, of the thoughts and wishes of their age, of their own situation here, or of the mysterious change before them.   They live precisely like brutes, to gratify, as far as their means allow, the appetites of their uncultivated bodies, and then die, to go they have never thought, cared, or wondered whither.

All this must seem exaggeration to those, who have not examined for themselves the reports of the Inspectors of Schools, or those of the Welsh Commissioners, or those of the visitors, chaplains, inspectors, and governors of our prisons, or those of the City Missionaries, or the admirable letters published in the " Times " and " Chronicle." But those persons, who have examined these reports, will know, that I have understated the deep ignorance of our poorer classes.

The reports, to which I allude, disclose a degree of ignorance, which must be quite incredible to all who have not given their attention to the study of these facts. I might fill volumes with quotations confirmatory of my statements, but as my space does not allow me to do more than state the fact, I am obliged to refer my readers to these reports for proof of the universal truth of what I have affirmed.

If these poor creatures commit what the more intelligent classes call " crimes against society," — if they are improvident and immoral,—if they have no love for the society which has left, if it has not made, them thus degraded,—and if they punish that society by burdening it with vice and pauperism, is it a matter of great surprise?

Brought up in the darkness of barbarism, they have no idea, that it is possible for them to attain any higher condition ; they are not even sentient enough to desire, with any strength of feeling, to change their situation ; they are not intelligent enough to be perseveringly discontented ; they are not sensible to what we call the voice of conscience ; they do not understand the necessity of avoiding crime, beyond the mere fear of the police and a gaol ; they do not in the least comprehend, that what is the interest of society is their own also ; they do not in the least understand the meaning, necessity, or effect of the laws ; they have unclear, indefinite, and undefinable ideas of all around them ; they eat, drink, breed, work, and die ; and while they pass through their brute-like existence here, the richer and more intelligent classes are obliged to guard them with police and standing armies, and to cover the land with prisons, cages, and all kinds of receptacles for those, who in their thoughtlessness or misery disturb the quiet and happiness of their more intelligent, and, consequently, more moral and prosperous neighbours, by plunder, assault, or any other deed, which law is obliged, for the sake of the existence of society, to designate a

" crime," although most of those who commit it do not in the least comprehend its criminality.

It is to this totally uneducated class, and to the class of those, who can only read and write very imperfectly, as Mr. Porter shows in the statistics I have quoted above, that the greatest part of our criminals belong. The majority of all our criminals have received no education, and cannot read or write at all; or have received so wretched an education, as only to be able to read or write very imperfectly. Scarcely any of the inmates of our prisons have received even a decent education. And yet, in the presence of such facts as these, 1850 years have passed since the birth of Jesus Christ, and scarcely anything worthy of mention has yet been done for the education of the English poor !

The very able correspondent of the " Morning Chronicle, " in one of his letters on the condition of the peasants in the rural districts of England, published on December 1st, 1849, says :—

" Taking the adult class of agricultural labourers, it is almost impossible to exaggerate the ignorance in which they live, and move, and have their being. As they work in the fields, the external world has some hold upon them through the medium of their senses; but to all the higher exercises of intellect, they are perfect strangers. You cannot address one of them, without being at once painfully struck with the intellectual darkness which enshrouds him. There is in general neither speculation in his eyes nor intelligence in his countenance. The whole expression is more that of an animal than of a man. He is wanting, too, in the erect and independent bearing of a man. When you accost him, if he is not insolent — which he seldom is — he is timid and shrinking; his whole manner showing that he feels himself at a distance from you greater than should separate any two classes of men. He is often doubtful when you address, and suspicious when you question him; he is seemingly oppressed with the interview, whilst it lasts, and obviously relieved, when it is over. These are the traits, which I can affirm them to possess as a class, after having come in contact with many hundreds of farm-labourers. They belong to a generation, for whose intellectual culture little or nothing was done. As a class, they have no amusements beyond the indulgence of sense. In nine cases out of ten, recreation is associated in their minds with nothing higher than sensuality. I have frequently asked clergymen and others, if they often find the adult peasant reading for his own or others' amusement ? The invariable answer is, that such a sight is seldom or never witnessed. In the first place, *the great bulk of them cannot read.* In the next, a large proportion of those who can, do so with too much difficulty to admit of the exercise being an amusement to them. Again, few of those who can read with comparative ease have the taste for doing so. It is but justice to them to say, that many of those who cannot read have bitterly regretted, in my hearing, their inability to do so. I shall never forget the tone, in which an old woman in Cornwall intimated to me what a comfort it would now be to her, could she only read her Bible in her lonely hours.

" Education has advanced him but little beyond the

position which he occupied in the days of William the Norman. The farm-labourer has scarcely participated at all in the improvement of his brethren. As he was generations gone by, so he is now — a physical scandal, a moral enigma, an intellectual cataleptic.

" Let it not be said, that this picture is too strongly drawn. *The subject is one, which does not admit of exaggeration.* Did space permit, or could any good purpose be served by it, I could adduce instances, almost innumerable, of the profound ignorance in which this class of British subjects is steeped. There is scarcely a field in the agricultural districts, which does not exhibit a living illustration of it. Search any county throughout the south and west, and the examples start up around you in hundreds. I have found it so in all those, which I have traversed — from Salisbury to the Land's-end — from Portland-bill to Oxford — in the vale of the Torridge, and in the vale of Aylesbury — by the Thames, the Severn, the Frome, the Stour, the Exe, the Camel, and the Plym. Where all is bad, it is sometimes difficult to point out the worst."

But what is the intelligence of the *partially instructed half* of our poorer classes? It is miserable. They can, perhaps, read and write, and they know something of the Scriptures; but that is all that the greatest part of even the instructed half understand. A few, but these are very few, are well educated, and know something of physical and political science, of the relations of their own nation with foreign nations, and of those truths of political economy, which all educated persons admit and understand, although often without knowing that they do so. But by far the greatest part of this partially instructed moiety know nothing of geography, nothing of the history of their country, nothing of science, nothing of the natural phenomena around them, nothing of political or of economical science, nothing of the history of the world, nothing of the relations of their own country with foreign countries, nothing of the necessity of having laws, and nothing of the laws by which they are governed; in short, the greatest part of even this partially instructed moiety of the poor have few ideas, beyond the most vulgar and crude notions of God and the devil, of heaven and hell, of everlasting happiness and everlasting burning; of our Lord Jesus, the sacrifice of an enraged Deity; and of those unpractical theories of equality, universal happiness, fraternity, and present oppression, which demagogues pour forth for their own selfish ends.

What is the character of the education which the majority of those poor children who go to school receive? Most of them are instructed either by poor ignorant women, who just know how to read, write, and cipher; or by poor men of the lowest attainments, who have taken to school-management, because they are fit for nothing else. A great part of the very best-built and endowed schools have no seats inside them; no separate rooms for the different classes; only one teacher for each school; no maps; very few books; and no apparatus for instruction. The poor children, all of them young, — for few remain at school beyond the age of ten, — are obliged to stand in many of these schools nearly the whole day, and are, in this fatiguing position, obliged, by the threat of a flogging, to learn the most beautiful passages of the Scriptures by heart ! Do my readers think that these passages, learned amidst such miserable associations, will have any beneficial influence in after life ? Do they think that children, who leave school at the age of twelve, even if the school be a good one, can carry away much that will be remembered afterwards to their moral improvement ?

I am quite convinced, that our dame schools, and those schools which are unfurnished, where the classes are unseparated, where the teachers are uneducated, and where the children are tortured by being made to stand the greater part of the day, are very much worse than no schools at all.

A poor boy, brought up under the kindly influences of his parents, however rude and unenlightened they may be, is much more likely to turn out a good citizen afterwards, than one who has been taught to hate instruction, the Bible, and moral and religious precepts, by being tortured daily in such wretched schools as those I have mentioned ; and yet such schools form the majority of all we have at present established !

But the small number of our schools, and the miserable character of the majority of them, are not the only obstacles to the progress of the education and to the improvement of the social condition of the poor in England. Almost as great an obstacle as the character or small number of the schools, is *the short time during which the children are left in schools.* The educational inspectors complain very much of this fact. It is said that the time during which the children have been left in school has been actually shortened of late years, owing, no doubt, to the increasing poverty of the lower orders.

The Rev. H. Moseley, government inspector of the Midland District, says *, " the general impression amongst those persons, who are likely to be best informed on the subject, is, *that the average age of the children who attend our elementary schools is steadily sinking.* We may be educating more, but they are, I believe, younger children, and stay with us a less time."

Mr. Moseley represents the age at which the majority of the children leave our schools to be about *nine;* Mr. Fletcher, another inspector, represents it at no more than *ten.* In Germany, the children remain in school to the end of their *fourteenth,* and in Switzerland to the end of their *fifteenth,* and often to the end of their *sixteenth* year. So that, not only are our schools and teachers too few in numbers, and incomparably worse than those of foreign countries, but our children only remain in the schools about four years, or less than one-half the period during which every child in Switzerland receives a first-rate education.

The Rev. H. Worsley, rector of Easton, in Suffolk, says † : —

" The low rate of wages for work, especially in the agricultural districts, may be alleged as the reason of the diminished term of a child's continuance at school; in some instances, perhaps, with justice ; but the general conclusion cannot be eluded, that parents place very low

* See Minutes of Committee of Education, 1846.
† See his admirable Essay on Juvenile Depravity, p. 14.

value on the education of their children. A very small pecuniary gain, to be derived from their children's labour, immediately outweighs, with the majority, all the benefits of instruction. Such low appreciation of a chief blessing is not confined to agriculture, or to manufacturing districts, but is common to all. The labourer, who can procure for his son employment with a farmer of the most trifling emolument, will at once remove him from school. The practice of what is called corn-keeping in country districts, in which small boys are mostly employed to defend the newly-sown corn or ripe grain from the attacks of birds, is a serious obstacle to the advance of instruction. During the whole of the Lord's day, the poor little fellow will be stationed in the cornfield, and must, of course, be absent, not only from the Sunday school, but also from church; and he may be thus occupied for months together. After so long an intermission of secular and religious instruction, (for in nine cases out of ten it cannot be supposed that he is taught at home,) the boy returns to the Sunday, perhaps weekly, school, manifestly no whit better in his general conduct for this long cessation from school duties, and with his small stock of previously obtained knowledge almost sheer forgotten."

Owing to these circumstances, the poor education, which we are giving, is rendered all the more imperfect, and ineffectual. The children leave the schools, at nine or ten years of age, with a mere smattering of knowledge, but with nothing more. Now, there is no saying more true than this, " that a little knowledge is a dangerous thing." It would be much safer, and much more expedient for the lower classes themselves, to give them *no* instruction, than to impart to them as little as we are doing by our present system.   The miserable instruction, which is being given in our present schools, is positively doing more harm than good, as it is actually tending to increase the criminality of our poorer classes.

The reports of crime, published by government, show, that the number of persons who are committed annually out of the class of poor *who can read and write imperfectly, i. e.* who have only received a little miserable instruction for about three years of their life, has IN-CREASED within the last ten years 7·43 per cent.

Talk of education not having yet done much for our poor! — why, we have scarcely begun anything like education in England.   Can you educate a citizen by taking a child of six years of age, and keeping him in such schools as those I have described from his *sixth* to his *tenth* year?   Can you educate a child by sending him to a dame school or to a ragged school, or to such a school as any of those I have described above, for *four* years?   The supposition is absurd.   And yet this is all we attempt in the case of most of even those children who go to school at all.

A good teacher ought to interest his scholars in the beauties of the Scripture history; to make them love the Bible; to teach them to read, write, and cipher, in order that afterwards they may continue their own education; to teach them the history of their own country and its great men, in order to inspire them with patriotism, with a love of their fellow-countrymen, with pride in their nation, and with that respect for high character which would lead them to seek a higher class of leaders, than those who pass off their ignorance and selfishness upon them now; to teach them to sing and chant, in order to provide them with a higher kind of amusement, which might tend to elevate their tastes, their social meetings in after life, and their amusements; and to train them in such habits of cleanliness and neatness, as would make filthy and incommodious houses, such as those I have described above, as intolerable to them, as they are to educated members of the middle classes of society.

I have shown that these ends are being actually attained throughout western Europe. I appeal to my readers, if we have even begun to realise them to any extent in England or Wales.

I am quite convinced, that if our schools and teachers were anything like what they ought to be in character and in numbers, and if our poor were only obliged and enabled to send their children to some school or another from their sixth to their fifteenth year, that by these means alone we should, in twenty years, make our labourers happy and prosperous, and get rid of the greatest part of our pauperism and crime, and of the outlay now required for its suppression.

If democracy should ever invade this country — and the march of events during the last half-century ought to show us that it will be in the midst of us in a few years — the people, among the first laws they will pass, will establish a great system of compulsory and gratuitous education, and will oblige all parents to send their children to school. The most stringent educational regulations that have been ever put in force are those of Switzerland and America.

The reports of the Welsh Commissioners, and of the Educational Inspectors, and the accounts given by teachers in the manufacturing districts of the north of England, disclose an amount of ignorance among the labouring classes which is almost incredible ; and this, be it remembered, exists contemporaneously with the frightful state, which the statistics quoted in this chapter disclose, and with a system of education, which depends for its support upon the efforts of charitable individuals, and upon the paltry sum of 125,000*l.* doled out annually by Government.

Why, in France, every parish is *obliged* by law to build at least one school, and to support a sufficient number of teachers; and, in addition to the enormous annual expenditure of the communes of France, in carrying out the above regulations, the government is now granting about 2,000,000*l.* per annum in order to assist the departments to carry on effectually the education of the people.

2. *The Neglect of the religious Education of our Poor.*

I have mentioned this before. I have said that the forms of worship of the English Church, and of the greater part of the dissenting sects, are not imaginative enough to attract an *ignorant* people, and that our labouring classes are much too ignorant to be capable of being attracted by, or of taking pleasure in, the simple and unadorned spirituality of our forms of worship. We must either adorn the spectacle, or we must *educate the people.* If we neglect to do one of these things, we must rest contented to see the poor of our towns remain as at present — outside the places of national or public worship, and uninterested in the religious worship and ceremonies, because their minds cannot understand them, and because their feelings are not excited by them.

In the towns, too, as I have shown, the English clergy require assistance, and the English Church requires another grade of workmen. We want a class of clergy, who could enter *daily* into the lowest haunts without disgust, and with whom the poor could converse *daily* without shyness or fear, and to whom they might relate their troubles without difficulty, and with a certainty of being understood, and of meeting with sympathy.

The greatest part of the poor of our towns are now never visited by a religious minister, or are visited so seldom that the minister always enters as a stranger. Even when the poor man is visited by a clergyman, it is by a man of so strangely different a rank of life, that the poor man knows his clergyman cannot comprehend the peculiar wants or difficulties of his life. The clergyman is, therefore, received with shyness, and with the constraint, which the visit of a great and wealthy man always inspires in the house of a poor and humble one. As the operatives in Lancashire are in the habit of saying, " there is no church in England for the poor, there is only a church for the rich."

How seldom, too, in the course of a year, are the poor of the cellars, garrets, or lodging-houses of the towns visited by any religious minister! How often are these poor creatures never visited at all! And yet how else is religion to be spread among the masses of our town poor? Sermons will not do it. Constant personal intercourse between the ministers of the Church and the poor can alone succeed in effecting this result. That intercourse, under the existing state of things, is often quite impossible. The number of clergy is too small. The social rank of the clergy is too much removed above that of the poor. Another class of clergy is required. Most of the town churches, too, are virtually closed to the poor. Go into the churches and see how little room is reserved for the poor. It is as if the churches were built exclusively for the rich; and as if the English Church thought it was of much less importance, that the poor should enjoy the consolations of religious worship, than that the rich should do so. In the Roman churches there are no closed pews and reserved places. In their churches, all men are treated as equals in the presence of their God. In the Roman churches, the poor are welcomed with an eagerness, which seems to say, — the church was meant especially for such as you; and in the Roman Church, many of the priests are chosen from the body of the poor, in order that the ministers of religious consolation may be able the better to understand the religious wants of their poor brethren.

Let the English Church take warning. In these democratic days we want institutions for the poor; and especially do we want religious institutions for the poor; and it is partly because we have in our towns no church, no religious ministers, and no effective religious minis-

tration for the masses of the poor, that they are still in
so wretched a condition.

The absence of the poorer classes from our churches
has been often remarked by foreigners. Amongst many
others, M. Leon Faucher, lately a minister of state in
France, says : —

" Place yourself on a Sunday in the midst of Briggate
Street, in Leeds ; of Mosley Street, in Manchester ; or
of Lord Street, or Dale Street, in Liverpool ; what are
the families whom you see walking to the churches
silently and gravely ? It is not possible to deceive
oneself ; *they belong almost exclusively to the middle
classes.* The operatives remain on their door-steps,
where they collect in groups until, the services in the
churches being concluded, the taverns will open. Religion is presented to them with so sombre an aspect,
and with such hard features,— she affects so well not to
appeal either to the senses, or to the imagination, or to
the heart, — that it ought not to be a matter of surprise
if she remain the patrimony and the privilege of the
rich." *

3. *The Game Laws.*

There can be no doubt whatsoever, that these laws
are one of the chief causes of the demoralisation of the
peasant classes.

I am far removed from any desire to see our country
gentry deprived of their healthy sports. I believe that
our system of sports is productive of certain good re

* Etudes sur l'Angleterre, tome première.

sults. It promotes the health and mental activity of
our legislators, of our professional men, and of our
gentry. It draws away from the towns to the healthy
pursuits of a country life, many who would otherwise
seldom seek the change. It often brings the landlords
into connection with their tenantry, in a kindly and
familiar manner, and tends to interest them in their
welfare in at least some small degree. It promotes the
friendly, useful, and healthy intercourse of people of the
richer classes, who often are drawn together by the plea
of sporting; and it mingles together gentlemen of the
highest intellectual culture, and of the most extended
political views, with others, who have spent their whole
life in the country, and who are often men of the lowest
intellectual culture, and of the most narrow and pre-
judiced views on questions of national expedience.

Such are some of the good effects of the system. Now
let us look at the other side of the picture.

No crimes are so much on the increase, and none are
tending to degrade the moral condition of the peasants
more, than offences against the game laws.

The following table will give an idea of the singular
manner in which the numbers of these offences have
been increasing of late years.

Years.			Proportions of Convictions for Offences against the Game Laws to every 100,000 Individuals.
1839	-	-	- 33·5
1840	-	-	- 33·2
1841	.	-	- 36·8
1842	-	-	- 46·1
1843	-	-	- 54·8

" The great increase of late years in poaching, is a striking feature in rural crime. In the three years from 1827 to 1830, no fewer than 8,502 persons were convicted under the game laws. The increase since that period has been startling. In 1843 the committals for this offence amounted to 4,529. In 1844–45, and up to May 1846, that is, during a period of eighteen months, the convictions were 11,372, which gives an average of 4,834 per annum."*

The peasants, who have no amusements, no gardens, no farms, and no chance of getting any, are irresistibly tempted to begin poaching. They cannot learn to regard a hare, a pheasant, or a partridge as the property of any particular person. They know, that the property in them is subject to perpetual change, at the will of the creature itself. One day it is the property of Squire Walters, and the next day of Squire Wyndham. Where it will be the following day no one knows. The sport of snaring them is a much greater pleasure and temptation to the poor, than the sport of shooting them is to the rich. The sport is immensely increased by the danger and the consequences of detection, and by the mode in which it is carried on. It is as exciting as smuggling. In the dark and stormy nights the young peasants venture by twos and threes into the strictly watched and solitary enclosures of their landlords; they are in constant risk of being discovered by the gamekeepers, and of being torn from their homes and consigned to gaol; they are tempted by the excitement of the enter-

* See Rev. H. Worsley's Essay on Juvenile Depravity.

prise, and by the desire to add something to the miserably scanty fare of their families. The poor fellows have no other amusement, and therefore take to this dangerous sport with the greater zest.

But what are the consequences of detection? Here comes the enormous evil resulting from these laws.

If detected, the young peasant, who is very often a man, who has never committed any other crime or offence against the laws; who has only yielded to the same kind of impulse as that which makes his landlord love sport; who has, in short, only done that, which we should all do without the least remorse, were we in his position; this poor fellow, who had no other amusement in which he could indulge, and who has been goaded on by misery and destitution, is caught by a gamekeeper, is carried off to the tribunal of the petty sessions, where his own landlord, who is interested in his punishment, or where some other neighbouring landlord, who is equally interested in his punishment, for the sake of his own sport, is sitting as judge! Before such an unfair tribunal the poor fellow is placed. *No jury is allowed him.* He is tried, judged, condemned, and sentenced by the landlords themselves, and is by them sent off to the county gaol, there to spend one, two, or six months, and often a whole year, in company with felons and criminals of the worst possible character. There he becomes inured to the contemplation of vice of all kinds, and of all degrees. There he gradually loses all horror of it; and thence he returns, hardened in villany, and prepared for the commission of deeds, from which he would have shrunk when he entered.

During the time of his incarceration, his poor wife and family are driven to the workhouse in order to escape starvation ; their household goods are all sold up ; their independence of character is ruined ; and the happiness of a whole family is often destroyed for ever. This is no fanciful picture. It is an occurrence of every day in the rural districts. About 5000 such committals take place every year in England and Wales !

An old baronet, himself a landed proprietor, and one of the greatest sportsmen of Norfolk, once said to me, — "If nothing else is done, I am convinced, that the jurisdiction in cases of offences against the game laws ought to be taken out of the hands of the landlords. It is very wrong, that those who are so strongly interested in punishing should be allowed to be the judges in cases of this description. I have constantly seen the most shameful injustice and cruelty practised by the magistrates in cases of this nature. Many times have I been obliged to interfere to protect a poor fellow, who had never done any other wrong in his lifetime, but who was being sentenced, for a trifling offence against the game laws, more severely than if he were a common felon."

For my own part I am convinced, as I have already observed, that these laws, as at present constituted, are demoralising our poor to an incalculable extent, and that they are capable of being easily altered, without depriving the landlords of their sport. I think two changes might be very advantageously introduced.

1. *All jurisdiction in matters of offences ought to be taken from the landlords themselves, and ought to be*

*transferred to some impartial tribunal, as for instance
that of the County Courts.* It is really monstrous, that
the magistrates, who are nearly all of them sportsmen
and game preservers, should be allowed to be judges in
cases of offences against the game laws; and it is still
more monstrous, that they should be allowed to exercise
summary jurisdiction in cases of this description, and
that they should be empowered to judge and sentence
the offender, without the intervention of any jury, and
according to the unfettered will of their own necessarily
biassed minds. Such a system is opposed to the spirit
of our constitution, and to every principle of civil liberty
and impartial justice.

2. *The punishment, in cases of offences against the
game laws, ought to be changed at once from imprisonment to a fine.* No judge should be allowed to im-
prison for poaching, except in cases of a *third* conviction;
but only to award a fine of not more than 1*l.* for the
first offence, and 3*l.* for the second. The fines ought to
be levied, not by the landlord, but by an officer of the
court. The court ought to be empowered to enable the
officer to distrain, in case the fine is not paid within a
certain time.

The punishments, which the landlords are now enabled
to adjudge at petty sessions, for offences against these
laws, are shamefully and ridiculously excessive. I will
enumerate a few of them: —

1. Any person, by night, unlawfully taking or destroying any game or rabbits, in any land, whether open
or inclosed, or on any public road, highway, or path, on
the sides thereof, or at the openings, outlets, or gates

from any such land into any such public road, highway, or path, or by night unlawfully entering or being
on any land, whether open or inclosed, with any gun,
net, or other instrument, for the purpose of taking or
destroying game, may be punished by the landlord-ma-
gistrates at petty sessions, without the intervention of a
jury —

For first offence, with three months' imprisonment, with
    hard labour, and at the expiration thereof may be
    required to find sureties, himself in 10*l*., and two
    sureties in 5*l*. each, or one in 10*l*., not so to offend
    again for one year ; and in case of not being able to
    find sureties, as is often the case, the poor fellow may
    be sent back to his felon associates in the gaol for
    six calendar months longer.

For a second offence, he may be imprisoned *a whole
    year*, and sureties to double the former amount may
    be required.

2. Where game has been killed out of season, the
offender may be sentenced, in the same manner as above,
to pay 1*l*. a head for every head of game so killed, and
in default of payment, may be imprisoned for two or
three calendar months.

3. Any person selling game without a certificate, may
be in the same manner sentenced to pay 2*l*. for every
head of game so sold, and in default of payment may be
imprisoned for two or three calendar months.

4. Any person killing game, without having taken
out a certificate, may be in the same manner sentenced
to pay 5*l*., and in default to be imprisoned for two or
three calendar months.

5. Any person taking the eggs of game, without having the right to do so, may be in the same manner fined 5s. per egg, and in default imprisoned for two or three calendar months.

6. Any person entering land in the day-time, in search of game, may be in the same manner fined 2l., and in default of payment imprisoned for two or three calendar months.

7. Any person killing game upon land, which he occupies himself, but upon which some other person has reserved the right of shooting, may be, in the same manner, fined 2l., and in addition 1l. for every head of game killed or taken, and in default, may be imprisoned for two or three calendar months.

Many of the poor fellows, who are thus imprisoned for the pardonable offence of poaching, return from the gaols with all the shame and dread of a prison destroyed, with all horror of felony too often destroyed also, and with a fatal familiarisation with criminals and crime. They return, to find their families too often in the workhouses, and their household furniture sold. They return, with an injured character, and with a very greatly increased difficulty of obtaining employment. Goaded on by a knowledge of these sad facts, and no longer restrained by their former dread of a prison and of the name of felon, they soon commit some greater crime than that of shooting or snaring a pheasant, and thus add to the sad length of our criminal lists, and to the numerous inmates of our crowded gaols.

4. *The System of Laws which affect Land in Great Britain and Ireland.*

I have shown, that these laws have had the effect of gradually annihilating the old English class of yeomen; — that they prevent the small shopkeepers, farmers, and peasants buying land; — that they tend to increase the size of farms, and to diminish their number;—that by acting in this manner they take away from the peasant every chance of rising in the social scale, unless he emigrates either to the manufacturing districts or to the colonies;—that they destroy the strong motives which would otherwise urge him to economise, to keep from excesses of all kinds, to defer his marriage, and to bear patiently present hardship for future good; — that they stimulate the increase of population in a most unhealthy and unnatural manner; — that they deprive the shopkeepers and town-labourers of the healthiest of all recreations, and of the most humanising of all employments; — that they deprive the shopkeepers of what would otherwise be the object and end of their labours, viz., the possibility of purchasing a small estate, and of retiring from the toil of business to the happiness of a rural life; — that they keep great tracts of country out of cultivation, which would otherwise be immediately bought up and cultivated by our peasants, or by our small farmers; — that they tend to accumulate enormous masses of wealth in a few hands, and by so doing to render the competition and toil of all the other classes of society very much more intense and painful; — that they entirely destroy the independence of the peasant, while they render him turbulent and discontented;—that they condemn the peasants to live in wretched hovels, and prevent their getting commodious houses, by preventing their building for themselves; — that they tend to destroy all respect for property among the peasants, and among the labourers of our smaller provincial towns; — that they are considered abroad as the real cause of the degradation of the Irish; — that they have deprived the people of that country of all security of tenure, of all interest in the proper cultivation of the soil, and in the preservation of order or of social tranquillity; — that they tend to drain that country of its wealth for the support of a foreign aristocracy; —that they have subjected the peasantry and farmers of that country to the will of agents, who are left to act according to their own unchecked pleasure; — that they are keeping nearly one-third of the rich soil of that island out of cultivation, while the peasantry are starving; — that they have destroyed almost every trace of manly virtue, independence, and energy in the Irish peasantry; — that they have prevented the introduction of capital into that country; — and that they have been one of the principal causes, if not the principal cause, of the degradation and pauperism of the peasants and labourers of the British Isles.

5. *The Gin Palaces.*

As I have before shown, the only amusement or relaxation which the English poor possess, in many parts of the country, is, the frequenting the taverns.

I have shown, that in Western Europe, the amusements of the poor are of a much healthier and a much higher order than those of our poor, and that they consist of musical concerts, village dances, village festivals and sports, gardening, and reading. I have said, that it is a common thing for the labourers of the towns to possess gardens of their own; that the peasants generally possess farms of their own; and that both peasants and town-labourers are educated, and understand music.

But, in England and Wales, generally speaking, the poor have no other resource for amusement, than the taverns. Generally speaking, the poor do not possess land or gardens; they do not understand music or dancing, while nearly all the old athletic pastimes of the villages are forgotten.

But no people have ever lived without amusements of some kind or other. According as they are in a moral or immoral condition, so will their amusements also be moral or immoral. And, on the other hand, it may be said to be a universal truth, that the character of the amusements of a people will always show the character of the people.

In the case of the English poor, the amusements are of a very degraded character, and, what is worse, they are degrading our people more and more.

The streets of our towns are crowded with gaudy, conspicuous buildings, the style of whose architecture has at last gained a name for itself. We call it the " gin-palace style." The interiors of these buildings are intended principally for night-work, though they are, alas! filled throughout the day. The ornaments are such as will produce the greatest effect by the glare of gas-light, and are flaring and disgusting in their painted finery, when the sun shines in upon them, and shows their real character.

In these " palaces," ale, beer, porter, and, more particularly, all kinds of spirits, are sold. These are sometimes drunk by the purchasers in the room, where they are sold, and sometimes in an adjoining or upper room.

These wretched resorts are paying so well, that larger and larger sums are spent every year in embellishing them, so that many in London and in the manufacturing districts have attained a singular degree of tawdry splendour.

The beer-houses, which are still more numerous than the gin-palaces, and which are to be found both in the towns and in the villages, differ from the gin-palaces in this respect — that the owners of the former have obtained from the magistrates licences to sell spirits, while the owners of the latter have not been able to obtain such licences, and are, consequently, unable to sell spirits, and are obliged to confine themselves to the sale of beer, ale, and porter.

The gin-palaces and beer-houses of the towns are the places where the prostitutes resort in search of gain or of stimulants. Many of these places are either brothels, or are connected with brothels kept in an adjoining house, and often by the owner of the gin-palace or beer-house.

In the manufacturing districts it is very common for the same house to serve both as drinking house and as brothel, and in the majority of cases the beer-houses are provided with rooms for the use of the prostitutes and their companions. Those who attend the police courts in our towns, and especially in our manufacturing districts, know but too well what infamous scenes are enacted almost every evening in these places.

There can be no doubt whatever that our legislation has *increased* the numbers of these hotbeds of crime and pauperism.*

In the beginning of the revolutionary war the duties on malt were *augmented*, and in 1825 the duties on spirits were *decreased*. It was thus that whisky was substituted for ale as the beverage of the Scotch, and that gin and brandy began to be generally drunk by the English poor.

The consumption of spirits immediately increased in a tremendous proportion. From 4,132,263 gallons, the consumption in 1825, it rose in one year to 8,888,648 gallons; that is, the consumption was *in one year* more than *doubled* by the change; and from that period, with the exception of the year next following, viz. 1827, the consumption has been progressively augmenting.

Since that time the noted beer-shop act has been passed. By that act, any one was enabled to obtain a licence to enable him to sell beer, whether the person desirous of doing so was a person of respectable character or not.

But this was the least of the evils, which were effected by that act. A clause, which was still more injurious, was that which prescribed that the liquor

---

* Almost the whole of the remainder of this section is taken from Mr. Worsley's and Miss Meteyard's Essays on Juvenile Delinquency.

must be drunk upon the premises of the beer-house, i. e. either in the beer-house or on a bench just outside the door.

This has the effect in many cases, where the poor would otherwise take the beer home to their own cottages, of forcing the young men who wish to have a little to drink, to sit down and take it in the society of the worst people of the neighbourhood, who always, as a matter of course, spend their leisure in the tavern. I am convinced that nothing can be more injurious in its effects upon the poor than this clause. It may be said to *force* the honest labourers into the society and companionship of the most depraved, and so necessarily to demoralise the young and honest labourers.

The following is the number of gallons of *native* proof spirits, on which duty was paid for home consumption in the United Kingdom, in the undermentioned years : —

Years.				Gallons.
1843	-	-	-	- 18,841,890
1844	-	-	-	- 20,608,525
1845	-	-	-	- 23,122,588
1846	-	-	-	- 24,106,697

To the above, must be added the number of gallons of foreign and colonial spirits retained for home consumption, as follows : —

Years.	No. of Gallons of Foreign, &c. Spirits.	No. of Gallons of Home and Foreign Spirits consumed in the United Kingdom
1843	3,161,957	22,026,289
1844	3,242,606	22,042,905
1845	3,549,889	26,672,477
1846	4,252,237	28,360,934

From the above statistics it appears, that the consumption of spirits in the United Kingdom is increasing much more rapidly than the population!

The number of licences granted to retailers of spirits or beer amounted, in 1845, to 237,345; that is, there was to be found, in 1845, a retailer of beer or spirits in every 115 of the population! Of the beer licences, 68,086 were for dwellings rated under 20*l.* per annum, and 35,340 were licences for premises rated under 10*l.* per annum! This shows how large a proportion of the beer-shops are situated in the poorest districts, for the use of the poorest classes.

The valuable return for 1847, issued by the Commissioners of *Metropolitan* Police, shows that 5,307 males and 3,697 females were committed in that year for drunkenness, and that 4,161 males and 3,709 females were committed in the same year for drunken and disorderly conduct in the metropolis alone! Thus the total number of persons committed in the metropolis in 1847 for drunkenness, was 16,847, of which 7,406 were females!

Between the years 1831 and 1843, there were taken into custody by the *metropolitan police* alone for drunkenness and disorderly conduct 482,936 persons, of whom 183,921 were females.

Some idea of the way in which some of our towns are crowded with beer-houses and gin-palaces may be formed from the following facts. A district of London is mentioned in the Twelfth Annual Report of the London City Mission (1847), comprising 400 families, which contains *one* butcher's shop, two bakers' shops, and *seventeen* beer-houses. Another report mentions, that in a *single* street near the docks, there are SIXTY-SEVEN gin-palaces, public-houses, and beer-shops. In a population of about 1,212,000, comprising the most important towns of the manufacturing districts of Yorkshire and Lancashire, there were found to be, in 1846, 14,300 public-houses!

The sum of money, which is frequently given as a premium for the good-will of a public-house doing a good business in London, is from 2000*l*. to 4000*l*.*

The total cost of the spirits and beer consumed in the United Kingdom was, in 1843, estimated to amount to 65,000,000*l*., *i. e.* the sum spent by the British nation in intoxicating liquors is greater by several millions than the whole revenue of the government!

Our judges have, over and over again, remarked in their charges to the grand juries, and in their sentences, that the chief and almost universal causes of nearly all the crimes for which offenders are prosecuted in our courts of justice, are the taverns and gin-palaces. If my space would allow, I could quote many of these dicta ; but the effect of drinking upon the amount of crime is proved still more clearly by the subjoined table.

In 1825, as I have before said, the duty on spirits was lowered from 12*s*. 7*d*. to 7*s*. the imperial gallon; and now mark the effect as shown in the following table.

---

* Report of Commission on Drunkenness, p. 10.

Years.	Annual Consumption of Spirits in England and Wales.	Poor Rates.	Crime in England and Wales.	Crime in London and Middlesex.
	Gallons.	£	Committed.	Committed.
High Duty. { 1823	4,225,903	5,772,962	12,263	2,503
1824	4,880,679	5,736,900	13,698	2,621
1825	4,132,263	5,786,989	14,437	2,902
Low Duty. { 1826	8,888,644	5,928,501	16,164	3,457
1827	8,005,872	6,441,088	17,924	3,381
1828	9,311,624	6,298,003	16,564	3,516

The above statistics would seem to prove that the amount both of crime and of pauperism is dependent in great measure upon the quantity of spirits consumed by the people.

The same fact is proved, wherever the records of the prisons have been well tabulated.

I have already mentioned the fact, that in the towns, the beer-houses and gin-palaces are generally either brothels or the constituted rendezvous of the prostitutes.

The following authorities bear me out in this assertion.

The Rev. H. Worsley, in his admirable report on juvenile depravity *, says, " The beer-shops and gin-palaces are the general centres of meeting, and serve as ' rendezvous ' to vagabonds, thieves, and prostitutes."

The Rev. Mr. Clay, the chaplain of Preston gaol, of whose enlightened efforts in behalf of the poor I cannot sufficiently express my admiration, says, in one of his last reports, " My last year's intercourse with the subjects of my ministry has made me acquainted with practices resorted to in certain beer-houses, which must be men-

* See Juvenile Depravity, p. 170.

tioned, in order to show what demoralising agencies are
added to those already existing in them,—viz. the keeping of prostitutes. From three entirely independent
sources, and at different times, I received statements
fully confirming each other, which leave no doubt of the
extent to which this profligate system is carried on.
Sixteen houses in one town, harbouring, or rather
maintaining, about fifty-four prostitutes, have been
named to me. But this is not the full amount of the
evil. The neighbourhood of these houses is corrupted.
Women — married momen — occupied, to all appearance,
with their own proper avocations, at home, hold themselves
at the call of the beer-house for the immoral purposes to
which I have referred."

The evidence of a police magistrate states*, — " A
very short time since, I fined a publican the utmost
penalty that the law would admit. It was proved that
he had thirty thieves and prostitutes in his house at
eight o'clock on the Sunday morning."

The evidence of Mr. Symons, on the state of Leeds,
says †, — " I went, accompanied by Inspector Childs
and three police officers, to visit the low places of resort
of the working classes of Leeds. We started soon after
nine o'clock, and visited about a score of beer and
public-houses, and as many lodging-houses. . . . .
In the beer-shops there were several mere children ;
and *in almost all were prostitutes.* In some of these
places we found a fiddle or other instrument played :
these places were thronged as full as they could hold.
In another, dancing was going on in a good-sized room

---

* Report on Drunkenness, p. 18.   † Juvenile Depravity, p. 174

upstairs, where I found a dozen couples performing a country-dance; *the females were all factory girls and prostitutes.* Not one of these dancers, boys or girls, was above twenty or twenty-one years of age, and most of them were sixteen or seventeen."

We have often, and as I think with great reason, cried shame upon France, for granting licences to the brothels in her towns; but by our present system of licensing beer-houses, we are in reality giving the sanction of law to, and encouraging the establishment of, the worst possible species of brothels for the demoralisation of the poorer classes of society.

The present unchecked system of beer-houses is producing greater evils every year. It is destroying the health and deteriorating the physical character of our labouring classes more and more; it is increasing the amount of pauperism and criminality; and it is stimulating political disaffection among the masses of the manufacturing districts, more than almost any other cause.

It is in the taverns, whether beer-houses or gin-palaces, that the lowest of the demagogues instil their doctrines into the minds of the young;—it is in the taverns, that the worst of the political publications are read aloud to ignorant audiences;—it is in the taverns, that the young peasants make friends with the hardened poachers and rick-burners of their neighbourhoods;—it is in the taverns, that the young men and young women of our towns are first habituated to the sight and manners of the prostitutes, and that they lose all horror of their condition;—it is in the taverns, that young boys and girls, of not more than fifteen or sixteen years of age, go to dance and amuse themselves, in company with all the worst frequenters of the place; — and it is in the taverns, that nine out of ten of all the inmates of our crowded gaols are first instructed in crime. Judges, magistrates, and police all agree in earnestly and continually deprecating the present system, and yet it is continued. And why? The only reason is, that it produces a considerable sum towards the expenses of government. It was for this reason that the duty was first lowered. But ought we not all of us to be willing to bear any amount of increased taxation, rather than ruin the moral and physical condition of our poor, for the sake of increasing our revenue, by any amount, however great?

We must do something to check this enormous evil, if we would not see the moral and physical character of our people completely ruined. My own opinion is : —

1. That we ought to give much greater powers to the magistrates to withdraw the licences from, and to close, any gin-palace or beer-house, the proprietor of which could be convicted of permitting excesses to be committed in his house.

2. That we ought not to allow any beer-house or gin-palace keeper to keep his house open, or to serve out or sell any spirits or beer, after eight o'clock in the evening, or at any time during the Sundays.

3. That in every town a certain number of the police ought to be chosen every week to act specially as inspectors of the taverns, to prevent indecencies or excesses, and to see that the law was obeyed.

4. That any tavern-keeper should be deprived of his

licence, who was convicted before a magistrate of suffering persons of different sexes to have criminal intercourse in his house, or of knowingly permitting certain indecent practices, not fit to be named here; or of allowing any child, of less than fifteen years of age, to enter the drinking-rooms, and to remain there more than five minutes in the course of any day.

Enactments such as these would put a stop to a great part of the demoralising effects of these wretched rendezvous of the lower orders.

But I do not think we should stop there. My own opinion is, and has always been, that we must sooner or later raise the duty upon spirits again. Such a step would be hailed with joy by millions of the poor themselves, however great an outcry it would raise among the gin-palace keepers.

6. *The Want of Classification in our Prisons.*

A good deal has been done of late years to improve our prisons, but a great deal remains to be done.

It is quite possible, and it is very common, for a poor boy or for a poor person of good character to do something, which society is obliged to designate a crime, and to punish severely, although, morally speaking, the person who committed the deed was almost innocent. Now, it is very important, that this class of offenders, and especially the younger portion of them, should be kept from the contamination of thoroughly depraved associates, during the period of their imprisonment. If a young or a comparatively guiltless offender is thrown into the society of abandoned companions in the gaols, the chances are ten to one that he will go out worse than he came in.

Our criminal records and our courts of justice are singular proofs of the truth of this assertion.

Moreover, it is an undeniable fact, that if the poor may only have companions in the gaols, they would often rather be in prison than out, especially during the winter months. It is no punishment, but a decided privilege to most of them. Any one, who will visit the prisons, and converse with the more talkative of the felons, may learn this from their own lips.

We have, in fact, gone from one extreme to another. A few years back the gaols were wretched, filthy, badly ventilated, small, and so miserable, as to be a dreadful punishment even to the poorest of the wretches sent to them. Now, they are large, capacious, well ventilated, well warmed, beautifully cleaned, and well arranged; the food is good, clean, and abundant; the beds are very comfortable; the health of the prisoners is very well attended to; they are very kindly treated; and are lodged *much* better, than they often are before they enter. All this is quite right; *but where is the punishment?* Solely the loss of liberty; and, in exchange for this, they find themselves comfortably housed, well though simply fed, without any labour worth calling hard, without any risk of going to bed supperless, and with plenty of companions.

Is it any wonder, that our criminal records should be full of instances of persons being convicted *three, four,* and *five* times, and that the prisoners at our quarter sessions should very often receive their sentence with actually a smile of pleasure?

For three reasons it is becoming absolutely necessary to introduce the separate system into all our prisons, and to do away altogether with the plan of imprisoning persons in company : —

1. To save the younger and more innocent prisoners from being contaminated by associating with the more hardened offenders.

2. To make our gaols a *punishment*, instead of being, as many of them are at present, an actual *premium* for the commission of crime.

3. To save our counties the expense of prosecuting, and committing, and imprisoning the same person *four* or *five* times in the course of as many years, and each successive time for a worse offence than the former one.

In Germany and in America they are substituting solitary confinement for the old plan of confining a number together. Wherever this system has been introduced, it has been found to work well. It keeps the less depraved prisoners from contamination; it makes the prison a real, though still a lenient, punishment; it affords excellent opportunities for the instruction and moral reformation of the prisoners; and, in the long run, it saves expense to the counties, by rendering recommittals and reimprisonments of the same persons much rarer than in those provinces where the prisoners are confined together.

END OF THE FIRST VOLUME.

LONDON:
SPOTTISWOODES and SHAW,
New-street-Square.

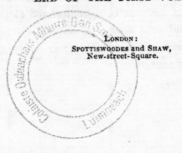